Jacqueline Evers-Vermeul and Elena Tribushinina (Eds.)
Usage-Based Approaches to Language Acquisition and Language Teaching

Studies on Language Acquisition

—

Edited by
Peter Jordens

Volume 55

Usage-Based Approaches to Language Acquisition and Language Teaching

Edited by
Jacqueline Evers-Vermeul
Elena Tribushinina

DE GRUYTER
MOUTON

ISBN 978-1-5015-1752-5
e-ISBN (PDF) 978-1-5015-0549-2
e-ISBN (EPUB) 978-1-5015-0542-3
ISSN 1861-4248

Library of Congress Cataloging-in-Publication Data
A CIP catalog record for this book has been applied for at the Library of Congress.

Bibliographic information published by the Deutsche Nationalbibliothek
The Deutsche Nationalbibliothek lists this publication in the Deutsche Nationalbibliografie;
detailed bibliographic data are available on the Internet at http://dnb.dnb.de.

© 2018 Walter de Gruyter Inc., Boston/Berlin
This volume is text- and page-identical with the hardback published in 2017.
Typesetting: RoyalStandard, Hong Kong
Printing and binding: CPI books GmbH, Leck

♾ Printed on acid-free paper
Printed in Germany

www.degruyter.com

Acknowledgments

This book would not have been possible without the effort of many people. First of all, many thanks to all the contributors for their interesting work and patience. We are also very grateful to Laurent Rasier for his valuable efforts at the earlier stages of the editorial process, and to Carla van Rooijen and Nina Sangers in assisting us during the compilation of the index. Many thanks go to all the colleagues who kindly agreed to review the chapters in this volume: Walter Daelemans, Sylvie De Cock, Gaëtanelle Gilquin, Dylan Glynn, Fanny Meunier, Antje Orgassa, Esther Pascual, Ted Sanders, Anne Vermeer and Daniel Wiechmann.

This volume grew out of the Anéla Spring Conference Cognitive Approaches to Applied Linguistics held at Utrecht University in April 2010. Several chapters are based on talks presented at this conference, and we are grateful to the audience for their feedback and inspiring discussions.

Finally, we owe thanks to several funding agencies. The work by Jacqueline Evers-Vermeul has been partly supported by a grant from the Education for Learning Societies at Utrecht University. The work by Elena Tribushinina has been partly supported by the Netherlands Organization for Scientific Research (NWO), grant 275-70-029 and by a Marie Curie International Research Staff Exchange Scheme Fellowship within the 7th European Community Framework Programme (grant number 269173).

DOI 10.1515/9781501505492-202

Table of contents

III Implications for language teaching and translation

List of contributors

Barend Beekhuizen
Department of Computer Science
University of Toronto
Sandford Fleming Building
10 King's College Road
Toronto, Ontario   M5S 3G4
Canada
barendbeekhuizen@gmail.com

Huub van den Bergh
UiL OTS – Utrecht University
Trans 10
NL-3512 JK   Utrecht
The Netherlands
h.vandenbergh@uu.nl

Rens Bod
University of Amsterdam
Postbus 94242
NL-1090 GE   Amsterdam
The Netherlands
l.w.m.bod@uva.nl

Jacqueline Evers-Vermeul
UiL OTS – Utrecht University
Trans 10
NL-3512 JK   Utrecht
The Netherlands
j.evers@uu.nl

Natalia Gagarina
Zentrum für Allgemeine Sprachwissenschaft
Schützenstraße 18
10117   Berlin
Germany
gagarina@zas.gwz-berlin.de

Steven Gillis
University of Antwerp
Prinsstraat 13
B-2000   Antwerpen
Belgium
steven.gillis@uantwerpen.be

Gaëtanelle Gilquin
Institut Langage et Communication
Université catholique de Louvain
Place Blaise Pascal 1
B-1348   Louvain-la-Neuve
Belgium
gaetanelle.gilquin@uclouvain.be

Hana Gustafsson
MultiLing Center for Multilingualism in
Society across the Lifespan
University of Oslo
PO Box 1102 Blindern
N-0317   Oslo
Norway
hana.gustafsson@iln.uio.no

Maria Mos
Tilburg University
Postbus 90153
NL-5000 LE   Tilburg
The Netherlands
maria.mos@tilburguniversity.edu

Elma Nap-Kolhoff
napkolhoff@gmail.com

Déogratias Nizonkiza
Centre for Academic and Professional
Language Practice
North-West University
(Potchefstroom Campus)
11 Hoffman Street
2531   Potchefstroom
South Africa
deogratias.nizonkiza@mcgill.ca

Rasmus Steinkrauss
LET – Applied Linguistics
University of Groningen
Postbus 716
NL-9700 AS   Groningen
The Netherlands
r.g.a.steinkrauss@rug.nl

Karen Sullivan
School of Languages and Cultures
University of Queensland
Brisbane, QLD 4072
Australia
ksull@uq.edu.au

Elena Tribushinina
UiL OTS – Utrecht University
Trans 10
NL-3512 JK   Utrecht
The Netherlands
e.tribushinina@uu.nl

Eva Valcheva
Freie Universität Berlin
Habelschwerdter Allee 45
14195 Berlin
Germany
valcheva@zedat.fu-berlin.de

Javier Valenzuela
Departamento de Filología Inglesa
University of Murcia
Campus de la Merced
Plaza de la Universidad s/n
30071   Murcia
Murcia
Spain
jvalen@um.es

Arie Verhagen
Leiden University
Van Wijkplaats 2
NL-2311 BX   Leiden
The Netherlands
a.verhagen@hum.leidenuniv.nl

Anne Vermeer
Tilburg University
Postbus 90153
NL-5000 LE   Tilburg
The Netherlands
anne.vermeer@uvt.nl

Marjolijn Verspoor
Department of English Language and Culture
University of Groningen
Postbus 716
NL-9700 AS   Groningen
The Netherlands
m.h.verspoor@rug.nl

Elena Tribushinina and Jacqueline Evers-Vermeul

Language acquisition and language teaching in the usage-based framework

1 Introduction

In the generative tradition, language acquisition in childhood and after puberty are seen as two fundamentally different processes. Children acquiring their first (L1) or second (L2) language are thought to have access to Universal Grammar (UG). The ease with which they acquire language – in terms of both acquisition rate and ultimate attainment – is explained by the fact that young learners only need input to set the parameters based on the input they hear and that the rest of the grammar is already available to them through the innate language acquisition device (Chomsky 1975, 1988; Pinker 1989). In contrast, post-puberal learners supposedly have either no access to UG or only a partial or indirect access (through L1), which is taken as an explanation of the slower acquisition rate and overall non-native outcomes. For example, one generative view argues that post-puberty L2ers are unable to acquire functional features that are not available in their L1 (Hawkins and Chan 1997).

A major problem of the generative account in our view is that the presence of UG is not falsifiable: It is not possible to look into the brain of a human being in the hope to find a language acquisition device. However, what *can* be done empirically is verifying that language acquisition from input, without positing an inborn grammar, is possible. This is exactly the path that language acquisition researchers working in the usage-based paradigm have embarked upon, inspired by Tomasello's pioneering work in the field (Tomasello 1992, 2000a, 2000b, 2003). That is why usage-based studies of language development are by definition empirical in nature.

This volume presents state-of-the-field research on language acquisition in naturalistic and instructed settings from the perspective of two major usage-based approaches: Cognitive Linguistics and Construction Grammar. Within the usage-based approach, language can be acquired from input due to the use of domain-general learning mechanisms, such as pattern-finding, analogy, generalization and entrenchment (Tomasello 2003). Input properties such as type and token frequencies, conceptual complexity and communicative significance play a crucial role in all kinds of acquisition. Therefore there is no need to postulate

Elena Tribushinina and **Jacqueline Evers-Vermeul**, UiL OTS – Utrecht University

DOI 10.1515/9781501505492-001

fundamentally different acquisition mechanisms for L1, L2 and foreign language (FL) acquisition. Both children and adults make use of the same learning mechanisms, and the same input properties are important determinants of acquisition across ages and populations (Ellis 2008).

Following this general spirit of the usage-based enterprise, we do not divide the chapters into parts according to the type of acquisition (L1, L2 in naturalistic and instructed settings). Rather, the book is divided into three parts based on the approach undertaken in the chapters. Part I contains mainly theoretical contributions reflecting on the applications of the usage-based paradigm in L1 and L2 research, and critically assessing the commonly used methodologies. Part II includes empirical studies examining the role of various factors influencing language development along the lines of Cognitive Linguistics and Construction Grammar. The factors investigated include input frequency, family size, communicative function, conceptual complexity and language transfer. The chapters in Part III take a more applied approach and discuss the implications of usage-based language acquisition research for teaching and translation practices.

This volume takes an integrative approach and shows that Cognitive Linguistics and Construction Grammar can provide a valuable unified framework for the study of different types of language acquisition in monolingual and bilingual contexts. Common to the chapters in the present volume is that they emphasize a win-win situation, in which language acquisition research greatly benefits from theoretical constructs developed in Cognitive Linguistics and Construction Grammar, and at the same time helps to fine-tune a usage-based theory of language. On the one hand, the usage-based paradigm provides a unified explanatory framework for the study of L1 and L2 acquisition. On the other hand, the contributions critically assess theoretical claims made in Cognitive Linguistics and Construction Grammar against solid empirical data, which leads to further refinement of the theory.

2 Theoretical and methodological foundations of language acquisition from a usage-based perspective

The first two chapters of the volume present theoretical considerations about usage-based studies of L1 and L2 acquisition, respectively. In *Advances and lacunas in usage-based studies of first language acquisition*, Elena Tribushinina and Steven Gillis discuss the basic tenets and advantages of L1 research within the framework of Cognitive Linguistics and Construction Grammar by comparing it with the generative approaches to child language development. The authors conclude that usage-based approaches present an attractive paradigm for studying child language because they are empirically driven and assume a tight bond between language and other aspects of child development. Language is not learnt in a vacuum; children are individuals with developing executive functions, theory of mind, motor abilities, etc. Therefore, usage-based approaches, where language is studied as an integral part of human cognition, appear more viable than approaches where language is treated as a separate module, isolated from the rest of the human brain (Fodor 1983). At the same time, Tribushinina and Gillis critically reflect on the lacunas in the current usage-based studies of L1 acquisition. The authors demonstrate that the role of input frequencies in the process of language development is sometimes exaggerated in the usage-based paradigm and that other important factors such as cue detectability and reliability, conceptual complexity, functional load and communicative function of linguistic items deserve much more attention than they have hitherto received. The chapter also sketches important avenues for future research. The authors suggest that investigations in the truly usage-based tradition should pay more attention to the bidirectional relationships between language and other facets of human cognition. It is also important to take a more dynamic approach to child-caregiver interactions and systematically study how children and caregivers influence each other over time. Putting such questions would inevitably require the use of more advanced longitudinal methods, such as growth curve analysis.

In the next chapter, *Applied cognitive linguistics and second/foreign language varieties: Towards an explanatory account*, Gaëtanelle Gilquin gives a broad overview of the field of applied cognitive linguistics, with special emphasis on L2/FL teaching and L2/FL learning. With two case studies, the author illustrates how adding a cognitive dimension may help gain deeper insight into the processes underlying L2 acquisition. The first case study, which deals with the use of *indeed* by French-speaking learners, demonstrates how linguists can benefit from the combined use of learner corpora and elicitation techniques. While a comparison of learner corpora with bilingual corpora uncovers the transfer errors typically made by L2 learners, elicitation tests aimed at determining the prototypical equivalents found in the learners' mental lexicons help explain why transfer takes place, and why learners tend to associate a word in the L2 with a translation that hardly ever corresponds to it in reality: learners transfer the conceptual representation of the L1 word onto the L2 equivalent, without realizing that the L2 word may have a different conceptual structure. The second case study shows that a Construction Grammar approach may explain the misuse of prepositional complements in institutionalized second-language varieties of

English (New Englishes). In particular, it gives valuable insights into the (probable) processes leading to the production of non-standard constructions such as *discuss about* or *take into seriousness*. Both case studies demonstrate that the explanatory power of cognitive linguistics represents a valuable complement to the descriptive adequacy of corpus linguistics. The chapter ends with some promising avenues for research in applied cognitive linguistics. These include adopting a longitudinal approach to the cognitive study of L2/FL varieties, examining the language L2 learners are exposed to, and establishing whether there are any cognitive processes that are common to any type of language evolution, including L1 acquisition, L2 acquisition, pidginization, and diachronic development. As the author argues, the resulting insights are only a first step, which can lead to practical applications: the better one understands why learners get something wrong, the easier it is to help them solve the problem, so that these insights can themselves result in improvements in L2/FL language teaching.

The remaining two chapters of Part I address methodological issues in (usage-based) language acquisition research. In *Acquiring relational meaning from the situational context: What linguists can learn from analyzing videotaped interaction*, Barend Beekhuizen, Rens Bod and Arie Verhagen introduce a new method that may prove particularly useful in research on early word learning in general and acquisition of relational vocabulary in particular. How does the child derive the meaning of a novel word, given that the world offers so many possible interpretations? Several word-learning mechanisms and constraints have been proposed in the literature. However, the authors maintain that all hypotheses about how children arrive at the meanings of new words are doomed to remain speculative as long as we do not know what kind of situational context children are exposed to in naturalistic settings at the moment they hear a novel word. This is exactly what the proposed method aims to pinpoint. Beekhuizen and colleagues traced the co-occurrence of relational words and their corresponding visual cues in a database of video-recorded mother-child interactions during a simple game. The authors developed a formalized coding scheme for capturing the situational context that was matched with the transcriptions of the concurrent utterances. The results have revealed that some relational terms (e.g. *passen* 'fit') have an excellent match with the corresponding features of the real-world situation, which means that it should not be too difficult for 16-month-olds to deduce their meaning from the visual context. Some other words, however, have a less reliable situational profile. For example, the preposition *in* was barely concurrent with the visual scene of containment, probably because the mothers encouraged the children to put things into the box and the actual event of putting-in only took place later. The authors conclude that some relational words clearly have correlates in the perceivable context, whereas others are probably acquired with more support from other learning mechanisms. These findings provide valuable insights into the situatedness of child-directed speech, which so far has been largely overlooked in studies of early word learning. This method appears particularly suitable for testing the usage-based claim that it *is* possible to learn a language without any innate devices or linking rules.

Given that usage-based approaches to language acquisition often examine longitudinal data, a sound methodology is crucial in order to be able to draw correct conclusions. In their contribution *Validity issues in longitudinal research*, Huub van den Bergh and Jacqueline Evers-Vermeul address three validity issues relevant to longitudinal studies, illustrating them with examples from actual research: attrition, measurement invariance and density of measurements. First, the authors show that attrition is seldom at random, and hence may seriously affect the representativeness of the sample. They argue that a research design with overlapping measurements, or splitting the data in separate sub-samples, can circumvent effects of attrition, although the application of such designs limits possibilities of interpretation. A second methodological issue is so-called measurement invariance, which refers to the question whether the same constructs are measured on different occasions. The authors recommend paying more attention to the construction of tests, because apparent differences between children at different ages might otherwise simply be due to differences in the exact capacity that is measured with each test. Once such tests are constructed, firmer conclusions on growth can be drawn. In their discussion of the third methodological issue, density of measurements, the authors argue that researchers should aim at collecting dense data during the acquisition period of the linguistic phenomenon under investigation, as well as during the periods before and after acquisition takes place. Only with such dense data sets can non-linear changes in development be established.

3 Driving forces of language development

The chapters in Part II present empirical research on monolingual and multilingual development using a range of methodologies. Rasmus Steinkrauss' contribution *L1 acquisition beyond input frequency* examines the role of input frequency as well as of non-frequency related factors in the acquisition of German *was ist das* 'what's that' and closely related wh-constructions. Analyzing a dense corpus from a German boy in the CHILDES database Steinkrauss first establishes a very strong correlation between abstract combinations (e.g. WH+V+NP) in the input and the child's use of such combinations between the age of 2;0 and 2;11.

At the level of specific constructions the correlations were lower, but still significant. The author then goes on to show that two remarkable exceptions to these correlations – questions starting with *was ist das* 'what's that' or *was ist denn* 'what's+PART' – can be explained by taking into account their communicative functions. It was found that *was ist denn* combinations in the input are tied to a specific situation of first attracting the child's attention to a new object by means of expressing (pretended) surprise and then asking what that object is, a communicative situation the boy never creates, which explains his virtual non-use of this construction. The boy's overuse of *was ist das* 'what's that' is tied to an overgeneralization of the most frequent function (i.e., inquiring for the name of an object) of this construction in the child's language production. Steinkrauss' findings present a nice example of what kind of insights can be obtained if communicative functions of linguistic constructions and/or their situatedness are taken into account.

In *Acquiring and processing morpheme constructions: The MultiRep Model*, Maria Mos reports the results of four experiments testing the predictions of the MultiRep Model, a theoretical model describing how morpheme constructions are acquired by generalizing over lexically-specific constructions and gradually arriving at more abstract schemas. A central assumption of this model is that the original item-specific constructions do not disappear once the child has derived a more general construction. The four experiments tapped into different levels of representation and revealed that children make use of either lexically-specific patterns or more general constructions, depending on the demands of the task at hand. This demonstrates that linguistic knowledge is massively redundant and contains co-existing constructions of different levels of representation. The findings also reveal an important role of token and type frequencies: children performed better with more frequent complex words and with words having more morphologically related words (family size), which is interpreted as evidence of gradual development from lexically-specific to more general morphological knowledge. The enormous differences between items and between participants observed across the four experiments also point in the same direction.

The remaining three chapters in Part II deal with the multilingual development of early L2 learners. One of the basic premises of the usage-based approach is that input frequencies are paramount in language acquisition. Hence, multilingual development presents an interesting test-lab for usage-based theories of language, because bilinguals grow up with more than one language and inevitably receive less input in each of their languages than monolingual peers. Furthermore, there is a competition of language systems in the bilingual mind, leading to cross-linguistic transfer. Does this mean that dual language development follows a qualitatively different path? Elma Nap-Kolhoff targets this question in her contribution *The development of Dutch object-naming constructions in bilingual Turkish-Dutch children receiving low amounts of Dutch language input.* Unlike most studies looking either at simultaneous bilinguals acquiring two languages from birth or child L2 learners exposed to a second language around age four, the focus of this chapter is on the acquisition of a second language very early in life (between ages two and three). The analysis of several longitudinal corpora demonstrates that there are both similarities and differences in the development of the object-naming construction in the speech of monolingual Dutch-speaking children and Turkish children acquiring Dutch as L2. In general, the results suggest that bilinguals follow the same developmental path as monolinguals. However, their acquisition pace is slower due to reduced input in Dutch and some of their productions reveal traces of cross-linguistic influence from Turkish. The author interprets the results as supporting the usage-based approach to language acquisition, where both the amount of input and entrenched patterns (e.g. from L1) are crucial determinants of language development.

The last two chapters of Part II focus on the acquisition of discourse connec-tives (such as *and* and *because*) by early sequential bilinguals and investigate whether conceptual complexity influences (the order of) connective acquisition in bilingual individuals. In his chapter *Acquisition order of connectives in stories of Dutch L1 and L2 children from 4 to 8,* Anne Vermeer conducts a longitudinal study using the narratives elicited with picture stories at five measurement occa-sions. His findings show a remarkable resemblance between the connective use by monolingual Dutch children and bilingual Dutch children from Turkish and Moroccan immigrant families where Dutch is not used as a home language. Using the technique of implicational scaling, in which the frequency rank orders of the various connectives are equated to the acquisition sequence of these connectives, the author shows that the connective use in both developmental trajectories exhibits an increase in cumulative complexity. These trajectories are in line with the cognitive approach presented by Evers-Vermeul and Sanders (2009): over time, children use more and more connectives (with girls out-performing the boys), but causal connectives are only used in any substantial way from the end of grade 1 onwards. More complex connectives, such as *voordat* 'before', *totdat* 'until' and *zodat* 'so that' were hardly ever used during the period under investigation.

Elena Tribushinina, Eva Valcheva and Natalia Gagarina take a similar approach. In their contribution, *Acquisition of additive connectives by Russian-German bilinguals: A usage-based approach,* the authors compare how L1 Russian L2 German children (aged 4 to 6) use additive connectives in elicited picture narratives, compared to monolingual Russian- and German-speaking peers. Their findings are consistent with the cumulative complexity approach to connective acquisition (Evers-Vermeul and Sanders 2009): children have more trouble using negative connectives, such as *but* and extensively rely on less complex connectives such as *and*. The results also reveal that there is quite some cross-linguistic influence in a bilingual mind. Traces of cross-linguistic transfer have been attested both in the L1 and in the L2 of the bilingual children. However, cross-linguistic influence only affects elements for which there is a counterpart in the other language (e.g. the Russian *i* 'and'), but not language-specific elements with no competitor item in the other language (e.g. the Russian *a* 'but/and'). The authors conclude that frequency of use and language dominance are crucial factors shaping language production of bilingual children, which is consonant with the basic tenets of Cognitive Linguistics and Construction Grammar.

4 Implications for language teaching and translation

The last three chapters of this volume demonstrate how theoretical assumptions and empirical findings from the usage-based studies of language acquisition can be applied to research on L2 instruction and translation practices. The first of these chapters, Hana Gustafsson and Marjolijn Verspoor's *Development of formulaic sequences in Dutch L2 learners of English*, investigates the effect of instruction setting on the development of L2 idioms. The authors longitudinally traced the use of conventionalized expressions in the writings of two groups of Dutch L1 English L2 speakers – children enrolled in the bilingual Dutch-English school program (the high-input group) and their peers from the regular monolingual program (the low-input group). In both groups there was an increase in the frequency and length of chunks as a function of time. However, the high-input group developed a greater range of idiomatic expressions than the low-input group. After 2.5 years of intensive exposure, the high-input group even approached a native-like proportion of chunks in their writing. These results lend support to the basic assumption of the usage-based theories that the amount of input is a principal predictor of L2 development.

Déogratias Nizonkiza's chapter, *Predictive power of controled productive knowledge of collocations over L2 proficiency*, also deals with the development of idiomatic competence in L2 learners of English. After discussing a variety of tests measuring L2 learners' proficiency in producing collocations, the author presents the results of his own controlled productive test (modeled after Laufer and Nation 1999), in which a sentence context was provided and the missing target word, the noun of a verb+noun collocation, had to be supplied. The main issue is to study to which extent the productive collocation proficiency develops with proficiency level, and whether word frequency plays a role as well. To this end, Nizonkiza tested three groups of university students from Burundi (L2 students of English in their first, second, respectively fourth year), taking test items from four word frequency bands: the 2000-, 3000-, respectively 5000-word frequency bands (Nation 2006), and the Academic Word List (Coxhead 2000). His findings suggest that performance on collocations follows frequency bands, with collocations of words from higher frequency bands mastered first. Level of proficiency plays a role as well: controled productive knowledge of collocations develops alongside L2 learners' general language proficiency, although growth is slow at low levels, and only increases at more advanced levels. Insights such as the ones obtained by Nizonkiza, can be applied in L2 language teaching, for example by developing a syllabus of collocations that takes into account both word frequency and L2 proficiency level.

Finally, in *Comparing word sense distinctions with bilingual comparable corpora: A pilot study of adjectives in English and Spanish*, Karen Sullivan and Javier Valenzuela stress the potential role of bilingual comparable corpora as an approach to comparative lexical semantics. They first discuss the benefits of analyzing different types of corpora – parallel corpora, translation corpora, monolingual corpora of learner data, and bi- or monolingual comparable corpora – for L2 acquisition and translation studies. Then, the authors present the results of their study, in which they sorted the senses of four adjectives (English *smooth* and *soft*, and Spanish *suave* and *blando*) on the basis of distributional data (e.g. whether adjectives occur in predicative or attributive position) in a bilingual comparable corpus. This allowed a hierarchical cluster analysis of the relatedness of the senses of each individual word, and a comparison of the networks of related senses in the two languages. Outcomes such as the ones presented by Sullivan and Valenzuela can serve as a guide for L2 students, translators or lexicographers interested in finding the best approximation for a given source-language meaning in a target language, in four ways. First, a comparison of sense clustering allows them to recognize which types of senses of an item in the L1 correspond most closely to particular items in the L2. Second, these analyses draw attention to mismatches between deceptively similar L1 and L2 items. Third and fourth, the clusters can help choose lexical items with the intended (positive or negative) connotation or with the appropriate metaphorical sense.

Taken together, these chapters stress that usage-based data can and should more frequently be analyzed in order to increase our insight into and improve the language teaching of specific linguistic phenomena. Consonant with these authors, we urge the field of Cognitive Linguistics and Construction Grammar to collect and analyze more corpus data of various sorts.

References

Chomsky, Noam. 1975. *Reflections on Language*. New York: Pantheon.

Coxhead, Averil. 2000. A new academic word list. *TESOL Quarterly* 34 (2): 213–238.

Ellis, Nick C. 2008. Usage-based an form-focused language acquisition: The associative learning of constructions, learned attention, and the limited L2 endstate. In *Handbook of Cognitive Linguistics and Second Language Acquisition*, Peter Robinson, and Nick C. Ellis (eds.), 372–405. New York: Routledge.

Evers-Vermeul, Jacqueline, and Ted Sanders. 2009. The emergence of Dutch connectives: How cumulative cognitive complexity explains the order of acquisition. *Journal of Child Language* 36 (4): 829–854.

Hawkins, Roger, and Cecilia Yuet-hung Chan. 1997. The partial availability of Universal Grammar in second language acquisition: The 'Failed functional features hypothesis'. *Second Language Research* 13, 187–226.

Laufer, Batia, and Paul Nation. 1999. A vocabulary-size test of controlled productive ability. *Language Testing* 16 (1): 33–51.

Nation, Paul. 2006. How large a vocabulary is needed for reading and listening? *Canadian Modern Language Review* 63 (1): 59–82.

Pinker, Steven. 1989. *Words and Rules: The Ingredients of Language*. New York: Basic Books.

Tomasello, Michael. 1992. *First Verbs: A Case Study of Early Grammatical Development*. Cambridge: Cambridge University Press.

Tomasello, Michael. 2000a. First steps toward a usage-based theory of language acquisition. *Cognitive Linguistics* 11 (1/2): 61–82.

Tomasello, Michael. 2000b. The item-based nature of children's early syntactic development. *Trends in Cognitive Sciences* 4: 156–163.

Tomasello, Michael. 2003. *Constructing a Language: A Usage-Based Theory of Language Acquisition*. Cambridge, MA. / London: Harvard University Press.

I Theoretical and methodological foundations of language acquisition from a usage-based perspective

Elena Tribushinina and Steven Gillis

1 Advances and lacunas in usage-based studies of first language acquisition

1 Introduction

A central question in language acquisition research is how language is acquired by children in naturalistic settings. For a long time, it has been assumed, within the influential generative tradition, that parental input to children is largely uninformative of the target grammar and, therefore, not sufficient to enable children to learn language, the so-called *poverty-of-the-stimulus* problem (Chomsky 1975, 1988; Pinker 1989, 1994; see also Lidz and Waxman 2004; Lidz, Waxman, and Freedman 2003). Hence, in order to explain "how you get from here to there" generative grammar posits an innate component within the learner that is supposed to guide a child through the acquisition process by structuring the impoverished input in a way that makes learning possible. This innate structure is a set of hard-wired domain-specific principles, i.e. principles specific to language. The generative view hinges on the so-called *continuity assumption* that a child's grammar is essentially a miniature of an adult grammar. Language development is then seen as a matter of maturation and selecting the relevant parameters that match the input in the ambient language.

The generative approach has more recently been contested by the usage-based theory of language acquisition (Tomasello 2000b, 2003), a view suggesting that it *is* possible to learn a language from the input by means of social skills and powerful generalization mechanisms. In this chapter we review major advances made in usage-based studies of (first) language acquisition over the past years, critically assess the current research agenda in this area and suggest some avenues for future investigations.

Since usage-based approaches to language acquisition largely rely on cognitive linguistic theories of language, we start this chapter with an overview of the major tenets of cognitive linguistics (Section 1.1) and then review key assumptions and directions of usage-based research on language acquisition (Section 1.2). We do not strive for a complete overview of usage-based language acquisition research (for comprehensive reviews the reader is referred to Behrens 2009 and Tomasello 2003). Instead, in this section we focus on the main assumptions

Elena Tribushinina, UiL OTS – Utrecht University
Steven Gillis, University of Antwerp

DOI 10.1515/9781501505492-002

of the usage-based theory of language acquisition and thereby set a stage for a critical assessment of its current applications further in the chapter. Section 2 reviews studies on the role of input frequencies in language acquisition. Section 3 reflects on the definitions and operationalizations of caregiver input. Section 4 explores the relationship between language acquisition and other aspects of child development (cognitive, social, motor) and evaluates the conformity of usage-based acquisition studies to the domain-general spirit of cognitive linguistics. Main conclusions are summarized in Section 5.

1.1 Cognitive linguistics as a usage-based approach to language

A keystone of cognitive linguistics is language use (Bybee 1985, 2007; Goldberg 1995, 2006; Langacker 1987, 1999). Unlike generative grammar, cognitive linguistics assumes that knowledge of language is not an abstract grammar, but rather a result of generalizations over actual use. More abstract patterns of various levels of complexity are thought to be grounded in individual usage events. Hence no level of language can be studied independently of language use. According to Langacker (1987, 1990), cognitive linguistics is a usage-based model of language due to the maximalist, non-reductive, and bottom-up character of the approach, as opposed to the minimalist, reductive, and top-down spirit of generative grammar.

A central assumption in usage-based studies of language is that there is no autonomous language faculty and that linguistic activities of human beings are based on the same cognitive principles as various non-linguistic abilities, such as perception, reasoning, memory and motor activity. This principle stands in stark contrast to the basic assumption of generative grammar that language is an autonomous module separated from other cognitive abilities.

Cognitive linguistics is a *maximalist* approach in the sense that it considers the linguistic system to be a massive and largely redundant inventory of form-function units of various sizes (e.g. small morphemes *vs.* lengthy idioms) and degrees of abstractness and productivity, rather than a self-contained set of rules. In this paradigm, both highly general constructions (Goldberg 1995, 2006) and completely idiosyncratic units can be part of the linguistic system. In addition, there are mixed constructions that are partly lexically specified and also contain open slots, such as the famous *What is X doing Y* construction (e.g. *What's that fly doing in my soup?*) studied by Kay and Fillmore (1999).

Cognitive linguistics is *non-reductive* in the sense that general rules (schemas) and individual instantiations of these rules (specific linguistic units such as words and multiword utterances) are considered as phenomena of the same kind. Thus, Langacker discards Pinker's (1989) idea that only those linguistic phenomena that do not fit the general rules should be listed in the lexicon as a *rule-list-fallacy*. In Cognitive Grammar, rules and lists are not mutually exclusive. The same construction can be represented both in the generalized form (as a schema/rule) and by specific instantiations. This implies that the same unit, say a specific morpheme, can be represented in many different combinations, which renders the system redundant. This is nicely illustrated by the experiments reported in Mos (*this volume*) demonstrating that language users exploit different representations depending on the demands of the task at hand.

Finally, cognitive linguistics is a *bottom-up* approach to language, since it posits that more general patterns are abstracted from specific instances and usage events. Accordingly, attention is given not only to general rules, but also to specific instantiations of these rules and to the process by which people generalize over specific expressions and arrive at more abstract schemas. In Goldberg's words, "speakers' knowledge of language consists of systematic collections of form-function pairings that are learned on the basis of the language they hear around them" (Goldberg 1995: 227). Thus, grammar for cognitive linguists is not a device for producing utterances, but rather an inventory of symbolic resources. Since different people are exposed to different usage events, cognitive linguistics envisages that the linguistic systems of individual speakers do not have to be the same. Language acquisition is then seen as a process of "mastering a large inventory of patterns of activity" (Langacker 2009: 628). Since all linguistic units at various levels are seen as form-function pairings, cognitive linguistics predicts that the same mechanisms apply to the acquisition of various linguistic phenomena.

1.2 Usage-based theory of language acquisition

Within the usage-based paradigm, there is no need to postulate an innate component of grammar in order to explain "how you get from here to there", since language learning is thought to be possible due to early emerging social skills (chiefly, intention reading) and powerful generalization (pattern-finding) capacities of young humans.

1.2.1 Intention reading and joint attention

Human infants are able to develop unique social skills. Herrmann et al. (2007) found that chimpanzees and two-and-a-half-year-old human children have comparable cognitive skills for dealing with the physical world (including space, quantities and causality). However, human children far outperform chimpanzees on tasks of the social world (social learning, communication, theory of mind). These sophisticated social skills are argued to be a major driving force behind a child's communicative development, including the acquisition of language.

In the usage-based theory of language acquisition, the utterance is considered to be the primary unit of early language acquisition. An utterance is defined as "a linguistic act in which one person expresses towards another, within a single intonation contour, a relatively coherent communicative intention in a communicative context" (Tomasello 2000a: 63). This definition captures an important idea that children do not merely parrot parental input. Rather they understand communicative intentions of their conversation partners and (re)produce linguistic sequences with the same communicative function as in the input. This process is known as *cultural learning* (Tomasello, Kruger, and Ratner 1993). Thus, intention-reading is argued to lay a crucial foundation for the acquisition of language. Pre-linguistic infants are able to discriminate sounds, but they do not learn to comprehend and produce linguistic utterances before around their first birthdays; this is when the ability to understand other people's intentions emerges.

Intention reading has been shown to play a critical role in early word-learning (Akhtar and Tomasello 2000; Baldwin et al. 1996). On this account, children do not try to grasp the abstract meaning of novel words. Rather they try to understand what their communication partner wants to draw their attention to and, therefore, direct their attention towards the same entity (object, action, property) on which the speaker is focusing. Put another way, for word learning it is crucial that children are able to enter into a state of joint focus with the adult. Hence, understanding intentionality of other people's communicative behavior is seen as a key social skill needed to be a successful word learner.

Brooks and Meltzoff (2008) related vocabulary growth to infant gaze following and pointing. Infants who followed the adult's gaze and looked longer at the object, as well as infants who were pointing during the experimental session (at 0;10–0;11) had a faster vocabulary growth between ages 0;10 and 2;0. In the same vein, Carpenter, Nagell, and Tomasello (1998) found that children with earlier emerging joint-attentional skills also start acquiring words at an earlier age.

Joint attention has been shown to play a crucial role not only in word learning, but also in understanding longer utterances. In fact, recent evidence suggests that joint attention even enables toddlers to understand indirect language and draw relevance inferences (Schulze, Grassmann, and Tomasello 2013; Tribushinina 2012). Until very recently, it was assumed that children develop the ability to understand relevance implicatures (and implicatures in general) only by the time they are six or seven (Bernicot, Laval, and Chaminaud 2007; Loukusa, Leinonen, and Ryder 2007; Verbuk and Schultz 2010). However, Schulze et al. (2013) demonstrated that three-year-olds are able to draw relevance inferences if this process constitutes a necessary part of an ongoing interaction and is supported by joint attention. Tribushinina (2012) replicated this result and showed that even two-year-olds can understand quite complex indirect utterances when implicature generation is supported by joint attention and constitutes an intrinsic part of natural communication. In a context of a shopping game, children without joint attention with the person producing the target utterance had trouble understanding that a negative utterance such as *I find it boring* is an indirect refusal to buy a product. By contrast, children having joint attention with the "customer" performed equally well on direct and indirect, positive and negative utterances. These findings are consonant with the general idea that intention-reading supported by joint attention plays a key role in language comprehension and language development.

1.2.2 Piecemeal learning and generalization

On the usage-based view, children are both conservative learners and quick generalizers (Goldberg 2006: 91). A child's conservativeness involves the finding that early constructions are highly concrete and item-specific; children seem to merely learn them as *prefabs* (Dąbrowska 2004a) from the input language. This means that early in development children reproduce utterances (or rather parts of utterances) stored in the ready-made form from the input in communicative situations that are similar to the ones in which the utterances were pronounced by the caregivers.

Furthermore, this acquisition is piecemeal. The fact that a child has mastered, say, a locative construction with one verb does not necessarily mean that she has also acquired the same construction with other verbs (Pine, Lieven, and Rowland 1998; Tomasello 1992). Tomasello (1992) studied early use of verbs in his daughter's speech and proposed the so-called *Verb Island Hypothesis*, according to which children learn morphosyntactic properties, such as argument structure, morphological marking and subject-verb agreement, for each verb individually. Similarly, research on morphologically rich languages has repeatedly shown that children gradually master some inflections with some verbs and other inflections with different verbs (e.g. Gathercole, Sebastián, and Soto 1999; Pizutto and Caselli 1992; Rubino and Pine 1998; Stoll 1998). This means that productive use of person in one tense does not necessarily imply a person distinction in another tense (Gathercole et al. 2002).

Although a lot of research in the usage-based paradigm focused on verbs, it should be mentioned that item-specific learning is not restricted to the verbal domain. For example, Clark and Nikitina (2009) report that the acquisition of the plural marker –s proceeds in a piecemeal, word-by-word manner. Some nouns are already used in the target plural form, whereas the plural of other nouns can still be expressed in a non-canonical way, for instance, by combining *two* with the singular form of a noun (e.g. *two cow*). Pine and Lieven (1997) found that early determiner-noun combinations are also lexically-specific. Some nouns are initially combined with *a*, some with *the*, and in many cases determiner-noun pairings are part of a larger rote-learnt construction such as [*in the* N]. Interestingly, even the distribution of fillers, which presumably function as proto-articles, was shown to be to a large extent lexically-specific. The study by Taelman, Durieux, and Gillis (2009) revealed that fillers in spontaneous speech of a Dutch-speaking child were particularly frequent after a number of 'anchor' words such as *is* 'is', *ook* 'also' and *niet* 'not', i.e. words often followed by articles in child-directed speech.

Taking a more global approach, Lieven, Salomo, and Tomasello (2009) traced all multi-word utterances in the speech of four two-year-olds and related these utterances to the child's own speech in the preceding six weeks (cf. Dąbrowska and Lieven 2005; Lieven et al. 2003). The majority of the child's utterances could be related to what she had said before. More precisely, 58–92% of utterance types were either exact repeats of the child's previous productions, or could be related to previous utterances through only one operation, usually a substitution of a semantically similar slot.

The most straightforward implication of item-based learning is that child grammars are qualitatively different from adult grammars, which goes against the continuity assumption of generative grammar. According to the usage-based view, children arrive at more abstract grammatical representations by generalizing over the stored instances. Their rules/schemas gradually grow in abstractness "as more and more relevant exemplars are encountered and assimilated to the construction" (Tomasello 2003: 316). The onset of the generalization process is usually heralded by relatively late overgeneralization errors (e.g. Dąbrowska and Lieven 2005; Lieven et al. 2003; Tomasello 1992, 2000b). In other words, children start making errors once they proceed to productive use on the basis of the generalizations drawn from the lexically-specific constructions. Although we do not yet know exactly how this generalization process unfolds, many researchers follow the idea proposed by Marchman and Bates (1994) that children need a 'critical mass of exemplars' of a particular construction before they can make generalizations and extract more abstract rules.

2 Frequency is not the key to all doors

Frequency is a central notion in usage-based research. Converging evidence from naturalistic and experimental studies strongly suggests that it is a significant factor in the process of language learning. Therefore, this section starts with a review of usage-based studies illustrating the important role of input frequencies in acquisition (Section 2.1). Research on the role of frequency in language acquisition has been extremely fruitful, which may in part be due to the fact that frequency is easy to operationalize and to analyze (see also Steinkrauss, *this volume*). This said, the increasing attention to frequencies seems to over-shadow the role of other important factors, such as transparency of form-function pairings, functional load, conceptual salience, complexity and communicative functions of linguistic units. We briefly review these factors in Section 2.2.

2.1 Type and token frequencies in language acquisition

The notion of frequency plays a central role in usage-based studies of language processing and acquisition. Since grammar is grounded in usage, it is assumed that each event of use leaves a trace in the processing system and, therefore, has an effect on the stored representation. Thus, repetitions strengthen representations, which means that frequently used items become entrenched and, therefore, more accessible. However, not only token frequency, i.e. the number of times a unit is used, is important. Type frequency, i.e. the number of distinct items represented by the pattern, has also been shown to be of paramount importance in language development. To quote Bybee (2007: 15), "a certain degree of type frequency is needed to uncover the structure of words and phrases" due to the fact the construction is experienced with different units occupying a slot. Put differently, diversity of exemplars enables a child to draw analogies and to generalize over the stored instances. Hence, it is argued that token frequency leads to entrenchment, whereas type frequency correlates with productivity (Bybee 2007; Dąbrowska 2004b; Goldberg 2006).

There has been a plethora of studies demonstrating the crucial role of frequency in language processing (Ellis 2002) and acquisition (Lieven 2010). The basic idea is simple: the more frequently children hear a linguistic item the sooner they will acquire it (Majorano, Rainieri, and Corsano 2012; Roy 2009). For example, the order of acquisition of individual verbs was shown to correlate strongly with the frequency of verb use in the input (Naigles and Hoff-Ginsberg 1998; Theakston et al. 2004). In a similar vein, Blackwell (2005) found that cumulative frequencies of adjectives in parental speech are significant predictors of the order in which adjectives are acquired. Goodman, Dale, and Li (2008) report similar results for a range of grammatical categories, including nouns, verbs, adjectives and closed-class words. Furthermore, on a more general level, the more speech children hear, the faster they acquire language (Hart and Risley 1995; Hoff 2003; Huttenlocher et al. 1991).

Frequency is not only important in the acquisition of individual words; the acquisition of grammatical phenomena is influenced by the frequency of use as well. For example, the more often a word is used in the plural form in the input, the faster children will start using the plural marking on that word (Zapf 2004). Input frequencies were also shown to be a crucial determinant in the acquisition of higher-level syntactic constructions. In one such study (Matthews et al. 2005) English-speaking children in two age groups (2;9 and 3;9) heard sentences with a non-canonical (SOV) word order, as in *Bear Elephant dabbed*. The verbs used in the sentences could be of high, medium or low frequency. The children were then asked to describe the scenes introduced by the experimenter. In their descriptions, the younger children were more likely to adopt the non-canonical word order with low-frequency verbs than with high-frequency verbs. Older children had a preference for the canonical word order, which seems to suggest that they had acquired the abstract SVO schema of their target language. In contrast, two-year-olds' knowledge of the English word order appeared to be lexically-specific. For high-frequency verbs they had already received enough evidence of the target SVO order (which enabled them to correct the non-target sentences), whereas in the case of low-frequency verbs they tended to "trust" the order modeled by the adult speaker. Thus, frequently used items play a major role in forming constructional schemas (see also Pine et al. 1998). Not only token frequencies of individual words are important, also frequency of an item's morphological family plays a role (see Mos, *this volume*).

Frequency of use can also account for varying paces of acquisition across languages. In a longitudinal study of spontaneous child speech, Rozendaal and Baker (2008) compared the acquisition of determiners by Dutch-, English- and French-speaking children. Children acquiring French were the fastest to acquire determiners and reached Brown's 90% criterion of acquisition (Brown 1973) between 2;6 and 2;9. The English-speaking subjects attained the 90% criterion later, between ages 3;0 and 3;3. The Dutch-speaking participants were the slowest and did not yet reach the 90% criterion by age 3;3. These cross-linguistic differences are consistent with the frequency of determiners in the three languages. Bare nouns are hardly used in the French input, and are more frequent in Dutch than in English. Thus, learners of French receive more evidence favoring the use of an element preceding a noun than toddlers acquiring English and Dutch. The study by Rozendaal and Baker (2008) also demonstrates that the distribution of determiners across pragmatic functions in spontaneous speech of two-year-olds largely reflects input frequencies. For instance, indefinite determiners are associated with non-specific reference in both child-directed speech and early child speech, whereas definite determiners are used for discourse-given referents.

To conclude, input frequencies account not only for the order of emergence and pace of acquisition, but also for usage patterns in child speech. Frequencies with which linguistic items are used by the child appear to be determined by the distributions in the input. However, the influence of parental input decreases as the child grows older and comes to use words more independently, which can be taken as a marker of acquisition (Tribushinina et al. 2013, 2014; Van Veen et al. 2009).

2.2 Other important factors

2.2.1 Detectability and reliability of cues

Children acquiring a language use multiple cues that inform them of the target language structure. The Competition model (Bates and MacWhinney 1987; MacWhinney 2001) posits that cue strength is determined by four basic properties: detectability, task frequency, availability and reliability. Two of these factors are closely tied to input frequencies: *task frequency* pertains to the frequency of a category, and *availability* involves frequency of a cue within a category. But frequency effects are mediated by two other essential factors – detectability and reliability of cues.

Detectability concerns the possibility to detect the presence of a cue in the input. A cue may be very frequent, but non-salient due to, for instance, phonological factors. In line with this assumption, Smoczyńska (1985) found that the case-inflectional systems in Russian and Polish that are almost identical on paper are acquired at a different pace. The reason is that Russian inflections, unlike the Polish ones, are phonologically reduced to a schwa and, therefore, less easily detectable in the flow of speech. This is why Polish-speaking children acquire noun cases much faster than their Russian-speaking peers.

Cue reliability specifies whether the cue is unambiguously associated with a given category. Greater ambiguity in form-function mappings results in more protracted learning, since there is more competition between the cues. A case in point is the acquisition of grammatical gender in Welsh. The Welsh gender system is fairly opaque, with no one-to-one correspondence between form and function; the same type of mutation can be associated with different gender classes. For instance, soft mutation marks feminine gender in local lexical concord and masculine gender in distant constructs. Therefore, Welsh-speaking children are still acquiring gender at 9 years of age (Thomas and Gathercole 2007). In contrast, children exposed to languages with more transparent form-function correspondences in the gender domain were shown to acquire grammatical gender rapidly and fairly effortlessly (Karmiloff-Smith 1979; Lew-Williams and Fernald 2007; Pérez-Pereira 1991; Rodina 2007; Seigneuric et al. 2007, *inter alia*).

Further support for the crucial role of cue reliability comes from cross-linguistic investigations demonstrating that input transparency may indeed be a significant predictor of acquisition. There is growing evidence that (noun and verb) morphology is acquired faster in languages with a large paradigm (e.g. Greek, Croatian), where separate forms are available for different meanings, than in languages with sparse morphology (e.g. English, Dutch) where the same form can represent several different meanings (Dressler 1997; Gillis 1998; Laaha and Gillis 2007; Xanthos et al. 2011).

2.2.2 Functional load

In addition to the frequency of particular elements in the linguistic input, also the frequency with which these elements bring about meaningful distinctions are thought to determine how soon and how fast they are acquired. In other words, "the more work" an element (e.g., phoneme, feature) does in a language, the sooner it will be acquired. For instance, input frequency has been shown to have an effect on the order of emergence and the accuracy of production of consonants in the speech of children acquiring English and Cantonese (Stokes and Surendran 2005). Intuitively speaking, it is clear that the more a child hears a particular segment, the sooner that segment will be acquired. In other words, *input frequency*, the relative frequency of a particular segment in the ambient language, determines its acquisition order (e.g. Stokes and Wong 2002; Tsurutani 2007). Alternatively, it could be argued that the more a segment is used in the ambient language to differentiate one word from another, the sooner it will be acquired. This notion of relative use, which can be traced back to Martinet (1955), is often referred to as the *functional load* of a particular language element, such as a segment or a segmental contrast. Functional load refers to the extent to which a language makes use of that element (Pye, Ingram, and List 1987; Stokes and Surendran 2005; Surendran and Niyogi 2006). For instance, Ingram (1989) estimates the functional load of the consonant /ð/ in English to be fairly low: if all instances of /ð/ became /d/, communication would hardly be hampered. If English lost the /d/–/ð/ contrast, listeners would not be able to distinguish *then* and *den* out of context, but such minimal pairs are not very frequent in English.

According to Pye et al. (1987) functional load significantly correlates with the order of acquisition of (word-initial) consonants in Quiché-speaking and English-speaking children. Stokes and Surendran (2005) report significant negative correlations between functional load and the order of acquisition in English-speaking children, meaning that segments that carry a smaller functional load tend to be acquired later. Corroborating evidence is also offered by Amayreh and Dyson (2000), Catano, Barlow, and Moyna (2009) and So and Dodd (1995).

Van Severen et al. (2013) investigated the frequency and the functional load of word-initial segments in a large corpus of child-directed speech. The language addressed to 30 toddlers acquiring Dutch between six months and two years of age was investigated relative to the order in which those segments were acquired by the children. In this study a decisive impact of functional load (and input frequency) on the age of acquisition of word-initial consonants was established as well: the higher the functional load of a word-initial consonant in the ambient language, the sooner that consonant was acquired by Dutch-speaking children. But Van Severen et al. (2013) also established that input frequency and functional load correlate significantly, which means that a segment with a high input frequency tends to have a high functional load. Therefore the question turns up whether input frequency has an additional predictive power for acquisition order when the effect of functional load is partialed out, and – mutatis mutandis – if functional load has an additional benefit once the effect of input frequency is partialed out. The analyses reported in Van Severen et al. (2013) reveal that functional load still correlates significantly with acquisition order when the effect of input frequency is removed from the statistical model. The reverse is not true: there is no additional benefit of input frequency when the effect of functional load is withdrawn: input frequency has only a small, non-significant additional impact on the age of consonant acquisition.

2.2.3 Conceptual salience

Goodman et al. (2008) correlated the age of acquisition of specific lexical categories (common nouns, people words, verbs, adjectives, closed-class words) with frequency of their use in the input. The results show that within each lexical category, there is a negative correlation between input frequencies and age of acquisition, i.e. words that are used more frequently by caregivers are acquired earlier. However, for all classes taken together, the correlation was positive, which means that higher parental frequencies appear to be associated with later acquisition. More specifically, common nouns were the least frequent category in the child-directed speech in the CHILDES corpora used in this study, but learned the earliest. And, conversely, closed-class words were the most frequent in the input, but the slowest to be acquired. In this case, input frequencies obviously fall short of explanatory power. To account for this pattern, we need to appeal to conceptual salience of various word classes. It is widely assumed that nouns are acquired earlier than relational words (e.g. verbs, adjectives, prepositions) because prototypical referents of nouns – objects – are salient and accessible enough for a child (Gentner 1982). Relatedly, Dressler, Lettner, and Korecky-Kröll (2010) argue that the order in which patterns of compounding are acquired is related to the salience of concepts involved – nominal compounds are acquired before verbal ones, which in their turn are acquired faster than adjectival compounds.

Some concepts, such as agentivity, causality, possession and number, are so salient that children may attempt to express them even before they have started acquiring the morphological form associated with that particular meaning (Bloom 1970; Braine 1976; Brown 1973; Clark 2001; Slobin 1985). For example, pre-linguistic babies were shown to have understanding of number, including one, two, three and many (see Dehaene 1997 for a literature review). Interestingly, children look for forms to express the meaning of more-than-one before they discover the plural morpheme (Clark and Nikitina 2009). Such emergent forms include a combination of numerals with bare nouns (e.g. *two duck*), quantifiers (e.g. *more*) and pointing gestures.

2.2.4 Conceptual complexity

Input frequencies appear to be a more consistent predictor of age of acquisition for production than for comprehension (Goodman et al. 2008). Comprehension of linguistic items is more often related to their complexity. For instance, color terms are used frequently by parents and children in the third year of life (Blackwell 2005; Nelson 1976). This does not mean, however, that children acquire color terms at the age of two years. Research has repeatedly shown that even four-year-olds use color terms haphazardly, often applying them to the wrong colors (Bornstein 1985; Cruse 1977). The probable explanation of this production-comprehension asymmetry is that color concepts are conceptually demanding for toddlers (Kowalski and Zimiles 2006).

There is also ample evidence that conceptual complexity determines the order in which linguistic items emerge in child speech (Clark 2003; Clark and Clark 1977). In one such study, Tribushinina (2013) demonstrated that the order of emergence of spatial adjectives is influenced by the conceptual complexity of the words. Overall, spatial terms frequently used by the caregivers are also the first ones to emerge in child speech. Nevertheless, there are also deviations from this pattern that cannot be explained by input frequencies. For instance, the Dutch adjective *dik* 'thick/fat' emerges later and is used by children less frequently than might be predicted on the basis of input frequencies. This mismatch can be presumably attributed to the finding that *dik* is a semantically complex adjective denoting a secondary horizontal dimension (Clark 1973). Thus the effect of input frequency on acquisition is in this case constrained by the conceptual complexity of the linguistic item (cf. Tomasello 2003: 175).

Likewise, Evers-Vermeul and Sanders (2009) present evidence that the order of connective emergence is determined by cumulative cognitive complexity (see also Tribushinina, Valcheva, and Gagarina, *this volume*; Vermeer, *this volume*). Connectives denoting positive relations (e.g. *and*, *because*) are usually acquired before the more complex negative connectives (e.g. *but*, *although*). Additive connectives (e.g. *and*) are less complex and, hence, emerge earlier than temporal (e.g. *after*) and causal connectives (e.g. *because*). Within the causal domain, the order of acquisition has also been shown to be related to the conceptual complexity of the coherence relations involved. Children are able to understand and mark objective causal relations before they come to comprehend and express more complex subjective relations, such as speech-act and epistemic causality (Evers-Vermeul and Sanders 2011; Spooren and Sanders 2008; Van Veen 2011).

Gathercole et al. (1999) studied the use of verbs in the longitudinal transcripts from two Spanish-speaking children around their second birthdays, and their mothers. The results demonstrate that not all forms frequently used by the mother are acquired early and used frequently in child speech. The verbal forms that are frequently used by both children and their caregivers – imperative, infinitive and third person singular present tense – are all unmarked and, therefore, relatively simple. The forms that are frequently used by the parents, but emerge relatively late in child speech – second person singular present tense, present continuous, imperfect and present perfect forms – are both linguistically and conceptually more complex than the unmarked forms. However, when language offers two or more forms with the same level of complexity expressing similar meanings, the most frequent form will be acquired first. In conclusion, input frequency appears to interact with linguistic and conceptual complexity in intricate ways.

2.2.5 Communicative importance

Some frequent constructions are not used by children simply because the communicative need to produce them does not arise in child speech. A case in point are two types of WH-questions discussed by Steinkrauss (*this volume*). Using a dense corpus from the German-speaking boy Leo, Steinkrauss demonstrates that the questions *was ist das* 'what's that' and *was ist denn* 'what's+PART' that are both very frequent in the input and very similar in terms of conceptual complexity, are not exploited by the child to the same extent. Leo over-uses the former question type and barely uses the latter. The explanation of this pattern, Steinkrauss suggests, is that *was ist denn* questions are usually used by the parents after a token of surprise (e.g. *Look!*) aimed to draw the child's attention, or as repetitions of earlier questions not answered by Leo. The need to express these meanings does not arise in Leo's speech; hence he does not produce *was ist denn* questions.

The experimental study reported in Stoll (2005) is also suggestive in this connection. This study revealed that Russian-speaking children acquire Aktionsarten in their prototypical contexts. Telic verbs (e.g. *priexat'* 'come') that have a broad range of applications, both in perfective and imperfective aspects, are acquired earlier than ingressive verbs (e.g. *zaplakat'* 'start to cry') that are prototypically embedded in longer sequences of events. Therefore, in order to comprehend and use ingressives children need to be (cognitively and linguistically) mature enough to be able to represent ordering of events. Furthermore, their narrative ability has to be sufficient to start producing contexts making ingressives communicatively justified. Hence, children do not start producing ingressives before the time the communicative need for this construction arises and before they are cognitively up to it.

2.2.6 Other factors

Maekawa and Storkel (2006) investigated the development of expressive vocabulary in three English-speaking children and found that word length, rather than frequency, is one of the earliest cues used by the children: Shorter words appear in child speech earlier than longer words. Phonotactic probability is another early cue whose influence diminishes over time. Interestingly enough, frequency and neighborhood density (number of similar forms) were among the later cues. This study also found a lot of variability in the use of these cues: whereas word length was a consistent predictor for all children in this study, there was more variation in the extent to which frequency, phonotactic probability and density could predict the development of expressive vocabulary.

2.2.7 Summary

To recapitulate, although both token and type frequencies of linguistic items have been shown to play a major role in the language acquisition process, some other relevant factors determining patterns of development in child speech are often overlooked in usage-based studies. These factors include but are not limited to detectability and reliability of cues, functional load, conceptual salience, cognitive complexity and communicative importance of linguistic items. These factors interact with input frequencies in intricate ways. Therefore, it is important to combine quantitative analyses of child speech and parental input with more qualitative analyses informed by broader linguistic theories. Counting linguistic forms without taking into account their meaning and function is likely to give an incomplete or even distorted picture of development. What is more, studying linguistic forms independent of their semantics and communicative functions contradicts the basic premises of the usage-based enterprise.

3 What is input?

Since a leading claim of usage-based acquisition studies is that it is possible to learn language from the speech that children are exposed to, a bulk of research attempts to demonstrate that patterns in child language (output) can be related to distributions in the parental speech (input). In view of the central role that input plays in usage-based investigations, a serious thought should be given to what *input* actually is. Researchers investigating input factors in child language development often assume that there is a unanimous definition of *input*. The matters are, however, more complex than they may seem at first glance. Furthermore, the term *input* as such may be inappropriate given the current state of knowledge in the field, as we will try to show in this section.

3.1 Operationalization and analysis of input

The terms *input* and *child-directed speech* are often used interchangeably, probably because input effects are usually studied in naturalistic longitudinal investigations of spontaneous parent-child interactions. In this type of research a target child is commonly recorded in conversation with the primary caregiver, usually the mother. However, research by Shneidman and colleagues reveals that for families with multiple speakers child-directed speech from *all* speakers, and not just the primary caregiver, is the best predictor of the child's receptive vocabulary (Shneidman et al. 2013). Hence, it is crucial to study input provided by all caregivers and probably also by siblings. What is more, children can also learn from ambient language that is not necessarily directed to them. In other words, they hear not only child-directed speech (baby talk, motherese), but also a lot of (overheard) adult-directed speech. Researchers barely take that kind of input into account and so far it is not clear how this can be practically done and what effects such input has on language development.

Yet another problem that is insufficiently taken into consideration is that caregiver speech is not stable. Research often relates the order and pace of acquisition to (cumulative) frequencies in the input. But *the input* does not exist, since parental speech changes over time. Many studies demonstrate that parents modify their speech to young children in ways that support language learning (Majorano et al. 2012; Roy 2009; Snow 1972). This is in line with the idea of "audience design" (Clark and Murphy 1982). For example, Tribushinina et al. (2014) demonstrate that the frequency of color terms in child-directed speech increases between ages 2 and 3, as children grow older and become more cognitively and linguistically mature. Likewise, Bellinger (1979) shows that parental directives become less imperative and less explicit as children gradually develop the capacity to understand indirect language. Using a very dense corpus of an English-speaking child Roy (2009) demonstrates that caregivers gradually decrease the length of utterances containing a particular word as the child approaches the zone of proximal development (Vygotsky 1978) for that word. And when the word emerges in child speech, caregivers start gradually increasing the length of utterances containing that word. This finding shows how amazingly sensitive caregivers are to the needs and the capacities of their child and how they fine-tune their speech to scaffold language learning.

Since parents adjust their speech to the maturational level of the child, it is questionable whether relating the acquisition of specific phenomena to cumulative frequencies in the input is the right thing to do (Van Veen et al. 2013). Researchers sometimes try to solve this problem by dividing the investigated period into sub-periods, such as trimesters and by relating child speech to child-directed speech in the same sub-period. Notice, however, that such divisions are purely arbitrary and may therefore obscure developmental patterns and relevant changes in the relation between child speech and child-directed speech.

A method that appears particularly useful in studying input effects is a growth curve analysis (Goldstein 1979; Rogosa, Brandt, and Zimowski 1982; Singer and Willett 2003, see also Van den Bergh and Evers-Vermeul, *this volume*). In this type of analysis, the occurrence of a language phenomenon is related to age in a regression model. Growth curve analysis allows for a statistical test of growth and differences in growth, not only in general but also with respect to different children. In other words, both average development (generalizations over children) and individual differences are quantified and tested. Since age is used as a continuous variable, there is no need to divide the investigated period into (arbitrarily defined) sub-periods. Growth curve analysis does not require data from many children, since individual parameters depend on the number of observations for each child. So even case studies of a single child can be statistically analyzed and contribute new insights into the acquisition process (e.g. Robinson and Mervis 1998; Van Veen et al. 2009). Furthermore, if different children (parents) are compared, there is no strict need to have the same number (and length) of the recordings, and these recordings do not need to be made at the same age for different participants.

Differences in growth curves can be related to other types of variables such as parental input. In one such study, Van Veen and colleagues modeled the probability of connective use in a dense corpus of the German-speaking boy Leo. The results suggest that frequency of connective use by the parents in the same recording (short-term input), as well as cumulative frequencies of connectives in child-directed speech of all previous recordings (long-term input) are significant predictors of the probability of occurrence of individual connectives in child speech (Van Veen et al. 2009).

Growth curve analysis can be used in a wide array of domains. For instance, it has already been applied to study growth in the number of word tokens (Evers-Vermeul 2005; Robinson and Mervis 1998; Tribushinina et al. 2013, 2014; Van Veen et al. 2009; Van Veen 2011), growth of expressive vocabulary (Brooks and Meltzoff 2008; Huttenlocher et al. 1991; Rescorla, Mirak, and Singh 2000; Tomblin et al. 2005) and receptive vocabulary (Scheffner Hammer, Lawrence, and Miccio 2008), changes in grammaticality judgments (Rice, Wexler, and Redmond 1999), degree of morphological productivity (Hadley and Holt 2006), morpheme use in obligatory contexts (Rice, Wexler, and Hershberger 1998; Robinson and Mervis 1998), and percentage of correct use (Rice et al. 2000).

3.2 A child is not a computer

It has become very normal to use the term *input* in (usage-based) studies of language acquisition, and its appropriateness is almost never called into question. Very often the counterpart term *output* is used with reference to child language. We would like to argue that the input-output metaphor is intrinsically flawed, since it suggests that a child is a kind of machine that you can feed with input in order to get target language as output. What this mainstream approach seems to ignore is the fact that already from the first days of life infants are different individuals (McAdams and Olson 2010). For example, even at birth there are differences between babies in the deployment of selective attention, and these differences increase with age (Ruff and Rothbart 1996). There are also differences in dispositional traits – some new-borns are cheerful, others generally distressed.

Early differences in attention, mood, response intensity and inhibition herald personal traits under development. Any dispositional trait is determined by a multitude of genes, but genes interact with the environment in complex ways (McAdams and Olson 2010; Sameroff 2010). Phenotypic differences between people influence the way the environment reacts to these people. For example, cheerful babies are more likely to evoke warm responses from other people; and these responses, in turn, create an environment that further reinforces initial temperamental dispositions, resulting in a snowball effect (Caspi, Roberts, and Shiner 2005).

Similarly, child language development is not a unidirectional input → output process. Parents attune their child-directed speech to the child's capacities and dispositional traits. Parental strategies that are congruent with the child's profile seem to reinforce further development. For example, research by Welch-Ross (1997) has shown that parents provide more elaborative conversations about past events with children possessing higher representational skills, and children with higher representational skills are more responsive in these conversations. Likewise, children with larger vocabularies solicit greater maternal responsiveness (Tamis-LeMonda et al. 1996), more frequent book-reading (Raikes et al. 2006) and highly elaborative parental speech (Lazaridis 2013). Maternal responsiveness, book-reading and high-elaborative parental style, in turn, stimulate further development of the child's language ability, showing a snowball effect.

It is of paramount importance to study child language acquisition as a bidirectional process in which the child interacts with the environment in complex ways. This approach would be in line with a basic tenet of contemporary developmental psychology positing a child's dynamic rather than passive relationship with experience (Sameroff 2010). The field is clearly in need of a comprehensive framework for studying such dynamic interactions in the language acquisition process.

4 How domain-general are usage-based studies?

As explained in Section 1.1, cognitive linguistics postulates a domain-general view of language as an integral part of human cognition, hinging on the same cognitive principles as perception, reasoning, memory and motor activity. It is then surprising how seldom usage-based investigations actually study language acquisition in relation to other aspects of child development, such as cognitive, motor and socio-emotional development.

As noticed above, there are huge individual differences between children from early on. For example, there are 16-month-olds with productive vocabularies of over 150 words, but there are also children producing no words at all at this age (Bates, Dale, and Thal 1995). There is, however, a general tendency to look at average tendencies and mean developments, irrespective of the obvious fact that the average child does not exist. Overall, the study of individual differences has not been viewed as critical to understanding fundamental mechanisms underlying language acquisition.

There are, however, a few exceptions. Some studies have sought explanation of individual differences in child-internal factors such as processing speed (Fernald and Marchman 2012) and joint-attentional capacities (Brooks and Meltzoff 2008), whereas other investigations concentrated on child-external factors such as quantity and quality of parental speech (see the review in Topping, Dekhinet, and Zeedyk 2013). The time is ripe for a comprehensive approach unifying these research lines. Only looking at various aspects of child development in tandem would genuinely correspond to the domain-general spirit of usage-based approaches. In the remainder of this section, we will discuss several studies demonstrating that language acquisition is related to other aspects of human development, including the development of executive functions, theory of mind and motor development, and critically assess some of the lacunas in this type of research.

4.1 Predictors of language ability

4.1.1 Executive function

The term *executive functions* is commonly used with reference to a range of cognitive processes that underlie goal-oriented behavior and hinge on the neural systems of the prefrontal cortex. Components of executive function are inhibition, shifting, working memory and planning ability (Best and Miller 2010). Research on the relation between executive function and language development has by and large focused on bilingual populations (e.g. Carlson and Meltzoff 2008; Poulin-Duois et al. 2011) and various clinical groups including children with specific language impairment (Henry, Messer, and Nash 2012), cochlear-implanted children and adolescents (Kronenberger et al. 2014), patients after head injury (Channon and Watts 2003), as well as individuals with autism (Landa and Goldberg 2005) and schizophrenia (Binz and Brüne 2010).

Less attention has been given to the role of executive functions in typical language development. In one such study, Rose, Feldman, and Jankowski (2009) investigated the relation between four basic cognitive processes – memory, processing speed, attention and representational competence – at 12 months and language skills at 12 and 36 months. Two of these domains (memory and representational competence) were shown to be related to language, both concurrently and predicatively. The specific memory measures that proved related to language development are (immediate and delayed) recognition and recall. Within representational competence, three skills appear to be related to language; these include tactual-visual cross-modal transfer (matching tactual perceptions to visual ones), symbolic play (acting out pretended scenarios) and object permanence (understanding that a hidden object continues to exist).

A disadvantage of such studies – which are usually performed by developmental psychologists rather than linguists – is that they generally use very gross language measures and that operationalization of *language ability* is often restricted to only one or two domains. For example, in the aforementioned study by Rose and collaborators only vocabulary skills were taken into account. Language skills at 12 months were assessed by means of the *CDI: Words and Gestures* questionnaire (MacArthur-Bates Communicative Development Inventories). At the age of 36 months, receptive language was assessed by means of the Peabody Picture Vocabulary Test (PPVT). Productive language was assessed by means of the ETS Test of Verbal Fluency, in which participants are asked to name as many things as possible within three different categories in thirty seconds. It is possible that other cognitive processes prove relevant to other aspects of language use, such as phonology, morphology and syntax.

4.1.2 Theory of mind

It has long been assumed that theory of mind, i.e. the ability to predict and explain other people's mental states, develops very late, around the age of four. However, more recent studies using methods suitable for research with toddlers and infants (such as violation-of-expectation and anticipatory-looking tasks) revealed that even the ability to attribute false beliefs to others, which is seen as one of the most difficult theory-of-mind tasks, is present already in the second year of life (Baillargeon, Scott, and He 2010). Other aspects of theory of mind also start emerging already in infancy.

It has been shown on numerous occasions that language development is related to the development of theory of mind, as it enables children to grasp communicative intentions of other people and to take others' perspectives into account (see, for instance, a meta-analysis in Milligan, Astington, and Dack 2007). A recent study by Norbury, Gemmel, and Paul (2014) reveals that children with specific language impairment (SLI) have as much (if not more) difficulty talking about other people's mental states as autistic children.

4.1.3 Motor development

Relatively little attention in the literature has been devoted to the relationship between language acquisition and motor development. In an overview article Iverson (2010) argues that motor development gives infants myriad opportunities to practice skills that are necessary for language acquisition and communicative development. For example, it is argued that the peak in the frequency of rhythmic arm movements (e.g. rattle-shaking) around the age of 28 weeks facilitates development of reduplicated babbling by providing an infant with an opportunity to practice the production of rhythmically organized actions and facilitates infants' awareness of correlations between their movements and resultant sound patterns. In a similar fashion, Iverson (2010) maintains that there is a close relationship between infants' increasingly sophisticated actions on objects and the vocabulary spurt. Development of object manipulation skills gives an infant an opportunity to learn about progressively more specific properties of objects and thereby to attribute increasingly specific meanings to objects. This process of connecting meaning with a referent is fundamental for word learning.

In the same vein, attainment of motor milestones, such as unsupported sitting and walking, was also shown to predict the acquisition of language (Oudgenoeg-Paz, Volman, and Leseman 2012). These motor developments change the child's interaction with objects and people in the environment. For example, unsupported sitting frees infants' hands and makes object exploration easier. Crawling and walking allows children to obtain objects that were previously out of reach. These changes also expose children to a new type of linguistic input (e.g. prohibitions) and motivate the acquisition of new communicative skills, such as communicating about distal referents.

Another piece of evidence supporting the relationship between linguistic and motor development is that language-impaired children commonly exhibit concomitant impairments in motor skill (see Hill 2001 for a review). Iverson and Braddock (2011) report that children with SLI perform more poorly than peers with typical language development on measures of fine and gross motor abilities, but make enhanced use of gestures probably as a means to compensate for poor language skills. Remarkably, even though children with SLI have a slower manual response to a stimulus, such as striking a key or touching a response pad (Windsor 2002; Windsor et al. 2001), they do not have a similar problem with eye-movements: When language-impaired children know the meaning of the word being processed, they look at the referent of that word as fast as their unimpaired peers do (Mak et al., 2016) and can even anticipate the upcoming object noun based on the semantics of the predicate verb (Andreu, Sanz-Torrent, and Trueswell 2013). This makes eye-tracking experiments by means of the visual world paradigm an excellent method for comparing language processing in impaired and unimpaired groups of learners.

4.2 What is still needed?

Although studies looking at the relationship between language and other aspects of child development are extremely valuable, we would like to suggest two directions for improvement.

4.2.1 Striving for a complete developmental picture

First, most investigations focus on the relationship between language and one more thing (e.g. working memory or theory of mind). There are hardly any in studies trying to look at child development as a complex process in which various aspects are inter-related. It would be very useful to look at several aspects of child development in tandem, as this could reveal that relationships between language development and, for example, cognitive development are mediated by a third factor. For instance, there is voluminous evidence that language and theory-of-mind development are closely related. Notice, however, that it is still possible that there is a third underlying factor (e.g. executive function) that brings about the development in both domains (Astington and Jenkins 1999; Hughes 1998).

A case in point is Lazaridis (2013), a study investigating factors that contribute to the child's developing understanding of *Temporally Extended Self*, i.e. understanding that self continues to exist through time despite any internal and external changes. The results of this investigation demonstrate that caregivers' conversational style predicts child language ability. Further, child language ability and caregivers' conversational style have a direct effect on child's cognitive maturity (mental age). In addition, this study shows that theory of mind is the only significant predictor of the emergence of the Temporally Extended Self, although caregiver conversational style partially mediates the effects of theory of mind. Lazaridis' investigation provides a good example of how various aspects of child development and parent-child interactions are intertwined in the maturational process. It is therefore very important to include several facets of child development within one study and scrutinize their complex interrelationships.

4.2.2 More attention to bidirectional relations

Second, researchers usually try to establish the influence of cognitive abilities on language development. However, there is increasing evidence that the relationship between language and other aspects of human development is bidirectional (see Christie and Gentner 2012 for a recent review). For example, children's linguistic development has been shown to interact with their developing categorization ability. On the one hand, ability to assign objects to categories stimulates learning labels for categories. But, on the other hand, exposure to linguistic labels draws a child's attention to the underlying concept and in this way facilitates categorization behavior (Gopnik and Meltzoff 1987).

A particularly interesting piece of evidence of how linguistic development may stimulate conceptual development comes from the study by Gopnik, Choi, and Baumberger (1996), which shows that categorization abilities arise later in children acquiring Korean compared to children exposed to English. The explanation offered by Gopnik and colleagues is that nouns, i.e. linguistic labels for object categories, are less prevalent in Korean than in English. Hence, English-speaking children get more cues of (at least) nominal categorization than their peers learning Korean. More recently, Borovsky and Elman (2006) presented evidence from computer simulations converging with Gopnik and Meltzoff's idea of the complex inter-relationship between word learning and developing categorization capacity.

Within usage-based approaches to language acquisition, it is well-established that analogical reasoning plays a crucial role in language learning: Semantic and grammatical categories are formed by comparing different uses of a linguistic item and generalizing over them. However, there is much less attention to the fact that relational language can bolster the development of analogical reasoning, because relational terms can "invite attention to a relational construal of a situation" (Gentner and Christie 2010: 273). For instance, Gentner, Anggoro, and Klibanoff (2011) found that children are better able to draw an analogy if relations underlying analogies are marked by relational nouns (e.g. "The first word is *dax*. The knife is the *dax* for the watermelon. Now it's your turn. Which one of these (paper, pencil, scissors) is the *dax* for the paper?") compared to descriptions without relational nouns (e.g. "The knife *goes with* the watermelon. Now it's your turn. Which one of these *goes with the paper in the same way?*").

Similarly, a series of experiments conducted by Loewenstein and Gentner (2005) revealed that pre-schoolers perform better on spatial relational mapping tasks if they previously heard spatial terms describing the task situation. This effect was contingent on the semantics of the spatial expressions involved; the locative nouns *top-middle-bottom* had a greater and earlier effect compared to the prepositions *on-in-under*. Although these two sets of spatial expressions can both be used with reference to the same locations, the nouns *top, middle* and *bottom* highlight an integrated system of relations within a single situation, whereas the corresponding prepositions convey separate figure-ground relations and are in this sense less connected with each other. As a result, children performed much better on the spatial mapping task in the noun condition compared to the preposition condition. Interestingly, even the presence of the word for *like* in children's vocabularies appears to influence the ability to compare and use analogy (Özçalişkan et al. 2009).

In the literature on the relation between language and theory of mind, there is also quite some evidence in favor of bidirectional relationships between language and cognition. Research shows, for example, that exposure to discourse elements related to mental states (e.g. evidentials, mental verbs, complement clauses) may trigger children's attention to other people's desires, beliefs and states of knowledge and thereby to the development of theory of mind (see De Villiers 2007 and references therein). For example, Hale and Tager-Flusberg (2003) report that explicit training on sentential complementation leads to an enhanced performance on false-belief tasks (see also De Villiers and Pyers 2002). Interestingly enough, other aspects of complex syntax, such as comprehension of relative clauses, appear to have no influence on the development of theory of mind. The special status of tensed complements can probably be attributed to the fact that they are commonly used to discuss contradictions between mental states and reality. A child needs to understand, for instance, that the sentence such as *Mary thought the earth was flat* can be true even if the proposition of the embedded clause is false. In this way, sentential complements may draw a child's attention to varying perspectives on the same piece of reality and on possible mismatches between reality and the propositions held in the mind.

In a similar vein, De Mulder (2011) has shown that the relation between theory of mind and linguistic development is bidirectional and not the same for different language phenomena. Earlier theory of mind was shown to predict later vocabulary, but earlier vocabulary also predicted later theory of mind. More specifically, children's performance on spatial terms (e.g. locative prepositions) proved to be a particularly good predictor of later theory of mind. De Mulder argues that spatial prepositions may force children to consider multiple perspectives on the same scene (e.g. what is *left* for me is *right* for the person in front of me) and thereby facilitate the development of theory of mind.

Not only specific linguistic elements, but also discourse practices as such may bootstrap the development of theory of mind. For example, Dunn et al. (1991) found that engagement in family talk about feeling states and, to a somewhat lesser extent, about causality was positively correlated with toddlers' performance on false-belief tasks at a later moment.

A recent study by Song, Spier and Tamis-LeMonda (2014) demonstrates that not only child language development, but also changes in child-directed speech involve a complex bidirectional relationship with the child's cognitive development. Mothers' language use at age 2;0 was associated with the growth of children's cognitive abilities between ages 2;0 and 3;0; and children's cognitive status at age 2;0 was in turn related to changes in maternal language use between ages 2;0 and 3;0.

In a nutshell, there is a growing body of research demonstrating the important role of attention to complex bidirectional relations between language acquisition and other aspects of child development. We believe that usage-based studies of language acquisition could benefit greatly from considering various aspects of child development in tandem and from studying complex interactions between linguistic, cognitive, socio-emotional and sensory-motor development.

5 Conclusion

Usage-based approaches have provided a plethora of useful insights into the process of child language acquisition. A major contribution of usage-based studies is that they have convincingly demonstrated that there is no need to postulate an innate grammar, since it *is* possible to get from here to there. Children *are* able to learn a language from child-directed speech and ambient language; this process is supported by unique social skills of human infants and constrained by the properties of caregiver speech, such as frequency, reliability of cues, functional load and communicative function. The contribution of usage-based studies to our understanding of the fundamental acquisition processes can hardly be overestimated.

However, this chapter has also revealed a number of lacunas in usage-based approaches to language development. An important avenue for future research would be investigations in the truly domain-general spirit of the usage-based approach, with more attention to complex bidirectional relations between language and other aspects of human development. Furthermore, there is a growing awareness that the input-output metaphor commonly used in studies of language acquisition is outdated and fundamentally flawed. Child and environment interact in multiple complex ways and influence each other in the developmental process. The field is in need of more longitudinal studies that would capture such non-trivial dynamic relationships between child and environment and pay more attention to individual differences. It is important to remember: the average child does not exist.

References

Akhtar, Nameera, and Michael Tomasello. 2000. The social nature of words and word learning. In *Becoming a Word Learner: A Debate on Lexical Acquistion*, Roberta M. Golinkoff, Kathy Hirsh-Pasek, Lois Blom, Linda B. Smith, Amanda L. Woodward, Nameera Akhtar, Michael Tomasello, and George Hollich (eds.), 115–135. Oxford: Oxford University Press.

Amayreh, Nameera, and Alice Dyson. 2000. The acquisition of Arabic consonants. *Journal of Speech, Language & Hearing Research* 41: 642–653.

Andreu, Llorenç, Mònica Sanz-Torrent, and John C. Trueswell. 2013. Anticipatory sentence processing in children with specific language impairment: Evidence from eye movements during listening. *Applied Psycholinguistics* 34: 5–44.

Astington, Janet Wilde, and Jennifer M. Jenkins. 1999. A longitudinal study of the relation between language and theory-of-mind development. *Developmental Psychology* 35: 1311–1320.

Baillargeon, Renée, Rose M. Scott, and Zijing He. 2010. False-belief understanding in infants. *Trends in Cognitive Science* 14: 110–118.

Baldwin, Dare A., Ellen M. Markman, Brigitte Bill, Renee N. Desjardins, Jane M. Irwin, and Glynnis Tidball. 1996. Infants' reliance on a social criterion for establishing word-object relations. *Child Development* 67: 3135–3153.

Bates, Elizabeth, and Brian MacWhinney. 1987. Competition, variation, and language learning. In *Mechanisms of Language Acquisition*, Brian MacWhinney (ed.), 157–193. Mahwah, NJ: Erlbaum.

Bates, Elizabeth, Philip Dale, and Donna Thal. 1995. Individual differences and their implications for theories of language development. In *Handbook of Child Language*, Paul Fletcher, and Brian MacWhinney (eds.), 96–151. Oxford: Basil Blackwell.

Behrens, Heike. 2009. Usage-based and emergentist approaches to language acquisition. *Linguistics* 47 (2): 383–411.

Bellinger, David. 1979. Changes in the explicitness of mothers' directives as children age. *Journal of Child Language* 6: 443–458.

Bernicot, Josie, Virginie Laval, and Stephanie Chaminaud. 2007. Nonliteral language forms in children: In what order are they acquired in pragmatics and metapragmatics? *Journal of Pragmatics* 39: 2115–2132.

Best, John R., and Patricia Miller. 2010. A developmental perspective on executive function. *Child Development* 81: 1641–1660.

Binz, Britta, and Marin Brüne. 2010. Pragmatic language abilities, mentalising skills and executive functioning in schizophrenia spectrum disorders. *Clinical Neuropsychiatry* 7: 91–99.

Blackwell, Aleka. 2005. Acquiring the English adjective lexicon: Relationships with input properties and adjectival semantic typology. *Journal of Child Language* 32: 535–562.

Bloom, Lois. 1970. *Language Development: Form and Function in Emerging Grammars*. Cambridge, MA: MIT Press.

Bornstein, Marc H. 1985. On the development of color naming in young children: Data and theory. *Brain and Language* 26: 72–93.

Borovsky, Arielle, and Jeff Elman. 2006. Language input and semantic categories: A relation between cognition and early word learning. *Journal of Child Language* 33: 759–790.

Braine, Martin D.S. 1976. *First Word Combinations* (Monographs of the Society for Research in Child Development 41). Chicago: University of Chicago Press.

Brooks, Rechele, and Andrew N. Meltzoff. 2008. Infant gaze following and pointing predict accelerated vocabulary growth through two years of age: A longitudinal, growth curve modelling study. *Journal of Child Language* 35: 207–220.

Brown, Roger. 1973. *A First Language: The Early Stages*. Cambridge, MA: Harvard University Press.

Bybee, Joan. 1985. *Morphology*. Amsterdam: John Benjamins. 2007. *Frequency of Use and the Organization of Language*. Oxford: Oxford University Press.

Carlson, Stephanie M., and Andrew N. Meltzoff. 2008. Bilingual experience and executive functioning in young children. *Developmental Science* 11: 282–298.

Carpenter, Malinda, Katherine Nagell, and Michael Tomasello. 1998. Social cognition, joint attention, and communicative competence from 9 to 15 months of age. *Monographs of the Society for Research in Child Development* 63 (4): 1–143.

Caspi, Avshalom, Brent W. Roberts, and Rebecca L. Shiner. 2005. Personality development: Stability and change. *Annual Review of Psychology* 56, 453–484.

Catano, Lorena, Jessica Barlow, and Marina Irene Moyna. 2009. A retrospective study of phonetic inventory complexity in acquisition of Spanish: Implications for phonological universals. *Clinical Linguistics & Phonetics* 23: 446–472.

Channon, Shelley, and Mike Watts. 2003. Pragmatic language interpretation after closed head injury: Relationship to executive functioning. *Cognitive Neuropsychiatry* 8: 243–260.

Chomsky, Noam. 1975. *Reflections on Language*. New York: Pantheon.

Chomsky, Noam. 1988. *Language and Problems of Knowledge: The Managua Lectures*. Cambridge, MA: MIT Press.

Christie, Stella, and Dedre Gentner. 2012. Language and cognition in development. In: *The Cambridge Handbook of Psycholinguistics*, Michael Spivey, Ken McRae, and Marc Joanisse (eds.), 653–673. Cambridge: Cambridge University Press.

Clark, Eve V. 1973. What's in a word? On the child's acquisition of semantics in his first language. In *Cognitive Development and the Acquisition of Language*, Timothy E. Moore (ed.), 65–110. New York and London: Academic Press.

Clark, Eve V. 2001. Emergent categories in first language acquisition. In *Language Acquisition and Conceptual Development*, Melissa Bowerman, and Steven C. Levinson (eds.), 379–405. Cambridge: Cambridge University Press.

Clark, Eve V. 2003. *First Language Acquisition*. Cambridge: Cambridge University Press.

Clark, Eve V., and Tatiana V. Nikitina. 2009. One vs. more than one: Antecedents to plural marking in early language acquisition. *Linguistics* 47 (1): 103–139.

Clark, Herbert H., and Eve V. Clark. 1977. *Psychology and Language: An Introduction to Psycholinguistics*. New York: Harcourt Brace Jovanovich.

Clark, Herbert H., and Gregory L. Murphy. 1982. Audience design in meaning and reference. *Advances in Psychology* 9: 287–299.

Cruse, D. Alan. 1977. A note on the learning of colour names. *Journal of Child Language* 4: 305–311.

Dąbrowska, Ewa. 2004a. *Language, Mind, and Brain: Some Psychological and Neurological Constraints on Theories of Grammar*. Edinburgh: Edinburgh University Press.

Dąbrowska, Ewa. 2004b. Rules or schemas? Evidence from Polish. *Language and Cognitive Processes* 19 (2): 225–271.

Dąbrowska, Ewa, and Elena Lieven. 2005. Towards a lexically specific grammar of children's question constructions. *Cognitive Linguistics* 16: 437–474.

Dehaene, Stanislas. 1997. *The Number Sense*. Oxford: Oxford University Press.

De Mulder, Hannah. 2011. *Putting the Pieces Together: The Development of Theory of Mind and (Mental) Language*. Utrecht: LOT. Available online: http://www.lotpublications.nl/Documents/272_fulltext.pdf.

De Villiers, Jill. 2007. The interface between language and Theory of Mind. *Lingua* 117 (11): 1858–1878.

De Villiers, Jill G., and Jennie E. Pyers. 2002. Complements to cognition: A longitudinal study of the relationship between complex syntax and false-belief-understanding. *Cognitive Development* 17: 1037–1060.

Dressler, Wolfgang U. (ed.). 1997. *Studies in Pre- and Protomorphology.* Wien: Verlag der Österr. Akademie der Wissenschaften.

Dressler, Wonfgang U., Laura E. Lettner, and Katharina Korecky-Kröll. 2010. First language acquisition of compounds. With special emphasis on early German child language. In *Cross-Disciplinary Issues in Compounding*, Sergio Scalise, and Irene Vogel (eds.), 323–344. (Current Issues in Linguistic Theory 311.) Amsterdam: John Benjamins.

Dunn, Judy, Jane Brown, Cheryl Slomkowski, Caroline Tesla, and Lise Youngblade. 1991. Young children's understanding of other people's feelings and beliefs: Individual differences and their antecedents. *Child Development* 62: 1352–1366.

Ellis, Nick C. 2002. Frequency effects in language processing. *Studies in Second Language Acquisition* 24: 143–188.

Evers-Vermeul, Jacqueline. 2005. *The Development of Dutch Connectives: Change and Acquisition as Windows on Form-Function Relations.* Utrecht: LOT. Available online: http://www.lotpublications.nl/Documents/110_fulltext.pdf.

Evers-Vermeul, Jacqueline, and Ted Sanders. 2009. The emergence of Dutch connectives: How cumulative cognitive complexity explains the order of acquisition. *Journal of Child Language* 36: 829–854.

Evers-Vermeul, Jacqueline, and Ted Sanders. 2011. Discovering domains: On the acquisition of causal connectives. *Journal of Pragmatics* 43: 1645–1662.

Fernald, Anne, and Virginia A. Marchman. 2012. Individual differences in lexical processing at 18 months predict vocabulary growth in typically developing and late-talking toddlers. *Child Development* 83: 203–222.

Gathercole, Virginia C. Mueller, Eugenia Sebastián, and Pilar Soto. 1999. The early acquisition of Spanish verbal morphology: Across-the-board or piecemeal knowledge? *International Journal of Bilingualism* 3: 133–182.

Gathercole, Virginia C. Mueller, Eugenia Sebastián, and Pilar Soto. 2002. The emergence of linguistic person in Spanish-speaking children. *Language Learning* 52 (4): 679–722.

Gentner, Dedre. 1982. Why nouns are learnt before verbs: Linguistic relativity versus natural partitioning. In: *Language Development. Vol. II: Language, Thought, and Culture*, Stan A. Kuczaj (ed.), 301–334. Hillsdale, NJ: Erlbaum.

Gentner, Dedre, Florencia K. Anggoro, and Rachel S. Klibanoff. 2011. Structure mapping and relational language support children's learning of relational categories. *Child Development* 82: 1173–1320.

Gentner, Dedre, and Stella Christie. 2010. Mutual bootstrapping between language and analogical processing. *Language and Cognition* 2: 261–283.

Gillis, Steven (ed.). 1998. *Studies in the Acquisition of Number and Diminutive Marking.* (Antwerp Papers in Linguistics 95.) Antwerp: Antwerp University.

Goldberg, Adele E. 1995. *Constructions: A Construction Grammar Approach to Argument Structure.* Chicago: University of Chicago Press.

Goldberg, Adele E. 2006. *Constructions at Work: The Nature of Generalization in Language.* Oxford: Oxford University Press.

Goldstein, Harvey. 1979. *The Design and Analysis of Longitudinal Studies: Their Role in the Measurement of Change.* London: Academic Press.

Goodman, Judith C., Philip S. Dale, and Ping Li. 2008. Does frequency count? Parental input and the acquisition of vocabulary. *Journal of Child Language* 35: 515–531.

Gopnik, Alison, Soonja Choi, and Therese Baumberger. 1996. Crosslinguistic differences in semantic and cognitive development. *Cognitive Development* 11 (2): 197–227.

Gopnik, Alison, and Andrew Meltzoff. 1987. The development of categorization in the second year and its relation to other cognitive and linguistic developments. *Child Development* 58: 1523–1531.

Hadley, Pamela A., and Janet K. Holt. 2006. Individual differences in the onset of tense marking: A growth-curve analysis. *Journal of Speech, Language, and Hearing Research* 49: 984–1000.

Hale, Courtney Melinda, and Helen Tager-Flusberg. 2003. The influence of language on theory of mind: A training study. *Developmental Science* 6: 346–359.

Hart, Betty, and Todd R. Risley. 1995. *Meaningful Differences in Everyday Experience of Young American Children*. Baltimore: Brookes.

Henry, Lucy A., David J. Messer, and Gilly Nash. 2012. Executive functioning in children with specific language impairment. *Journal of Child Psychology and Psychiatry* 53: 37–45.

Herrmann, Esther, Josep Call, Maria Victoria Hernández-Lloreda, Brian Hare, and Michael Tomasello. 2007. Humans have evolved specialized skills of social cognition: The cultural intelligence hypothesis. *Science* 317: 1360–1366.

Hill, Elisabeth L. 2001. Non-specific nature of specific language impairment: A review of the literature with regard to concomitant impairments. *International Journal of Language and Communication Disorders* 36: 149–171.

Hoff, Erika. 2003. The specificity of environmental influence: Socioeconomic status affects early vocabulary development via maternal speech. *Child Development* 74: 1368–1378.

Hughes, Claire. 1998. Executive function in preschoolers: Links with theory of mind and verbal ability. *British Journal of Developmental Psychology* 16: 233–253.

Huttenlocher, Janellen, Wendy Haight, Anthony Bryk, Michael Seltzer, and Thomas Lyons. 1991. Vocabulary growth: Relation to language input and gender. *Developmental Psychology* 27: 236–248.

Ingram, David. 1989. *First Language Acquisition*. Cambridge: Cambridge University Press.

Iverson, Jana. 2010. Developing language in a developing body: The relationship between motor development and language development. *Journal of Child Language* 37: 229–261.

Iverson, Jana, and Barbara A. Braddock. 2011. Gesture and motor skill in relation to language in children with language impairment. *Journal of Speech, Language, and Hearing Research* 54: 72–86.

Karmiloff-Smith, Annette. 1979. *A Functional Approach to Child Language: A Study of Determiners and Reference*. Cambridge: Cambridge University Press.

Kay, Paul, and Charles Fillmore. 1999. Grammatical constructions and linguistic generalizations. *Language* 75: 1–33.

Kowalski, Kurt, and Herbert Zimiles. 2006. The relation between children's conceptual functioning with color and color term acquisition. *Journal of Experimental Child Psychology* 94: 301–321.

Kronenberger, William, Bethany G. Colson, Shirley C. Henning, and David B. Pisoni. 2014. Executive functioning and speech-language skills following long-term use of cochlear implants. *Journal of Deaf Studies and Deaf Education* 19 (4): 456–470.

Laaha, Sabine, and Steven Gillis (eds.). 2007. *Typological Perspectives on the Acquisition of Noun and Verb Morphology*. (Antwerp Papers in Linguistics 112.) Antwerp: Antwerp University.

Landa, Rebecca J., and Melissa C. Goldberg. 2005. Language, social, and executive functions in high functioning autism: A continuum of performance. *Journal of Autism and Developmental Disorders* 35: 557–573.

Langacker, Ronald W. 1987. *Foundations of Cognitive Grammar.* Vol. 1. Theoretical prerequisites. Stanford, CA: Stanford University Press.

Langacker, Ronald W. 1999. *Concept, Image, and Symbol: The Cognitive Basis of Grammar.* Berlin & New York: Mouton de Gruyter.

Langacker, Ronald W. 2009. A dynamic view of usage and language acquisition. *Cognitive Linguistics* 20 (3): 627–640.

Lazaridis, Mary. 2013. The emergence of a Temporally Extended Self and factors that contribute to its development: From theoretical and empirical perspectives. *Monographs of the Society for Research in Child Development* 72 (2): 1–120.

Lew-Williams, Casey, and Anne Fernald. 2007. Young children learning Spanish make rapid use of grammatical gender in spoken word recognition. *Psychological Science* 18: 193–198.

Lidz, Jeffrey, and Sandra Waxman. 2004. Reaffirming the poverty of the stimulus argument: A reply to the replies. *Cognition* 93: 157–165.

Lidz, Jeffrey, Sandra Waxman, and Jennifer Freedman. 2003. What infants know about syntax but couldn't have learned: Experimental evidence for syntactic structure at 18 months. *Cognition* 89: B65–B73.

Lieven, Elena. 2010. Input and first language acquisition: Evaluating the role of frequency. *Lingua* 120: 2546–2556.

Lieven, Elena, Heike Behrens, Jennifer Speares, and Michael Tomasello. 2003. Early syntactic creativity: A usage-based approach. *Journal of Child Language* 30: 333–370.

Lieven, Elena, Dorothé Salomo, and Michael Tomasello. 2009. Two-year-old children's production of multiword utterances: A us agebased analysis. *Cognitive Linguistics* 20 (3): 481–507.

Loewenstein, Jeffrey, and Dedre Gentner. 2005. Relational language and the development of relational mapping. *Cognitive Psychology* 50: 315–353.

Loukusa, Soile, Eeva Leinonen, and Nuala Ryder. 2007. Development of pragmatic language comprehension in Finnish-speaking children. *First Language* 27: 279–296.

MacWhinney, Brian. 2001. The Competition Model: The input, the context, and the brain. In *Cognition and Second Language Instruction*, Peter Robinson (ed.), 69–90. New York: Cambridge University Press.

Maekawa, Junko, and Holly L. Storkel. 2006. Individual differences in the influence of phonological characteristics on expressive vocabulary development by children. *Journal of Child Language* 33 (3): 439–459.

Majorano, Marinella, Chiara Rainieri, and Paola Corsano. 2012. Parents' child-directed communication and child language development: A longitudinal study with Italian toddlers. *Journal of Child Language* 40: 836–859.

Mak, Willem M., Elena Tribushinina, Julia Lomako, Natalia Gagarina, Ekaterina Abrosova, E., and Ted Sanders. 2016. Connective processing by bilingual children and monolinguals with specific language impairment: Distinct profiles. *Journal of Child Language*, published online: 05 February 2016, DOI: 10.1017/S0305000915000860.

Marchman, Virginina, and Elizabeth Bates. 1994. Continuity in lexical and morphological development: A test of the critical mass hypothesis. *Journal of Child Language* 21: 339–366.

Martinet, André. 1955. *Economie des changements phonétiques.* Bern: Francke.

Matthews, Danielle, Elena Lieven, Anna Theakston, and Michael Tomasello. 2005. The role of frequency in the acquisition of English word order. *Cognitive Development* 20: 121–136.

McAdams, Dan P., and Bradley D. Olson. 2010. Personality development: Continuity and change over the life course. *Annual Review of Psychology* 61: 517–542.

Milligan, Karen, Janet W. Astington, and Lisa A. Dack. 2007. Language and theory of mind: Meta-analysis of the relation between language ability and false-belief understanding. *Child Development* 78: 622–646.

Naigles, Letitia R., and Erika Hoff-Ginsberg. 1998. Why are some verbs learned before other verbs? Effects of input frequency and structure on children's early verb use. *Journal of Child Language* 25: 95–120.

Nelson, Katherine. 1976. Some attributes of adjectives used by young children. *Cognition* 4: 1–31.

Norbury, Courtenay F., Tracey Gemmel, and Rhea Paul. 2014. Pragmatic abilities in narrative production: A cross-disorder comparison. *Journal of Child Language* 41 (3): 485–510.

Oudgenoeg-Paz, Ora, Chiel J.M. Volman, and Paul P.M. Leseman. 2012. Attainment of sitting and walking predicts development of productive vocabulary between ages 16 and 28 months. *Infant Behavior and Development* 35: 733–736.

Özçalişkan, Şeyda, Susan Goldin-Meadow, Dedre Gentner, and Carolyn Mylander. 2009. Does language about similarity play a role in fostering similarity comparison in children? *Cognition* 112: 217–228.

Pérez-Pereira, Miguel. 1991. The acquisition of gender: What Spanish children tell us. *Journal of Child Language* 18: 571–590.

Pine, Julian, and Elena V.M. Lieven. 1997. Slot and frame patterns and the development of the determiner category. *Journal of Child Language* 18: 123–138.

Pine, Julian, Elena V.M. Lieven, and Caroline F. Rowland. 1998. Comparing different models of the development of the English verb category. *Linguistics* 36: 4–40.

Pinker, Steven. 1989. *Words and Rules: The Ingredients of Language*. New York: Basic Books.

Pinker, Steven. 1994. *The Language Instinct*. New York: William Morrow and Co.

Pizutto, Elena, and Maria Cristina Caselli. 1992. The acquisition of Italian morphology. *Journal of Child Language* 19: 491–557.

Poulin-Dubois, Diane, Agnes Blaye, Julie Coutya, and Ellen Bialystock. 2011. The effects of bilingualism on toddlers' executive functioning. *Journal of Experimental Child Psychology* 108: 567–579.

Pye, Clifton, David Ingram, and Helen List. 1987. A comparison of initial consonant acquisition in English and Quiché. In: *Children's language*. Vol. 6, Keith Nelson, and Anne van Kleek (eds.), 175–190. Hillsdale, NJ: Lawrence Erlbaum.

Raikes, Helen, Barbara Alexander Pan, Gayle Luze, Catherine S. Tamis-LeMonda, Jeanne Brooks-Gunn, Jill Constantine, Louisa Banks Tarullo, H. Abigail Raikes, and Eileen T. Rodriguez. 2006. Mother-child bookreading in low-income families: Correlates and outcomes during the first three years of life. *Child Development* 77 (4): 924–953.

Rescorla, Leslie, Jennifer Mirak, and Leher Singh. 2000. Vocabulary growth in late talkers: Lexical development from 2;0 to 3;0. *Journal of Child Language* 27: 293–311.

Rice, Mabel L., Kenneth Wexler, and Scott Hershberger. 1998. Tense over time: The longitudinal course of tense acquisition in children with specific language impairment. *Journal of Speech, Language, and Hearing Research* 41: 1412–1431.

Rice, Mabel L., Kenneth Wexler, Janet Marquis, and Scott Hershberger. 2000. Acquisition of irregular past tense by children with specific language impairment. *Journal of Speech, Language, and Hearing Research* 43: 1126–1145.

Rice, Mabel L., Kenneth Wexler, and Sean M. Redmond. 1999. Grammaticality judgments of an extended optional infinitive grammar: Evidence from English-speaking children with specific language impairment. *Journal of Speech, Language, and Hearing Research* 42: 943–961.

Robinson, Byron F., and Carolyn B. Mervis. 1998. Disentangling early language development: Modeling lexical and grammatical acquisition using an extension of case-study methodology. *Developmental Psychology* 34: 363–375.

Rodina, Yulia. 2007. Semantics and morphology: The acquisition of grammatical gender in Russian. Unpublished Ph.D. diss., University of Tromsø.

Rogosa, David, David Brandt, and Michele Zimowski. 1982. A growth curve approach to the measurement of change. *Quantitative Methods in Psychology* 92: 726–748.

Rose, Susan A., Judith F. Feldman, and Jeffery J. Jankowski. 2009. A cognitive approach to the development of early language. *Child Development* 80 (1): 134–150.

Roy, Deb. 2009. New horizons in the study of child language acquisition. *Proceedings of Interspeech 2009*. Brighton, England.

Rozendaal, Margot I., and Anne E. Baker. 2008. A cross-linguistic investigation of the acquisition of the pragmatics of indefinite and definite reference in two-year-olds. *Journal of Child Language* 35: 773–807.

Rubino, Rafael, and Julian Pine. 1998. Subject-verb agreement in Brazilian Portuguese: What low error rates hide. *Journal of Child Language* 25: 35–60.

Ruff, Holly Alliger, and Mary Klevjort Rothbart. 1996. *Attention in Early Development: Themes and Variations*. New York: Oxford University Press.

Sameroff, Arnold. 2010. A unified theory of development: A dialectic integration of nature and nurture. *Child Development* 81: 6–22.

Scheffner Hammer, Carol, Frank R. Lawrence, and Adele W. Miccio. 2008. Exposure to English before and after entry into Head Start1: Bilingual children's receptive language growth in Spanish and English. *The International Journal of Bilingual Education and Bilingualism* 11: 30–56.

Shneidman, Laura A., Michelle E. Arroyo, Susan C. Levine, and Susan Goldin-Meadow. 2013. What counts as effective input for word learning? *Journal of Child Language* 40 (3): 672–686.

Schulze, Cornelia, Susanne Grassmann, and Michael Tomasello. 2013. 3-year-old children make relevance inferences in indirect verbal communication. *Child Development* 84: 2079–2093.

Seigneuric, Alix, Daniel Zagar, Fanny Meunier, and Elsa Spinelli. 2007. The relation between language and cognition in 3- to 9-year-olds: The acquisition of grammatical gender in French. *Journal of Experimental Child Psychology* 96: 229–246.

Singer, Judith D., and John B. Willett. 2003. *Applied Longitudinal Data Analysis: Analyzing Change and Event Occurrence*. Oxford, NY: Oxford University Press.

Slobin, Dan I. 1985. Cross-linguistic evidence for Language-Making Capacity. In *The Cross-Linguistic Study of Language Acquisition*: Vol. 2, Dan I. Slobin (ed.), 1157–1256. Hillsdale, NJ: Lawrence Erlbaum Associates.

Smoczyńska, Magdalena. 1985. The acquisition of Polish. In *The Cross-Linguistic Study of Language Acquisition*: Vol.1, Dan I. Slobin (ed.), 595–686. Hillsdale, NJ: Lawrence Erlbaum.

Snow, Catherine. 1972. Mothers' speech to children learning language. *Cognitive Development* 43: 549–565.

So, Lydia, and Barbara Dodd. 1995. The acquisition of phonology by Cantonese-speaking children. *Journal of Child Language* 22: 473–495.

Song, Lulu, Elizabeth T. Spier, and Catherine Tamis-LeMonda. 2014. Reciprocal influences between maternal language and children's language and cognitive development in low-income families. *Journal of Child Language* 41 (2): 305–326.

Spooren, Wilbert, and Ted Sanders. 2008. The acquisition order of coherence relations: On cognitive complexity in discourse. *Journal of Pragmatics* 40: 2003–2026.

Stokes, Stephanie, and Dinoj Surendran. 2005. Articulatory complexity, ambient frequency and functional load as predictors of consonant development in children. *Journal of Speech, Language, and Hearing Research* 48: 577–591.

Stokes, Stephanie, and Man Wong. 2002. Vowel and diphthong development in Cantonese-speaking children. *Clinical Linguistics & Phonetics* 16: 797–617.

Stoll, Sabine. 1998. The acquisition of Russian aspect. *First Language* 18: 351–378.

Stoll, Sabine. 2005. Beginning and end in the acquisition of the perfective aspect in Russian. *Journal of Child Language* 32: 805–825.

Surendran, Dinoj, and Partha Niyogi. 2006. Quantifying the functional load of phonemic oppositions, distinctive features, and suprasegmentals. In *Competing Models of Linguistic Change: Evolution and beyond*, Ole Nedergaard Thomsen (ed.), 43–58. Amsterdam: John Benjamins.

Taelman, Helena, Gert Durieux, and Steven Gillis. 2009. Fillers as signs of distributional learning. *Journal of Child Language* 36: 323–353.

Tamis-LeMonda, Catherine S., Marc H. Bornstein, Lisa Baumwell, and Amy Melstein Damast. 1996. Responsive parenting in the second year: Specific influences on children's language and play. *Early Development and Parenting* 5 (4): 173–183.

Theakston, Anna L., Elena V.M. Lieven, Julian M. Pine, and Caroline F. Rowland. 2004. Semantic generality, input frequency and the acquisition of syntax. *Journal of Child Language* 31: 61–99.

Thomas, E.M., and Virginia C. Mueller Gathercole. 2007. Children's productive command of grammatical gender and mutation in Welsh: An alternative to rule-based learning. *First Language* 27: 251–278.

Tomasello, Michael. 1992. *First Verbs: A Case Study of Early Grammatical Development.* Cambridge: Cambridge University Press.

Tomasello, Michael. 2000a. First steps toward a usage-based theory of language acquisition. *Cognitive Linguistics* 11 (1/2): 61–82.

Tomasello, Michael. 2000b. The item-based nature of children's early syntactic development. *Trends in Cognitive Sciences* 4: 156–163.

Tomasello, Michael. 2003. *Constructing a Language: A Usage-Based Theory of Language Acquisition.* Cambridge, MA. / London: Harvard University Press.

Tomasello, Michael, Ann Cale Kruger, and Hilary Horn Ratner. 1993. Cultural learning. Target Article for *Behavioral and Brain Sciences* 16: 495–511.

Tomblin, J. Bruce, Brittan A. Barker, Linda J. Spencer, Xuyang Zhang, and Bruce J. Gantz. 2005. The effect of age at cochlear implant initial stimulation on expressive language growth in infants and toddlers. *Journal of Speech, Language, and Hearing Research* 48: 853–867.

Topping, Keith, Rayenne Dekhinet, and Suzanne Zeedyk. 2013. Parent-infant interaction and children's language development. *Educational Psychology: An International Journal of Experimental Educational Psychology* 33: 391–426.

Tribushinina, Elena. 2012. Comprehension of relevance implicatures by pre-schoolers: The case of adjectives. *Journal of Pragmatics* 44: 2035–2044.

Tribushinina, Elena. 2013. Spatial adjectives in Dutch child language: Towards a usage-based model of adjective acquisition. In *The Construal of Spatial Meaning: Windows into Conceptual Space*, Carita Paradis, Jean Hudson, and Ulf Magnusson (eds.), 263–286. Oxford: Oxford University Press.

Tribushinina, Elena, Huub van den Bergh, Marianne Kilani-Schoch, Ayhan Aksu-Koç, Ineta Dabašinskienė, Gordana Hrzica, Katharina Korecky-Kröll, Sabrina Noccetti, and Wolfgang U. Dressler. 2013. The role of explicit contrast in adjective acquisition: A cross-linguistic longitudinal study of adjective production in spontaneous child speech and parental input. *First Language* 33 (6): 594–616.

Tribushinina, Elena, Huub van den Bergh, Dorit Ravid, Ayhan Aksu-Koç, Marianne Kilani-Schoch, Katharina Korecky-Kröll, Iris Leibovitch-Cohen, Sabine Laaha, Bracha Nir, Wolfgang U. Dressler, and Steven Gillis. 2014. Development of adjective frequencies across semantic classes: A growth curve analysis of child speech and child-directed speech. *Language, Interaction and Acquisition* 5 (2): 185–226.

Tsurutani, Chiharu. 2007. Early acquisition of palato-alveolar consonants in Japanese: phoneme frequencies in child-directed speech. *Journal of the Phonetic Society of Japan* 11: 102–110.

Van Severen, Lieve, Joris Gillis, Inge Molemans, Renate van den Bergh, Sven De Maeyer, and Steven Gillis. 2013. The relation between order of acquisition, segmental frequency and function: the case of word-initial consonants in Dutch. *Journal of Child Language* 40: 703–740.

Van Veen, Rosie. 2011. *The Acquisition of Causal Connectives: The Role of Parental Input and Cognitive Complexity*. Utrecht: LOT. Available online: http://www.lotpublications.nl/Documents/286_fulltext.pdf.

Van Veen, Rosie, Jacqueline Evers-Vermeul, Ted Sanders, and Huub van den Bergh. 2009. Parental input and connective acquisition in German: A growth curve analysis. *First Language* 29: 267–289.

Van Veen, Rosie, Jacqueline Evers-Vermeul, Ted Sanders, and Huub van den Bergh. 2013. The influence of input on connective acquisition: A growth curve analysis of English 'because' and German 'weil'. *Journal of Child Language* 40 (5): 1003–1031.

Verbuk, Anna, and Thomas Schultz. 2010. Acquisition of Relevance implicatures: A case against a Rationality-based account of conversational implicatures. *Journal of Pragmatics* 42: 2297–2313.

Vygotsky, Lev S. 1978. *Mind in Society: The Development of Higher Psychological Processes*. Cambridge, MA: Harvard University Press.

Welch-Ross, Melissa K. 1997. Mother-child participation in conversation about the past: Relationships to preschoolers' theory of mind. *Developmental Psychology* 33 (4): 618–629.

Windsor, Jennifer. 2002. Contrasting general and process-specific slowing in language impairment. *Topics in Language Disorders* 22 (3): 49–61.

Windsor, Jennifer, Rochelle L. Milbrath, Edward J. Carney, and Susan E. Rakowski. 2001. General slowing in language impairment: Methodological considerations in testing the hypothesis. *Journal of Speech, Language, and Hearing Research* 44: 446–461.

Xanthos, Aris, Sabine Laaha, Steven Gillis, Ursula Stephany, Ayhan Aksu- Koç, Anastasia Christofidou, Natalia Gagarina, Gordana Hrzica, F. Nihan Ketrez, Marianne Kilani-Schoch, Katharina Korecky-Kröll, Melita Kovačević, Klaus Laalo, Marijan Palmović, Barbara Pfeiler, Maria D. Voeikova, and Wolfgang U. Dressler. 2011. On the role of morphological richness in the early development of noun and verb inflection. *First Language* 31 (4): 461–479.

Zapf, Jennifer. 2004. Frequency in the input and children's mastery of the regular English plural. In *Proceedings of the Annual Boston University Conference on Language Development 27*, Barbara Beachley, Amanda Brown, and Frances Conlin (eds.), 834–845. Somerville, MA: Cascadilla Press.

Gaëtanelle Gilquin

2 Applied cognitive linguistics and second/ foreign language varieties: Towards an explanatory account

1 Introduction

Applied cognitive linguistics is a relatively recent addition to the theory of cognitive linguistics. One of the first book-length treatments of this topic is a collection of articles brought together in two volumes edited by Martin Pütz, Susanne Niemeier and René Dirven in 2001 and entitled *Applied Cognitive Linguistics*. In the introduction to the first volume, the editors note that "[e]ven if cognitive linguistics is a rapidly expanding linguistic paradigm, the impact of this new and revolutionary linguistic theory on various branches of applied research and on their pedagogical implications is only now beginning to be felt" (Pütz, Dirven, and Niemeier 2001: xiv). More than a decade later, despite the progress that has been made, it is still true that some branches of applied linguistics have not yet fully benefited from what Gibbs and Perlman (2006: 211) aptly call the "cognitive linguistic revolution" (cf. Achard and Niemeier 2004: 9; Gries and Wulff 2005: 184; Boers and Lindstromberg 2006: 305; Pütz 2007: 1139–1140). In this chapter I would like to focus on one such branch, namely second/ foreign language learning, and show that introducing a cognitive dimension into the analysis (in the present case, a corpus analysis) may enhance its explanatory power.

The chapter starts by giving a broad overview of the field of applied cognitive linguistics, with special emphasis on second/foreign language teaching (which has attracted quite some attention in the cognitive literature) and second/foreign language learning (which tends to have been neglected). In Section 3, two case studies are used to illustrate how cognitive linguistics can account for some of the non-standard characteristics found in second and foreign language varieties. The first case study deals with transfer in English as a foreign language, using the concepts of prototypicality and psychotypology, whilst the second one adopts a Construction Grammar approach to study the misuse of prepositional complements in institutionalized second-language varieties of English (New Englishes). The case studies, which both rely on corpus data, also serve to

Gaëtanelle Gilquin, Université catholique de Louvain

DOI 10.1515/9781501505492-003

demonstrate that the explanatory power of cognitive linguistics represents a valuable complement to the descriptive adequacy of corpus linguistics, and that the combination of the two frameworks has much to offer from an applied perspective. The chapter ends with a brief discussion of what I see as promising avenues for research in applied cognitive linguistics, as well as some concluding remarks.

2 An overview of applied cognitive linguistics

The term 'applied cognitive linguistics', like the term 'applied linguistics', can be understood in various ways, from a very broad definition to a more restricted one. *The Oxford Handbook of Cognitive Linguistics*, for example, edited by Dirk Geeraerts and Hubert Cuyckens in 2007, has a section entitled 'Applied and interdisciplinary perspectives', which includes papers on lexicography, critical discourse analysis, cultural studies, cognitive poetics, philosophy, and psychology. Much narrower is Pütz's (2007: 1139) definition, in which applied cognitive linguistics is restricted to "the acquisitional and pedagogical implications of Cognitive Linguistics in Second and Foreign Language Teaching/Learning", and hence excludes the acquisition of a first language. Taking a middle-ground position, one can adapt the definition of applied linguistics found in the *Encyclopedic Dictionary of Applied Linguistics* (Johnson and Johnson 1998: 9), according to which applied linguistics refers "somewhat exclusively to the field of language teaching and learning, rather than to any field where language is a relevant consideration", and thus define applied cognitive linguistics as the field concerned with the implications of cognitive linguistics for first (L1) and second (L2) language teaching and learning.

The implications of cognitive linguistics for first language acquisition have been explored in some detail over the last few years, and studies have demonstrated that the cognitive approach makes it possible to gain a better understanding of the processes underlying the acquisition of one's mother tongue. In this section, however, I will not deal with first language acquisition (the reader is referred to, e.g., Tomasello 2003 or Tribushinina and Gillis, *this volume*), but will focus instead on second/foreign language teaching (Section 2.1) and second/foreign language learning (Section 2.2).

2.1 Cognitive linguistics and second/foreign language teaching

In Littlemore's (2009: 1) *Applying Cognitive Linguistics to Second Language Learning and Teaching*, we can read that "[c]ognitive linguistics is a relatively new discipline which is rapidly becoming mainstream and influential, particularly in the area of second language teaching." That the author mentions second language teaching, rather than second language learning, is probably not a coincidence, for the pedagogical applications of cognitive linguistics have far outnumbered the cognitive investigations into second/foreign language learning (see also Boers and Lindstromberg 2006 and De Rycker and De Knop 2009 for reviews of research into the pedagogical applications of cognitive linguistics).

In the two volumes on applied cognitive linguistics referred to earlier (Pütz et al. 2001a, 2001b), a large number of papers deal with the didactic applications of cognitive linguistics, and two subsequent collective volumes, published in 2008, specifically concentrate on this issue, one by Boers and Lindstromberg on vocabulary and phraseology instruction, and another one by De Knop and De Rycker on pedagogical grammar. The most frequently studied phenomena in this context are metaphors, idioms, phrasal verbs, and polysemous words (with metaphor often being a key element in the analysis of the other phenomena as well). Usually, the methodology proposed relies on the concept of semantic motivation, which claims that, although language is not fully predictable, it is not completely arbitrary either. It is argued that a number of forms can be motivated, i.e. retrospectively explained, that they somehow "make sense" (cf. Lakoff 1987: 448). The expression *She was fuming*, for example, can be explained by referring to the conceptual metaphor 'anger is fire' (anger is often understood in terms of fire, cf. *to be spitting fire, to be smouldering with anger*; Kövecses 2001: 93). The meaning of the idiom *jump the gun* (to start doing something too soon, especially without thinking about it carefully) can be motivated by revealing its original context of use, i.e. that of a contender in a running contest who leaves the blocks before the starting pistol has been fired (Boers and Lindstromberg 2006: 313). In phrasal verbs, the particle *across* normally describes motion from one side of a surface to another (cf. *walk across the road*). In *get one's ideas across*, it refers to figurative motion, the ideas crossing the space between the speaker and a human receiver (Rudzka-Ostyn 2003: 193). The polysemous verb *keep*, in its central sense, implies possession of an object, cf. *keep the change*. The motivation for using the same verb in *keep a secret* lies in the fact that when someone keeps a secret, they do not let anyone else know/have it (Csábi 2004: 243). The same sort of reasoning has been applied to the different uses of prepositions (see, e.g., Evans and Tyler 2005).

Such motivational explanations are believed to help learners remember the words or expressions thus presented more easily. However, this belief sometimes seems more like an act of faith than a decision buttressed by empirical evidence. Tyler and Evans (2001: 98), talking about the teaching of tenses, state: "We

believe that insights from cognitive linguistics have real merit in offering more systematic, motivated accounts of how English works" [emphasis added]. They also claim that "by assuming the perspective and methodology of cognitive linguistics it is possible to relate the non-temporal senses associated with tense with the time-reference meaning in a plausible way. This approach, **we suggest, should** facilitate language teaching by providing a systematic model of the links among the semantics of tense markers" [emphasis added] (Tyler and Evans 2001: 66). Other linguists, by contrast, take the time to experiment before making any judgement. Their findings, in some cases, augur well. Thus, Verspoor and Lowie (2003) show that an experimental group of learners who were taught figurative senses of polysemous words according to cognitive principles (i.e. by relating them to a core sense) performed significantly better than the control group. A study by Boers (2004) provides more mixed results, in that it questions the beneficial effects of the cognitive approach on vocabulary retention in the long term: while experimental students performed significantly better than the control group in a task involving metaphor awareness when the task took place as part of an immediate post-test, the results were no longer significantly different a year later, when both groups had to perform a similar task. As for Condon (2008), although she is generally favourable to the cognitive linguistic approach in teaching, she notes that one should be wary of the potentially negative effects of this approach. Her own qualitative data on the teaching of English phrasal verbs show that:

> if the item has not been fully mastered, an active recall task may prompt the learners to retrieve the incorrect verb particle combination from memory but they believe the combination to be correct because they can justify their choice with an over-generalised Cognitive Linguistic explanation. This has the potential to lead to a situation in which the learner may be worse off than before with regard to certain phrasal verbs, because not only have they failed to learn the phrasal verb, but they are now unaware that they do not know it. (Condon 2008: 306)

All in all, however, the results are pretty encouraging, and as Boers and Lindstromberg (2006: 305) put it, "[a]lthough most controlled experiments reported so far have tended to be small-scale, taken collectively they are beginning to constitute a fairly robust body of evidence in favour of C[ognitive]L[inguistics]-inspired pedagogy." This is an interesting conclusion for second/foreign language teaching, but also an important one for cognitive linguistics for, as Langacker (2008: 8) points out, "its effectiveness in language teaching [is regarded] to be an important empirical test for the framework."

2.2 Cognitive linguistics and second/foreign language learning

While language instruction is certainly a very important aspect when it comes to non-native varieties of a language, the question of the processes underlying the acquisition of a second or foreign language is equally important for, as Ellis (2003: 95) rightly points out, "one cannot properly understand something without knowing how it came about." It is possible that the findings made by cognitive linguists for first language acquisition (see Tribushinina and Gillis, *this volume*) are to some extent applicable to second language acquisition (SLA). Ellis (2003: 87), talking about connectionist models, notes that "[t]o the considerable degree that the processes of learning L1 and L2 are the same, these L1 simulations are relevant to SLA." However, he adds that "[t]he problem, of course, is determining this degree and its limits" (Ellis 2003: 87). This uncertainty means that L1 studies are not sufficient and that similar efforts for L2 acquisition cannot be dispensed with. In Sanz's (2005: 3) words, "[l]ike their counterparts in the field of first language (L1) acquisition, scholars in the field of second language acquisition (SLA) need to explain both the nature of language and how it is acquired, that is, what is learned and how it is learned."

A review of the literature reveals that, in contrast to what happens with teaching, relatively few studies have sought to investigate second/foreign language learning from a truly cognitive perspective, i.e. using the tools and concepts of cognitive linguistics (and, one could add, with a sound empirical basis). In this respect, it is quite symptomatic, for instance, that the *Handbook of Cognitive Linguistics and Second Language Acquisition* (Robinson and Ellis 2008), which, of all books, should contain examples of cognitive approaches to the acquisition (or learning) of a second or foreign language, does not really offer much in terms of genuine integration of cognitive linguistics and SLA. Some of the chapters simply provide a general overview of certain cognitive concepts, with no or little consideration for SLA, e.g. Taylor's (2008) chapter on prototypicality, which hardly refers to acquisition at all. Goldberg and Casenhiser (2008), in a chapter entitled *Construction learning and second language acquisition*, only deal with first language acquisition, except for a paragraph in the conclusion which alludes to the "clear, but as yet untested, implications for second language learning and pedagogy" (Goldberg and Casenhiser 2008: 210). The handbook also includes some clearly SLA-oriented papers, but these sometimes seem to lose sight of the cognitive linguistic aspect and its relation to SLA. Gries's (2008) chapter on *Corpus-based methods in analyses of Second Language Acquisition data*, for instance, demonstrates that as a theoretical paradigm cognitive linguistics is compatible with the methodology of corpus linguistics, and then goes on to show how corpora can be exploited (in general and in SLA), but does not really relate SLA to cognitive linguistics. Truly cognitive SLA studies represent a minority in Robinson and Ellis's (2008) handbook, and not all of them rely on a sound empirical basis.

The few studies that have adopted a cognitive linguistic framework to tackle an SLA issue, however, have proved that this combination is a very fruitful one, especially when it is backed up by empirical evidence. To illustrate this, I would like to describe three related studies that examine L2 acquisition processes empirically and from a Construction Grammar perspective. Gries and Wulff (2005) performed several experiments in order to determine whether foreign language learners have mental representations of constructions, as claimed (and demonstrated) for native speakers by proponents of Construction Grammar (e.g. Bencini and Goldberg 2000). In one of their experiments, which they replicated from Bencini and Goldberg's (2000) study, they asked German learners of English as a foreign language to sort a number of sentences (see Table 1) on the basis of their overall meaning. The learners could adopt different strategies to sort these sentences, focusing on the verb (*throw, take, cut, get*), focusing on the construction (transitive, ditransitive, resultative, caused motion), or using a combination of these two methods. Although one could have expected learners to resort to the more transparent verb-based sorting, Gries and Wulff discovered that they actually preferred the construction-based sorting in a majority of cases, which suggests that learners, like native speakers, are able to abstract away from the utterances they hear to produce mental representations of constructions.

Table 1: Stimuli used in Gries and Wulff's (2005) sorting study.

Construction	Stimuli
Transitive	Anita threw the hammer.
	Audrey took the watch.
	Barbara cut the bread.
	Michelle got the book.
Ditransitive	Chris threw Linda the pencil.
	Paula took Sue a message.
	Jennifer cut Terry an apple.
	Beth got Liz an invitation.
Resultative	Lyn threw the box apart.
	Rachel took the wall down.
	Nancy cut the tire open.
	Dana got the mattress inflated.
Caused motion	Pat threw the keys onto the roof.
	Kim took the rose into the house.
	Meg cut the ham onto the plate.
	Laura got the ball into the net.

Liang (2002, cited in Goldberg 2006) conducted a similar experiment with Chinese learners of English and found out that the higher the learners' proficiency, the more likely they were to opt for construction-based sorting. This, interestingly, is in line with the usage-based trend in Construction Grammar (and in cognitive linguistics in general), according to which the more instances of a construction a learner gets exposed to, the more likely s/he is to generalize (see also Section 3.2). Finally, Valenzuela Manzanares and Rojo López (2008), besides replicating Bencini and Goldberg's (2000) experiment with Spanish learners of English (and with similar results), also used data from a learner corpus to investigate learners' lexical preferences in certain constructions and compare them with native speakers' preferences. Studies like these, however, are few and far between, and, although there are indications that interest in such issues may be growing (see Pütz and Sicola 2010 for another example), there is still a long way to go before cognitive linguistics has revealed (and realized) its full potential for second/foreign language learning.

3 The explanatory power of cognitive linguistics in SLA

In this section, I would like to make my own, modest contribution to the neglected field of 'cognitive second language acquisition' by showing how adding a cognitive dimension may help gain deeper insights into the processes underlying the acquisition of an L2. In particular, I would like to argue that cognitive linguistics holds explanatory power for SLA, which allows it, among other things, to account for some of the distinctive features displayed by second and foreign language varieties. As an additional aim, since I will be using corpora as a resource to investigate L2 production, I would like to show that the explanatory efficacy of cognitive linguistics represents an ideal complement to the descriptive adequacy offered by the methodology of corpus linguistics.

Two case studies will contribute to achieving this double objective. The first one will deal with transfer and rely on the concepts of prototypicality and psychotypology, whilst the second one will adopt a Construction Grammar approach to study innovation in the use of prepositional complements. These two case studies will also give me the opportunity to illustrate the analysis of two types of non-native varieties, namely English as a foreign language (EFL), found in settings where English is learned through formal instruction in countries that do not have English as an official language, and English as a second language (ESL), representing institutionalized varieties of English that are emerging in countries where English is an official or semi-official language (also referred to as 'New Englishes').[1]

3.1 Prototypical transfer in foreign language varieties

The concept of transfer, according to which learners may transfer features from one language (usually their mother tongue) to another, has a long history in applied linguistics. The early studies of transfer used to have a very thin empirical basis, being typically based on just a few texts produced by learners from a specific population and, most of the time, no contrastive data at all except those coming from the linguist' intuition. This often led to broad generalizations, hasty conclusions, and, more generally, lack of reliability (see Gilquin 2008a). With the advent of corpora, transfer studies came to rely on more data, more representative and more reliable. Two types of corpora appeared to be particularly relevant to the investigation of transfer: learner corpora, which contain data produced by language learners, and bilingual corpora, which are made up of data in two different languages (either translations of each other, or simply texts that are comparable in terms of register, topic, etc.).

The Integrated Contrastive Model (see Granger 1996; Gilquin 2001) proposes to combine these two types of corpora, as well as two methodologies they can be exploited with (contrastive analysis and contrastive interlanguage analysis), in an attempt to make more reliable claims about transfer. Contrastive analysis, which consists in comparing different languages in comparable corpora of original texts or in parallel corpora of source texts in one language and their translations in another language, enables the linguist to make predictions about the learner's interlanguage: identity between the L1 and the L2 is hypothesized to lead to error-free use by the learner, whereas mismatches between the L1 and the L2 are hypothesized to result in errors in the interlanguage through transfer of the L1 patterns into the L2. Next to this predictive power, the model also has diagnostic power. Through contrastive interlanguage analysis, that is, the comparison of learner data with native data or with data produced by learners from other mother tongue backgrounds, one can identify the specific features of the interlanguage of one or several learner populations, and then try to explain these features by examining the bilingual data. A slightly refined version of the

---

1 The term ESL is also used to refer to the situation of a learner of English living and learning English in an English-speaking country (e.g. in Great Britain or in the USA). Here, I restrict the term to countries where English is not a native language, but an official (or semi-official) one. In Kachru's (1985) model of the three concentric circles, this corresponds to the outer circle, whereas EFL corresponds to the expanding circle.

model (see Gilquin 2008a) suggests adding one type of comparison, viz. a comparison between the learner's interlanguage and his/her native language, in order to establish transfer with even more certainty.

While this model is a powerful one and, unlike the first transfer studies, is based on authentic and representative data, it presents some problems. In particular, it exclusively relies on performance data, which show what learners produce, and hence only provides indirect information about competence (what learners actually know). It also neglects the cognitive dimension of transfer, that is, what happens inside the learner's mind. This is especially striking in the way the equivalence between the L1 and the L2 is determined in the model, namely by resorting to texts produced by expert (native) writers and translators, instead of considering the (sometimes incorrect) equivalents found in the learner's mental lexicon, which is what one should arguably do when studying an essentially cognitive phenomenon like transfer. Consider the case of false friends (see also Lowie and Verspoor 2004). While in a parallel corpus, the French word *actuellement* may be linked to English translations such as *at present, these days, nowadays, now, at the moment,* or *presently* (with perhaps stronger links with some of these translations), in the learner's mental lexicon it may very well be that the word *actuellement* is (incorrectly) linked with *actually.* In the normal course of events, such a correspondence will never appear in a corpus of translations produced by expert (native) writers and translators, and could only emerge through a more experimental approach.

Transfer being a phenomenon that takes place first and foremost in the learner's cognitive system, it is important to consider what Kellerman (1983) calls the learner's psychotypology, that is, the learner's perception of the target language and of its relation with (and especially distance from) his/her mother tongue. In other words, as against corpus data, which reflect the objective distance between the L1 and the L2, psychotypology looks into the subjective distance between the two languages. Studies which have taken into account the element of psychotypology have underlined its importance (see, for example, Singleton 1987), but such studies are still, unfortunately, too rare. In what follows, I suggest combining the concept of psychotypology with that of prototypicality, and using elicitation techniques to probe into learners' competence and to integrate subjective distance (i.e. learners' perceptions) into the study of transfer.

Prototypicality implies that some members of a category are more representative of the category – more 'prototypical' – than others, which are more peripheral or marginal. The prototype is the most representative exemplar, the one most typically associated with the category. Prototypes have been shown to exist for natural categories (e.g. fruit or birds, cf. Rosch 1975), but also for linguistic categories (e.g. meanings or constructions, cf. Taylor 2003). The noun *ring*, for instance, is said to prototypically refer to a circular object (Langacker 2002: 2), and transitivity, which is traditionally defined by the presence or absence of an object, also presents prototype effects (cf. Hopper and Thompson 1980). Following these examples, it is reasonable to assume that in the mental lexicon of those who know (or learn) a foreign language, a word in one's mother tongue is prototypically associated with a certain equivalent in the foreign language. To come back to an earlier example, a French translator may know that the word *actuellement* has several translations in English, including *at present*, *these days, nowadays, now, at the moment*, and *presently*, but for some reason (which may have to do with his/her experience of the English language, orthographic or phonological resemblance, or other reasons), the translator may prototypically associate *actuellement* with, say, *at the moment*. That is, when asked to translate the word *actuellement*, s/he would spontaneously produce the phrase *at the moment* rather than any other possible translation. Note that, except perhaps for expert translators (especially those who are used to working with parallel corpora), the prototypical equivalent of a word does not necessarily correspond to its most frequent translation (see Gilquin 2008b for a similar remark about prototypicality in general). In this sense, the notion of prototypicality is closely akin to that of psychotypology: the prototypical equivalence established between two words reflects, not objective, but subjective closeness.

In order to elicit this perceived 'prototypical equivalent', I used the technique of the "first-come-to-mind" item (Ungerer and Schmid 2006: 41), which has also been employed in psychology to identify prototypes. In her psychological experiments, Rosch (1975) established prototypicality, among others, by asking subjects to name the first member of a category that they could think of (e.g. the first vehicle or the first piece of furniture that came to mind). The most frequently named entity across individuals was considered the prototype. Likewise, I asked learners to name the first L1 equivalent of an L2 word (or vice versa) that they could think of (e.g. "What is the first French equivalent of *besides* that you can think of?" or "What is the first English equivalent of *donc* that you can think of?"). The equivalent most frequently given by the subjects was regarded as the perceived prototypical equivalent.

My case study focuses on the use of *indeed* by French-speaking learners of English. On the basis of a simple corpus analysis, we can say that it presents all the signs of transfer. Table 2, based on data from the International Corpus of Learner English (ICLE, see Granger et al. 2009) and on the academic component of the British National Corpus (BNC_Acad), shows that *indeed* is significantly overused by French-speaking learners when compared to native speakers (836.78 vs 297.44 occurrences per million words, $\chi^2 = 131.29$, p < .001), and that its frequency in the French component of ICLE (ICLE-FR) is very different from its frequency in all the other components, none of which displays a significant overuse of the adverb.

In addition, a comparison of the results in Table 2 for native speakers (BNC_Acad) and French-speaking learners (ICLE-FR) with a corpus of native French (Corpus de Dissertations Françaises, CODIF, see Gilquin 2001) reveals that the intuitive equivalent of *indeed* in French, *en effet*, is much more frequent than its English counterpart: 1,209 occurrences per million words, as against 297 for *indeed* in native English (see Figure 1). In fact, its frequency is closer to that of *indeed* in ICLE-FR (837 occurrences per million words), which might point to a quantitative transfer (cf. Mougeon and Beniak's (1991) concept of "covert transfer"). This, together with the idiosyncratic behavior of French-speaking learners compared to the other populations of learners, suggests that transfer is a very plausible explanation for the overuse of *indeed* in French-speaking learners' production.

Table 2: Frequency of *indeed* in learner and native English (absolute and relative frequency per million words).

L1	Absolute frequency	Relative frequency
French	115	836.78
Dutch	53	323.36
English	4787	297.44
Japanese	5	233.09
Swedish	11	227.18
Finnish	20	157.98
German	17	153.31
Chinese	4	145.71
Italian	7	144.98
Polish	15	88.27
Spanish	6	60.06
Turkish	6	57.14
Russian	9	53.56
Czech	4	30.43

The problem, however, lies in the results of a corpus-based contrastive analysis that seem to refute this explanation. French-English parallel corpus data from the Poitiers-Louvain Échange de Corpus Informatisés (PLECI, see Gilquin 2001) uncover a very low degree of correspondence between *indeed* and *en effet*, with only four out of forty-eight occurrences of *indeed* translated as *en effet*. Thus, cases of correspondence like (1) are relatively rare. An equivalent such as *même*, in fact, is even more common than *en effet* in the corpus data, e.g. (2). This lack of correspondence between *indeed* and *en effet* in the bilingual corpus

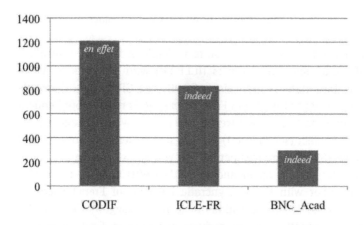

Figure 1: Relative frequency (per million words) of *indeed/en effet* in native French (CODIF), French learner English (ICLE-FR) and native English (BNC_Acad).

testifies to the great objective distance between the two expressions. This distance, according to Ellis (1994: 327), should act as a constraint on transfer, thus making transfer unlikely in this case. We are therefore faced with a problem, since the bilingual corpus predicts absence of transfer, whereas the learner corpus shows quite clear traces of transfer.

(1) **Indeed,** *it is in this period that poets step forth and speak with distinct, individual voices.*
'C'est à ce moment-là, **en effet**, que les poètes entrent en scène et s'expriment chacun d'une voix distincte, singulière.' (PLECI-ng003)

(2) **Indeed,** *a cable under Walker's signature is said to have been sent to Washington.*
'Un câble signé Walker serait **même** parvenu à Washington.'
(PLECI-mod01)

This apparent contradiction can be resolved by considering the subjective correspondence between *indeed* and *en effet*, rather than the objective correspondence transpiring from the translation corpus data. In an attempt to establish subjective correspondence, and more precisely the perceived prototypical equivalent of *indeed*, twenty-three French-speaking learners of English, with profiles similar to those represented in ICLE-FR, were asked to give the first equivalent of *indeed* that came to their minds. The answers clearly show that *en effet* is the most prototypical equivalent of *indeed*, since it was chosen by twenty of the informants.

Two learners translated it by *en fait* ('in fact'), and one by the rather formal adverb *certes* ('admittedly'), each of which occurs twice in the parallel corpus data. This perceived closeness between *indeed* and *en effet* explains why there is no constraint on transfer, and why, therefore, transfer is possible, although the two expressions are, objectively (i.e. in the corpus data), quite different.

This 'prototypical-psychotypological' approach would be the first step of the explanatory account of transfer. After explaining why transfer takes place, one would have to explain why learners tend to associate a word in the L2 with a translation that hardly ever corresponds to it in reality. In the case of *indeed*, I suspect that this may be teaching-induced. Instructed learners are still very often given lists of words in the target vocabulary with their translations in the native language (often limited to one translation per word), and typically, the translation of *indeed* in such lists would be *en effet*. Teaching-induced effects may be combined with conceptual factors, especially in the case of content words: the learner transfers the conceptual representation of the L1 word onto the L2 equivalent, without realizing that the L2 word may have a different conceptual structure; the L2 expression is thus encoded according to the conceptual system of the L1. A good example of conceptual transfer can be found in Jarvis and Pavlenko (2008: 124), who explain that, although the word *cup* is the equivalent of *chashka* in Russian, the two words differ in terms of the contents of the conceptual category. While in English a paper cup is considered a (peripheral) member of the conceptual category of cups, this is not the case in Russian, where the word *stakany* 'glasses' (or rather, a derived form of it, *stakanchiki*, meaning 'little glasses') is used to refer to a paper cup. An English learner of Russian using the term *chashka* to refer to this object would thus be guilty of conceptual transfer (see also Danesi 2008). Such conceptual problems could be investigated by means of techniques like word association, as advocated by Verspoor (2008), who uses bilingual word associations to demonstrate that Vietnamese, Dutch, and English speakers may have different conceptualizations when it comes to an apparently simple word like *career*.

To summarize this first case study, we have seen that, in the investigation of transfer, one can benefit from the combined use of learner corpora, which reflect learners' performance, and elicitation techniques, which give more direct access to their competence. More particularly, it has been argued that the comparison between mother tongue and target language should rely on elicitation tests aimed at determining the prototypical equivalents found in the learner's mental lexicon. The case study of the use of *indeed* by French-speaking learners has shown that such a cognitively-oriented model can explain cases of transfer which could not be accounted for by means of a model exclusively relying on corpora.

3.2 Innovative constructions in second language varieties

The second case study is a Construction Grammar approach to innovation in institutionalized second-language varieties of English (ESL). Construction Grammar holds that grammar is an inventory of constructions, i.e. form-function pairings, which have their own meanings. In the by now classic example *He sneezed the napkin off the table*, it is the construction in which the word occurs which gives *sneeze* a caused motion reading (Goldberg 1995: 9). In line with its usage-based view, Construction Grammar also holds that repeated exposure to a construction leads to its entrenchment in the cognitive system (cf. Bybee 2008): the more instances of a particular construction one gets exposed to, the more likely one is to form an abstract representation of the construction. For instance, after hearing or reading sentences such as *Mary pushed the trolley to the car, She threw the ball onto the roof, He took the dog into the house* or *Joe moved the saucepan onto the table*, a person may form a representation of the caused motion construction, consisting of a subject, a verb, an object, and an oblique argument, and expressing the fact that the causer argument directly causes the theme argument to move along a path designated by the directional phrase. This construction, in turn, will enable the person to create sentences similar to the above.

In what follows, I will focus on the case of *discuss about*, a form which is unacceptable according to the rules of standard English and should normally be replaced by the simple transitive verb *discuss something* (see, e.g., Turton and Heaton 1996: 101). Yet, the form *discuss about* is regularly found in non-native varieties of English, especially in institutionalized second-language varieties of English. Thus, Mukherjee (2007: 175) notes about Indian English that an "interesting phenomenon at the lexis-grammar interface is the formation of new prepositional verbs such as *approach to, comprise of, **discuss about**, order for, and visit to*" [emphasis added]. Nesselhauf (2009), using data from the International Corpus of English (ICE), found fourteen occurrences of *discuss about* in the Indian component of the corpus, nine in the Singaporean component, and seven in the Kenyan component. She states that the form is also reported for Nigerian and Zambian English. My own investigations brought to light eighteen occurrences of *discuss about* in ICE Hong Kong, eight in ICE Philippines, and seven in ICE Tanzania, e.g. (3). What is interesting is that, although this form is perhaps not extremely frequent, it is shared by several institutionalized varieties of English which are unlikely to have influenced each other or to have been influenced by the same language such as the speakers' L1. One can therefore expect this feature to be linked to general cognitive processes, rather than being due to the influence of some other language (including a substrate language).

(3) *That was the year when Margaret Thatcher representing Britain went up to
     China to **discuss about** the future of Hong Kong with the Chinese officials.*
     (ICE-HK-S2A-031)

The processes underlying this innovation can be explained if we accept the
assumption that non-native speakers, like native speakers, may have mental
representations of certain constructions (cf. Section 2.2) and if we use the framework of Construction Grammar and its usage-based approach, combined with
the tools of corpus linguistics (see Hartford 1989 for an account which is somewhat similar in spirit, but not grounded in the theory of Construction Grammar).
First, it should be noticed that, when it comes to constructions with verbs of
speaking, one is more likely to have entrenched the constructions related to
verbs like *talk* or *speak* than the constructions related to *discuss*. This is because,
as appears from Table 3, which is based on data from the British National
Corpus, the verb *talk* (and, to a lesser extent, *speak*) is much more frequent
than the verb *discuss*, especially in speech. This means that one is more likely
to transfer the patterns of *talk* to the verb *discuss* than the other way round.

Table 3: Relative frequency (per million words) of the verbs *talk,*
speak, and *discuss* in the whole BNC and in the conversational
component of the BNC.

Verb	BNC (all)	BNC (conversational)
Talk	301.32	682.35
Speak	254.82	220.40
Discuss	151.23	16.40

Among the different constructions associated with the verb *talk*, it is the [V *about*
NP] construction that is most likely to influence the use of *discuss*. Again, we can
turn to corpus data to explain why this is so. Figure 2 represents part of a Word
Sketch, which summarizes the different constructions in which a target word
commonly occurs and which shows the verbs, adjectives, nouns, etc. recurring
in a certain grammatical slot of the construction (see Kilgarriff and Tugwell
2002 and www.sketchengine.co.uk).

The Word Sketch is based on the BNC and displays the most frequent patterns that the verb *talk* occurs in. It appears that the [V *about* NP] construction
(pp_about-p) is the most frequent one, with a total of 5,074 occurrences (and an
overall 'salience score' of 216.8).[2]

---

2 Salience in the Sketch Engine is "a statistical measure of how salient a word or lemma is in a
given context, given the frequency of the word and the context. This is measured with logDice"
(Sketch Engine help file).

talk British National Corpus freq = 29332

and/or	913 0.5	unary rels		pp_about-p	5074 216.8	pp_to-p	3462 16.7	part_over-a_obj	41 13.4
laugh	69 8.5	prep_wh	334 69.7	sex	36 6.16	stranger	17 6.48	time	8 0.27
joke	9 7.57	prep_ing	618 32.8	thing	148 5.52	mum	30 6.16		
talk	88 7.14	prep_Sing	223 29.9	weather	18 5.49	daddy	11 6.09	part_trans	345 4.2
listen	24 6.59	np_adv	212 9.4	childhood	9 5.0	doctor	38 5.83	through	45 7.35
relax	9 6.46			poetry	9 4.98	mate	11 5.66	over	137 7.13
pray	7 6.32			past	14 4.92	guy	12 5.54	round	15 5.29
drink	17 6.23			feeling	23 4.84	people	272 5.51	down	56 4.64
walk	36 6.12			experience	38 4.79	reporter	9 5.47	about	8 4.08
sing	13 5.95			boyfriend	6 4.76	journalist	11 5.33	out	32 2.89
sit	40 5.67			percent	6 4.64	outsider	6 5.3	up	35 2.8
smile	9 5.25			future	20 4.63	press	23 5.25	back	7 1.72

subject	2777 3.4	pp_with-p	373 2.9	part_intrans	188 1.3	object	1710 1.1	pp_in-p	389 1.1
Clare	10 5.96	boss	6 4.64	through	18 6.05	nonsense	68 9.4	riddle	10 8.86
speaker	20 5.79	mouth	10 4.11	back	40 4.24	rubbish	25 7.63	whisper	12 8.13
Emma	7 5.71	friend	8 2.16	over	18 4.21	gibberish	10 7.53	sleep	9 5.68

Figure 2: (Truncated) Word Sketch of the verb *talk* in the BNC: frequencies (underlined) and salience scores.

Not only is *talk* more frequently associated with the *about* construction, but it turns out that the *about* construction is often associated with verbs expressing the conveying of information on a certain subject. Consider Figure 3, from the Erlangen Valency Patternbank,[3] a database based on Herbst et al. (2004) that provides a list of all the patterns of a number of verbs, adjectives, and nouns. Figure 3 shows all the verbs from the database that occur with the [V *about* NP] construction in a large corpus (the Bank of English). Besides *talk*, we find verbs such as *speak, tell, chat,* or *write,* all of which express the conveying of information on the subject of something.

Given this, it is not surprising that non-native speakers of English should be influenced by the construction [TALK *about* NP] when trying to use the verb *discuss.* Instead of using the standard construction [V NP] (*discuss something*), which is a construction more prototypically used to express causation (e.g. *kill somebody* or *break something,* cf. Kemmer and Verhagen 1994: 126), they use a construction that is typically associated with the conveying of information,

---

3 The Erlangen Valency Patternbank is available at http://www.patternbank.uni-erlangen.de/.

Active patterns:

NP + VHC $_{act}$ **+ about_NP**

Passive patterns:

NP + VHC $_{pass}$ **+ about | (+ by_phrase)** with verbs marked in grey

advise (A recommend) - argue (A dispute) - argue (B discuss) - ask (A inquire) - care (A consider important) - chat - complain - cry (A ... tears) - deceive - decide - dream - enquire - fight - forget - forget (special use 2) - go (idiomatic phrasal verb) - go (θ) - hang (idiomatic phrasal verb) - hear (B ... news) - hesitate - inquire - joke - joke (α) - knock (idiomatic phrasal verb) - know (A INFORMATION) - know (special use 1) - laugh - lay (C attack) - learn (A acquire a skill / knowledge) - learn (B discover) - lie [lied lied] - mention - mind (B be bothered) - mind (D never ..) - phone - pray - pretend - protest - read - realize (A become aware) - realize (A become aware) - reason - remember (A PERSON/EXPERIENCE) - remember (B TASK) - ring (B telephone) - see (E organize) - see (special use 9) - set (D start) - set (E attack) - shout (α) - sing - smile - speak (B FORMAL ADDRESS) - speak (D TOPIC) - talk (B TOPIC) - talk (D SPEECH) - talk (special use 3) - teach - tell (A INFORMATION) - think (A THOUGHT) - think (B consider) - warn - whisper - wonder - wonder (α) - worry - write

Figure 3: The [V *about* NP] construction in the Erlangen Valency Patternbank.

yielding the non-standard form *discuss about something*. In fact, the ESL speakers in this case may be said to select a constructional template that corresponds better to the meaning of the verb *discuss*, thus bringing syntax and semantics more in line with each other. Figure 4 illustrates this process of 'remapping'. Other examples of innovative constructions, taken from Nesselhauf (2009) and Gilquin (2009) and which could be explained in similar ways, include *comprise of* (probably built by analogy with *consist of*), *demand for* (which uses the construction of *ask for*), *enter into a place* (imitating the pattern of *go into* or *come into*), or *complete up* (where the particle *up* is telic, presenting an action or event as being complete, as in *eat up* or *dry up*).

One way this approach could be extended is through the concept of blending, as suggested by Waara (2004). Blending, following Fauconnier (1997), "is the combination of two inputs in mental space that yield a third mental space that is called the 'blend'" (Waara 2004: 52). In our case, the two mental spaces could be two constructions, the combination of which yields a 'blended construction'. For example in (4), a sentence produced by a Tswana learner (see

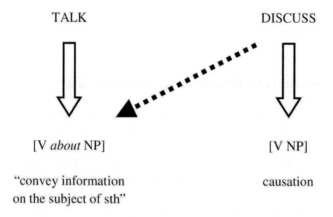

Figure 4: Remapping of the verb *discuss* on the model of the *talk* construction.

Gilquin and Granger 2011),[4] *take into seriousness* can be interpreted as a blend of *take into consideration*, the first input, and *take seriously*, the second input (cf. Figure 5).

(4) *Africa is by and by moving towards its last grave, this is due to the following unoticed [unnoticed] facts, yet not **taken into seriusness [seriousness]**.* (ICLE-TS-NOUN-0286.1)

In summary, this second case study has shown that the use of Construction Grammar (and/or conceptual blending theory) may explain some of the innovations found in institutionalized second-language varieties of English, and at the same time account for their presence in several non-related varieties. In particular, we have seen that the cognitive approach gives valuable insights into the (probable) processes leading to the production of non-standard constructions like *discuss about* or *take into seriousness*. More generally, as was the case with the first study (Section 3.1), the explanatory efficacy of the cognitive framework appears to be a nice complement to the descriptive adequacy offered by corpus linguistics.

---

4 Note that, although the sentence is taken from the International Corpus of Learner English, an essentially EFL corpus, the situation of the Tswana learners is close to an ESL one, because they have access to English-speaking media and are instructed through the medium of English from the fifth grade in primary school.

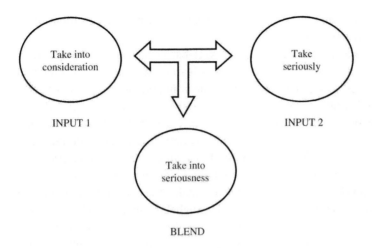

INPUT 1

INPUT 2

BLEND

Figure 5: Conceptual blending of *take into seriousness.*

4 Some promising avenues for research

Before turning to the conclusion of this chapter, I would like to briefly discuss some avenues for research that seem particularly promising from an applied cognitive linguistic perspective. The first one would be to adopt a longitudinal approach to the cognitive study of second/foreign language varieties, making it possible to see how a second or foreign language develops from a cognitive point of view. This evolution could then be compared to that of L1 acquisition. The main obstacle to implementing this type of evolutionary approach is a lack of appropriate data. As Ellis (2003: 73) observes with respect to constructions, "[t]here are lamentably few longitudinal acquisition data for SLA that are of sufficient detail to allow the charting of construction growth." The LONGDALE (Longitudinal Database of Learner English) project, when completed, should provide the kind of data that are necessary for such studies. This project, initiated in 2008 by the Centre for English Corpus Linguistics at the University of Louvain, Belgium, aims at building a large longitudinal database of learner English with data produced by learners from a wide range of mother tongue backgrounds, followed over a period of at least three years (from year 1 to year 3 of their studies at university).[5] Ideally, this time window would need to be expanded

---

5 See http://www.uclouvain.be/en-cecl-longdale.html for more information about the LONGDALE project.

further, so as to cover the whole cognitive development of L2 learners, from beginner to advanced level.

Next, one should strive for a truly usage-based model in L2 acquisition. Cognitive linguistics asserts that language is learned from usage (cf. Ellis and Robinson 2008: 5). In this regard, it is of crucial importance to know precisely what language learners are exposed to. It will always be an approximation, of course, as experience of a language is necessarily personal, but using a general corpus of native English to approximate EFL learners' experience with language (cf. Lowie and Verspoor 2004) may not be close enough (see also Gries 2008: 416 on this issue). A better approximation could be found in a corpus such as TeMa (see Meunier and Gouverneur 2009), which contains the pedagogical material of textbooks selected among bestsellers on the English language teaching market. Better still, one should expand the context by also taking into account classroom conversation for instance, including not only the teacher's talk, but also what the other students say. Ultimately, it is the whole of a person's interactions that one should attempt to record, as suggested by Adolphs, Knight, and Carter (2009) for native English, creating a database that reflects the exposure to TV programs in the target language, radio broadcasts, emails, websites, etc.

Finally, it would be interesting to broaden the paradigm by considering different types of language development together and comparing them from a cognitive linguistic perspective. One of Ellis's (2003) above-mentioned quotations suggests that the processes of L1 and L2 learning may be (at least partly) similar. Parallels have also been drawn between ESL and EFL (Nesselhauf 2009), as well as between ontogeny and phylogeny (Osawa 2003), i.e. between L1 acquisition (language learning) and historical development (language change). It might be interesting to establish whether there are any cognitive processes that are common to any type of language evolution, including L1 acquisition, L2 acquisition, pidginization, and diachronic development. We might thus be able to propose a unified developmental model, taking account of the specificity of each type of development.

5 Conclusion

This chapter has examined the role of the cognitive approach in applied linguistics, and more precisely in the study of second and foreign language varieties. The first conclusion to be drawn is that applied cognitive linguistics is in need of further research, especially as far as the processes underlying the acquisition of a second or foreign language are concerned. Ideally, such research should rely on a sound empirical basis, which could involve corpus data and elicitation data, as I have illustrated here, but also more sophisticated experimental techniques such as reaction time measurements or eye tracking.

Secondly, the two case studies have underlined the relevance of combining cognitive linguistics with corpus linguistics and the complementarity of the two frameworks: corpora offer privileged access to the final state of the production, whilst the cognitive approach gives insights into the actual acquisition processes (see also Ellis 2003: 64); corpora reflect performance, whilst cognitive linguistics is closer to competence; and corpus linguistics provides descriptive adequacy, whilst cognitive linguistics allows for explanatory efficacy. This last point proves the relevance of cognitive linguistics for second language acquisition (SLA), over and above foreign language teaching (FLT), where applied cognitive linguistics has been most prevalent up to now.

Of course, insights into language acquisition processes such as those revealed by cognitive linguistics are only a first step, which can lead to practical applications. The better one understands why learners get something wrong, the easier it is to help them solve the problem, so that these insights can themselves result in improvements in second/foreign language teaching, in the form of "well-informed language pedagogy", as Odlin (2008: 333) calls it. The explanatory power of applied cognitive linguistics, in other words, allows for anticipation, diagnosis, and remediation (Verspoor 2008: 263), all of which are important aspects of the learning and teaching of a language. This alone should encourage both SLA and FLT specialists to engage more actively in the field of applied cognitive linguistics.

References

Achard, Michel, and Susanne Niemeier. 2004. Introduction: Cognitive linguistics, language acquisition, and pedagogy. In *Cognitive Linguistics, Second Language Acquisition, and Foreign Language Teaching*, Michel Achard, and Susanne Niemeier (eds.), 1–11. Berlin/New York: Mouton de Gruyter.

Adolphs, Svenja, Dawn Knight, and Ronald Carter. 2009. Redefining context in communication: A multi-modal perspective. Paper presented at the 30th ICAME conference, Lancaster.

Bencini, Giulia M.L., and Adele E. Goldberg. 2000. The contribution of argument structure constructions to sentence meaning. *Journal of Memory and Language* 43 (4): 640–651.

Boers, Frank. 2004. Expanding learners' vocabulary through metaphor awareness: What expansion, what learners, what vocabulary? In *Cognitive Linguistics, Second Language Acquisition, and Foreign Language Teaching*, Michel Achard, and Susanne Niemeier (eds.), 211–232. Berlin/New York: Mouton de Gruyter.

Boers, Frank, and Seth Lindstromberg. 2006. Cognitive linguistic applications in second or foreign language instruction: Rationale, proposals, and evaluation. In *Cognitive Linguistics: Current Applications and Future Perspective*, Gitte Kristiansen, Michel Achard, René Dirven, and Francisco J. Ruiz de Mendoza Ibáñez (eds.), 305–355. Berlin/New York: Mouton de Gruyter.

Boers, Frank, and Seth Lindstromberg (eds.). 2008. *Cognitive Linguistic Approaches to Teaching Vocabulary and Phraseology*. Berlin/New York: Mouton de Gruyter.

Bybee, Joan. 2008. Usage-based grammar and second language acquisition. In *Handbook of Cognitive Linguistics and Second Language Acquisition*, Peter Robinson, and Nick C. Ellis (eds.), 216–236. New York/London: Routledge.

Condon, Nora. 2008. *Investigating a Cognitive Linguistic Approach to the Learning of English Phrasal Verbs*. Ph.D. diss., Université catholique de Louvain.

Csábi, Szilvia. 2004. A cognitive linguistic view of polysemy in English and its implications for teaching. In *Cognitive Linguistics, Second Language Acquisition, and Foreign Language Teaching*, Michel Achard, and Susanne Niemeier (eds.), 233–256. Berlin/New York: Mouton de Gruyter.

Danesi, Marcel. 2008. Conceptual errors in second-language learning. In *Cognitive Approaches to Pedagogical Grammar: A Volume in Honour of René Dirven*, Sabine De Knop, and Teun De Rycker (eds.), 231–256. Berlin/New York: Mouton de Gruyter.

De Knop, Sabine, and Teun De Rycker (eds.). 2008. *Cognitive Approaches to Pedagogical Grammar: A Volume in Honour of René Dirven*. Berlin/New York: Mouton de Gruyter.

De Rycker, Antoon, and Sabine De Knop. 2009. Integrating cognitive linguistics and foreign language teaching: Historical background and new developments. *Journal of Modern Languages* 19 (1): 29–46.

Ellis, Nick C. 2003. Constructions, chunking, and connectionism: The emergence of second language structure. In *The Handbook of Second Language Acquisition*, Catherine J. Doughty, and Michael H. Long (eds.), 63–103. Oxford: Blackwell Publishing.

Ellis, Nick C., and Peter Robinson. 2008. An introduction to cognitive linguistics, second language acquisition, and language instruction. In *Handbook of Cognitive Linguistics and Second Language Acquisition*, Peter Robinson, and Nick C. Ellis (eds.), 3–24. New York/London: Routledge.

Ellis, Rod. 1994. *The Study of Second Language Acquisition*. Oxford: Oxford University Press.

Evans, Vyvyan, and Andrea Tyler. 2005. Applying cognitive linguistics to pedagogical grammar: The English prepositions of verticality. *Revista Brasileira de Linguistica Aplicada* [Brazilian Journal of Applied Linguistics] 5 (2): 11–42.

Fauconnier, Gilles. 1997. *Mappings in Thought and Language*. Cambridge: Cambridge University Press.

Geeraerts, Dirk, and Hubert Cuyckens (eds.). 2007. *The Oxford Handbook of Cognitive Linguistics*. Oxford: Oxford University Press.

Gibbs, Raymond W. Jr., and Marcus Perlman. 2006. The contested impact of cognitive linguistic research on the psycholinguistics of metaphor understanding. In *Cognitive Linguistics: Current Applications and Future Perspectives*, Gitte Kristiansen, Michel Achard, René Dirven, and Francisco J. Ruiz de Mendoza Ibáñez (eds.), 211–228. Berlin/New York: Mouton de Gruyter.

Gilquin, Gaëtanelle. 2001. The Integrated Contrastive Model: Spicing up your data. *Languages in Contrast* 3 (1): 95–123.

Gilquin, Gaëtanelle. 2008a. Combining contrastive and interlanguage analysis to apprehend transfer: Detection, explanation, evaluation. In *Linking up Contrastive and Learner Corpus Research*, Gaëtanelle Gilquin, Szilvia Papp, and María Belén Díez-Bedmar (eds.), 3–33. Amsterdam/Atlanta: Rodopi.

Gilquin, Gaëtanelle. 2008b. What you think ain't what you get: Highly polysemous verbs in mind and language. In *Du fait grammatical au fait cognitif. From Gram to Mind: Grammar as Cognition*, Vol. 2, Jean-Rémi Lapaire, Guillaume Desagulier, and Jean-Baptiste Guignard (eds.), 235–255. Pessac: Presses Universitaires de Bordeaux.

Gilquin, Gaëtanelle. 2009. The (non-)use of phrasal verbs in L2 varieties of English. Paper presented at the 30th ICAME conference, Lancaster.

Gilquin, Gaëtanelle, and Sylviane Granger. 2011. From EFL to ESL: Evidence from the *International Corpus of Learner English*. In *Exploring Second-Language Varieties of English and Learner Englishes: Bridging a Paradigm Gap*, Joybrato Mukherjee, and Marianne Hundt (eds.), 55–78. Amsterdam/Philadelphia: John Benjamins Publishing Company.

Goldberg, Adele E. 1995. *Constructions: A Construction Grammar Approach to Argument Structure*. Chicago: University of Chicago Press.

Goldberg, Adele E. 2006. *Constructions at Work: The Nature of Generalization in Language*. Oxford: Oxford University Press.

Goldberg, Adele E., and Devin Casenhiser. 2008. Construction learning and second language acquisition. In *Handbook of Cognitive Linguistics and Second Language Acquisition*, Peter Robinson, and Nick C. Ellis (eds.), 197–215. New York/London: Routledge.

Granger, Sylviane. 1996. From CA to CIA and back: An integrated approach to computerized bilingual and learner corpora. In *Languages in Contrast: Papers from a Symposium on Text-based Cross-linguistic Studies*, Karin Aijmer, Bengt Altenberg, and Mats Johansson (eds.), 37–51. Lund: Lund University Press.

Granger, Sylviane, Estelle Dagneaux, Fanny Meunier, and Magali Paquot. 2009. *International Corpus of Learner English: Handbook and CD-ROM, Version 2*. Presses universitaires de Louvain: Louvain-la-Neuve.

Gries, Stefan Th. 2008. Corpus-based methods in analyses of second language acquisition data. In *Handbook of Cognitive Linguistics and Second Language Acquisition*, Peter Robinson, and Nick C. Ellis (eds.), 406–431. New York/London: Routledge.

Gries, Stefan Th., and Stefanie Wulff. 2005. Do foreign language learners also have constructions? Evidence from priming, sorting, and corpora. *Annual Review of Cognitive Linguistics* 3 (1): 182–200.

Hartford, Beverly S. 1989. Prototype effects in non-native English: Object-coding in verbs of saying. *World Englishes* 8 (2): 97–117.

Herbst, Thomas, David Heath, Ian Roe, and Dieter Götz. 2004. *Valency Dictionary of English*. Berlin/New York: Mouton de Gruyter.

Hopper, Paul J., and Sandra A. Thompson. 1980. Transitivity in grammar and discourse. *Language* 56 (1): 251–299.

Jarvis, Scott, and Aneta Pavlenko. 2008. *Crosslinguistic Influence in Language and Cognition*. New York/London: Routledge.

Johnson, Keith, and Helen Johnson (eds.). 1998. *Encyclopedic Dictionary of Applied Linguistics: A Handbook for Language Teaching*. Oxford: Basil Blackwell.

Kachru, Braj B. 1985. Standards, codification and sociolinguistic realism: The English language in the outer circle. In *English in the World: Teaching and Learning the Language and Literatures*, Randolph Quirk, and Henry G. Widdowson (eds.), 11–30. Cambridge: Cambridge University Press.

Kellerman, Eric. 1983. Now you see it, now you don't. In *Language Transfer in Language Learning*, Susan Gass, and Larry Selinker (eds.), 112–134. Rowley, MA: Newbury House.

Kemmer, Suzanne, and Arie Verhagen. 1994. The grammar of causatives and the conceptual structure of events. *Cognitive Linguistics* 5 (2): 115–156.

Kilgarriff, Adam, and David Tugwell. 2002. Sketching words. In *Lexicography and Natural Language Processing: A Festschrift in Honour of B.T.S. Atkins*, Marie-Hélène Corréard (ed.), 125–137. Euralex. Available online at http://www.kilgarriff.co.uk/Publications/2002-KilgTugwell-AtkinsFest.pdf.

Kövecses, Zoltán. 2001. A cognitive linguistic view of learning idioms in an FLT context. In *Applied Cognitive Linguistics II: Language Pedagogy*, Martin Pütz, Susanne Niemeier, and René Dirven (eds.), 87–115. Berlin/New York: Mouton de Gruyter.

Lakoff, George. 1987. *Women, Fire, and Dangerous Things: What Categories Reveal about the Mind*. Chicago: University of Chicago Press.

Langacker, Ronald W. 2002. *Concept, Image, and Symbol: The Cognitive Basis of Grammar*. 2nd ed. Berlin/New York: Mouton de Gruyter.

Langacker, Ronald W. 2008. The relevance of Cognitive Grammar for language pedagogy. In *Cognitive Approaches to Pedagogical Grammar: A Volume in Honour of René Dirven*, Sabine De Knop, and Teun De Rycker (eds.), 7–35. Berlin/New York: Mouton de Gruyter.

Liang, Junying. 2002. Sentence comprehension by Chinese Learners of English: Verb-centered or construction-based. MA thesis, Guangdong University of Foreign Studies.

Littlemore, Jeannette. 2009. *Applying Cognitive Linguistics to Second Language Learning and Teaching*. Basingstoke: Palgrave Macmillan.

Lowie, Wander, and Marjolijn Verspoor. 2004. Input versus transfer? The role of frequency and similarity in the acquisition of L2 prepositions. In *Cognitive Linguistics, Second Language Acquisition, and Foreign Language Teaching*, Michel Achard, and Susanne Niemeier (eds.), 77–94. Berlin/New York: Mouton de Gruyter.

Meunier, Fanny, and Céline Gouverneur. 2009. New types of corpora for new educational challenges: Collecting, annotating and exploiting a corpus of textbook material. In *Corpora and Language Teaching*, Karin Aijmer (ed.), 179–201. John Benjamins Publishing Company: Amsterdam/Philadelphia.

Mougeon, Raymond, and Edouard Beniak. 1991. *Linguistic Consequences of Language Contact and Restriction: The Case of French in Ontario, Canada*. Oxford: Oxford University Press.

Mukherjee, Joybrato. 2007. Steady states in the evolution of New Englishes: Present-day Indian English as an equilibrium. *Journal of English Linguistics* 35 (2): 157–187.

Nesselhauf, Nadja. 2009. Co-selection phenomena across New Englishes: Parallels (and differences) to foreign learner varieties. *English World-Wide* 30 (1): 1–25.

Odlin, Terence. 2008. Conceptual transfer and meaning extensions. In *Handbook of Cognitive Linguistics and Second Language Acquisition*, Peter Robinson, and Nick C. Ellis (eds.), 306–340. New York/London: Routledge.

Osawa, Fuyo. 2003. Syntactic parallels between ontogeny and phylogeny. *Lingua* 113 (1): 3–47.

Pütz, Martin. 2007. Cognitive linguistics and applied linguistics. In *The Oxford Handbook of Cognitive Linguistics*, Dirk Geeraerts, and Hubert Cuyckens (eds.), 1139–1159. Oxford: Oxford University Press.

Pütz, Martin, René Dirven, and Susanne Niemeier. 2001. Introduction. In *Applied Cognitive Linguistics I: Theory and Language Acquisition*, Martin Pütz, Susanne Niemeier, and René Dirven (eds.), xiii–xxiv. Berlin/New York: Mouton de Gruyter.

Pütz, Martin, Susanne Niemeier, and René Dirven (eds.). 2001a. *Applied Cognitive Linguistics I: Theory and Language Acquisition*. Berlin/New York: Mouton de Gruyter.

Pütz, Martin, Susanne Niemeier, and René Dirven (eds.). 2001b. *Applied Cognitive Linguistics II: Language Pedagogy*. Berlin/New York: Mouton de Gruyter.

Pütz, Martin, and Laura Sicola (eds.). 2010. *Cognitive Processing in Second Language Acquisition: Inside the Learner's Mind.* Amsterdam/Philadelphia: John Benjamins Publishing Company.

Robinson, Peter, and Nick C. Ellis (eds.). 2008. *Handbook of Cognitive Linguistics and Second Language Acquisition.* New York/London: Routledge.

Rosch, Eleanor. 1975. Cognitive representations of semantic categories. *Journal of Experimental Psychology: General* 104 (3): 192–233.

Rudzka-Ostyn, Brygida. 2003. *Word Power: Phrasal Verbs and Compounds. A Cognitive Approach.* Berlin/New York: Mouton de Gruyter.

Sanz, Cristina. 2005. Adult SLA: The interaction between external and internal factors. In *Mind and Context in Adult Second Language Acquisition. Methods, Theory, and Practice*, Cristina Sanz (ed.), 3–20. Washington, DC: Georgetown University Press.

Singleton, David. 1987. Mother and other tongue influence on learner French: A case study. *Studies in Second Language Acquisition 9* (3): 327–345.

Taylor, John R. 2003. *Linguistic Categorization.* 3rd ed. Oxford: Oxford University Press.

Taylor, John R. 2008. Prototypes in cognitive linguistics. In *Handbook of Cognitive Linguistics and Second Language Acquisition*, Peter Robinson, and Nick C. Ellis (eds.), 39–65. New York/London: Routledge.

Tomasello, Michael. 2003. *Constructing a Language: A Usage-Based Theory of Language Acquisition.* Cambridge, MA: Harvard University Press.

Turton, Nigel D., and Heaton, J.B. 1996. *Longman Dictionary of Common Errors.* 2nd ed. London: Longman.

Tyler, Andrea, and Vyvyan Evans. 2001. The relation between experience, conceptual structure and meaning: Non-temporal uses of tense and language teaching. In *Applied Cognitive Linguistics I: Theory and Language Acquisition*, Martin Pütz, Susanne Niemeier, and René Dirven (eds.), 63–105. Berlin/New York: Mouton de Gruyter.

Ungerer, Friedrich, and Hans-Jörg Schmid. 2006. *An Introduction to Cognitive Linguistics.* 2nd ed. Harlow: Pearson Education.

Valenzuela Manzanares, Javier, and Ana María Rojo López. 2008. What can language learners tell us about constructions? In *Cognitive Approaches to Pedagogical Grammar: A Volume in Honour of René Dirven*, Sabine De Knop, and Teun De Rycker (eds.), 197–230. Berlin/New York: Mouton de Gruyter.

Verspoor, Marjolijn. 2008. What bilingual word associations can tell us. In *Cognitive Linguistic Approaches to Teaching Vocabulary and Phraseology*, Frank Boers, and Seth Lindstromberg (eds.), 261–289. Berlin/New York: Mouton de Gruyter.

Verspoor, Marjolijn, and Wander Lowie. 2003. Making sense of polysemous words. *Language Learning* 53 (3): 547–586.

Waara, Renee. 2004. Construal, convention, and constructions in L2 speech. In *Cognitive Linguistics, Second Language Acquisition, and Foreign Language Teaching*, Michel Achard, and Susanne Niemeier (eds.), 51–75. Berlin/New York: Mouton de Gruyter.

Barend Beekhuizen, Rens Bod and Arie Verhagen

3 Acquiring relational meaning from the situational context: What linguists can learn from analyzing videotaped interaction

1 The difficulties of acquiring relational meaning[1]

The acquisition of linguistic expressions of relational meaning is typically re-garded as a difficult task (Gentner 1978; Gleitman 1990).[2] What hampers this process, as compared to the acquisition of expressions of object reference, is not so much the complexity of relational concepts per se, which children seem to understand well before their first birthdays for many types of relational con-cepts (Casasola, Bhagwat, and Ferguson 2006; Mandler 2006; Sootman-Buresh, Woodward, and Brune 2006), but the question which subset of the large set of relations perceivable in situational context should be mapped to a linguistic expression. Furthermore, as especially Gleitman (1990) argues, not all relations expressed are directly perceivable, as some pertain to mental states of inten-tional agents and others are simply not present in the here-and-now of the speech situation. As Gleitman succinctly puts it (p. 5): "[T]here is *not enough* information in the whole world to learn the meaning of even simple verbs, or ... there is *too much* information in the world to learn the meaning of ... verbs."

In this chapter, we evaluate Gleitman's double problem. Is the context indeed too poor or too rich for the learner to find situational, contextual correlates for

1 Corresponding author: Barend Beekhuizen, University of Toronto. Email address: barend-beekhuizen@gmail.com. The work reported here is part of the first author's Ph.D. project Constructions Emerging, funded by NWO. The second and third authors have made significant contributions to the development of the described method. The authors would like to thank Marian Bakermans and Rien van IJzendoorn of the department of Child Studies at Leiden University for allowing us to use their data, as well as the two anonymous reviewers for their valuable comments.

2 As a working definition of *relational*, we adopt Gentner and Kurtz's (2005: 153) explanation that "[e]ntity categories can be thought of as first-order partitions of the world (Gentner 1982) and relational categories second-order ways of organizing and linking those first-order partitions".

Barend Beekhuizen, University of Toronto
Rens Bod, University of Amsterdam
Arie Verhagen, Leiden University

DOI 10.1515/9781501505492-004

the linguistic items he perceives that can help him bootstrap the meaning of those items? We address this question for a broad class of word types, both relational (verbs and prepositions) and non-relational (nouns and adjectives) ones.[3] We do so by using a corpus of child-directed language that contains precise information on the behavior of the participants and several states in the world. This information is derived from annotations of the behavior of the caregiver and the child, based on videotaped interaction in the setting of a simple game.

Note that our focus is mainly on the situation rather than on cognition. Work by Gentner and colleagues on relational categories (see e.g. Gentner and Kurtz 2005) has provided us with much insight in the cognitive mechanisms at work when acquiring relational meanings of words. This chapter looks at the other side of the same coin: what information is available in naturalistic situations on which these mechanisms operate. Is there any relation between two objects that could be construed as "containment" present in the environment in which the language-learning child operates when the word *in* is uttered?

We believe the development and use of methods like these, in combination with computational modeling techniques, is paramount for the development of a more comprehensive usage-based theory. If we assume that the interaction between caregivers and children is the locus of the development of the acquisition of things like construal and symbolic mappings, we must at least have a decent understanding of what happens in those situations. Without analyzing actual behavioral data, we do not know what information is available, and any form of theorizing about the mechanisms used in the acquisition of symbolic mappings can effectively not be evaluated, as the interpretive step from a controlled experiment tapping into the hypothesized mechanisms and the situation "in the wild" is unwarranted. It is exactly this understanding that is currently too weakly present in acquisitionist research.

This precise method has, to the best of our knowledge, not been used before in language acquisition research, but similar work has been done on object reference using video data in which the present objects and social cues such as eye gaze and pointing were coded (Frank, Goodman, and Tenenbaum 2009; Frank, Tenenbaum, and Fernald 2013). Because of this, we discuss the considerations in developing the data in some detail first (Section 2). In Section 3 we then address the question of the usefulness of the context for acquiring relational meaning by looking at a quantitative measure of association between linguistic elements and aspects of the situation in which these elements are produced. We

---

3 We realize that it is the case that there are verbs that have non-relational meanings, as well as nouns and adjectives that have relational ones. The particular items we study do not belong to these types.

limit ourselves to verbs, and other relational elements that encode conceptualizations of physical relations and actions.[4]

2 Developing a corpus of contextualized language

If we want to understand how informative the situations are for the language-learning child, we need to have material that captures the situational context of every utterance in detail and that is situated in a relatively ecologically valid setting. Regular corpora contain little information on the context, and deriving information about the context from the language in order to find associations between the two, which is often done in computational modeling studies of word-meaning acquisition, leads to circularity.

Because of this lack of data, we decided to develop a dataset on the basis of videotaped interactions in Dutch between children and their mothers, which was recorded for other purposes. The child-directed language was transcribed by the first author, and the situation was described according to a formalized coding scheme by two assistants. In the following sections, we discuss the choices and the justification for them, as well as the coding procedure and evaluation in some detail, so as to provide other researchers with a starting point for doing similar research.

2.1 The nature of the underlying data

Our material consists of 32 videotaped fragments, each containing a unique mother-daughter dyad playing a full game of putting blocks into holes of a toy. The mothers are all middle-class, native speakers of Dutch who were living in or close to the Dutch town of Leiden at the time. The fragments are on average 4 minutes and 54 seconds long, ranging from 3 minutes and 12 seconds to 7 minutes and 5 seconds. The game starts with the observer giving the toy to the mother, and ends with the mother returning the toy to the observer. The observer

---

4 This is not to say that verbs encoding mental states, intentions and dispositions have no ground in the child's situational understanding independently of language. From a very young age, children have a basic understanding of intentions and emotions (Behrend and Scofeld 2006; Tomasello 2003) that might become associated with certain verbs. Barak, Fazly, and Stevenson (2012) provide an interesting first step towards modelling the acquisition of such meanings.

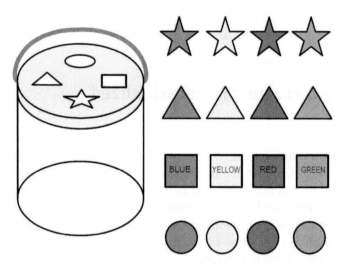

Figure 1: The toy and the twelve blocks.

does not take part in the interaction, so the mother and the daughter are jointly focused on playing the game.

The game-related objects are displayed in Figure 1. The game typically takes place on the table or on the floor, and there are few non-game objects that are manipulated during the game. A typical game consists of the mother or daughter opening the bucket and getting all blocks out. Then the daughter tries to fit each of them back in, sometimes with the help of the mother, but always with verbal comments, suggestions and questions by the mother. Several children lose interest after a while and wander off, while others are so excited about their success that the game is played two or three times during the fragment.

All children were around sixteen months at the time of the recording. This means that their ages are within a desirable time window for this type of observational study. Before the age of one, we cannot expect children to understand the symbolic nature of language. When children's early intentional understanding enters the picture, they are able to start learning linguistic symbols (Tomasello 2003: 21–28). However, as we get closer to the child's second birthday, chances increase of the child himself being able to talk, in which case the child is often directing the conversation by means of single-word utterances triggering responses from the caregiver. The age of sixteen months squarely falls within the period in which children understand the symbolic, communicative nature of language, but are just beginning to connect word forms and meanings. Because of this, we can make the assumption that this is actually the kind of situated child-directed language input that children receive.

2.2 Developing a coding scheme

What aspects of the situational context are worth taking into account? The participants perform various actions related to the game, and hence the spatial states of the game objects change continuously. The most straightforward aspects of the scenes we could describe thus are changes in spatial relations between objects and the behavior of participants leading to these changes. We found that with nine predicates, we were able to cover almost all of the participants' behavior in the fragments. The top nine predicates, given in Table 1 and described as English verbs, reflect the building blocks of object manipulation: there are descriptions of bringing an object under manual control (**reach** and **grab**), and of letting go of this control (**let go**). In between, one can do all sorts of things with objects: **move** them from one location to another, position them vis-à-vis a location, exert **force** upon them and letting them go (as in pushing, throwing) and showing them to another participant. Furthermore, we can **point** to non-held objects. Situations that do not fit into this set of categories are assigned the label **other**, and in case of doubt between two existing codes, the label **unclear** could be used. Finally, when one of the participants' behavior is not visible, because that participant is outside of the camera frame or behind some occluding object, the predicate **out-of-view** is assigned. For a more detailed description of these predicates, we point to the coding manual.[5]

Each of these predicates dictates a number of roles together with which they form a semantic predicate-argument structure. The predicate **grab**, meaning to bring something under one's manual control, has a grabber and a grabbed object, and possibly an instrument of grabbing other than the hands (a spoon, the mouth), **move** has a mover, a moved object and a source and goal location. The second column of Table 1 describes the valency of the predicates. As to the fillers of these roles, all roles marked with subscript O require objects to fill them, whereas the S subscripts describe a role to be filled with a spatial predicate. The objects either come from a closed class of descriptions of game-related objects (Table 2) or are assigned freely but consequently by the coder, in the case of objects that are not part of this closed set.

---

5 Available at https://github.com/dnrb/publications/blob/master/annotation_guidelines.pdf

Table 1: Behavioral predicates and their roles.

predicate	arguments
reach	(theme$_{O/S}$, [instrument$_O$])
grab	(theme$_O$, [instrument$_O$])
show	(theme$_O$, recipient$_O$, [instrument$_O$])
position	(theme$_O$, location$_S$, [instrument$_O$])
move	(theme$_O$, source$_S$, goal$_S$, [instrument$_S$])
hit	(theme$_O$, [instrument$_O$])
let_go	(theme$_O$, [instrument$_O$])
force	(theme$_O$, source$_S$, goal$_{O/S}$ [instrument$_O$])
point	(theme$_O$, recipient$_O$, [instrument$_O$])
other	n.a.
unclear	n.a.
out-of-view	n.a.

Table 2: Object labels for game-related arguments.*

predicate	arguments
to	toy
bu	bucket
ha	handle
li	lid
ho(ci|sq|st|tr)$_1$	hole in the lid with a certain shape$_1$
b(bl|re|gr|ye)$_1$(ci|sq|st|tr)$_2$	block with a certain color$_1$ and shape$_2$
mo	mother
ch	child
ob	observer
table	table
floor	floor
air	air

* ci = circle, sq = square, st = star, tr = triangle, bl = blue, re = red,
gr = green, and ye = yellow.

Independent spatial predicates are used in the case of some arguments (sources, goals, locations) and in order to describe salient events of the game. The spatial relations are given as English prepositions, but, again, rely upon descriptions that the coders used when coding the states. The four relations that are coded, are **in** for containment, **on** for horizontal support, **at** for all other forms of physical contact between two objects and **near** for all forms of non-contact but a salient proximity between two objects. Two pairs of game-related objects are independently described because of their relation to the success of the participants. The first is the lid being on or not-on (**off**) the bucket, and the second that of each of the blocks being in or not-in (**out**) the bucket. These relations are only coded if there is a change in situation.

When developing a set of predicates and objects like this, two important questions arise. First: does the handcrafted set have the right degree of granularity? Second, and perhaps more important: does the set reflect perceivable relations and not leave out perceivable relations. Regarding the first question, the set of primitives was developed so as to be as specific as possible, while still being codable by an instructed coder. In evaluating the coding procedure, there are some demarcation issues between predicates that can be solved by decomposing them further, but doing so would involve methods beyond coding video data to obtain the information.

As to the question whether the coding scheme is not too specific: our aim was to code primarily the physical behavior, and as little intention as possible. Actions at a larger scale, such as getting something out of something, often consist of parts that are simple predicates like **grab** and **move**, but are as a whole intentional, goal-directed actions. Inferring these from the perceived simple action schemas is a future direction we are currently looking into (see also Section 2.5).

Turning to the perceptual availability of the predicates, we believe the behavioral predicates reflect very basic, primitive sensory-motor experiences that are available from at least 12 months of age (Meltzoff and Moore 1995). These may then be grouped into culture-specific gestalts, combining properties of the shape of the manipulated object, the presence and nature of instruments etc. (see for an approach to the way languages encode these types of features Narasimhan and Kopecka 2012), but as such, we expect the basic building blocks of these analytically complex concepts to be perceptually available independent of culture.

The same holds, mutatis mutandis, for the spatial relations and properties and category labels of objects. Especially in the case of the former, the work by Baillargeon and Wang (2002) shows that notions like 'containment', 'nearness' and 'physical contact' have developed well before the child's first birthday. The predicate **on**, denoting horizontal support, is arguably more problematic. Choi (2006) presents evidence that children understand support relations later than containment relations, a fact that she ascribes to the many ways in which there can be a support relation, such that a common conceptual core is harder to abstract. Also, some potential perceptual sources of spatial relations that are encoded in different languages, such as pointwise vs. surface contact, tight fit vs. loose fit, are not coded in the data. Again, decomposing spatial relations into more primitive notions of relations (e.g. contact, surroundedness of figure by ground on both the horizontal and vertical axes, similarity in shape) combined with properties of the figure and the ground (mass-like or discrete, animacy) can provide a promising avenue (see e.g. Feist 2000 for such an approach), but coding observational data with such fine-grained distinctions (as opposed to setting up experimental situations) might prove too difficult for coders. Summarizing: the coded predicates are all available, but might not reflect all perceptually available relations. Nevertheless, we believe that we can still address the question whether the context is not too rich, as we code perhaps not all, but at least many predicates that function as noise for learning a word.

2.3 The coding procedure

The predicate-argument structures described above were coded using ELAN, a piece of software for video annotation.[6] Regular intervals of three seconds were created, so that the coders had to describe the events that took place within that window of time. Predicates taking place in two subsequent windows were only coded in the window in which they started. The behavior of the mother and the child was coded on different tiers, as were the spatial states of the game objects.

The coders, a second-year and a fourth-year student at Leiden University, were paid as research assistants and worked in total 56 and 64 hours respectively on the project and were supervised by the first author. They received six hours of training. The first two hours were spent on an in-depth explanation of the predicates, arguments and objects, after which the coders and the first author jointly coded a fragment in four hours. After this, the coders reported to feel confident about the task. Apart from the training, they received a manual with a reference sheet to be used during the coding itself. This document contained detailed descriptions about the predicates, decision trees for anticipated demarcation problems and a general instruction about the workflow using ELAN. The coders and the supervisor had contact at every working day about unclear cases and more general issues.

2.4 Coding the behavioral data: insights and figures

The coders worked for 56 and 64 hours on coding fragments. In this time, they coded 23 and 19 fragments, respectively. Each coder did one fragment twice and there was an overlap of three fragments between the coders. Five fragments

---

6 Developed by The Language Archive at the Max Planck Institute for Psycholinguistics, Nijmegen, and publicly available from http://tla.mpi.nl/tools/tla-tools/elan/. For a description, see Brugman and Russel (2004).

were discarded due to a low visibility of the actions (three cases) or children who failed to play the game for most of the time (two cases). On average, coding a fragment took the coders two hours and thirty-four minutes, with barely any difference between the coders (2 hours and 31 minutes, and 2 hours and 38 minutes respectively). This resulted in 175 minutes of coded material, out of which 157 minutes were useful, unique fragments. The average rate of coding thus was approximately 37 minutes of coding time per one minute of video.

The coders reported few problems with the procedure. Recurrent difficulties were the difference between **force** (i.e. moving without grabbing) and **hit**, which indeed is a distinction along a continuum, viz. that of the duration of the impact, which is more pointwise in hitting and more durative in forcing. This can be overcome if the dimensions of the manual contact are split out: one has to decide upon a cut-off point for the length of the impact to demarcate **force** from **hit**.

Also, the difference between **position** and **move** was felt to be unclear at times. Again, these predicates seem to form a continuum, with the amount of motion with respect to the ground being low for the former and high for the latter predicate. Truly distinguishing them would require the interpretation of intentions of the agents: one positions something in order to establish a different relation between the undergoing object and the location, whereas one moves something to change the object's location from a source to a goal location.

In order to evaluate the reliability of the coding, we calculated the inter- and intra-coder agreement. Three games were coded by both coders and each coder did one fragment twice. We measure the agreement by checking, for each predicate and for each time frame of three seconds whether at least one instance of that predicate was coded. A good measure for agreement is Cohen's kappa (Cohen 1960), which looks at the extent to which two codings of the same situation deviate (either two codings of one situation by the same coder or two codings of one situation by two different coders). A κ of 1 means perfect agreement, and a κ of 0 complete disagreement. This measure is often used in studies using human coders (e.g. Carletta 1996). Table 3 lists the Cohen's kappa scores for each predicate. A $\kappa \geq .80$ is generally taken to be the standard for very reliable coding (though often lower scores, above $\kappa \geq .60$ are taken to be acceptable as well).

We can see that several predicates are coded very reliably: **show, move, let go, point** and **grab**. The figures for **hit** are reasonably good, but the predicate is very infrequent, and all scores of 1.00 for this predicate are due to single predicates. **Reach** was coded unreliable across coders, but reliably within. This was due to the fact that one coder regarded them to be 'implied' by other predicates

(**grab, hit** and sometimes **force**) and only coded **reach** when these other predicates did not apply.

Table 3: Cohen's kappa per fragment and coder.

		inter-coder agreement per fragment			intra-coder agreement	
predicate	agent	1	2	3	coder 1	coder 2
reach	mother	.00	.29	.50	.80	.82
	daughter	.57	.35	.75	.66	.78
show	mother	1.00	1.00	.91	.91	1.00
	daughter	.80	1.00	.91	.91	1.00
move	mother	.77	.92	.85	.81	.92
	daughter	.79	.93	.86	.85	.91
position	mother	.70	.00	.69	.80	.00
	daughter	.59	.38	.69	.67	.39
hit	mother	.00	1.00	1.00	1.00	1.00
	daughter	.66	1.00	1.00	.75	.00
let_go	mother	.96	.84	.89	.90	.88
	daughter	.85	.83	.79	.92	.84
force	mother	1.00	1.00	1.00	1.00	1.00
	daughter	.00	.75	1.00	.27	.00
point	mother	.56	.89	1.00	.89	.89
	daughter	.59	.89	1.00	.90	.89
grab	mother	1.00	.90	.87	.81	.83
	daughter	.85	.82	.85	.85	.87
out		.00	1.00	1.00	1.00	.79
off		1.00	.83	1.00	1.00	1.00
in		.49	.92	1.00	.91	.87
on		.83	.91	.49	1.00	1.00

Position, finally, was coded variably between coders and within coders. This
may have to do with the fact that, as the coders reported, position and move
were found difficult to discriminate. How to create a more transparent coding
scheme for the motion-positioning continuum remains to be seen. For now,
we will retain the predicate, but in future work, this action will need to be
demarcated clearer for the coders. The space predicates, finally, were coded
reliably overall, except for two low scores, one for **out** and one for **in**. In the first
case, one coder coded **out** in the time window after the one in which the other
coder coded it, so effectively, they agree upon the predicate, but placed in a
different time frame. Part of the explanation of the low score for **in** is the disagreement on positioning: one coder used more **position** labels (as opposed to
non-actions) and in many cases the positioning took place in the air.

2.5 Deriving information

The codings resulting from this process were paired with all utterances that take place within each time window, to give us a corpus of child-directed language enriched with detailed situational information. Table 4 gives us a sample of this corpus.

Table 4: A sample of the coding and transcribed language paired.

time	type	action/utterance*
0'00	situation	hold(mo,li)
	language	een. nou jij een.
	gloss	one. now you one.
0'03	situation	position(mo,to,on-floor) grab(ch,byetr)
		move(ch,byetr,on-floor,near-hoci)
	language	nee daar.
	gloss	no there.
0'06	situation	point(mo,hotr,ch) hold(mo,li) position(ch,byetr,near-hoci)
	language	nee lieverd hier past ie niet.
	gloss	no sweetheart here fits he not.
0'09	situation	point(mo,hotr,ch) letgo(mo,lid) move(mo,byetr,near-hoci,near-hotr)
		grab(ch,bblst) move(ch,bblst,on-floor,in-air) grab(mo,byetr) letgo(ch,byetr)
	language	hier in. kijk e(en)s. een twee.
	gloss	here in. look once. one two.

* to = toy, li = lid, ho = hole, b = block, bl = blue, ye = yellow, st = star, ci = circle,
tr = triangle, mo = mother, ch = child.

Given the fine-grained descriptions of the behavior of the participants, it is possible to derive more information about the situation without having to code it manually. An important aspect of understanding a situation is understanding the intentions and goals of the participants. Although intentions are not directly perceivable, they can be inferred from the actions the participants partake in (cf. Fleischman and Roy 2005). It is likely that a person grabbing a block has some goals involving that block. Suppose we assume that the participants understand the global outline of the game, we could say that one participant's grabbing of a block can make the other participant infer that the first participant has (or: should have) the goal of putting that block in the bucket through the hole. We are currently exploring this direction further.

On a lower, less intentional level, it is interesting to know whether there is a match in shape or not between a block and a hole when a participant moves and positions a block next to a hole. Furthermore, the blocks can be split out in such a way that **grab (mother, blue-triangular-block)** is given as **grab**(e_i,e_j), **blue**(e_j), **triangular**(e_j), **block**(e_j), **mother**(e_i).

2.6 The language

The child-directed language used in the 157 minutes of useable material consists of 7,842 word tokens in 2,492 utterances, on average 3.14 words per utterance. Many utterances consist of merely *ja* 'yes' or *goed zo!* 'well done!'. The word tokens contain 480 types and 355 word lemmas (i.e. lemmas without inflectional and diminutive morphological marking).[7] Table 5 gives an overview of lemma statistics split over some categories. Nouns and adjectives are lumped, because many adjectives are used nominally. We can see many game-related lemmas in the top of the frequency distributions of the verbs, nouns and adjectives, and prepositions and spatial particles.

3 A first exploration

3.1 Data

To see if the situational context can be informative for the child trying to assign a meaning to a word, we investigate the association between coded aspects of the situation and certain lemmas. If we can find a strong association between certain lemmas and aspects of the situation related to their meaning, we can establish that the situational context is rich enough and not too rich to learn the meaning, or at least point the child in the right direction.

The starting point is a corpus of pairs of utterances (U) and situations (S), based on the 157 minutes of coded and transcribed interactional data discussed in the previous section. An utterance consists of the string of all lemmas $w_1 \ldots w_n$, and the situations are represented as a set of features $f_1 \ldots f_n$ that are present within the three-second time window in which the utterance takes place. So, every datapoint d is a pair U, S, where $U = w_1 \ldots w_n$ and $S = \{f_1 \ldots f_n\}$.

---

7 We take a type to be a unique transcribed representation of the speech, including diminutives and different sorts of inflection. A lemma, on the other hand, is taken to be the core word (whether it is a compound, another derivation or a mono-morphemic element). Examples of different types belonging to the same lemma are *ster* 'star', *sterren*, 'star.PL' and *sterretje*, 'star. DIM', that are all types related to the lemma *ster* 'star'. No methodological problems were found in determining the types and lemmas.

Table 5: Lemma frequencies split out over part of speech type and ranked, and total number of lemmas and tokens per part of speech type.*

verbs		nouns/ adjectives		prepositions/ spatial particles		other	
lemma	*n*	lemma	*n*	lemma	*n*	lemma	*n*
doen 'do'	260	*goed* 'good'	197	*in* 'in'	287	*ja* 'yes'	361
gaan 'go'	205	*mooi* 'beautiful'	58	*op* 'on'	54	*die* 'that'	306
zijn 'be'	185	*ander* 'other'	49	*uit* 'out'	43	*zo* 'like that'	288
kijken 'look'	178	*moeilijk* 'difficult'	46	*met* 'with'	25	*maar* 'but'	259
moeten 'should'	127	*mama* 'mom'	36	*af* 'off'	15	*d'r* 'there (red.)'	191
proberen 'try'	70	*keer* 'time'	26	*door* 'through'	15	*hier* 'here'	168
komen 'come'	60	*deksel* 'lid'	25	*van* 'of'	10	*eens* 'PRT'	162
kunnen 'can'	51	*blok* 'block'	24	*voor* 'for'	10	*nee* 'no'	158
pakken 'grab'	40	*rond* 'round'	23	*aan* 'on, at'	9	*een* 'a'	147
passen 'fit'	38	*leuk* 'nice'	19	*naar* 'towards'	8	*je* 'you (red.)'	143
zullen 'shall'	35	*ster* 'star'	17	*bij* 'at'	6	*hij* 'he'	138
zitten 'sit'	33	*makkelijk* 'easy'	15	*om* 'in order to'	4	*dat* 'that'	132
halen 'get'	32	*puzzel* 'puzzle'	13	*na* 'after'	3	*he* 'huh'	115
hebben 'have'	30	*gat* 'hole'	11	*neer* 'down'	5	*nog* 'still'	112
maken 'make'	28	*spel* 'game'	11	*heen* '-ither'	5	*niet* 'not'	106
draaien 'turn'	26	*stuk* 'piece'	10	*naast* 'next to'	2	*we* 'we (red.)'	105
stoppen 'stick'	18	*vierkant* 'square'	9	*achter* 'behind'	1	*nou* 'PRT'	98
zien 'see'	13	*emmer* 'bucket'	8	*boven* 'above'	1	*één* 'one'	96
weten 'know'	12	*meid* 'girl'	8	*buiten* 'outside'	1	*daar* 'there'	86
willen 'want'	12	*groen* 'green'	7	*dichtbij* 'close'	1	*deze* 'this'	85
74 lemmas		103 lemmas		20 lemmas		158 lemmas	
1640 tokens		765 tokens		505 tokens		4932 tokens	

* The gloss PRT is given when the word primarily function as a discourse particle for which no translation equivalent exists in English. (red.) means that this is a conventional, reduced form that is morpho-syntactically distinct from the full form.

For this exploration, we simplified the representation of the situation. Whereas we coded the information as predicate-argument structures, we discarded all arguments and used the predicates as atomic features. The predicate-argument structure **grab** (**mother, bucket**) and **on** (**lid, bucket**) thus become **grab** and **on** respectively. Apart from the behavioral predicates and spatial predicates that take place at a certain point in time, the following features are also included:

- properties of blocks and holes present among the arguments of the predicates coded at that moment in time (e.g. **red, star**);
- category labels for all objects that are arguments of those predicates (e.g., **mother, block, table**);
- two derived predicates: **match** and **mismatch**, that apply if there is a coded spatial relation between a block and a hole in the time window and there is either a match in the shape of both or a lack thereof, respectively.

In total, this procedure gives us 89 feature types, with an average of 12.2 features per situation.

To give a fuller example, consider the utterance in (1), which is paired with the situation in (2).

(1) *allemaal   even   d'r   uit   halen*
     all   PARTICLE   there   out   remove.INFINITIVE
     'Let's get them all out.'

(2) **reach (mother, bucket) grab (mother, bucket) move (mother, bucket, on-floor, in-air) position (mother, bucket, in-air) out (blocks, bucket)**

From the predicate-argument structures, we extract for the purpose of this study the features listed above. This gives us the situation S given in example (4). The lemmas of the words in the utterance in (1) are given in (3).

(3) U = (allemaal, even, d'r, uit, halen, gewoon, zo)

(4) S = {reach, grab, move, position, air, block, bucket, floor, mother, blue, green yellow, red, in, on, out, round, square, star, triangle}

3.2 Associating language and situation

Suppose we are interested in seeing whether the lemma *ster* 'star' is associated with the (non-relational) feature **star**. We check in our dataset of utterance-situation pairs for every sentence whether the lemma *ster* is used in the utterance (*ster* $\in U$) and whether the feature star is present in the situation (**star** $\in S$). This gives us the 2 × 2 table given in Table 6.

Table 6: 2 × 2 table for the lemma ster and the feature **star**.

	star $\in S$	star $\notin S$	row sum
ster $\in U$	16	1	17
ster $\notin U$	748	1727	2475
column sum	764	1728	2492

What we can see here is that the lemma *ster* is used almost exclusively in situations in which the feature **star** is present, that is: in situations in which a star-shaped object is an argument to an action or space predicate taking place at that time. However, in an overwhelming majority of cases in which the feature **star** is present, the lemma *ster* is not used. Despite this fact, we can see that the lemma and the feature are clearly associated: there is a higher chance of finding the feature if the lemma is present than if the lemma is not present (94.1% vs. 30.2%) and a slightly higher chance of finding the lemma if the feature is present than if it is not present (2.1% vs. 0.1%).

This association is reflected in a highly significant association using the Fisher exact test (p = 6.6399e−8). Note that the association between lemmas and features resembles that between syntactic environments and words in certain slots in collostructional analysis (Stefanowitsch and Gries 2003). Where Stefanowitsch and Gries establish behavioral profiles for constructions, we use the same statistics to show what the situational profiles are for lemmas. Following Stefanowitsch and Gries (2005), we take the negative natural logarithm of the Fisher exact *p*-value as a more readily interpretable association measure. This effectively means that the lower the probability of this and more extreme distributions, the higher the association value. For the feature **star** and the lemma *ster*, the association value is −ln 6.6399e−8 = 16.53. Note that, as we use the natural logarithm, association values greater than 2.995 and 4.605 reflect associations significant at α = .05, resp. α = .01.

Importantly, the Fisher exact test and derived association value will inform us about both poverty and excessive richness of the context. If the intended meaning is not grounded in some perceivable feature (i.e. the context is too poor) the lemma will be associated with other features that make little sense from an adult point of view. On the other hand, if there are too many features consequently present in the situational context of a lemma, the lemma will be associated about equally with all of them. A high association between a lemma and a feature thus means that that feature is found more often with that lemma than with other lemmas and that that lemma is found more often with that feature than with other features.

Now, we can calculate the association values between the lemma at hand (i.c. *ster*) and all possible features. Doing so and sorting the features on their association values with *ster*, from high to low, we can determine the situational profile for the lemma (Table 7).

What we see is that the lemma is most strongly associated with what we conceive to be its meaning, namely the feature **star**. Apart from that, we find noise, with the second strongest association being between the lemma and the feature **air**. We can repeat this procedure for a range of lemmas. Table 8 gives the top three strongest associated features for the four words referring to the colors of the blocks, and Table 9 does so for the words referring to the shape of the blocks.

What we can see from these tables, is that in five out of eight cases, the arguably correct feature is the one with the strongest association with the lemma. The cases in which the correct feature is not associated with the lemma are either very low in frequency (*blauw* (n = 3), *driehoek* (n = 4)), or have an 'unfortunate' split in time windows (three out of nine cases of groen). This means that the child grabbed a green block, and a second later, just within the next time window the mother comments on the block, using the lemma *groen*. Because the child was not *doing* anything with the block in the time window in which the utterance was produced, there is no predicate in which it is involved and hence **green** is not included in *S*.

Table 7: Features with the highest association values with the lemma *star*.

feature	association value
star	16.53
air	7.35
in	6.04
move	3.59
ball	3.39

Table 8: Lemmas for color and features most strongly associated with them.

rood 'red'		*groen* 'green'		*blauw* 'blue'		*geel* 'yellow'	
feature	assoc.	feature	assoc.	feature	assoc.	feature	assoc.
red	3.99	move	3.11	circle	3.43	yellow	4.49
let_go	2.06	lid	2.79	out	2.53	let_go	1.65
in	1.91	green	2.6	mother	1.91	mother	1.45

Table 9: Lemmas for shape and features most strongly associated with them.

vierkant 'square'		*driehoek* 'triangle'		*rond* 'round'		*ster* 'star'	
feature	assoc.	feature	assoc.	feature	assoc.	feature	assoc.
square	5.17	yellow	3.23	round	19.35	star	16.53
force	4.42	point	2.39	floor	6.25	air	7.35
match	3.44	mother	1.65	mismatch	4.26	in	6.04

3.3 Relational terms and their situational contexts

In this section, we investigate to what extent the situation can guide a learner towards the meaning of relational terms. We consider eight lemmas that relate to aspects of the game. Linguistic items that do relate to the limited world of the game are action verbs, spatial prepositions and terms referring to properties of the blocks and holes (colors and shapes, as we have discussed in the previous section). Let us turn to the former two categories now.

The utterances contain many verbs pertaining to game-related actions. We find verbs of placement, like *stoppen* 'put in', and *halen* 'remove, get'. Then there are verbs of manipulation, such as *duwen* 'push', *pakken* 'grab' and *draaien* 'turn, rotate'. Finally, of interest are verbs denoting relations between blocks and holes, such as *horen* 'belong' and *passen* 'fit'. For all of these relations, a range of modals and light verbs is also used, especially in combination with certain argument-structure constructions and spatial particles. We will not go into these in this exploration. Here, we discuss four verbs, namely *halen*, *pakken*, *passen* and *proberen* 'try'. The former three are members of the categories of placement verbs, manipulation verbs and verbs pertaining to stative relations. The latter is a frequently used verb in the game situation but has no clear corre-late in the coded predicates. We discuss it to see what sort of situational profile it displays.

The prepositions and verbal particles also form an interesting category. The caregivers often talk about the spatial relations of the game objects, especially in combination with the three types of verbs discussed above (someone pushing something in something, someone getting something off something, something fitting in something). Four prepositions we will discuss are *in* 'in', *op* 'on', *uit* 'out' and *af* 'off'.

What are the situational profiles for the eight items we selected? Tables 10 and 11 present the top five most strongly associated features per lemma.

Table 10: Four verbs and the features most strongly associated with them.

passen 'fit'		*pakken* 'grab'		*halen* 'get'		*proberen* 'try'	
feature	assoc.	feature	assoc.	feature	assoc.	feature	assoc.
mismatch	35.69	hit	4.87	bucket	24.82	square	10.95
hole	23.37	unknown1	4.13	out	19.18	block	9.02
near	19.56	unknown2	3.45	on	7.02	mismatch	7.11
block	11.92	cheek_child	2.77	off	6.07	child	5.53
circle	11.04	observer	2.23	floor	4.95	show	5.29

Table 11: Four prepositions/particles and the features most strongly associated with them.

in 'in'		*op* 'on'		*af* 'off'		*uit* 'out'	
feature	assoc.	feature	assoc.	feature	assoc.	feature	assoc.
square	5.17	yellow	3.23	round	19.35	star	16.53
force	4.42	point	2.39	floor	6.25	air	7.35
match	3.44	mother	1.65	mismatch	4.26	in	6.04

Turning to the verbs first, we find two verbs that have readily interpretable situational profiles. The four most strongly associated features for *passen* 'fit' are all elements of the meaning we would like to assign to the verb. Used mostly with negation, *passen* is about the match or mismatch ('doesn't fit') between a figure (i.c. the block) and a ground (i.c. the hole) that is salient because the two are in some relevant relation to each other (i.c. nearness, as the child is trying to fit the block in the hole). The fact that the precise figure and ground are associated is obviously due to the nature of the game: the only things that fit or don't fit are blocks and holes.

The lemma *halen* 'remove, get' is in our corpus always used with either *af* 'off' or *uit* 'out'. The things that are typically removed are the lid from the bucket and the blocks from the bucket. Now, the verb *halen* is indeed associated strongly with features related to these two situations: the bucket is a pivotal object out of which or off of which objects are removed. These objects then enter into a new spatial relationship with another object (typically a support relation with the floor, hence on and floor). As the mode of removal varies (grabbing and moving by hand, positioning the bucket in such a way that the blocks fall out), no specific feature pertaining to the behavior (e.g., move, position) is associated with *halen*.

It may be argued that if a child acts in a certain way when a certain word is used, the child understands that word. Suppose the mother says *Go take the lid off*, and the child subsequently takes the lid off. It does not follow logically that the child does so by having an understanding of the particle verb *take off*, the auxiliary *go* and the noun *lid*. In fact, in situations like the ones occurring in this corpus, it is clear what is expected from the participants. An openable and closeable container with blocks that fit in certain holes and not others needs hardly any instruction to be played with. When the toy is given to the mother and the mother shows the child the toy, and says *Go take the lid off*, the child will just as readily start taking the lid off as when the mother makes a comment about the toy (e.g. *That's a nice puzzle!*) or produces another adhortative utterances (e.g. *Let's do this puzzle*).

For the other two verbs, the situational context is not so clear. This is to be expected from a verb denoting an intention, such as *proberen*, for which encoding the intentional states of the agents might provide a way out, but not so much for a highly concrete verb like *pakken*. We expect *pakken* to become associated with the feature **grab**, but in only in 57.5% of utterances containing *pakken*, that feature is present, whereas it is also present in 52.2% of all utterances not containing *pakken*.

What then, is the situational action *pakken* relates to? Out of the forty cases of utterances in which the lemma occurs, thirty-one have a grabbing event that can be identified with the utterance within a time frame of two three-second windows before and after the window in which the utterance was produced. An example is the utterance in example (5), produced within the fifteen-second fragment of situational context in Table 12. The mother comments on the choice of the daughter to grab the red, round block and does so a few seconds after the action referred to takes place.

(5) *pak* *je* *weer* *de* *zelfde*
      grab you   again   the   same
      'You picked the same one again!'

Table 12: The situational context of the utterance *Pak je weer dezelfde*.

time	Predicates*
−2	reach(child,bgrsq)
−1	grab(child,breci) move(child,breci,on-floor,in-air)
0	move(child,breci,in-air,at-hoci)
1	letgo(child,breci) in(breci,bucket)
2	reach(child,bgrsq) grab(child,bgrsq)

* ho = hole, b = block, re = red, gr = green, sq = square, ci = circle.

Widening the window thus seems to make the situation available in which the referred action takes place. Nevertheless, if a learner used a window this wide, the feature **grab** would be present in 93.9% of the utterance-situation pairs. This presents a great amount of noise for the learner, and so if a child is to learn the meaning of *pakken*, other cues must be used. Now, it falls outside of the scope of this exploration to go much deeper into this matter, but as other cues we can imagine bootstrapping the meaning from pre-established object reference: if we know that the pronoun *die* 'that' refers to a certain block, it should be more likely for the lemma *pakken* to be associated with predicates in which that specific block is an argument. The use of these advanced cues can only start when the child has a basic understanding of other referential expressions in the utterance, and hence cannot be the initial drive behind verb learning. This position resembles that of the Emergentist Coalition Model (Hollich, Hirsh-Pasek, and Golinkoff 2000; Poulin-Dubois and Forbes 2006), in which the validity of different cues for acquiring word meanings changes over ontogenetic time. Another route to pursue would be to look at argument-structure constructions, see if those can be associated with certain clusters of meanings and then use that information to bootstrap the meaning of the verb. This is essentially the idea of syntactic bootstrapping (Gleitman 1990; Naigles 1990), but then from an emergentist perspective: both argument-structure constructions and verbs are acquired through use and mutually reinforce each other's acquisition.

For the prepositions, we see a similar pattern: some have relatively strong associations with the (correct) spatial features and the typical figure and ground objects in those relations (*af* and *uit*). For *op*, the highest four features are object categories (three of which are typical objects found in a support relation), and the fifth is the correct meaning of *op*. Although the feature **on** only comes fifth, it ranks higher than all other spatial, or in general relational features, and we can hence say that the situational context does provide some evidence for the acquisition of the preposition *op*.

The most frequent (r = 286) preposition, *in*, however, shows hardly any interesting associations. The reason why the lemma is not associated with the feature **in** is the same as for *pakken*: the feature is highly frequent in general, and hence there are many occurrences of the feature in which the lemma is not used. Furthermore, in only 51.7% of all instances of *in*, a change of state resulting in a containment relation took place. This might be due to the fact that mothers often encourage their child by saying *doe 'm daar maar in* 'go put it in there', when the actual putting-in only takes place half a minute later. This can be seen from the fact that the accompanying pointing gesture is highly associated with the lemma *in*. What cues there are that might guide the child towards the intended meaning of *in*, remains to be seen. In any event, the learner would have to be able to suppress a lot of noise in the data and perhaps ignore several uninformative instances of the lemma. Perhaps the a priori salience of the containment relation (Choi 2006) helps finding the intended meaning as well.

4 Conclusion and directions

It seems that some relational terms are used in a way that an ideal learner can associate them with the correct features. Others, like *pakken*, *proberen* and *in* do not have any clearly associated features that we would recognize to be valid meaning representations from an adult point of view. Interestingly, *pakken* is a highly concrete verb, denoting a single, atomic predicate in our representation (i.e. **grab**), but there is too much noise for the feature and lemma to be associated. We suggested that other cues might help understand the meaning of *pakken*. In the case of a preposition with a relatively accessible intended meaning like *in*, the situational context provides little help in acquiring that meaning, at least if we see learning as naïve association. How a preposition like *in* is acquired from the situational context, remains to be seen.

It thus seems that Gleitman's disjunction is partly right. Some relational meanings do have clear correlates in the perceivable situation and are highly associated with the lemmas denoting these meanings. We discussed eight lemmas, five of which were strongly associated with features related to the meaning they were intended to convey. This should be enough to get a learner (at least) started learning terms with relational meanings. One of the other three, *pakken* 'grab', also has grabbing events in its context, only taken a little wider (six seconds before and six seconds after the time frame of the utterance). Surprisingly, *in* 'in' has no good association with the feature denoting a containment relation. For the lemmas for which the situational context does not provide reliable grounding, Gleitman's argument still holds: additional cues are needed to explain their acquisition.

In this study, we presented a method for studying the situational context of child-directed language in more detail. We discussed the decisions and the process, as this is an often overlooked aspect of the study of child language. The main reason for developing such a dataset is to evaluate claims about the excessive richness (size of the hypothesis space) and the poverty of the situational context. We re-evaluated the statement that the situational context contains both too much information to find the right correlate for a word and too little – with the intended relation or action not being present. On the basis of the developed dataset, we concluded that for several relational meanings, the situational context does contain features that are very significantly associated with the word that refers to the relation captured in that feature. Other predicates and prepositions are less strongly associated with features related to their meaning. For these words, it is indeed the case that the hypothesis space is often too big, in the sense that the feature is often present when utterances nót containing the word are produced, so that the association becomes weaker. Nevertheless, the association can form a starting point for word learning, which is later supplemented with additional cues (other words in the sentence, syntactic frames, social cues, better understanding of the task), a position that has been worked out in more detail in the Emergentist Coalition Model (Hollich et al. 2000).

What this study shows, is that it is possible to *get started* on learning relational semantics on the basis of mere association. The relevance of this analysis for usage-based theorizing is that domain-specific biases for word learning are not needed to start developing a lexicon. However, learning the symbolic mappings remains difficult, and there often is too much information in the situation. One challenge for usage-based approaches is to develop accounts of structured learning (as opposed to merely associative learning) where constructions (for example) play a role in bootstrapping word meanings, and to apply this in a structured way to naturalistic data like the dataset presented in this chapter.

Using the atomic-feature representation, we plan to work with actual word learning models (e.g. Fazly, Alishahi, and Stevenson 2010) in order to see if the meaning can indeed be learned by a cognitively realistic incremental model. A next step would be to see if it is possible to have a computational learner induce a simple, (semi-)productive grammar that can be used to interpret unseen utterances.

In our exploration we left aside interesting, but more complex issues, such as the relation between the nature of the child-directed language and the output. For prepositions, it would be interesting to see if there is a correlation between the availability of situational context guiding the learner in the correct direction and the age of acquisition or the overextension patterns of certain lemmas. Examples are the prepositions *af* 'off of' and *uit* 'out of' (Bowerman 1995) or the set of *op* 'canonical support', *aan* 'support by hanging and attachment' and *in* 'containment' and the overextension of *op* to *aan*-situations [Bowerman 1993]).

Modeling known phenomena, whether they were established by experimental method or by observation, gives us a greater insight in the cognitive mechanisms underlying them. However, in order to model the acquisition of meaning, a detailed understanding of the context is needed, especially given claims about the nature of that context. With the development of a dataset, we hope to encourage research in language acquisition that takes the situatedness of actual child-directed language into account in a systematic way.

References

Baillargeon, Renee, and Su-Hua Wang. 2002. Event categorization in infancy. *Trends in Cognitive Sciences* 6 (2): 85–93.

Barak, Libby, Afsaneh Fazly, and Suzanne Stevenson. 2012. Modeling the acquisition of mental state verbs. In *Proceedings of the NAACL-HLT Workshop on Cognitive Modeling and Computational Linguistics (CMCL)*.

Behrend, Douglas A., and Jason M. Scofeld. 2006. Verbs, actions, and intentions. In *Action Meets Word: How Children Learn Verbs*, Kathryn Hirsh-Pasek, and Roberta M. Golinkoff (eds.), 286–307. Oxford, UK: Oxford University Press.

Bowerman, Melissa. 1993. Typological Perspective on Language Acquisition: Do Crosslinguistic Patterns Predict Development. In *Proceedings of the Twenty-fifth Annual Child Language Research Forum*, Eve V. Clark (ed.), 7–15. Stanford, CA: CSLI Publications.

Bowerman, Melissa. 1995. Learning how to structure space for language: A crosslinguistic perspective. In *Language and Space*, Paul Bloom, Mary. A. Peterson, Lynn Nadel, and Merill F. Garett (eds.), 385–436. Cambridge, MA: MIT Press.

Brugman, Hennie, and Albert Russel. 2004. Annotating multimedia/multi-modal resources with ELAN. In *Proceedings of the Fourth International Conference on Language Resources and Evaluation (LREC)*, 2065–2068. Paris: European Language Resources Association.

Carletta, Jean. 1996. Assessing agreement on classification tasks: The kappa statistic. *Computational Linguistics* 22 (2): 249–254.

Casasola, Marianella, Jui Bhagwat, and Kim T. Ferguson. 2006. Precursors to verb learning: Infant's understanding of motion events. In *Action Meets Word: How Children Learn Verbs*, Kathryn Hirsh-Pasek, and Roberta M. Golinkoff (eds.), 160–190. Oxford, UK: Oxford University Press.

Choi, Soonja. 2006. Preverbal spatial cognition and language-specific input: Categories of containment and support. In *Action Meets Word: How Children Learn Verbs*, Kathryn Hirsh-Pasek, and Roberta M. Golinkoff (eds.), 191–207. Oxford, UK: Oxford University Press.

Cohen, Jacob. 1960. A coefficient of agreement for nominal scales. *Educational and Psychological Measurement* 20 (1): 37–46.

Fazly, Afsaneh, Afra Alishahi, and Suzanne Stevenson. 2010. A probabilistic computational model of cross-situational word learning. *Cognitive Science: A Multidisciplinary Journal* 34 (6): 1017–1063.

Feist, Michele I. 2000. On *in* and *on*. An investigation into the linguistic encoding of spatial scenes. Ph.D. diss., Northwestern University.

Fleischman, Michael, and Deb K. Roy. 2005. Why verbs are harder to learn than nouns: Initial insights from a computational model of intention recognition in situated word learning, In *Proceedings of the 27th Annual Meeting of the Cognitive Science Society*.

Frank, Michael C., Noah D. Goodman, and Joshua B. Tenenbaum. 2009. Using speakers' referential intentions to model early cross-situational word learning. *Psychological Science* 20 (5): 578–585.

Frank, Michael C., Joshua B. Tenenbaum, and Anne Fernald. 2013. Social and discourse contributions to the determination of reference in cross-situational word learning. *Language, Learning, and Development* 9: 1–24.

Gentner, Dedre. 1978. On relational meaning: The acquisition of verb meaning. *Child Development* 49: 988–998.

Gentner, Dedre. 1982. Why nouns are learned before verbs: Linguistic relativity versus natural partitioning. In *Language Development*. Vol. 2. *Language, Thought, and Culture*, Stan A. Kuczaj II (ed.), 301–334. Hillsdale, NJ: Lawrence Erlbaum Associates.

Gentner, Dedre, and Kurtz Kenneth. J. 2005. Relational categories. In *Categorization Inside and Outside the Lab*, Woo-Kyoung Ahn, Robert L. Goldstone, Bradley C. Love, Arthur B. Markman, and Phillip Wolff (eds.), 151–175. Washington, DC: Amer Psychological Association.

Gleitman, Lila. 1990. Sources of verb meanings. *Language Acquisition* 1 (1): 3–55.

Hollich, George. J., Kathryn Hirsh-Pasek, and Roberta M. Golinkoff. 2000. Breaking the language barrier: An emergentist coalition model for the origins of word learning. *Monographs of the Society for Research in Child Development* 65 (3): 1–135.

Mandler, Jean M. 2006. Actions organize the infant's world. In *Action Meets Word: How Children Learn Verbs*, Kathryn Hirsh-Pasek, and Roberta M. Golinkoff (eds.), 111–133. Oxford, UK: Oxford University Press.

Meltzoff, Andrew N. and M. Keith Moore. 1995. Infants' understanding of people and things: From body imitation to folk psychology. In *The Body and the Self*, José L. Bermúdez, Anthony Marcel, and Naomi Eilan (eds.), 43–69. Cambridge, MA: MIT Press.

Naigles, Letitia R. 1990. Children use syntax to learn verb meanings. *Journal of Child Language* 17 (2): 357–374.

Narasimhan, Bhuvana, and Anetta Kopecka. (eds.). 2012. *Events of putting and taking: A cross-linguistic perspective.* Amsterdam: John Benjamins.

Poulin-Dubois, Diane, and James N. Forbes. 2006. Word, intention, and action: A two-tiered model of action word learning. In *Action Meets Word: How Children Learn Verbs*, Kathryn Hirsh-Pasek, and Roberta M. Golinkoff (eds.), 262–285. Oxford, UK: Oxford University Press.

Sootman-Buresh, Jennifer, Amanda L. Woodward, and Camille W. Brune. 2006. The roots of verbs in prelinguistic action knowledge. In *Action Meets Word: How Children Learn Verbs*, Kathryn Hirsh-Pasek, and Roberta M. Golinkoff (eds.), 208–227. Oxford, UK: Oxford University Press.

Stefanowitsch, Anatol, and Stefan T. Gries. 2003. Collostructions: Investigating the interaction of words and constructions, *International Journal of Corpus Linguistics* 8(2): 209–243. 2005. Covarying collexemes. *Corpus Linguistics and Linguistic Theory* 1 (1): 1–43.

Tomasello, Michael. 2003. *Constructing a language: A Usage-Based Theory of Language Acquisition*, Cambridge, MA: Harvard University Press.

Huub van den Bergh and Jacqueline Evers-Vermeul
4 Validity issues in longitudinal research

1 Introduction

Usage-based studies, just like developmental studies taking a different theoretical approach, are interested in changes in responses with age, which is why data are gathered at different points in time on the phenomenon studied. For instance, if we aim to assess growth in language use by young children, we would like to describe differences in the language development of individual children and extract inter-individual patterns from the observed intra-individual differences in language development (compare, Baltes and Nesselroade 1979: 7). And, of course, in a later phase we try to explain differences in growth between (groups of) children.

In order to assess growth with age, two principally different types of research designs are being used: longitudinal designs and cross-sectional designs. In longitudinal designs the same respondents' skills are measured on multiple occasions, whereas in cross-sectional designs different subjects' skills are measured at different occasions. In other words, if we were to study the language development of young children we could follow a random sample of children during a period of interest (a longitudinal design), or measure the responses of different samples of children at different ages (a cross-sectional design).

For example, in Figures 1 and 2 the spelling scores of students in the first grades of primary education are presented. In both figures the spelling scores (y-axis) of students are plotted against the number of months elapsed since the start of spelling education (x-axis) in the first grade.

In Figure 1 the spelling skills of the same nine students are measured on six occasions according to a longitudinal design. It is obvious that each student can be followed during the period under investigation: each line represents the proficiency of one of the nine students in this study. For instance, student X has a high spelling score at the beginning, but shows a remarkable lack of growth and has the lowest spelling score at the final measurement occasion. Student Y starts as an average student, but shows a (relatively) large increase in spelling skills during this study. Due to the longitudinal design each student is followed during all six measurements and the data allow for a prediction of spelling

Huub van den Bergh and **Jacqueline Evers-Vermeul**, UiL OTS – Utrecht University

DOI 10.1515/9781501505492-005

scores to time points outside the investigated period. For instance, student X is a student likely to be at risk if his spelling scores keep developing at this pace.

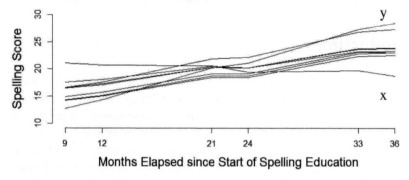

Figure 1: Results of a study on the development of spelling skills by students in the first grades of primary education according to a longitudinal design (data from Boland 1991).

In Figure 2 the same data are presented as if they were gathered according to a cross-sectional design. There are six measurement occasions, and hence the spelling skills in six samples of nine students have been measured.

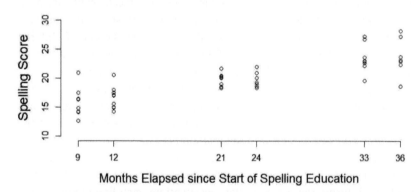

Figure 2: Results of a study on the development of spelling skills by students in the first grades of primary education according to a cross-sectional design (data from Boland 1991).

Longitudinal and cross-sectional designs each have their merits and drawbacks. Cross-sectional studies are less time-consuming, as different samples can be measured simultaneously, whereas in longitudinal studies measurements have to be made during the whole period under investigation. Perhaps this is one of the reasons why cross-sectional designs are preferred in so many studies in linguistics and language learning.

However, longitudinal designs have more opportunities for interpretation of research results. Although the average pattern of spelling skills is the same in Figures 1 and 2, the cross-sectional study does not allow for conclusions on the development of spelling skills of individual students. Consequently, interpretation is limited to differences in scores within measurement occasions and differences in means between occasions. Interpreting differences in terms of development can lead to erroneous conclusions regarding the development of spelling skills.

This drawback of cross-sectional designs does not imply that longitudinal studies have to be preferred at all cost. There are many threats to validity in longitudinal studies as well. In the remainder of this chapter we will discuss three such threats. First, we will look at attrition (Section 2), as many longitudinal studies can be characterized by the attrition of respondents. This can influence research results considerably (compare, Chatfield, Brayne, and Matthews 2005). Second, we will discuss measurement invariance (Section 3), which concerns the question whether the same skills are measured at different occasions. In our experience measurement invariance is a neglected issue in many studies on the development of language. Third, we will turn to the density of measurements in longitudinal studies (Section 3). Each of the validity issues will be illustrated with examples from actual research, along with conclusions about consequences for interpretation and suggestions for circumventing these issues.

2 Attrition

Both longitudinal and cross-sectional research designs have their merits and difficulties. For instance, longitudinal research is well known for the attrition of subjects: longitudinal studies in which less than two third of the respondents are tested at all occasions are the rule rather than the exception. In Section 2.1 we examine the potential threats of attrition to the representativeness of the sample. In Section 2.2 we discuss the consequences of selecting overlapping measurements as a way to minimize attrition.

2.1 Attrition and representativeness of the sample

Unfortunately, attrition is seldom at random. Consequently, the resulting data are often not a valid reflection of the population they come from, and hence the conclusions might be biased. For instance, Boland (1991) performed a longitudinal study on spelling skills. A total of 564 students in the first grades of primary education (age 6 through 8) participated in this study. However, a complete data set of six measurements is available for only 355 students (62%). Hence, for 199 students (38%) spelling scores at one or more measurement occasions are missing. An important question is whether the attrition can be considered to be at random. If it is, there is no need to worry about the representativeness of the data, and the research results can be generalized to the population of students in the first grades of primary education. If, however, attrition is not at random, the sample of students at later occasions is different from the original sample. Hence, generalization of the results might become problematic.

In Figure 3 the average estimated (standardized) spelling scores of Boland's study are presented as a function of time elapsed since the start of spelling education in the first grade. This study has six measurement occasions: at 9, 12, 21, 24, 33 and 36 months after the start of spelling education. The solid line is the estimated growth if attrition of (spelling measurements of) students does not influence the results. That is, if attrition of (spelling measurements of) students is assumed to be completely at random. The dashed line shows the average change in spelling scores for students who have taken spelling tests at all six measurement occasions. If attrition (of spelling measurements of) students is completely at random, the two lines would coincide.

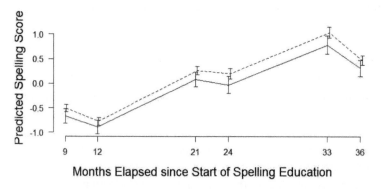

Figure 3: Average development of standardized spelling scores for all 564 students (solid line) and for 355 students without missing observations (dashed line; vertical lines represent 95% confidence intervals for means).

The solid line in Figure 3 represents the average growth in spelling proficiency of all students (N = 564) in the sample. It clearly shows that, on average, the spelling score decreases from the 9th month till the 12th month, after which an increase is shown until the 21st month, followed by a small decrease in scores until the 24th month after the start of spelling education, etc. Note that periods with a negative average growth nicely correspond to summer holidays. During summer holidays students receive no (spelling) education, which is why a decrease in spelling scores might be expected. In periods in which children do receive education (i.e. from 12 till 21 months, and from 24 till 33 months) an increase in spelling achievements is shown. The vertical lines represent the 95%-confidence intervals of the averages. For instance, the mean of the first spelling measurement of all students (solid line) shows a 95%-confidence interval that ranges from −.81 to −.53.

The estimated growth in spelling scores makes it clear that attrition plays a substantial role; the estimated growth curve of the sample of students present at all six measurements occasions (dashed line in Figure 3) is different from that of the complete sample (solid line Figure 3). Hence, the attrition of (spelling measurements of) students does not seem to be completely at random. The differences in averages suggest that especially poor spellers are likely to be more absent at measurements. A statistical test shows that at all measurement occasions the difference in mean scores between students who are tested at all six occasions and students with fewer than six measurements appears to be significant ($t > 5.89$, $df > 441$, $p < .001$); on average students with complete measurements outperform students with one or more missing measurements.

A second cue for the non-randomness of the attrition can be found in the size of the confidence intervals; each of the confidence intervals for the entire sample is larger than the corresponding confidence intervals for students with complete measurements ($\chi^2 > 13.71$, $df = 1$, $p < .001$). As confidence intervals are based on the variance in scores (and the number of observations), this means that the variance between students' spelling skills in the entire sample is larger than the variance in the sample in which only students are present with spelling scores at all six occasions. Hence, not only low performing students are more likely to be absent at one or more measurement occasions – as can be inferred from the average difference between the two lines – but also (some) high per-forming students, as can be inferred from the differences in confidence intervals.

In short, we have to be very careful in generalizing the results of this study to the population of students, as attrition proved to be not at random. There could be several reasons why students did not participate in every test: their parents could have moved, or they could have been ill at specific measurement occasions. An additional problem in this specific case is that especially during the first years of primary education low achieving students are referred to special education, and hence drop out of regular education. As a result the population might change from grade 1 to 2 and from grade 2 to 3. Afterwards one can only guess about the exact reasons, and hope that attrition has not influenced the generalizability from the sample to the population, and that attrition has not influenced differences between means (and variances) at different occasions. This is an argument for very laborious procedures to minimize attrition of data.

2.2 Using overlapping measurements as a way to minimize attrition

One way to deal with attrition is to limit the number of observations per student. If, for instance, the spelling skills of students would be measured at only two occasions, the attrition rate is of course likely to be lower. This idea to limit the number of observations of individual participants has been proposed several times (e.g. Shadish, Cook, and Campbell 2002; van den Bergh, Eiting, and Mellenbergh 1992). Following this advice, one could choose a different research design, one with overlapping measurements, in order to circumvent attrition as much as possible. An example of such a design is presented in Table 1.

Table 1: Example of a design with overlapping observations (X: planned observations).

Sample	Measurements				
	End grade 1	Begin grade 2	End grade 2	Begin grade 3	...
1	X	X			
2		X	X		
3			X	X	
4				X	X
...					X

In Table 1 an example is given of a design in which students' skills are measured at only two occasions. By applying such a design with overlapping measurements attrition can be minimized. This design also allows for a check on the equivalence of samples, because consecutive samples have one measurement in common.

A design with overlapping measurements can also be applied afterwards, by cutting the entire sample in two or more sub-samples. Such samples can be optimized in order to limit attrition as much as possible (compare, van den Bergh et al. 1992). In the present example on growth in spelling skills we could draw a random sample of students who have taken the spelling test at the first and second occasion (i.e. month 9 and 12), another sample of students who took the tests at the second and third occasion (month 12 and 21), a third sample of students who took the tests at the third and fourth occasion, and so on. If we apply this design, the scores of only 55 students who took the spelling tests at only one occasion are not taken into account. This is a large improvement, compared to the 199 students with incomplete observations in the original study. The results for the average development of spelling scores are presented in Figure 4.

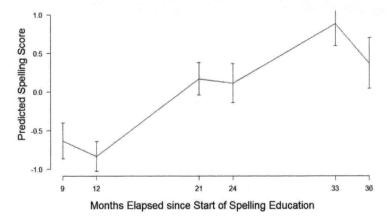

Months Elapsed since Start of Spelling Education

Figure 4: Average development of standardized spelling scores after sampling in order to minimize attrition (vertical lines represent 95% confidence intervals for means).

The average development of spelling skills according to the latter analysis holds the middle between the two previous ones (presented in Figure 3). This suggests that in this design with overlapping measurements the effect of attrition is more or less equal across measurement occasions. The size of the confidence intervals, however, stands out. They are much larger than in both samples in the previous analysis. This is the price we have to pay for cutting the sample in five separate sub-samples.

Development and changes in development are more than just differences in averages. In fact, the average student does not exist, and the development of individuals – and differences between them – is at the heart of longitudinal research. Therefore, not only the average development has to be studied, but also the individual (estimated) growth curves. Here, we use the data from the spelling study to illustrate that applying a design of overlapping measurements affects not only the interpretation of averages, but also that of individual differences. In Figure 5 individual growth curves for the development of 355 students are plotted according to the original longitudinal design: each line represents the development of one student.

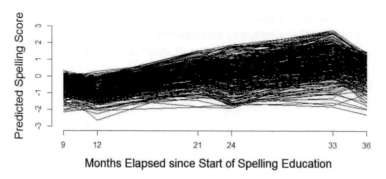

Figure 5: Individual growth curves according to a longitudinal design.

On the basis of the longitudinal data in Figure 5, several observations can be made. First, it is apparent that the development of spelling skills in the first grades of primary education differs between students; some students hardly appear to learn to spell correctly, whereas others show a clear development in spelling scores.

Second, the individual curves show a crisscross change in the period under investigation. This indicates that the change in spelling scores differs between children and that each child develops (more or less) at his or her own pace. Nevertheless, the data suggest a fair correlation between different measurement occasions. For instance, the correlation between spelling scores at the first and the final measurement equals .40, and the correlation between two successive measurements never drops below .64. A useful next step would be to explain these differences in individual growth trajectories – at least partly – with characteristics of students and characteristics of the spelling education these students received.

Third, for most children a summer holiday drop in spelling scores can be shown. However, for some children, especially the good spellers, such a summer holiday drop is absent. This difference appears to be related to socio-economic status; students with disadvantaged socio-economic backgrounds have a larger summer holiday drop than students with higher socio-economic backgrounds who do not show a severe summer holiday drop in spelling scores (van den Bergh and Kuhlemeier 1992).

Fourth, the differences between students in spelling scores seem to increase. Education does not appear to decrease or minimize differences between students, but rather to increase differences in spelling skills (see, Anastasi (1976) for a similar but more general conclusion).

In Figure 6 the original sample of 564 students is divided into five sub-samples of around 102 students. That is, again a design over overlapping measurements is used, in order to minimize effects of attrition.

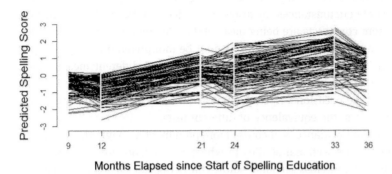

Months Elapsed since Start of Spelling Education

Figure 6: Individual growth curves according to a cross-sectional design with repeated measurements.

Due to the cross-sectional design with repeated measurements we now have five samples to study the development in students' spelling skills. For each combination of successive measurement occasions there are about a hundred lines indicating the skills of just as many students. Note that due to the sampling criteria, the development of each student is observed at exactly two occasions. Hence, it is impossible to make inferences concerning the whole period, other than changes in average development. This implies that, next to the loss in precision, due to the smaller sample sizes, we cannot make individual predictions other than those based on mean values. Nevertheless, trends such as increasing differences between spelling skills of children over measurement occasions, and remarkably large differences in development during summer holidays become apparent.

All in all, attrition appears to influence the results to a considerable degree. Splitting the data in separate sub-samples might decrease the influence of attrition, but decreases the precision of parameter estimates, and makes inferences on the development of individual participants difficult if not impossible. The only real solution is to minimize attrition during the study as much as possible.

3 Measurement invariance

A second threat to the validity of longitudinal studies is so-called measurement invariance. Measurement invariance refers to the question whether different tests, or the same test at different measurement occasions, measure the same construct (irrespective of measurement error; e.g. Cheung and Rensvold 2002; Jöreskog 1971). If respondents in a longitudinal study take the same test over and over again, differences between measurement occasions might be due to age (and the intermediate circumstances) or to memory effects and/or to test sophistication. If different constructs are being measured at different occasions, the differences between measurement occasions cannot be interpreted unambiguously.

However, if the respondents take different tests at different measurement occasions, we do not know whether exactly the same skill/knowledge is being measured at these occasions. Special analysis and special measures are necessary in order to test the equivalence of different tests.

Measurement invariance is of course more prominent in longitudinal research than in purely cross-sectional studies in which respondents are only measured once. Nevertheless, in cross-sectional studies measurement invariance is relevant as well. If, for instance, the same test is taken by 6-year-olds, 8-year-olds and adults, one might wonder whether the same constructs are tested in all three samples. A simple math problem such as 10+10 is difficult for the youngest age group, but the correct answer is not more than cognition for adults who do not have to do any real arithmetic but just 'know' the answer. Hence, in both longitudinal studies and cross-sectional studies measurement invariance can lead to difficulties in the interpretation of research results.

In a well-planned longitudinal study, checks on measurement invariance are crucial. In the above-mentioned study of Boland (1991) each student took three spelling tests at each occasion. By repeating one test on successive occasions, Boland created possibilities for checks on measurement invariance. In this case this boils down to testing the equality of correlation matrices of different occasions in which the same test was taken.

A completely different approach was taken by Klein Gunnewiek (2000). She studied the syntactic (and morphological) development of Dutch students learning German in the first years of secondary education according to a longitudinal design. In fact, her study is a test of Pienemann's (1994, 1998) processability theory, which makes strong claims about the order of acquisition of syntactic structures by learners of German as a foreign language. This theory boils down to the hypothesis that more complex structures can only be processed if less complex structures have been acquired. Complex syntactic structures require processing of more information, which is further apart (such as V-End), than the information in less complex structures (with, for instance, a canonical subject-verb order). An example of a V-End sentence is presented in (1): the finite verb *bin* 'am' is positioned at the end of the subordinate clause. A simpler syntactic structure can be found in (2), where the finite verb *spielen* 'play' is in its canonical position immediately after the subject (examples are taken from Klein Gunnewiek 2000: 63 respectively 61).

(1) *Ich traüme, wenn ich am Strand* **bin**
     I dream, when I at the beach **am**
     'I dream when I am at the beach'

(2) *Silvia und Anette* **spielen** *mit Puppe*
     'Silvia and Anette **play** with puppets'

It follows from the processability theory that only once a 'simple' structure A has been acquired a more complex structure B can be processed. Hence, if we were to test structure A and B in a longitudinal study, we would expect hardly any development in the use of structure B until some development has been shown in the use of structure A. This is called the implication hypothesis (Pienemann 1994, 1998).

Pienemann (1994, 1998) used a cross-sectional design to study the occurrence of syntactic structures in the oral communication of several learners of German as a foreign language. He concluded that these learners did not use, for instance, V-End structures unless they had lived quite some years in Germany. In order to make a comparison between different learners of German, Pienemann drew heavily on his implication hypothesis. Hence, if a learner used a V-End structure, less complex structures (such as SVO) were assumed to have been acquired, even if empirical evidence is lacking. In this case the cross-sectional design makes the implication hypothesis a necessity in order to interpret cross-sectional data in a longitudinal way.

Klein Gunnewiek (2000) studied the development of the use of syntactic structures by Dutch students in their initial phases of learning German. She assessed the (correct) use of different syntactic structures in the first twenty-five weeks of education in German as a foreign language. According to theory she needed to collect relatively dense measures of students' syntactic proficiency. Therefore she decided to measure students learning German seven times in this twenty-five-week period. This of course begs for memory effects; if the same students take the same test seven times in such a short time, they are likely to remember the items and/or their answers of previous occasions. This is why Klein Gunnewiek needed different tests to measure the use of V-End at different occasions.

In order to circumvent memory effects she constructed three versions of the same test. These three versions were constructed on the basis of the results of a pretest on a large sample of students (who did not participate in the actual study). In a large test-construction phase Klein Gunnewiek selected items that were shown to measure exactly the same constructs, with equal means and variances, and hence were shown to be parallel tests (compare, Gulliksen 1950). Only if she was able to construct parallel tests, she could interpret differences in scores between these tests taken at different measurement occasions in terms of differences in syntactic skills. Measurement invariance between tests is essential in this case.

Pienemann's theory on the acquisition of German as a foreign language states that a complex structure such as V-End can only be processed if other, more simple, syntactic structures have been acquired. Hence, V-End sentences should be acquired in later phases in the learning process. According to the processability theory Klein Gunnewiek expected she could only show any development in the use of V-End during later weeks of her study. Parts of her results are summarized in Figure 7.

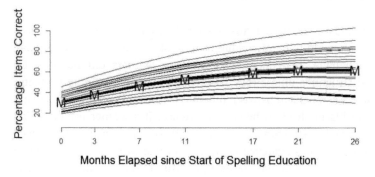

Figure 7: Development in the use of V-End structures by Dutch students (N = 24) learning German as a second language (solid bold line (M): average development).

Students took tests on V-End structures at the start of the school year (test A), after three weeks of Education in German (test B), after seven weeks (test C), after eleven weeks (test A), after seventeen weeks (test B), etc. In Figure 7 it appears that on average (solid line: M) the percentage of correct answers of V-End items increases steadily from (around) 30% to 60% correct. Except in terms of growth, this steady increase can also be interpreted in terms of successfulness of the procedures that were used in constructing the different test. If the tests were not really parallel, a continuous growth without any in- or decreases related to test would be unlikely.

From Figure 7 it can also be derived that the pace of development decreases over time; in the first weeks students learn more than in the final weeks. These results are contrary to the predictions of the processability theory, which would expect only an increase once other, simpler structures have been acquired.

Figure 7 shows the development of each individual student. It becomes clear that without exception the correct use of V-End structures increases during the period under investigation. The amount of increase, however, differs between students, causing the between-student variance to increase over time. It also shows that the ranking of students hardly changes during the first half year of learning German as a second language. Hence, high starters are also the ones who learn a lot.

Especially the finding that V-End structures develop throughout the period under investigation clearly contradict the processability theory, which can only be shown in a study that does not rely on the implication hypothesis to be true in order to interpret the results.

4 Density of measurements

The number of measurement occasions should always be related to the research question at hand. In order to assess the (language) growth of individuals at least two measurements are necessary. However, with exactly two measurements only a linear change with time can be shown. If we study children's language development and would like to show this development is not linear, more than two observations of children are necessary. For example, if we have a hypothesis about a temporary plateau in growth, this cannot be empirically tested in a study with only two measurements.

Many studies aim at explaining (differences in) language development. For instance, usage-based theorists are interested in the question whether language development is related to the input children receive (cf. Tribushinina and Gillis, *this volume*). If it is, we would expect a non-linear relation between language development and (parental) input. If a toddler hears a certain phrase, s/he might not be able to produce a phrase like this yet or her/his level of development might not allow this yet. But if a child has mastered this linguistic element, parental input will not influence the use of this element either. The child will only be sensitive to (parental) input during the period in which he is actually acquiring this specific linguistic element. In order to show a relation between input and children's speech, many observations are needed. This density of measurements especially holds for the period at which an influence of parental speech is expected, but also for the periods before acquisition starts and after acquisition ends.

Here, we will use some data from van Veen's (2011) study to illustrate the importance of measurement density. The hypothesis we are testing is a non-linear one: before acquisition starts and after acquisition ends, there will be no influence of child-directed speech on the child's speech. That is: input is only expected to affect children's output during the period in which they are acquiring the linguistic phenomenon under investigation.

Van Veen (2011) studied the use of causal connectives (see also, van Veen, Evers-Vermeul, Sanders, and van den Bergh 2009, 2013, 2014). Among other connectives she analyzed the causal connective *because* in child language and in child-directed speech in the CHILDES database (MacWhinney 2000). We have chosen two children from this data set: one with rather dense measurements (i.e. 210 observations in the age of 874–1539 days), and one with less dense measurements (i.e. 88 observations in the age of 454–1454 days).

In Figure 8 the probability of a child using *because* is presented as a function of his age: [p(*because*) = f(age)] (see, van den Bergh et al. 2009 or Long 2011 for statistical details). The actual measurement occasions are indicated with o's. Figure 8 shows that child A has relatively dense recordings of his speech throughout the observed period. However, the first measurement was taken relatively late (at the age of 874 days), when this child had already started to use *because*. For child B the observations are relatively dense at early ages; the first measurement is when she is 454 days old. When she gets older the measurements gradually become less dense. This is at least one of the explanations for the (relative) plateau between 900 and 1100 days. Especially during the period of interest, the period in which the use of *because* changes, the density of the measurements is low: after 900 days there are only 16 recordings of child B.

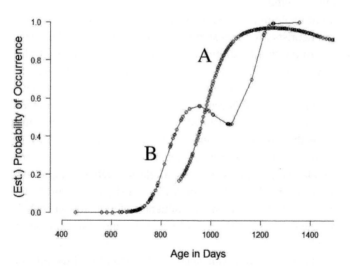

Figure 8: Growth curves for the use of *because* with age in the speech of two children (x-axis) (solid line: average growth; o: actual observations).

From Figure 8 it can easily be inferred that the probability to encounter the causal connective *because* increases as both children get older. For child A there is a marked increase in the use of *because* right from the first measurement, until around 1200 days after which he uses *because* in almost every (recorded) conversation. For child B there is no evidence of acquiring *because* during the first measurements: the probability to encounter *because* in the child's speech is almost 0.0. This changes when this child is 770 days old and a sharp increase can be seen in the occurrence of *because* in her speech. Unfortunately, after the start of using *because* the recordings of child B get more sparse.

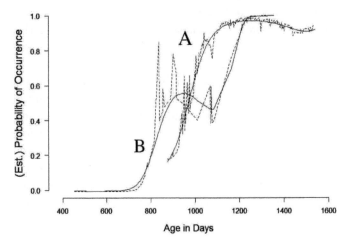

Figure 9: Growth curves for the use of *because* with age in the speech of two children (x-axis) (solid line: average growth; dashed line: effect of *because* in child-directed speech on child's speech).

The dashed line in Figure 9 indicates the influence of both age and the production of *because* in child-directed speech on the child's use of *because*: [p(*because*) = f(age, *because* in child-directed speech)]. For child B it is easy to infer that during the early recordings there is hardly any influence of *because* in the input on her uttering *because* as a causal connective; there is hardly any discrepancy between the average line indicating the child's use of *because* and the dashed line adding the effect of *because* in child-directed speech. Around 800 days the influence of child-directed speech becomes apparent. The peaks and dips in the dashed line show that this child's use of *because* depends on the production of this causal connective by the adult speech partner. If the adult is likely to say *because* relatively often, so will child B, and if the adult refrains from using *because*, so will this child. This seems to hold up until child B is (around) 1100 days old, after which the occurrence of *because* in child-directed speech does not seem to influence the child's production of *because* anymore. It has to be noted though that from this point onwards the measurements are really getting sparse, so there is no way of telling whether the occurrence of *because* in child-directed speech is not influencing the child's use of *because* anymore, or whether there are just too few observations to show a (significant) effect of child-directed speech.

For child A there are no measurements before he started to utter *because*. Right from the start of the observations there is clearly an influence of *because* in child-directed speech on child A's use of *because*; if the child-directed speech contains (relatively) many instances of *because*, so does the child's speech, and if his speech partner does not produce *because*, neither will the child. This dependency seems to hold upon to (around) 1200 days, after which the dependency of input is (significantly) less marked.

In conclusion, for one child it can be shown that at first, the occurrence of *because* in child-directed speech does not influence the child's production of *because*, and that in later phases the child is prone to use *because* more if it occurs in child-directed speech. For another child the measurements before using *because* are absent, and relatively dense measures were only made when the child had already started to utter *because*. All in all, it seems likely that the production of *because* in child-directed speech influences the child's use only during a specific period. Nevertheless, it should be noted that for none of the children under investigation there are enough observations during the period of acquisition to test this hypothesis.

5 Conclusions

In this chapter, we have discussed three validity issues in longitudinal research: attrition, measurement invariance, and density of measurements. Each of these issues relevant for usage-based and other developmental studies, was illustrated with examples from actual research.

It has been shown that attrition of (proficiency measurements of) subjects can have an effect on the results. Of course, attrition rates increase with the number of measurements. We have shown how a different research design, with overlapping measurements, can circumvent effects of attrition, but the application of such designs limits possibilities of interpretation.

Crucial in longitudinal research is so-called measurement invariance, which refers to the question whether the same constructs are measured on different occasions. In order to obtain such tests we need to pay more attention to the construction of tests. However, once such tests are constructed, firmer conclusions on growth can be drawn.

Density of measurements is also extremely relevant. By means of an example we have shown that non-linear changes in development can only be established with a dense data set. Preferably, researchers should aim at collecting data during the acquisition period of the linguistic phenomenon under investigation, but also during the periods before and after acquisition takes place.

References

Anastasi, Anne. 1976. *Psychological Testing*. 4th ed. New York: Macmillan.

Baltes. Paul B., and John R. Nesselroade. 1979. History and rationale of longitudinal research. In *Longitudinal Research in the Study of Behavior and Development*, John R. Nesselroade, and Paul B. Baltes (eds.), 1–39. New York: Academic Press.

Boland, Theo. 1991. Lezen op termijn [Reading in the long run]. Ph.D. diss., Nijmegen University.

Chatfield, M. D., Carol E. Brayne, and Fiona E. Matthews. 2005. A systematic literature review of attrition between waves in longitudinal studies in the elderly shows a consistent pattern of dropout between differing studies. *Journal of Clinical Epidemiology* 58 (1): 13–19.

Cheung, Gordon W., and Roger B. Rensvold. 2002. Evaluating goodness-of-fit indexes for testing measurement invariance. *Structural Equation Modeling* 9 (2): 233–255.

Gullikson, Harold. 1950. *Theory of Mental Tests*. New York: Wiley.

Jöreskog, Karl. G. 1971. Statistical analysis of sets of congeneric tests. *Psychometrika* 36 (2): 109–133.

Klein Gunnewiek, Lisanne. 2000. *Sequenzen und Konsequenzen: Zur Entwicklung niederländischer Lerner im Deutschen als Fremdsprache*. Amsterdam: Rodopi.

Long, Jeffrey. D. 2011. *Longitudinal Data Analysis for the Behavioral Sciences using R*. Thousand Oaks, CA: Sage.

MacWhinney, Brian. 2000. *The CHILDES Project: Tools for Analyzing Talk*. 3rd ed. Mahwah, NJ: Lawrence Erlbaum Associates.

Pienemann, Manfred. 1994. Towards a theory of processability in second language acquisition. Unpublished manuscript. Canberra: Australian National University.

Pienemann, Manfred. 1998. *Language Processing and Second Language Development: Processability Theory*. Amsterdam: John Benjamins.

Shadish, William R., Thomas D. Cook, and Donald T. Campbell. 2002. *Experimental and Quasi-experimental Designs for Generalized Causal Inference*. Boston, MA: Houghton Mifflin.

van den Bergh, Huub, and Hans Kuhlemeier. 1992. A three level growth model for educational achievement: Effects of holidays, socio-economic background and absenteeism. *Multilevel Modelling Newsletter* 4 (1): 7–10.

van den Bergh, Huub, Mindert H. Eiting, and Gideon J. Mellenbergh. 1992. Incomplete repeated measurement designs in longitudinal studies. *Methodika* 6 (2): 118–130.

van den Bergh, Huub, Gert Rijlaarsdam, Tanja Janssen, Martine Braaksma, Daphne van Weijen, and Marion Tillema. 2009. Process execution of writing and reading: Considering text quality, learner and task characteristics. In *Quality Research in Literacy and Science Education: International Perspectives and Gold Standards*, Mack C. Shelly, Larry D. Yore, and Brian B. Hand (eds.), 399–426. Dordrecht: Springer.

van Veen, Rosie. 2011. *The Acquisition of Causal Connectives: The Role of Parental Input and Cognitive Complexity.* Utrecht: LOT. Available online: http://www.lotpublications.nl/Documents/286_fulltext.pdf.

van Veen, Rosie, Jacqueline Evers-Vermeul, Ted Sanders, and Huub van den Bergh. 2009. Parental input and connective acquisition in German: A growth-curve analysis. *First Language* 29 (3): 267–289.

van Veen, Rosie, Jacqueline Evers-Vermeul, Ted Sanders, and Huub van den Bergh. 2013. The influence of input on connective acquisition: a growth curve analysis of English *because* and German *weil. Journal of Child Language* 40 (5): 1003–1031.

van Veen, Rosie, Jacqueline Evers-Vermeul, Ted Sanders, and Huub van den Bergh. 2014. "Why? Because I'm talking to you!" Parental input and cognitive complexity as determinants of children's connective acquisition. In *The Pragmatics of Discourse Coherence: Theories and Applications*, Helmut Gruber, and Gisela Redeker (eds.), 209–242. Amsterdam/Philadelphia: John Benjamins.

II Driving forces of language development

II. Driving forces of language development

Rasmus Steinkrauss
5 L1 acquisition beyond input frequency

1 Introduction

In recent years, the frequency of linguistic forms in spoken language has increasingly been recognized as one of the main factors shaping language development. This applies to language development both in the language community and in the individual speaker (e.g. Bybee 2006; Croft 2000). For example, in the area of first language (L1) acquisition, the frequency of linguistic structures in a child's ambient speech has repeatedly been shown to possess strong explanatory power for the linguistic development of that child (Lieven 2010).

Due to an emphasis on input frequency in some lines of L1 research, attention has shifted away from more qualitative factors in acquisition, although these are believed to influence L1 development as well (Lieven 2010; Lieven and Tomasello 2008). The present chapter therefore focuses explicitly on these factors and looks at L1 acquisition beyond input frequency. It will be shown that the explanatory power of input frequency is limited, and that previously learnt linguistic knowledge, communicative interest, and the conditions of use of linguistic structures may override the impact of input frequency, even in the early stages of L1 acquisition.

1.1 The role of frequency

A major work highlighting the role of frequency in language development is Bybee's (1995) book on morphology and linguistic change. In this book, she draws a distinction between the token frequency and the type frequency of linguistic items. Token frequency denotes the frequency of a specific linguistic item, while type frequency refers to the frequency of a linguistic pattern. For example, a speaker might use three different combinations of *what* and an auxiliary verb (e.g. *what is, what was* and *what does*) in a speech sample. The type frequency of the *what*+AUX pattern is in this case three. The token frequency on the other hand is the number of times each individual combination occurs in the sample – for example, it would be twelve for *what does* if that combination occurred twelve times.

Rasmus Steinkrauss, University of Groningen

DOI 10.1515/9781501505492-006

The frequency of linguistic items and patterns influences their respective representation in the minds of speakers. Generally speaking, it is assumed that items that frequently occur together are eventually stored as one linguistic unit, while patterns that occur frequently are stored as a linguistic construction with open slots (Bybee 2006). Taking the above example, if one of the three *what*+AUX combinations would be extremely frequent in the speech, i.e. show a high token frequency, a speaker would store that two-word combination as a single unit, much in the way as if it was one word. If none of the combinations would be frequent and the *what*+AUX pattern instead exhibits a high type frequency, with a lot of different auxiliary verbs in the second place and only *what* staying constant, a speaker would come to represent this pattern as a *what*+AUX construction. That construction would incorporate a fixed item, *what*, and an open slot in which to insert auxiliary verbs. Importantly, these two types of representation are not mutually exclusive. A speaker might store a few frequent *what*+AUX combinations as fixed units, ready for use, and at the same time possess a schematic *what*+AUX construction with a slot, enabling her to assemble also less frequent *what*+AUX combinations.

Because of these different types of representation, the frequency of linguistic items and patterns in the speech has certain effects for both language change and language acquisition. For example, in processes of language change, because high-frequency items and structures are repeated so frequently and acquire a special representational status compared to less frequent structures, they are more likely to undergo phonetic reduction, resist structural change, and lose transparent semantic connections to similar constructions (Bybee 2006). In L1 acquisition, input frequency has a measurable effect on what children produce in their early phases of development. The following section discusses various findings in this respect.

1.2 Wh-question acquisition

A well-researched area with respect to the influence of input frequency is the L1 acquisition of wh-questions. In English, wh-questions usually start with a wh-pronoun followed by a form of an auxiliary verb.[1] Because the number of wh-pronouns and auxiliary verbs is restricted and there are only a few different inflected forms of auxiliary verbs, the number of possible WH+AUX combinations is limited. In addition, some of the combinations are very frequent. If input frequency is an important factor for acquisition, one may expect children who

---

1 I.e. excluding echo wh-questions such as *He did what?*

acquire English as L1 to quickly develop unit-like representations of the frequent WH+AUX combinations and subsequently produce these combinations from early on. This is exactly what has been found. In their wh-question development, English-learning children start out with fixed phrases such as *what's this* or specific WH+AUX combinations such as *where is...* (Dabrowska 2000; Dabrowska and Lieven 2005; Klima and Bellugi 1966), and the combinations they produce first are those that tend to be highly frequent in their ambient speech (Rowland et al. 2003). The WH+AUX combinations they use seem to be fixed, because children do not freely combine any wh-pronoun with any form of auxiliary verb even if either of the words already occurs in their speech in other combinations. In addition, children's questions starting with the frequent WH+AUX combinations show fewer errors than wh-questions starting with other combinations (see also Rowland 2007; Rowland and Pine 2000, 2003). Taken together, the findings suggest that children initially operate with specific WH+AUX combinations that they have extracted from their ambient speech, possibly aided by the fact that the WH+AUX combinations occur in a salient position at the beginning of wh-questions. Input frequency thus seems to have a direct impact on children's processing and production of language.

After an initial phase of wh-question production based on specific linguistic items (for item-based learning, see, e.g. Lieven and Tomasello 2008; Tomasello 1992), English-learning children gradually abstract more schematic representations of wh-questions. For example, the fixed string *What's+Mommy+doing* that the child observed by Dabrowska (2000) produced around the age of 2;0 had step by step developed into a more abstract *What+is+NP+V* construction by the age of 3;0.[2] Such a development from specific to abstract constructions is assumed to be an effect of children's accumulated linguistic experience. As children hear more and more wh-questions, the variation in the different parts of the construction, e.g. the wh-pronouns and the verb forms, grows. This variation is not random: wh-pronouns will always be in the first position, auxiliary verbs in second position, and so on. Children will gradually detect these patterns and develop open slots for the positions in the construction. In such a way, children get increasingly more creative over time and depart more and more from the specific question structures they have heard in the input (Dabrowska and Lieven 2005).

The finding that variation in the input fosters the development of abstract linguistic knowledge is supported by a case study of a boy learning German. As German shows more variation in the verb types and verb forms allowed after

---

2 Children's age is given in the format years;months or years;months.days in this study. 2;0 thus means 2 years.

wh-pronouns, the type frequency of verbs after wh-pronouns is higher than in English. As a consequence, the boy in this case study developed an abstract WH+V construction quicker than typical English-learning children and relied on specific WH+V combinations only to a very limited extent (Steinkrauss 2009).

To sum up, the frequency of linguistic structures in the input has found to be a powerful explanation for children's course of language acquisition, not only in the area of wh-questions, but also in other fields of L1 development (Cameron-Faulkner, Lieven, and Tomasello 2003; Theakston et al. 2001, 2002). The success of input frequency as an explanatory factor supports cognitive linguistic approaches to language. These assume that L1 acquisition succeeds on the basis of information that children can extract from their ambient language and the linguistic interactions they experience. For this kind of acquisition, only general (learning) skills such as pattern recognition and intention reading are needed. This renders the postulation of language-specific, innate knowledge aiding in the process of language acquisition unnecessary (Tomasello 2003).

Language acquisition that relies on non-domain-specific skills and on learning from linguistic interactions is often characterized as being 'usage-based' (Lieven and Tomasello 2008; Tomasello 2000). This means that language is assumed to be learnt from the use that it is put to in the specific situations that a specific learner experiences. Because of this, children's linguistic environment, particularly the make-up of the input children receive, has received strong attention from cognitive linguistic researchers. There seems to be a general consensus that apart from the frequency of linguistic forms in the input, other aspects such as their saliency, semantic transparency, formal complexity, or the situations in which they occur play a role in the acquisition process (see Lieven and Tomasello 2008 and Tribushinina and Gillis *this volume* for an overview). However, these aspects have been addressed much less than input frequency – maybe because input frequency is comparatively easy to measure and very informative on its own.

1.3 Goal of the chapter

The goal of this chapter is therefore to focus explicitly on non-frequency related factors in acquisition. This will be done by analyzing a very dense corpus of a boy learning German and identifying two wh-question constructions that are not produced in the way that may be expected from their input frequency. In order to explain these differences between input and production, I will concentrate on the specific conditions of use of these constructions, and on how these conditions interact with two non-frequency factors that have both been discussed in the previous literature: the role of children's previous linguistic knowledge in the acquisition of new linguistic knowledge, and the role of children's communicative interests.

At least in later stages, when children have already acquired some linguistic constructions, it can be assumed that this knowledge may influence the acquisition of new constructions. The idea is supported by results from Morris, Cottrell and Elman (2000), who found that their connectionist model of wh-question acquisition could only generalize to a particular wh-construction when it had first learnt a group of related constructions. Inspired by this finding, Abbot-Smith and Behrens (2006) predicted that a construction might be acquired faster when a child already knows (semantically or syntactically) related, but simpler constructions, and that a construction might be acquired slower when the child does not know such supporting constructions or is already using another construction that fulfills the same communicative purpose. They tested this prediction in a case study on the acquisition of two German passive and one future construction and found it fully confirmed. The future construction was even learnt slowly in spite of potentially supporting constructions because the child had already acquired another, semantically highly similar construction.

That delay in acquisition because of the use of a construction with a very similar meaning suggests that semantics and pragmatics may also affect which constructions a child produces, independent of input frequency. This idea has been discussed by Cameron-Faulkner et al. (2003: 864) and Tyack and Ingram (1977: 222), and is backed up by some evidence from Clancy (1989), who compared the wh-question acquisition of two children. She found that only one child primarily used her wh-questions to actually elicit information from her interlocutors, while the other child simply used wh-questions to accompany her own play. While both children clearly understood the frequent and simple *what is* questions from early on, only the information-seeking child also asked *what is* herself, and even used other, functionally equivalent questions with a much lower input frequency. This points to communicative interest driving the children's actual production.

The present chapter looks at the acquisition of wh-questions by a German-learning boy. Wh-questions were chosen because children's production of wh-questions has repeatedly been shown to be quite item-based and heavily influenced by input frequency, at least in English (see Section 1.2). When studying acquisitional factors beyond input frequency, it is useful to identify cases where input frequency only plays a limited role in production. To achieve this, the present study makes use of the earlier finding that the input and production frequencies of constructions tend to be highly correlated. In other words, children use constructions in their own speech with about the same relative frequency as in the input (see also Behrens 2006 for input-production correlations on the level of linguistic structure; Cameron-Faulkner et al. 2003; Forner 1979; Theakston et al. 2001). Whenever the production strongly deviates from this trend, we may assume that other factors than input frequency play a role.

To find these differences between input and production, all wh-questions in the boy's ambient speech are extracted, their frequencies calculated, and subsequently compared to their production frequencies in the boy's speech. It will be shown that while there is a significant overall correlation between input and production, some wh-constructions clearly deviate from this pattern. Their production is thus not related to their input frequency. In order to investigate the causes for this, the use in interaction of these and other, related constructions is subsequently studied closely, and it will be argued that it is the use of these constructions, the boy's related linguistic knowledge, and his communicative interests that influence the boy's production more than input frequency. With this two-step approach, the study thus combines a quantitative with a thorough qualitative approach.

After a short description of the data and the method, I will present the results of the input-production comparison and investigate the deviant constructions.

2 Data and method

The participant of the current study is a monolingual German boy, Leo, growing up in Germany. The recordings were collected by the Max-Planck-Institute for Evolutionary Anthropology under the supervision of Heike Behrens and include both the child's and the ambient speech. The boy's language development was recorded from 1;11.15, the onset of multiword speech, up to 5;0. The present study draws on the recording period between 2;0 and 3;0. During that time, the sampling is particularly dense. Five one-hour recordings per week were made and the parents kept a daily diary in which they noted all new and complex syntactic structures that had not been captured by the audio recordings. The mother was the primary caretaker of the child and was paid for taking the diary notes and making the audio recordings. In some sessions, either the father or a research assistant took over the recording. All three adults speak clearly articulated standard High German. They were Leo's main caretakers in that period, and since Leo did not attend kindergarten in that year, the dataset offers a representative sample of what the child heard.

Each recording was digitized and transcribed in SONIC-Chat (MacWhinney 2000) with transcription guidelines developed for German by Behrens (cf. Behrens 2006 for a description of the data) and then coded morphosyntactically, including information on the word class. Half of the information was coded automatically using the mor-program of CLAN. Disambiguation and further coding was carried out manually by Behrens and two trained research assistants.

The present study focuses on the Leo's acquisition of wh-questions. To find all utterances in the data that clearly were wh-questions, all utterances ending with a question mark, containing a wh-pronoun, or coded as containing an interrogative pronoun or determiner were extracted automatically and revised manually. The following types of wh-questions were excluded in this process: oblique wh-questions, completions of preceding wh-questions, wh-questions embedded as relative clauses, *was* 'what' and *wie* 'how' tag questions, wh-pronouns that preceded an utterance and just expressed puzzlement, echo questions and other questions without inversion, indirect speech and citations, and rhetorical questions not directed to another speaker. This yielded 20,024 input utterances and 1,005 production utterances containing wh-questions.

To pull out the actual wh-questions, all other material in an utterance was discarded if necessary. The discarded material preceding a wh-question was mostly just one word (mainly conjunctions, interjections, vocatives and unsuccessful starts); longer strings often included repetitions of the previous discourse or short descriptions of the situation. In all cases, the discarded material was separated from the actual wh-question either by a pause, a syntactic boundary, or a conjunction. Likewise, material following the actual wh-question was excluded from analysis, such as vocatives, tags, and further specifications of the question. Also, relative clauses were excluded in cases where the matrix wh-question was already syntactically complete, as were reformulated parts, repetitions, and hesitation markers. In cases with several wh-questions in one utterance, only the first wh-question was kept. Finally, dialectal pronunciation variants and shortened words were changed into their standard variants (e.g. *'n* was changed manually to either the particle *denn* or the article *ein* 'a').

When comparing input and production frequencies of wh-questions, it cannot reasonably be expected that the child will produce precisely the same questions that he has heard in the input, up to the last word. On the basis of the earlier findings on wh-acquisition (see the Introduction), it can rather be assumed that the child builds up representations of the word combinations occurring at the beginnings of wh-questions and use those in his own productions. This is because the first words in wh-questions are the ones that show the least variation and therefore exhibit a high token frequency.

Therefore, all combinations of up to three words at the beginnings of wh-questions were extracted, and their frequency was measured. Importantly, each question was allowed to contribute to the frequency count of only one combination to avoid using one particular utterance more than once in the later correlation analyses. For example, the question *was ist das da* 'what's that there' was counted only once as contributing to the combination *was ist das* and not also to shorter combinations such as *was ist* or *was*. This methodology is in line with that of earlier studies on input/production frequencies (Cameron-Faulkner et al. 2003; Stoll, Abbot-Smith, and Lieven 2009). In order to analyze whether Leo's speech is similar to the input not only at the level of specific word combinations but also at an abstract level (see Behrens 2006), the frequencies of the structural combinations in the first three words of wh-questions, such as WH+V+N or WH+V+ADV, were measured as well.

In total, there are many more different combinations in the input than in Leo's speech (Table 1). This is not surprising because Leo's caregivers ask more wh-questions than Leo does. Many combinations in the input never occur in production, and conversely, some of the combinations in Leo's production never occur in the input.

Table 1: One- to three-word combinations in input and production; 2;0–2;11.

	Number of combinations (type frequency)	
Combination type	Input	Production
Abstract, e.g. WH+V+NP	76	30
Words, e.g. *was ist das*	3866	315

After measuring the input and production frequencies of all occurring combinations, the frequencies of all combinations occurring in the input were correlated with their frequencies in production (which were zero for those combinations that were produced by the adults but not by Leo). In keeping with earlier studies on input-production correlations (Cameron-Faulkner et al. 2003; Theakston et al. 2001), a Pearson product-moment correlation coefficient was calculated on the pairs of relative input and production frequencies of each combination. The relative frequency of a combination was calculated as the proportion of wh-questions that a particular combination accounts for in input or production.

Finally, to detect combinations that were not produced as often as their input frequency would predict, all outliers from the correlations were identified. For each combination, the absolute difference between input and production frequency was calculated. All combinations with an input-production difference above the double standard deviation of all input-production differences were considered outliers.

3 Results and discussion

3.1 Input and production frequencies

The frequencies of wh-combinations are highly correlated in input and production. Leo's production thus mirrors the input: he generally uses the same combinations as in the input and with the same frequencies.[3,4] This confirms earlier findings that input and production frequencies tend to be correlated.

The correlation coefficient is higher for abstract combinations ($r = .97$, $p < .001$) than for the word combinations ($r = .56$; $p < .001$). Leo's production is thus more similar to the input at an abstract, structural level than at the level of the specific constructions that are actually used. The different correlation coefficients for abstract and word combinations are a consequence of the greater inclusiveness of abstract combinations. A combination such as WH+V subsumes many different questions. This means that even if the specific questions are different in input and production, their abstract form can still correspond and lead to a high correlation. Figures 1 and 2 illustrate the correlations in Leo's speech.

The majority of combinations cluster in the lower left corner because many combinations have a relatively low input and production frequency, but there is also a combination that is very frequent both in the input and in Leo's speech (dot in upper right corner). In case of the word combinations, there is one combination that Leo produces only rarely although it is frequent in the input (dot in lower right corner).

Cases such as the latter suggest that factors other than input frequency also influence Leo's production. To identify these cases, the absolute difference between the relative frequency of a combination in the input and in Leo's speech was calculated, and all combinations in which the absolute difference between input and production frequency was greater than the double standard

---

3 The input-production correlation is not an expression of the input frequencies being influenced by the production frequencies. This was ascertained by carrying out three pairwise correlations for the relative input frequencies at 2;1 compared to 2;6, for 2;6 compared to 2;11, and for 2;1 compared to 2;11, separately for all wh-pronouns, for the 30 most frequent two-word combinations, and for the 30 most frequent three-word combinations. All correlations were highly significant at .001, and the correlation coefficients are very high ($r > .95$ for the wh-pronouns, $r > .87$ for the two-word combinations, and $r > .65$ for the three-word combinations). This means that the input frequencies stayed stable over time, independent of Leo's production frequencies (see Steinkrauss 2009: 53–61 for details).
4 The correlation coefficients stay the same when correlating all combinations in production with their frequencies in the input. This indicates that combinations that occur only in the input or only in Leo's speech do not impact the overall correlations. At a general level, the combinations that Leo does not produce are thus very infrequent in the input, and vice versa.

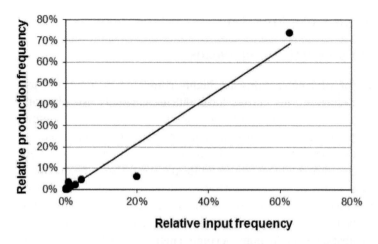

Figure 1: Relative input and production frequencies (and linear trend) of abstract combinations.

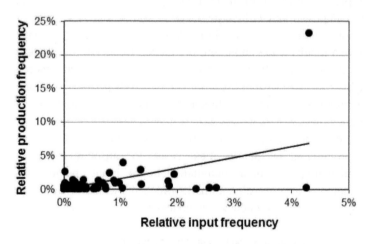

Figure 2: Relative input and production frequencies (and linear trend) of word combinations.

deviation were considered outliers. Table 2 lists the outliers and shows that Leo uses one abstract combination and three word combinations more often than in the input, and one abstract and two word combinations less often than in the input.

There seems to be an obvious pattern in these combinations. Compared to the input, Leo produces too many WH+V+NP questions and too few WH+V+ADV questions. At a lexically specific level, this translates to too many *was ist das* 'what's that', *was ist die* 'what is the_{fem.sg}' and *was das* 'what that' questions

Table 2: Combinations that Leo uses relatively much more or much less often than they appear in the input.

Used more often than in input	Relative (absolute) frequency in...			
	...input		...production	
WH+V+NP	62.7%	(12601)	73.7%	(741)
was ist das 'what is that'	4.3%	(864)	23.3%	(234)
was ist die 'what is the*fem.sg*'	1.0%	(210)	4.0%	(40)
was das 'what that'	0.02%	(4)	2.7%	(27)
Used less often than in input				
WH+V+ADV	20.0%	(4012)	6.2%	(62)
was ist denn 'what's ADV'	4.3%	(855)	0.3%	(3)
was hast du 'what have you'	2.3%	(539)	0.3%	(3)

(the latter is a common contraction of *was ist das* in Leo's speech), and to too few *was ist denn* questions.

Just looking at the abstract combinations, there appears to be a structural difference between input and production. In a universal grammar framework, the comparatively limited production of WH+V+ADV questions might be interpreted as the non-availability of certain structural positions in Leo's grammar.

With a less syntax-centered approach however, one may contribute the underuse of WH+V+ADV questions simply to the near lack of *was ist denn* questions in Leo's speech. In the input, the majority of WH+V+ADV questions contains *denn* (2,772 out of 4,012 questions), and of these again, *was ist denn* is the most frequently used combination (855 out of 2,772 questions). Leo however produces only three questions starting with *was ist denn.* Importantly, this underuse is not due to a general lack of questions with *denn.* Although the word is of low phonological saliency as it is unstressed and often shortened to *'n*, Leo still produces some WH+V+*denn* questions. But he hardly produces the most frequent of them in the input: *was ist denn.*

The overuse of WH+V+NP questions on the other hand may be attributed to two factors. First, Leo produces relatively many more *was ist das* questions than in the input, and these questions boost his number of WH+V+NP questions. Second, there are indications that the variation in the German input that Leo has received has enabled him to develop an abstract WH+V+NP construction relatively quickly. With this construction, he can freely produce many different WH+V+NP combinations in addition to the frequent *was ist das.* This is expressed by a strong increase in type as well as token frequency of WH+V+NP questions after 2;7 (see Steinkrauss 2009: 109–120).

What initially appears to be a structural difference between the wh-questions in the input and Leo's own questions then comes down to an overuse of *was ist das* and a near non-use of *was ist denn* questions. This difference in Leo's use of the two combinations is even more remarkable as both combinations are

a) the most frequent types of WH+V+NP and WH+V+ADV questions in the input respectively;

b) the most frequent word combinations in the input that form a syntactically complete question;

c) virtually equally frequent in the input: *was ist das* occurs 864 times, *was ist denn* 855 times (see Figure 3).

What might be the reason for this difference? It cannot be input frequency, because that is the same for both combinations. Therefore, the remainder of this chapter will investigate functional reasons, focusing on the use of *was ist das* and *was ist denn* in the input and by Leo, and the role that Leo's communicative interest and his knowledge of semantically related constructions might play.[5]

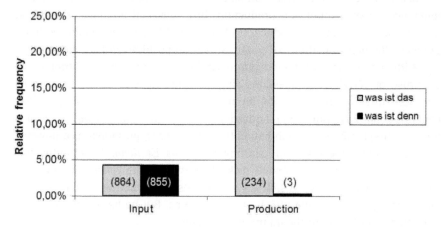

Figure 3: Relative frequencies of the combinations was ist das and was ist denn in input and production (absolute frequencies indicated in brackets).

---

5 Due to reasons of space, this chapter will not discuss the other outliers in detail. In short, the overuse of *was ist die* can be attributed to Leo's development of an abstract WH+V+NP construction; his underuse of *was hast du* to the fact that these Leo uses *hast* in all questions as an auxiliary for a verb in German Perfekt tense. Perfekt questions of any kind are rarely produced before 3;0 however. See Steinkrauss (2009) for details.

3.2 The use of *was ist das* and *was ist denn* in the input

To investigate the functional difference between *was ist das* and *was ist denn*, the use of *was ist das* and *was ist denn das* 'what's that' questions in the input will be compared. These two questions were chosen over other questions starting with *was ist das / was ist denn* because they are both very frequent and very short and thus of similar saliency and (structural) complexity. They are also very similar in meaning, and the precise differences between their conditions of use show up better.

To compare the two questions, three sessions between 2;0 and 3;0 were chosen (2;0.29, 2;1.12 and 2;1.23): two sessions containing particularly many questions of either one of the two types, and one session containing particularly many of both question types.[6] In total, 49 *was ist das* and 43 *was ist denn das* questions were investigated. Questions starting with *und* 'and' or ending with an additional *hier* 'here', *da* 'there', a vocative, or a trailing article (e.g. *was ist das da, ein?*) were included in the analysis.

All questions and the surrounding discourse (transcripts and audio recordings) were gone through carefully. An open coding procedure was adopted: whenever it was felt that a feature in the data could tell something about why a question was used, that feature was added to the coding procedure and all questions were recoded for that feature. This analysis is qualitative and not all features could be coded for all questions. For example, one feature was whether the object that the particular *was ist (denn) das* question was asked about had previously been mentioned or attended to non-verbally in the directly preceding interaction, thus whether the object was 'old' or 'new' in the given discourse situation. In most cases, this was relatively easy to determine, but in some cases, it was not. In such cases, the individual question was not coded for that feature. All in all, seven features were found to influence the use of *was ist das* and *was ist denn das* questions, and a quite clear pattern of use emerged from the data. The pattern of use of *was ist das* questions is described first.

3.2.1 Was ist das?

Was ist das 'what's that' questions are more often asked about 'old' than 'new' topics. The object that the question is about has thus already been introduced to

---

6 All sessions are from the beginning of Leo's third year of life. This is because there are more *was* questions in this period than later on. They therefore represent the most frequent and thus most typical use of *was* that Leo experiences.

the conversation when the *was ist das* question is finally asked. In total, three types can be distinguished:

a) the topic is old; *was ist das* is the first *was ist (denn) das* question on the topic (14 instances);
b) the topic is old; *was ist das* is a subsequent *was ist (denn) das* question on the topic (12 instances);
c) the topic is new (16 instances).

In cases where the topic is old but the *was ist das* question is the first instance of a *was ist (denn) das* question on the topic, the object has mostly been introduced into the conversation with what are here called 'completion questions', i.e. declarative utterances such as *that's a...*, uttered with a rising interrogative intonation. They introduce a new object, but its name is left out so that Leo may complete the utterance. The completion question thus directs Leo's attention to the new object and the caregivers wait for Leo to react. When he does not answer (correctly), his caregivers then often ask *was ist das*. See excerpt (1).

(1) Age 2;1.12 (Leo and research assistant)
    Assistant: **und das is(t) eine...**
                'and that's a...'
    Assistant: **was is(t) das?**
                'what's that?'
    Assistant: *eine...*
                'a...'
    Leo: *eine Lampe.*
                'a lamp.'
    Assistant: *eine Lampe.*
                'a lamp.'

In cases where the topic is old but the *was ist das* question is not the first instance of a *was ist (denn) das* question, the question is usually a follow-up question to the first *was ist (denn) das* question. It is asked when Leo does not answer, answers unintelligibly, etc.

When the object in question is new, *was ist das* questions are simply the first questions about that object. Sometimes, they start with *und* 'and'. They are mostly asked in situations where Leo and his caregivers play with several objects or look at a picture, and where many *was ist (denn) das* questions are asked about several objects in a row. Excerpt (2) contains a *was ist das* question

introducing a new topic, and a subsequent *und was ist das* question about the
following new topic.[7]

(2) Age 2;0.29 (Leo and research assistant playing)
     Assistant: *oh, jetzt haben wir hier sogar ein Haus, guck mal!*
                  'oh, now we even have a house here, look!'
     Leo: *xxx spielen.*
                  'play.'
     Assistant: **hm, was is(t) das?**
                  'hm, what's that?'
     Leo: *da da Laster.*
                  'there there truck.'
     Assistant: **das is(t) (ei)n Laster, und was is(t) das da, Leo?**
                  'that's a truck, and what's that there, Leo?'
     Leo: *Auto.*
                  'car.'

3.2.2 Was ist denn das?

Was ist denn das questions differ from *was ist das* questions because they contain
denn. *Denn* as a modal particle only occurs in questions. Its meaning is hard
to translate, but its function is to relate a question to a preceding event in the
conversation. By using *denn*, a speaker therefore indicates that his question is
particularly motivated or justified. Wegener (2002) argues that this function of
denn evolved from its originally locative meaning *from there*. Via a temporal
meaning it acquired a causal meaning (*denn* 'therefore' = as a consequence of a
prior event), which in turn motivates the use of *denn* as a modal particle, where
denn expresses that an utterance is a consequence of something prior in the
discourse.

In the input, most *was ist denn das* questions are about a new topic (20
instances), and in these cases, they are very often (15 instances) immediately
preceded by an expression of (often simulated) surprise or something like *guck
mal* 'look' to attract Leo's attention, as in excerpts (3) and (4).

---

7 In this and the following excerpts, *xxx* denotes unintelligible material, and PART indicates
the use of the particle *denn* in the original utterance.

(3) Age 2;1.23 (Leo and mother playing the 'Concentration' or 'Memory' card game where cards that are laid face down are turned face up. Mother turns up a new card)

Mother: **oh.**
'oh.'
Mother: **huh.**
(surprised sound)
Mother: **was is(t) (den)n das, Leo, weisst du das?**
'what is that PART, Leo, do you know?'
Leo: *xxx.*
Mother: *eine Espressokanne ist das.*
'that's an espresso pot.'

(4) Age 2;0.29 (Leo and mother talking about what they are drawing)

Leo: *xxx Monde.*
'moons.'
Mother: **hey, Leo, guck mal, was is(t) (den)n das?**
'hey, Leo, look, what's that PART?'
Leo: *(Ele)fant (ele)fant.*
'elephant elephant.'

When a *was ist denn das* question is asked about an old topic, the question is nearly always a subsequent question (14 out of 16 instances), meaning that another *was ist (denn) das* question has already been asked about the same object. These questions are mostly follow-up questions when Leo does not answer, or when he answers incorrectly.

To summarize the findings from a different angle, we can say that a new topic (object of the question) is introduced into the conversation by the caregivers in one of the following ways:

a) with a simple *was ist das* question;
b) with a *und was ist das* question in situations where several questions about new topics are asked in a row;
c) with completion questions such as *that's a...* When Leo does not answer as he should, the completion questions are followed by a *was ist das* question;
d) by attracting Leo's attention with *guck mal!* 'look' or an expression of surprise, followed by a *was ist denn das* question.

When Leo does not answer any of these first *was ist (denn) das* questions, a subsequent *was ist (denn) das* question is asked which is mostly a simple repetition of the first question.

We thus find a functional division between *was ist das* and *was ist denn das* questions. Both are used, but *was ist das* questions are asked in a wider range of circumstances. A *was ist das* question seems to be an all-purpose question that can be used to introduce a new topic directly or asked in conjunction with *und* in several questions in a row, or after a topic has been introduced in another way, e.g. with completion questions. *Was ist denn das* questions on the other hand are mainly asked after first attracting Leo's attention with *look* or a (feigned) expression of surprise, or as repetitions of earlier *was ist denn das* questions when Leo does not answer. As predicted by the literature, the use of *denn* thus often depends on something prior in discourse, namely that surprise or *look* expression.

This functional difference between *was ist das* and *was ist denn das* might be the reason why Leo hardly ever produces *was ist denn das*. *Was ist das* is the more general and versatile question and could be enough for Leo's communicative needs.

Also, and maybe more importantly, it is questionable whether the very special situation in which *was ist denn das* is commonly used ever arises for Leo. The use of *was ist denn das* questions by Leo's caregivers is not a goal in itself but a consequence of them trying to catch Leo's attention. To get and keep his interest in an object and to move the conversation forward, the caregivers feign surprise or request Leo to look at something. If they then want to ask a question about that object, they almost exclusively use a *was ist denn das* question.

The fact that the caregivers are so consistent in their use of a construction is an interesting finding in itself because it shows the high extent to which speaking is routinized. Although they could probably ask many lexically and syntactically different questions to reach the same communicative goal in a given situation, this is not what the caregivers do: there are 24 instances in the input where a surprised sound or *look*-expression designed to catch Leo's attention is followed by a *was ist (denn) das* question, and in 21 of these cases, the question contains *denn*. The range of *was ist… das…* constructions that seem conventional in that situation is thus severely limited.

For the current analysis this means that for Leo it would not be necessary (or, rather: conventional) to ask a *was ist denn das* question if the circumstances under which a topic-introducing *was ist denn das* question is asked never arise for Leo. In other words, if Leo never tries to direct his caregivers' attention to an object with a surprised sound or *look*-expression in order to ask a question about that object, he would not need a *was ist (denn) das* question. And as a consequence, he would not produce *was ist denn das* questions about an old topic either, because these are mainly subsequent questions to previous *was ist denn das* questions. This idea will be explored in the following section.

3.3 Leo's expressions of surprise

There are very few expressions in Leo's production that are explicitly marked as expression of surprise (mostly *oh*): only nine in total before 3;0. Crucially, all of them express real surprise, not the simulated surprise that we often find preceding *was ist denn das* questions in the input. They are not deliberately designed to attract the parent's attention, and they are never followed by any *was* question from Leo.[8] This also applies to all other instances of *oh* in Leo's speech, except two *oh*'s that are followed by a *was ist das* question but where the *oh* is not an expression of surprise. The finding is not unexpected, taking into account that feigning surprise to get someone's attention (to then ask a question) is not a trivial accomplishment and probably too early to be expected from a child between 2;0 and 3;0.

The findings are similar for the *look*-expressions in Leo's speech. In total, there are 197 imperatives of *gucken* 'look', often realized as *guck mal*, and two imperatives of *schauen* 'look' before 3;0. All are mainly used to attract the caregiver's attention to something that Leo knows, such as in excerpt (5).

(5) Age 2;0.7 (Leo and mother)
    Leo: *xxx guck guck guck.*
              'look look look!'
    Leo: *xxx xxx.*
    Mother: *hm?*
              'huh?'
    Leo: *Hund los [?].*
              'dog loose [?]'
    Mother: *das ist ein Hund, genau.*
              'that's a dog, exactly.'

Look is thus not used to direct the caregiver's attention to something that Leo does not know yet and wants to ask a question about, and accordingly, there is never a *was* question following a *look*-request in Leo's speech.[9]

We can therefore state that the situation that so often leads to a *was ist denn das* question in the input speech never arises in Leo's speech. He does not try to direct his interlocutors' attention with (feigned) surprise or *look!* to something he does not know, and never asks a *was* question following any of these expressions. I would like to suggest that this is an important part of the reason why we

---

8 In the same or the next eight utterances.
9 In the same or the next eight utterances.

find virtually no *was ist denn das* questions in Leo's production. The other part of the reason is Leo's use of *was ist das* questions.

3.4 The use of *was ist das* in production

Leo uses *was ist das* as the standard construction to elicit information about an object (mostly its label). The construction is very successful in the sense that Leo mostly receives the answer he wants. Leo also extends the conventional use of *was ist das* in ways that suggest that the construction is some kind of standard utterance for him that he can use to contribute a meaningful turn and elicit a following turn. This function of *was ist das* as a standard interrogative construction is further promoted by its chunk-like nature. All this suggests that *was ist das* is sufficient to serve Leo's communicative goals and can therefore function as the sole type of *was ist (denn) das* questions.

In total, there are 229 *was ist das* questions in Leo's speech between 2;0 and 3;0. This includes 27 instances of questions transcribed as *was das* (literally *what that*) which are contractions of *was ist das* to *was 's das*.

Section 3.2 identified several main areas of use for *was ist das* in the input. Such a diversification does not exist in Leo's speech. As in the input, Leo uses *was ist das* as a simple question for information about some object and repeats it when a first question is not answered. But unlike in the input, Leo also uses *was ist das* when asking several questions in a row. In the input, these questions are often introduced with *und*. Leo, in contrast, uses only a few *und was ist das* questions with a very inarticulate *und* in two-thirds of all cases (12 out of 19 *und was ist das*), and the questions are not used systematically. Also, unlike in the input, Leo never asks completion questions, but uses *was ist das* directly to elicit a label.

The way in which Leo uses *was ist das* thus resembles the most general way in which parents use the construction as well – to elicit information about an object. This function of *was ist das* as the standard question is exploited for further, unconventional functions. Leo sometimes asks *was ist das* although he clearly knows the answer, or while the answer to his previous *was ist das* is still being given, or possibly as an expression to distract his caregivers. An example is extract (6), in which Leo asks a *was ist das* question about the same object several times, and finally asks *was ist das* again about something different, just to give the answer himself.

(6) Age 2;10.4 (Leo and mother)
    Leo: *ja, was is(t) das?*
              'yes what's that?'
    Mother: *das ist… Salzteig-Ringe.*
              'that's… salt dough cracknels'
    Leo: *ach, was is(t) das was is(t) das was is(t) das?*
              'oh what's that what's that what's that?'
    Mother: *ein Salzteig-Ring, Leo.*
              'a salt dough cracknel, Leo.'
    (A few minutes later:)
    Leo: *ja, was is(t) das?*
              'yes what's that?'
    Mother: *Salzteig-Ringe, Leo.*
              'salt dough cracknels, Leo.'
    Leo: *was is(t) das was is(t) das was is(t) das?*
              'what's that what's that what's that?'
    Leo: *das is(t) eine Maus.*
              'that's a mouse.'
    Mother: *hm, ja, das stimmt.*
              'well yes, that's true.'

Also, Leo sometimes changes the topic directly after his question without waiting for an answer, and he does not complain or wonder when his parents ignore his question, as the interaction in (7) illustrates.

(7) Age 2;9.4 (Leo and mother)
    Mother: *wo is(t) ein Bahnhof für die Flugzeuge?*
              'where's a station for the planes?'
    Leo: *da.*
               'there.'
    Mother: *ah.*
               'I see.'
    Leo: *da.*
               'there.'
    Leo: **was is(t) das?**
              'what's that?'
    Mother: *haben Flugzeuge nich(t) eher Flughäfen, Leo?*
              'don't planes normally have airports, Leo?'
    Mother: *Bahnhöfe haben doch eigentlich eher Züge, oder?*
              'normally stations are for trains, aren't they?'

> Leo: *ja, ein Bahnhof-Flugzeug.*
> 'yes, a station plane.'
> Mother: *ein Bahnhofsflugzeug?*
> 'a station plane?'
> Leo: *ja, da können Flugzeuge reinfahren.*
> 'yes, planes can drive in there.'

In excerpt (8), Leo asks *was ist das*, gets an answer, asks the question again twice and then immediately changes the topic.

(8) Age 2;10.4 (Leo and mother)
> Mother: *den Hampelmann nochmal angucken?*
> 'look at the jumping jack again?'
> Leo: *was is(t) das was is(t) das?*
> 'what's that what's that?'
> Mother: *das is(t) der Hampelmann von der Rückseite.*
> 'that's the back of the jumping jack.'
> Leo: *doch was is(t) das?*
> 'but what's that?'
> Leo: *was is(t) das?*
> 'what's that?'
> Leo: *weiter den [=? die] Hampelmann basteln.*
> 'go on build the jumping jack.'

Several more instances of these kinds in the data suggest that *was ist das* is a standard construction for Leo, which is not used as a conventional question but also to simply provide a meaningful turn (and elicit a following turn, if desired). Interestingly, Leo often repeats *was ist das* several times rapidly within the same utterance, without waiting for an answer. This also suggests that Leo simply uses the question as some 'ready-made' turn.

That interpretation is supported by the fact that *was ist das* seems to be a chunk in Leo's repertoire. It is nearly always produced with the same specific intonation: fast, without a pause and with a single intonation contour, exhibiting a heavy main stress and a strong rising-falling pitch on *das* and secondary stress on *was*. The impression is that close to 90% of all *was ist das* questions (187 of 213 questions) are pronounced like this.[10] This points to a well-entrenched

---

10 Of the 229 *was ist das* questions between 2;0 and 3;0, 213 were recorded on tape; the rest are diary questions.

routine and is an indication that the question constitutes a fixed phrase for Leo. It is a single, possibly even unanalyzed *wasistdas* construction (Hickey 1993; Peters 1983; Plunkett 1993).

4 Summary and conclusions

The present study has shown that the explanatory power of input frequency for what a child produces is limited. This is true even for the second year of life of the child, a time in which the knowledge of multiword linguistic constructions is just starting. This is not to say that there is no relation between input and production frequencies. To the contrary, this study confirms earlier findings that the frequencies are significantly correlated. This is true particularly at an abstract level: the production was structurally very similar to the input. At the level of specific constructions however, the correlations were much lower, and several constructions were not produced with the same relative frequencies as in the input. The study identified the most striking exceptions to the correlation, concentrating on two wh-question types: questions starting with *was ist das* 'what's that' and questions starting with *was ist denn* 'what's+PART'. Both are extremely frequent in the input, they are very similar in meaning, comparable in cognitive complexity, and, importantly, have virtually the same input frequencies. Still, only *was ist das* is produced to a considerable extent and even produced far too much compared to its input frequency, while questions with *was ist denn* are practically absent from the boy's production.

The reason for this difference has been shown to lie in the specific circumstances of use of these question types, and the way in which the boy's communicative interest and his knowledge of semantically similar questions interact with this usage. In the case of *was ist denn*, it was found that the questions in the input are tied to a specific situation of use in a surprisingly consistent way: they are mainly used after first attracting the boy's attention to a new object by means of expressing (pretended) surprise and then asking what that object is. The *denn* in the question refers to that prior event of surprise in the discourse. The boy however never creates this special communicative situation. It is not in his interest and probably not in his power to mark surprise in such a way that his parents attend to a new object that he can then ask a question about – his (linguistic) expressions of surprise are all genuine and not planned. The strict circumstances of use for this construction and the boy's communicative interests therefore lead to a near non-production of that question.

The low use of *was ist denn* may additionally have to do with the boy's over-use of *was ist das*. From the different functions of this question in the input, the boy takes the most frequent one, to ask for the identity of an object, and over-extends it to other, unconventional areas. This way, he uses the question *was ist das* as a (initially prefabricated) question that can not only elicit information, but also be used to drive a conversation forward even if the question is locally unmotivated, to distract his interlocutor's attention from the current topic, or to simply supply a turn. The question can therefore answer to many communicative needs of the boy, especially in the context of play. This 'one fits all' use of *was ist das* also manifests itself in the fact that the question remains unchanged when used as a follow-up question. In the input, these questions often start with *und* or contain *denn*. Leo's broad use of *was ist das* thus seems to leave little room for the development of other *was ist das*-like questions at this stage. The overuse of *was ist das* and the underuse of *was ist denn* might thus partly be related, and both can be traced back to the questions' respective conditions of use and the boy's communicative needs.

The current study has two important limitations. First, this is a case study, meaning that no firm conclusions can be drawn for a wide range of children. At the same time, it is only in case studies that detailed qualitative investigations of language use in interaction can be carried out. There are no a priori reasons to assume that the mechanisms and factors found to be at work in the acquisition process of the boy studied here do not also play a role in the acquisition processes of other children. Second, due to the nature of the corpus, only spontaneous productions were used in this study as manifestations of the boy's linguistic abilities. But it is important to realize that production does not equal acquisition. Actually, the fact that Leo reacts to his caregivers' *was ist denn* questions indicates that he has probably acquired the question type in some way, even if he does not use it himself. This limitation applies to all studies that investigate input-production relations, not only this one. What this study strongly suggests however is that additional factors than frequency influence acquisition. This finding should therefore be further investigated by studies using a different kind of data, e.g. input data and elicited production data.

To conclude, while input frequency is undoubtedly an important factor in acquisition, it should not be overlooked that the frequency of a form only tells us something about one side of a linguistic construction. The other side, inseparable from form, is a construction's function which is firmly grounded in its use in interaction. The latter should therefore be taken into account in usage-based studies of language acquisition even if frequency effects may go a long way in explaining linguistic behavior.

References

Abbot-Smith, Kirsten, and Heike Behrens. 2006. How known constructions influence the acquisition of other constructions: The German passive and future constructions. *Cognitive Science* 30 (6): 995–1026.

Behrens, Heike. 2006. The input-output relationship in first language acquisition. *Language and Cognitive Processes* 21 (1–3): 2–24.

Bybee, Joan. 1995. Regular morphology and the lexicon. *Language and Cognitive Processes* 10 (5): 425–455.

Bybee, Joan. 2006. From usage to grammar: The mind's response to repetition. *Language* 82 (4): 711–733.

Cameron-Faulkner, Thea, Elena V. M. Lieven, and Michael Tomasello. 2003. A construction based analysis of child directed speech. *Cognitive Science* 27 (6): 843–873.

Clancy, Patricia M. 1989. Form and function in the acquisition of Korean wh-questions. *Journal of Child Language* 16 (2): 323–347.

Croft, William. 2000. *Explaining Language Change: An Evolutionary Approach.* Harlow: Longman.

Dabrowska, Ewa. 2000. From formula to schema: The acquisition of English questions. *Cognitive Linguistics* 11 (1–2): 83–102.

Dabrowska, Ewa, and Elena V. M. Lieven. 2005. Towards a lexically specific grammar of children's question constructions. *Cognitive Linguistics* 16 (3): 437–474.

Forner, Monika. 1979. The Mother as LAD: Interaction between order and frequency of parental input and child production. In *Studies in First and Second Language Acquisition*, Fred R. Eckman, and Ashley J. Hastings (eds.), 17–44. Rowley: Newbury House Publishers.

Hickey, Tina. 1993. Identifying formulas in first language acquisition. *Journal of Child Language* 20 (1): 27–41.

Klima, Edward S., and Ursula Bellugi. 1966. Syntactic regularities in the speech of children. In *Psycholinguistics Papers: The Proceedings of the 1966 Edinburgh Conference*, John Lyons, and Roger J. Wales (eds.), 183–219. Edinburgh: Edinburgh University Press.

Lieven, Elena V. M. 2010. Input and first language acquisition: Evaluating the role of frequency. *Lingua* 120: 2546–2556.

Lieven, Elena V. M., and Michael Tomasello. 2008. Children's first language acquisition from a usage-based perspective. In *Handbook of Cognitive Linguistics and Second Language Acquisition*, Peter Robinson, and Nick C. Ellis (eds.), 168–196. New York: Routledge.

MacWhinney, Brian. 2000. *The CHILDES project: Tools for Analyzing Talk.* 3rd ed. Mahwah, NJ: Lawrence Erlbaum.

Morris, William C., Garrison W. Cottrell, and Jeffrey Elman. 2000. A connectionist simulation of the empirical acquisition of grammatical relations. In *Hybrid Neural Symbolic Integration*, Stefan Wermter, and Ron Sun (eds.), 175–193. Berlin: Springer.

Peters, Ann M. 1983. *The Units of Language Acquisition.* Cambridge: Cambridge University Press.

Plunkett, Kim. 1993. Lexical segmentation and vocabulary growth in early language acquisition. *Journal of Child Language* 20 (1): 43–60.

Rowland, Caroline F. 2007. Explaining errors in children's questions. *Cognition* 104 (1): 106–134.

Rowland, Caroline F., and Julian M. Pine. 2000. Subject-auxiliary inversion errors and wh-question acquisition: 'What children do know?'. *Journal of Child Language* 27 (1): 157–181.

Rowland, Caroline F., and Julian M. Pine. 2003. The development of inversion in wh-questions: A reply to Van Valin. *Journal of Child Language* 30 (1): 197–212.

Rowland, Caroline F., Julian M. Pine, Elena V. M. Lieven, and Anna Theakston. 2003. Determinants of acquisition order in wh-questions: Re-evaluating the role of caregiver speech. *Journal of Child Language* 30 (3): 609–635.

Steinkrauss, Rasmus. 2009. Frequency and function in wh question acquisition: A usage-based case study of German L1 acquisition. Groningen Dissertations in Linguistics. Groningen: University of Groningen.

Stoll, Sabine, Kirsten Abbot-Smith, and Elena V. M. Lieven. 2009. Lexically restricted utterances in Russian, German and English child directed speech. *Cognitive Science* 33 (1): 75–103.

Theakston, Anna, Elena V. M. Lieven, Julian M. Pine, and Caroline F. Rowland. 2001. The role of performance limitations in the acquisition of verb-argument structure: An alternative account. *Journal of Child Language* 28 (1): 127–152.

Theakston, Anna, Elena V. M. Lieven, Julian M. Pine, and Caroline F. Rowland. 2002. Going, going, gone: The acquisition of the verb 'go'. *Journal of Child Language* 29 (4): 783–811.

Tomasello, Michael. 1992. *First Verbs: A Case Study of Early Grammatical Development.* Cambridge: Cambridge University Press.

Tomasello, Michael. 2000. First steps toward a usage-based theory of language acquisition. *Cognitive Linguistics* 11 (1–2): 61–82.

Tomasello, Michael. 2003. *Constructing a Language: A Usage-based Theory of Language Acquisition.* Cambridge, MA: Harvard University Press.

Tyack, Dorothy, and David Ingram. 1977. Children's production and comprehension of questions. *Journal of Child Language* 4 (2): 211–224.

Wegener, Heide. 2002. The evolution of the German modal particle *denn*. In *New Reflections on Grammaticalization*, Ilse Wischer, and Gabriela Diewald (eds.), 389–394. Amsterdam/ Philadelphia: John Benjamins.

Maria Mos

6 Acquiring and processing morpheme constructions: The MultiRep Model

1 Introduction

What does our knowledge of morphemes look like? To answer this question, it is useful to investigate how this knowledge develops: in what ways children's representations of morphemes are built up. This development is described in this chapter with the MultiRep Model, which is then tested empirically.

The first part of this chapter introduces the MultiRep Model. This is a model describing the path along which morpheme constructions are acquired, taking a usage-based approach.[1] The starting point is a holophrase, a simple form-meaning pairing. Upon encountering more sequences of language that are similar in form, meaning and/or distribution, children may develop more general and abstract representations. Crucially, the assumption is that these abstractions do not replace lexically specific knowledge, but are stored alongside these representations. The result is then, that speakers have both knowledge about specific instantiations and more pattern-like constructions at their disposal.

The MultiRep Model is tested empirically in the second part of the chapter, which reports on four experiments done by children in grades 4 and 6 (ages 9–12). It will be shown that these children employ different representations, depending on the demands of the task they are facing. Offline experiments with existing words, allowing speakers to tap into their lexically specific knowledge, show strong frequency effects. This indicates that the participating children do in fact use their knowledge of these specific instantiations, rather than rely on abstract templates. Reaction times in a lexical decision task suggest a strong

---

1 Describing language acquisition as an input-based development of patterns is not new (see, e.g. Tomasello 2003). In defining the morphological patterns, I make use of Goldberg's (1995, 2006) notion of constructions, and Langacker's (1987) representational conventions. The MultiRep Model is a redundancy model: it assumes massive parallel storage of specific and more abstract representations as the result of the bottom-up development of these representations. This focus differs from the network outlined by Goldberg (1995), who describes Construction Grammar as using normal inheritance with real copying: "each construction is fully specified, but is redundant to the degree that information is inherited from (i.e. shared with) dominating constructions" (Goldberg 1995: 74).

Maria Mos, Tilburg University

DOI 10.1515/9781501505492-007

influence of frequency too, not only of the lexical item, but also of its morphological family. When faced with the task of evaluating novel instantiations, however, participants must turn to a more general construction. Performance shows frequency effects here as well; this time of characteristics of the slot in the construction.

The MultiRep Model implies that knowledge of a morpheme construction is multi-facetted. This means that the question when a child has acquired (a) morpheme construction(s) requires further specification: which kinds of representation are to be included in the assessment? What levels of representation are activated with a particular type of experiment or test? The final section of this chapter touches on these issues.

2 The representation of morpheme constructions: A developmental path

The first step in language acquisition is a holophrase: the form is an unanalyzed chunk, with one meaning.[2] This is true for morphologically complex words as well, and is represented in Figure 1.[3]

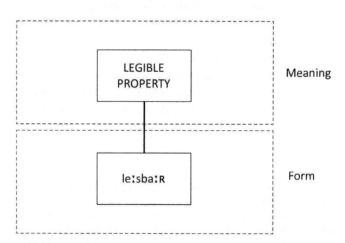

Figure 1: Representation of (internally unanalyzed) morphologically complex word.

---

2 This is a common assumption in usage-based approaches to language acquisition (viz. Tomasello 2003, and Tribushinina and Gillis, *this volume*).
3 At least initially. Once partially schematic representations have been acquired, it is possible that a new form is immediately recognized as an instantiation of this pattern.

Throughout this chapter, Langacker's (1987) conventions are applied: the boxes represent units, with vertical lines indicating symbolic relationships. For each representation, two levels are distinguished: a form level (the lower box or boxes, with phonological representations) and a meaning level (the top half, with semantic representations in capitals).

As children hear the linguistic unit in Figure 1 (*leesbaar* 'legible') more often, they may find that it occurs regularly with the same types of entities. It is not possible to predict how many encounters a child needs to recognize the recurrent patterns; this quantity varies for different children and depends on other contextual factors. Based on the input they get, children may infer that this particular unit is mainly used to describe a property of script (handwriting, fonts, smudgy number plates, etc.) or of written messages (notes, their own essays, etc.) This information becomes part of the representation, as represented in Figure 2.

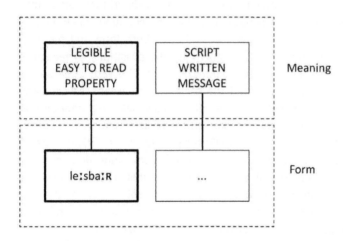

Figure 2: Representation of distributional knowledge for *leesbaar.*

At this stage, children will discover which other linguistic units co-occur with this lexical item. Note that the phonological part of the entity this property is ascribed to is left unspecified. The representation given here is one of a partially specific construction: one element is lexically specific while another is phonologically unspecified (represented as ... in the figures). Different lexical units may fill this unspecified slot, as long as they match with the semantic notions given in the top right box in Figure 2. No ordering is assumed, as this depends on the larger structure, such as the attributive or predicative use of *leesbaar.*

So far, the representations of *leesbaar* do not take into account any pre-existing linguistic knowledge, but this is a simplification. By the time children learn *leesbaar*, they already know hundreds if not thousands of other words. Priming effects (cf. Feldman 2000; McNamara 2005) show that words which are either similar in form or in meaning activate each other. Speakers can recognize words more quickly if they have been exposed recently to lexical items that are linked to this word. Duñabeitia, Perea, and Carreiras (2008) show that priming also occurs for partially abstract patterns with affixes. Priming effects are generally described in terms of activation: the use of a specific lexical item partially activates other items it is linked to. This then results in shorter recognition times for those items. Such activation patterns facilitate processing, since we have so many lexical items in our inventory. In language use, we find that the use of one lexical item can be a strong predictor for the occurrence of another; some items co-occur very frequently. If one of these items is recognized, it makes sense to already partially activate the other, because it is very likely to occur next.

As children encounter the same unit (in our case *leesbaar*) more often, they will not only extend their representation to include common combinatorial patterns, but may also recognize that it is similar in both form and meaning to other units, e.g. *lezen* (to read). This opens up the possibility to recognize the internal structure of the hitherto unanalyzed unit. The verb *lezen* shares elements in both the phonological and the semantic units with *leesbaar* and possibly also collocates, frame elements etc. It is a reasonable assumption that links between different representations exist on the basis of shared elements in meaning, form and distribution. Bybee (1995) suggests the same: "Words entered in the lexicon are related to other words via sets of lexical connections between identical and similar phonological and semantic features. These connections among items have the effect of yielding an internal morphological analysis of complex words,... their morphological structure emerges from the connections they make with other words in the lexicon" (Bybee 1995: 428–429).

The existence of links at multiple levels may lead to the analysis of *leesbaar* as consisting of two elements. This is depicted in Figure 3. The top half of Figure 3 shows that there are three points of similarity between *leesbaar* (top left) and the verb *lezen* (top right): there is a partial overlap in form in the morpheme *lees-*, there are shared aspects of meaning in that both refer to the action of reading, and there are common collocates since both words co-occur with references to written material. Such similarities serve to form links between the two words. As more and more links between *leesbaar* and *lezen* are made, the representation of *leesbaar* is extended to include a first morphemic analysis (bottom half). At this point it is important to emphasize that the original representation is not "overwritten" or deleted, but a new level is added.

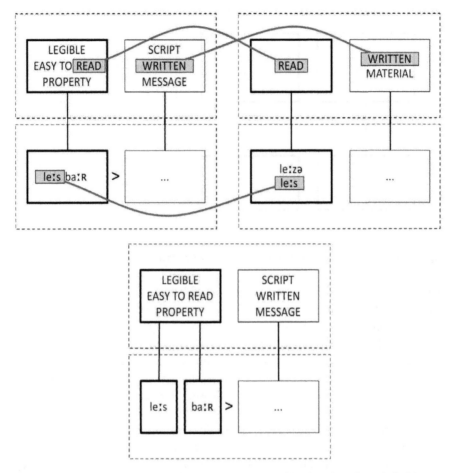

Figure 3: Representation of the initial morphemic analysis of leesbaar based on similarities with *lezen*, through links at the level of form, meaning and distributional properties. The resulting morphemic analysis is depicted in the bottom half of the representation.

The starting point for the morphemic analysis here are the links with the lexical representation for *lezen*. This initial morphemic analysis does not yet include a clear representation of the semantic contribution of both morphemic elements. For this to develop, a child needs to encounter other lexical units with *-baar*. These will have similarities in both form (the actual morpheme) and meaning (some notion of potentiality) to *leesbaar*. Over time, this will allow for the development of a representation in which the semantic contribution of both morphemes is present, as depicted in Figure 4 (collocates and other stored information are not presented in this figure for reasons of clarity). The phonological components are now ordered, represented by the ">" mark.

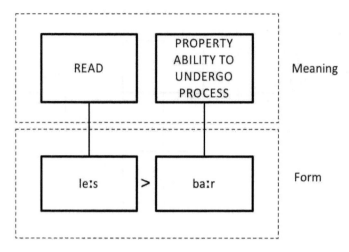

Figure 4: Representation of morphological analysis of *leesbaar*.

Finally, on the basis of this representation of *leesbaar* and other lexical units with the same affix and similar meanings, a partially schematic representation may develop of the *-baar* construction (Figure 5). This contains the phonemic and semantic representation of *-baar*, a maximally schematic phonemic representation of the item *-baar* is combined with, and an underspecified semantic representation for this item, which includes the similarities between the items on which this schematic representation is based. If *-baar* occurs in very different contexts, children may well develop more than one (semi)specific representation or mini-construction (cf. Boas 2008). These different representations are of course linked through strong overlap at least on the form side.

It is this final representation that speakers of a language can use when they encounter lexical items with the affix that are new to them and when they productively form novel instantiations of the construction. The semantics of *leesbaar* includes the notion 'property'. Through this, it can be linked to a more general representation of adjectives. In this way even very general and abstract categories like basic word class can be part of the same system of representations. There is no essential difference between concrete lexical representations and (much) more general ones, other than the fact that not all elements are equally specific.

Speakers of a language may not develop an abstract representation of the kind depicted in Figure 5 for all morpheme constructions, and the levels of representation need not be the same for all speakers. Someone who does not have a representation as given in Figures 3–5, i.e. with a morphemic structure, may still be a fluent speaker and a fully native-like user of the word *leesbaar*.

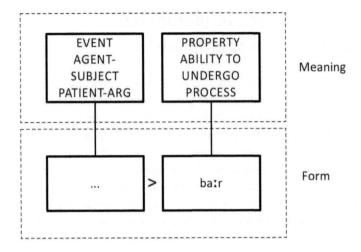

Figure 5: Partially schematic representation of -*baar*.

In fact, speakers who do have a representation as in Figure 5 will also have representations like Figure 3. It may not be possible to distinguish between these speakers in terms of their production and understanding of this lexical item. It is only when novel forms with -*baar* come into play, that a representation without morphemic boundaries cannot suffice. The development described for *leesbaar* above provides a path along which all constructions may be acquired.

For all constructions acquired up to the level of partially schematic representations, a language user ends up with multiple representations for the same structure (i.e. lexically specific and more abstract). Psycholinguistic research seems to indicate that language users access different levels of representation depending on the linguistic task they execute. A model that depicts these different levels as separate, albeit linked representations can account for this finding. An open question, deserving of more empirical attention, is in which contexts people make use of specific or more abstract levels of representation. Our hypothesis is that people will make use of the representation that maps most easily on the input they receive. Often, this will result in the activation of very specific representations, because these require less processing of the input from the complex and abstract representation to a mapping of the concrete form to meaning. The experiments reported on in the following section try to shed more light on this issue.

3 Measuring knowledge of morpheme constructions: Four experiments

Research investigating children's proficiency in using morphologically complex words tends to show a clear developmental pattern with gradual growth in adult-like performance (e.g. Anglin 1993) rather than all-or-nothing scores. This finding, repeated in the experiments reported on below, seems to point out that more abstract levels of representation develop gradually and may not be activated (consistently) when the task allows for the use of more specific representations. The experiments described in this section differ in the extent to which the participating children can use such specific representations, which depends on whether test items include instantiations they might have come across before or novel instantiations. The tasks also vary in the amount of time the participants get to respond: a lexical decision task (experiment 3) is an online task, requiring immediate reactions, while the other tasks leave time to consciously reflect on the response. This distinction is often linked to implicit (online task) and explicit (offline task) knowledge (cf. Ellis 2005; Hulstijn 2005). Differences in performance between tasks can therefore indicate that some representations may not be accessible for all types of tasks. Finally, experimental tasks differ in the extent to which they require metalinguistic knowledge to execute them, but also in whether it is necessary to put this knowledge into words while doing the task. A definition task (cf. experiment 2 below), for example, consists of verbalizing this knowledge, whereas an acceptability task (experiment 4) does not. Deciding how acceptable an expression is, is a metalinguistic job, but since you do not need to express your considerations in words, it might be less taxing than a definition task. Table 1 gives an overview of where the four experiments fall on each of these dimensions. The next sections provide detailed descriptions of the tasks and participants' performance.

Table 1: Overview of experimental tasks.

	Possibility to use lexically specific representations	Time to reflect on response	Necessity to verbalize knowledge
Word formation task	Present: known derived form	Yes	No
Word definition task	Absent: known stems, unknown derived form	Yes	Yes
Lexical decision task	Present: activation of known items	No	No
Acceptability task	Absent: novel instantiations	Yes	No (but indication of degree)

3.1 Experiment 1: Word formation task

The first experiment has a long tradition in language acquisition research, going back to Berko's (1958) seminal work. Using a range of elicitation techniques, a number of researchers have tried to investigate children's proficiency with regard to morphological affixes by presenting them with a mono-morphemic word, and asking them to produce a derived or inflected form. Children's responses provide an answer to the question to what extent children are able to manipulate words morphologically in such a way that it fits a given sentence context. This experimental, offline task measures explicit knowledge.

3.1.1 Method

3.1.1.1 Participants
Sixty-nine fourth-graders (mean age 9;4) from three different primary schools in Amsterdam participated in the experiment. In a questionnaire, more than half of the participating children reported using another language than Dutch on a regular basis in their home environment (N = 38), with 19 different languages mentioned.

To assess children's vocabulary size, the receptive word meaning task in the TAK (*Taaltoets Allochtone Kinderen Bovenbouw*, Language Test for Migrant Children grades 4–6, Verhoeven and Vermeer, 1993) was administered.

3.1.1.2 Test items
The test consisted of 14 sentences with 15 affixes in total, i.e. one test item combined two morpheme constructions (*on-* and *-baar*). Five different frequent morpheme constructions were part of three test items each: the prefix *on-* and suffixes *-eren*, *-er*, *-heid* and *-baar*. Table 2 contains an example for each affix, also listing an English near-equivalent.

Table 2: Affixes in the word formation task.

Affix	Stem	Derivation	English equivalent
on-	*Aardig* (kind)	*Onaardig* (unkind)	un-
-eren	*Fantasie* (fantasy)	*Fantaseren* (fantasize)	-ize
-er	*Inbreken* (break in)	*Inbreker* (burglar)	-er (ag. noun)
-heid	*Duidelijk* (clear)	*Duidelijkheid* (clarity)	-ity / -ness
-baar	*Lezen* (to read)	*Leesbaar* (legible)	-able

For each test item, the stem occurred at least five times in the Schrooten and Vermeer (1994) corpus, which indicates that these are words that children are likely to have encountered in school and will therefore be familiar. The frequency of the stems (the monomorphemic word that was given) and the derivations was determined using the Corpus of Spoken Dutch (Corpus Gesproken Nederlands, CGN). This is a 10 million-word corpus of contemporary Dutch. Table 3 contains the frequency data for each stem and derivation, based on lemma searches, including token frequencies of the different inflectional forms.[4]

Table 3: Frequency data for test items word formation task.

Item	Stem	Frequency stem	Frequency derivation
Kopiëren	Kopie	115	177
Inbreker	Inbreken	45	18
Fantaseren	Fantasie	68	23
(Dromen)vanger	Vangen	327	96
Adviseren	Advies	269	117
Onaardig	Aardig	1014	29
Leesbaar	Lezen	5539	20
Ongeduldig	Geduld(ig)	117	46
Verkoudheid	Verkouden	67	36
Duidelijkheid	Duidelijk	2319	135
Onhoorbaar	Horen	7494	16
Hoorbaar	Horen	7494	47
Bijter	Bijten	168	3
Hardheid	Hard	1817	7
Herhaalbaar	herhalen	361	1

The format of the task is a basic fill-the-gap procedure: the test items consist of a single mono-morphemic word, followed by a sentence with a gap in it. The participants had to fill in the gap, using the word at the beginning (see Figure 6 for an example).

> *Fantasie: Ze zegt dat haar vader drie auto's heeft, maar volgens mij zit ze*
> *maar een beetje te ... (fantaseren)*
> Fantasy: She says that her father three cars has, but according to me sits she
> but a little to ... (fantasize)
> 'She says that her father owns three cars, but I think she's just making that up.'

Figure 6: Example test item word formation task.

---

4 A full overview of all test items for each of the four experiments can be found under the header "onderzoek: lexicon & morfologie" at www.annevermeer.com.

3.1.1.3 Procedure

Prior to the task, the researcher introduced herself and the project in each class. The task started with a short oral introduction, after which all children did the pen-and-paper test individually, in their regular classroom. Using two examples with different affixes, it was explained that they had to change the word at the beginning of each sentence so that it fit in the gap. The children were allowed to take as much time as they needed; the task took approximately ten minutes.

3.1.2 Results

All responses were scored as either correct or incorrect. One item contained two suffixes and was scored twice: once for the first, and once for the second affix. The task was reliable (Cronbach's α = .85). Participants' mean score on the 15-item task was 8.38 (SD 3.77). At first glance, it seems that the monolingual children (mean 10.00, SD 3.42) outperformed their bilingual classmates (mean 6.97, SD 3.52). Because vocabulary size may influence performance on this task, an analysis of variance was done with TAK-scores as covariate. The apparent difference in scores between both groups turns out to be entirely attributable to the difference in vocabulary size. While the difference between the two groups in TAK scores is highly significant (F (1, 67) = 39.55, p < .001), the distinction between bilingual and monolingual children is not (F (1, 67) = 0.00, p = .99). Both measures (TAK and word formation) are strongly correlated (r = .70). Taken together, these figures suggest that performance on the word formation task is strongly influenced by vocabulary size.

There is considerable variation in the scores, indicating that not all children consistently used abstract representations. If this had been the case, a ceiling effect would have been observed, i.e. with all scores near the maximum of 15. This does not exclude the possibility that some children always provide the correct answer, while others consistently do not. A closer look at the distribution of scores over each morpheme construction serves to distinguish between this all-or-nothing hypothesis and a more gradual development. Performance on the test items ranged from 11 to 65 children providing the correct answer per item (with 69 participants). If the participating children always used abstract representations, correlations on test items with the same affix construction would have to be higher than the correlation between different items. This is not the case: correlations between items with different affixes (N = 89) are .26 (SE .015) on average, and .33 (SE .036) between items with the same affix (N = 15). This difference is not significant in a 2 samples Kolmogorov-Smirnov test (Z =.98, p = .29).

Looking at the relation between frequency of occurrence and item scores, the correlation between the frequency of the derivation and task performance is reasonably strong ($r = .54$). No such relation is found with the frequency of the stem ($r = -.23$), while the relative frequency of the items correlates strongly with scores ($r = .65$). This means that performance was highest for those derived items that occur frequently compared to their stems. This frequency effect indicates that participants do not use abstract representations in executing the task, but mainly retrieve specific complex words.

It could be argued that a correct response to at least one item with a particular affix suffices to indicate that a child is able to manipulate that affix. For that reason, a score was created for each affix indicating for each participant whether they had provided minimally one correct answer. For each of the five constructions tested, at least two thirds of the 69 participants were able to manipulate the affix successfully once or more (66, 64, 54, 50 and 46 for the -eren, -er, on-, -baar and -heid constructions, respectively).

The answer to the research question whether the participating children are able to manipulate words morphologically in such a way that it fits a given sentence context has to be affirmative, but it is clearly not the case that they can do this for any instance of a given affix construction. Performance strongly depends on the relative frequency of the test items, suggesting that the explicit knowledge children have to draw upon mainly relates to specific representations of complex items.

3.2 Experiment 2: Definition task

Like the word formation task, a definition task is a classic experiment to investigate children's linguistic proficiency, especially their vocabulary skills. With regard to morphologically complex words, a definition task can shed light on the question to what extent children make use of this morphological structure in coming up with a definition for the item. If they are aware of a morpheme construction, and are able to put its meaning into words, they can define morphologically complex words that are new to them. If they are not familiar with the construction, or perhaps unable to formulate its meaning, they may still realize that there is morphological structure, for instance because they recognize the stem, which is usually more frequent than the derivation.

In the current experiment, children were confronted with very complex words and were asked to tell the researcher what they thought this word meant. Their responses provide an answer to the question whether, in the absence of any linguistic context (e.g. a story or a conversation), children are able to deduce and verbalize the meaning of a novel complex word from their knowledge of its stem and the morpheme construction(s) it instantiates. This offline task measures metalinguistic knowledge.

3.2.1 Method

3.2.1.1 Participants

The same 69 fourth-graders that participated in the word formation task also took part in the definition task, in individual oral sessions. Due to recording problems, the responses of 22 participants were lost. Of the remaining 47 children, 29 are monolingual and 18 are bilingual.

3.2.1.2 Test items

The test consisted of 14 words, ranging from two to five morphemes (mean length 3.1) and nine to seventeen letters in length (mean length 12.1). For each of these words, the stems occur as mono-morphemic words in Dutch (sometimes with small phonological or orthographic adaptations, e.g. *meubel – meubileren* 'furniture – furnish'). Four out of the five morpheme constructions tested in the word formation task (the *on-, -er, -heid* and *-baar* constructions) each occurred four times in the test items, with *-eren* occurring three times. Five items instantiated two constructions. For those test items that combined more than one of the five affix constructions investigated, these were analyzed separately, i.e. for *adresseerbaar* (addressable), which contains both *-baar* and *-eren*, the responses were coded twice: once for the *-baar* construction and once for the *-eren* construction. None of the test items occurred in the Schrooten and Vermeer (1994) corpus, indicating that these are not frequent words in the linguistic input children get. In the corpus of spoken Dutch (CGN), six of the words occurred at least once, but none more than six times. Because of the choice to use real rather than pseudo words, it was impossible to exclude the possibility that one or more words are known by some of the children tested. All test items can be found on www.annevermeer.com.

3.2.1.3 Procedure

This task was administered individually, with the children and the researcher in a room separate from the rest of the class. Each child filled out a brief questionnaire about her/his language background first, then did the lexical decision task (see Section 2.3), followed by the word definition task.

The researcher explained that she had a number of 'big' and sometimes 'strange' words, that the child might or might not know. She wondered whether the child could figure out what the words might mean. She then presented the words one by one, by saying the word out loud and showing them a card with the word printed on it. Shuffling the stack of cards for each child randomized the order in which the words were presented. With each word, the researcher asked "what do you think that X means" or a variant of that question. If children said that they didn't know or did not say anything, she prompted by asking whether there was a part of the word that the children recognized. If that too failed to elicit a response, the researcher moved on to the next word. Children's responses were recorded using a small tape recorder. The task took approximately five minutes.

3.2.1.4 Analysis
Children's responses were coded on a four-point scale, based on the extent to which they showed the ability to identify and define the affix construction. In addition, all responses were also coded simply for reference to the construction that was tested. This second score is a measure of the extent to which children showed the ability to provide a definition for the morpheme construction.

3.2.2 Results

With 19 test items scored on a 0 to 3 scale, the maximum score was 57. On average, children scored 37.85 (SD 6.95). This means that they got 66% of the maximum amount of points. When only references to the affix construction were counted (maximum score = 19), the average is 6.34 (SD 3.44), or only 33% of the points. This means that, whereas a majority of responses showed some awareness of morphological structure, it was much less likely that this response included a reference to the affix construction.

Performance on the definition task correlated with the vocabulary size measure ($r = .49$). The difference between monolingual (mean 38.45, SD 7.11) and bilingual children (mean 36.89, SD 6.76) is not significant (t (46) = 0.74, $p = .46$). The high standard deviations indicate considerable individual differences; it was clear in administering the task that some children felt much more comfortable than others to give formulating a definition a try.

There were considerable differences in performance on different affix constructions. Table 4 ranks them in order of the percentage of responses that contained an explicit reference to the affix (i.e. the "3" scores in the analysis).

Table 4: Percentage of responses on definition task with reference to the affix.

Morpheme construction	Percentage responses with reference to affix
-er	65.3
on-	47.9
-eren	31.9
-baar	22.3
-heid	15.4
Total	33.4

These constructions vary on a number of points: one (*on-*) is a prefix while the other four are suffixes. With two constructions, the resulting word is an adjective (*on-* and *-baar*), one forms a verb (*-eren*) and two are used to make a noun (*-er* and *-heid*). They also differ semantically, in the abstractness of their meaning. It is relatively easy to refer to the meaning of some constructions, such as the agentive *-er* construction ("someone who…"). Since only five different constructions were tested and these differ in various ways, it is impossible to pinpoint the cause of variation in scores exactly. This is, however, a point that deserves further research.

In contrast to the word formation task, performance on the definition task was clearly influenced by the specific construction that was tested in each item. This cannot be interpreted, however, as evidence of use of abstract representations for these constructions, because lexically referring to the meaning of the morpheme constructions is more difficult for some than for others. Any mention of 'not' was analyzed as a reference to *on-* for items with that affix, but for *-baar* children had to say that something 'could be done' or 'was possible'. Although this is probably related to differences in difficulty of the constructions, it is not the same. If children are aware of both *on-* and *-baar* they may still score more points on the *on-* items because it is easier to verbalize the definition.

The answer to the question whether children are able to assign meaning to new words on the basis of the morphemes they contain is: not always. There is considerable variation between children, between different morpheme constructions and between items: correlations on scores between different items did not differ significantly between items with the same or different morpheme constructions. Correlations between items with different affixes ($N = 144$) are .08 (SE .02) on average, and .16 (SE .03) between items with the same affix ($N = 27$). This difference is not significant (t (169) = 1.91, $p > .05$). In other words, children who referred to the affix in one item with *on-* did not necessarily do the same for another item with the same suffix. To account for this, we must assume that the abstract representation is not always available, or that the representation contains a smaller generalization: one that captures some items, but not others.

3.3 Experiment 3: Lexical decision task; the Family Size effect

Both experiments described in the preceding sections tap into explicit knowledge that children have about complex words. There are other tasks, however, that allow us to investigate the role of morphological structure online, while lexical items are being processed. One such experiment is the lexical decision task. In a lexical decision task, participants see a string of letters, for which they must decide as quickly as possible whether it represents an existing word. Both the response (yes or no) and the reaction time (in milliseconds) are recorded. The speed with which a word is recognized or rejected depends on a large number of factors. One obvious aspect is word frequency: the more frequent a word is, the shorter the reaction time (hereafter RT). The measure for word frequency, which is, crucially, always based on a corpus, usually includes not only the frequency of the word that is given as a test item (e.g. *werk* 'work'), but also its inflectional variants (e.g. *werkje* 'work-DIM').

In this experiment, the main variable of interest is the morphological family size. This notion was introduced by Schreuder and Baayen (1997). The family size (hereafter FS) is the number of derivations and compounds a word occurs in. For Dutch, the word with the largest FS is *werk* 'work'. In Celex, a 40 million word corpus of written Dutch, this word has more than 500 family members, ranging from *werkster* 'cleaning lady' (literally: work-female agentive noun) to *huiswerk* 'homework' (Baayen, Piepenbrock, and Gulikers 1995). Baayen and Schreuder found that, other things being equal, words with a large FS are recognized faster than words with a small FS. Note that this is a type effect: RTs are not so much influenced by the frequency of the family members, but by the number of different family members. Since family size was first recognized as a factor that influences recognition, the variable has been explored further. De Jong, Schreuder, and Baayen (2000) replicated the finding that RTs are not influenced significantly by the frequency of family members, but by the number of derivations and compounds in which a word occurs (see Mos 2010, Chapter 1 for a more extensive overview).

The lexical decision task has been used successfully in research on children's linguistic abilities. Experiments investigating the effects of morphological family size have focused on adult speakers. The lexical decision task is an online task, which directly taps in to the processing of words. It is a time-pressured task, and, especially in comparison with the word definition task discussed in the previous section, requires little metalinguistic awareness.

3.3.1 Method

3.3.1.1 Participants
The same 69 fourth-graders that participated in the word formation task also did the lexical decision task. All children had normal or corrected to normal eyesight.

3.3.1.2 Test items
The nominal test items in De Jong et al. (2000) experiment 1 were the starting point for this task. In De Jong's design, twenty words with a large family size and twenty words with a small family size were selected using Celex (Baayen et al. 1995). The two groups of test items were matched for lemma frequency and length. The test items did not include long words (mean length 5.0 letters, with a range of 3 to 7 letters) and all items were monomorphemic. Celex is a corpus of written Dutch, composed of fiction and non-fiction books for adults. Since the input that children receive is rather different, these counts were contrasted with those from another corpus, *Woordwerken* (Schrooten and Vermeer 1994). *Woordwerken*, with nearly 1.8 million tokens, is considerably smaller than the 42-million word corpus Celex. It consists of texts in children's books, text-books used in primary schools and verbal interaction between teachers and pupils. In this way, *Woordwerken* reflects what children are likely to encounter in school. On the basis of a comparison between the family size counts from each corpus, a number of test items had to be replaced (cf. Mos 2010: 87–88). The final test items were 20 words with a large family size, 20 words with a small family size and 40 non-words. The test items can be found on www.annevermeer. com.

3.3.1.3 Procedure
The experiment was made using E-Prime (Schneider, Eschmann, and Zuccolotto 2002). The participating children executed this task individually, on a Dell Latitude D600 Laptop, in a quiet room, in the same session as the word definition task was administered.

First, the children read a brief explanation on the computer screen. This introduction contained a simple description of the task. The children were told that they would have to determine as quickly and as accurately as they could whether the letters they were about to see in the middle of the screen formed a word or not. If they thought they saw a word, they had to press the button with the green sticker on it; the no-button had a red sticker on it. Before entering the main experiment, the participants did a short practice session (10 items). Only if they responded correctly to at least 7 of these could they proceed with the main session. Each stimulus was preceded by an asterisk for 500 ms, both in the practice and in the main task. The stimulus disappeared from the screen as soon as the participant pressed one of the buttons or after three seconds, if none of the buttons had been pressed. The experiment took approximately five minutes.

3.3.1.4 Variables

For the test items, two length measures and two frequency variables were identified: the number of letters and syllables, lemma frequency and family size. Family size was included in the design as a dichotomous variable: test items had either a large or a small FS, following the research design of De Jong et al. (2000). In order to reliably observe the effects of FS, the other three item variables were matched between the two groups of test items. The mean length in letters (5.00 [SD 1.17] for large FS and 5.05 [SD 1.15] for small FS) and syllables (1.55 [SD 0.61] for large FS and 1.75 [SD .79] for small FS) were not significantly different for the two groups. Similarly, mean lemma frequency, which includes token counts of all inflectional variants of a word, was not significantly different for large FS and small FS test items (frequency per million words in Celex was 35.70 [SD 27.65] and 38.10 [SD 35.51] respectively).

3.3.1.5 Analysis

An initial item analysis showed that performance was below 70% for 11 items (3 non-words, 7 small FS items and 1 large FS item), which were removed from all further analyses. The mean frequency in Celex for the two groups was still not significantly different (37.37 [27.36] per million words for large FS items and 39.85 [37.10] for small FS items).

Two children scored less than 70% correct on this task. Their responses were excluded from the analyses. All incorrect responses and reaction times under 300 ms and RTs over two standard deviations above a participant's mean were also discarded.

3.3.2 Results

Table 5 below lists the mean reaction times for all remaining responses. An analysis of variance shows that the 33 ms difference between small FS test items and large FS words is significant (F (1, 1968) = 7.05, p < .01). On average, words with a large family size are recognized faster than words with a small family size which are matched for lemma frequency and length.

Table 5: Mean reaction times on correct responses lexical decision task.

Stimulus type	N (correct responses)	Mean reaction time (ms)	SD (ms)
Small FS	779	1171	276
Large FS	1191	1138	262
Non-words	1924	1402	327

The children who participated were much slower than the adults taking part in De Jong's experiment whose mean RT was 521 ms (SD 48) for small FS items and 502 (SD 51) for large FS items. Moreover, the correlation between the mean reaction times per stimulus for both experiments is very low (r = .12, p = .59). This indicates that the factors determining speed of recognition are not the same for adults and children. It has been suggested that children do not come across the same words frequently as adults do (Van der Werf, Hootsen, and Vermeer 2008). If that is really the case, this might explain the relative differences in recognition times for adults and children here: words that are frequent for children are possibly not very frequent for adults and vice versa. The *Woordwerken* corpus is too small to investigate this hypothesis in more detail, but this is clearly a point that would benefit from further research.

Performance on the separately measured vocabulary size task coincides with speed of recognition: children with a large vocabulary on average have shorter RTs (F (1, 66) = 10.91, p < .01). This means that children with high scores on the vocabulary size test are more adult-like in their reaction times, possibly because they know more words, or because they have more deeply entrenched lexical representations of items. This correlation seems indicative of a path of development and shows knowing more words aids in the recognition of a stimulus.

Contrary to the effect on overall speed of recognition, there is no relation between vocabulary size and the FS effect (F (1, 66) = 0.55, p =.46). This can be taken to indicate that the family size effect is there regardless of the number of words these children know. Similarly to the experiments described above, the differences in RT between monolingual and bilingual children were not significant when effects of vocabulary size were controlled for (F (1, 65) = 0.75, p = .39).

In sum, the FS effect as measured by De Jong et al. (2000) is replicated for children aged 9;4, although their mean RTs are considerably slower. The children take approximately twice as long as adults in responding, which may be tied to their smaller linguistic repertoire, encompassing both vocabulary size and level of entrenchment: performance on a separate vocabulary test was significantly related to speed of recognition. Replicating the effect found for adults indicates that the way in which knowledge of lexical items is structured is not essentially different for children around this age.

3.4 Experiment 4: Acceptability task

For the previous experiments, participants could make use of lexically specific representations. In order to test use of a partially abstract representation of the Dutch morpheme -*baar* construction, a task was developed in which participants had to rate the acceptability of novel instantiations of -*baar*. This experiment focuses on the participant structure of the verbs. Corpus analyses show that verbs with certain participant structures (i.e. transitive verbs with Agent and Patient participant roles) are much more likely to occur with -*baar* than other verbs (cf. Backus and Mos 2011). If people make a consistent distinction in the acceptability of forms that corresponds to the participant structure of the verb they contain, this indicates that they have a representation for the construction that includes information about the types of verbs with which it can be combined.

The experiment conducted is a magnitude estimation task (Sorace 1996; Wulff 2009). This is a specific type of judgment task, in which participants make up their own acceptability scale. Participants are told to assign a random number to a first stimulus, and then grade subsequent stimuli relative to the previous one. Participants are free to distinguish as many grades of acceptability as they like, unlike grammaticality judgment tasks using Likert scales. Magnitude estimation can be used to determine whether people consistently distinguish between types of stimuli theoretically postulated to be different, in our case between verbs with different thematic role assignments. To our knowledge, magnitude estimation tasks have not been done before with children. There is evidence that children in primary school are able to perform grammaticality (cf. McDonald 2008) and acceptability judgment tasks (Sorace et al. 2009). For this experiment, a group of adult participants was added to the research design in order to obtain a measure of adult native-speaker knowledge.

3.4.1 Method

3.4.1.1 Participants
The adult participants were 72 native speakers of Dutch (aged 18–82, mean age 43). All were born in the Netherlands and participated on a voluntary basis. The 148 participating children were sixth-graders ("groep 8" in the Dutch school

system), mean age 12;3 years. They came from three primary schools in Tilburg, a city in the south of the Netherlands. All children participated on a voluntary basis, with parental consent. Thirty-eight children reported speaking another language than Dutch on a regular basis.

3.4.1.2 Test items

Test items contained an instance of the -*baar* construction (always used predicatively).[5] Filler items were made up from other ways to express potentiality, such as 'it is possible that'. In the test items, five categories of verbs were used, with four verbs in each category (three in the smaller set of test items for children) and all verbs occurring once with -*baar*. The five verb categories, listed in Table 6, were based on corpus analyses (cf. Mos 2010, Chapter 3; Backus and Mos 2011).

Table 6: Verb categories in the acceptability task.

	Category	Example
I	Prototypical transitive verbs, with Agent-Subject and Patient-Object	*Schrijven* (write)
II	Optionally transitive verbs with Agent-Subject and Patient-Object or Undergoer-Subject roles	*Smelten* (melt)
III	Optionally transitive verbs with a (generally) implicit second argument	*Schreeuwen* (yell)
IV	Non-prototypical transitive verbs, with Stimulus-Experiencer roles and BE-perfect	*Lukken* (succeed)
V	Non-prototypical transitive verbs, with Stimulus-Experiencer roles and HAVE-perfect	*Verbazen* (amaze)

3.4.1.3 Procedure

The adult participants received an email with a link to a website. A short introduction informed them that this experiment was set up to find out what kinds of sentences people rate as 'better' or 'worse', where 'bad' sentences were defined as unintelligible or ungrammatical – thus pointing at both form and meaning. The participants were told that they were to rate each sentence on how 'good' it seemed to them, with higher numbers reflecting better sentences. They were then introduced to the experimental technique with a number of examples, first with non-linguistic stimuli (oddly-shaped objects whose size they had to grade relative to one another), then with sentences in which one or more word order restrictions were violated. Before starting they were told that the sentences in

---

5 Other constructions were tested in the same experiment (cf. Mos 2010, Chapter 3). The analysis here is limited to -*baar* items.

the experiment all contained information about something that was possible. They were instructed to read each sentence carefully, but not think too long about the number they filled in. From the logged data, it was clear that participants spent between 12 and 22 minutes on the task. Test items appeared in random order, different for each participant.

The children did the experiment at school. They were told the experiment was designed to find out what kinds of sentences are 'better' or 'worse'. For that reason, they would have to rate a number of sentences. They too were introduced to the technique by practicing assigning numbers to differently sized objects first, and then given a practice trial with sentences containing word order violations. The instructions for the task were slightly modified, in order to make sure that the children understood what they were asked to do. These modifications only included simplifications in sentence structure and word choice. Each child worked at an individual computer, taking approximately 20 minutes to complete the task.

3.4.2 Results

For each participant, scores were recoded into Z-scores to make a direct comparison of individual scores possible. Although participants reported feeling unsure about being consistent in their grading, the test was found to be reliable (Cronbach's α = .85 for adults, α = .93 for children). The acceptability data of children and adults were analyzed separately because of the differences between the two test versions, which included a smaller set of test items for children, slight differences in the formulation of the instruction and the setting in which participants took place. Since the sphericity assumption is not met (the Mauchly test is significant), Huynh-Feldt corrected F-values will be reported.

Figure 7 provides an overview of adults' and children's mean Z-scores for each of the five verb types. For adults, the effect of verb category is significant (F (2.63, 186.59) = 189.07, $p < .001$). Pairwise comparisons show all differences to be significant. The same applies for children's data: the effect of verb type is significant (F (1.00, 147.00) = 10,58, $p < .001$). Again, pairwise comparisons show significant differences between all pairs. One element in the distribution of scores is particularly striking: a clear distinction in acceptability between verb categories I, II and III on the one hand and IV and V on the other. This distinction is present in adults' and children's responses alike. Categories I–III have in common that they are regularly expressed with an Agent-Subject. In addition they are expressed with an obligatory Patient (category I), an optional Patient (II) or an implicit Patient (III). Clearly, the acceptability of novel instantiations does not so much require an expressed Patient, but depends on this argument's interpretability.

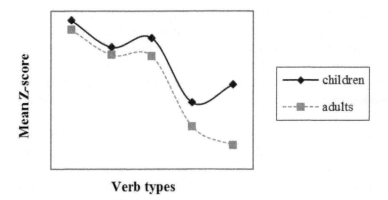

Figure 7: Mean Z-scores in acceptability for test items with -baar, for each of the five verb categories as listed in Table 6.

To the extent that the experimental task contained novel instantiations of the construction, it forced participants to make use of abstract representations they may have had for this pattern. The acceptability ratings that the participants provided showed a pattern related to the verb types that the test items contained. This can be interpreted as evidence for the existence of an abstract representation for the morpheme construction: the consistency in rating differences can only come about if participants had a general representation available to them against which test items could be compared. This experiment has therefore been successful in triggering the use of partially specific representations for the -*baar* construction, both in children and in adults.

4 Discussion

The results of the four experiments reported on above demonstrate clear frequency effects. This is easily accounted for in the MultiRep Model. Correlations between task performance and vocabulary size, a recurrent finding in these experiments, point at the gradual development of representations. The MultiRep Model assumes that knowledge about morpheme constructions develops in a bottom-up fashion: based on the input children receive, they will first acquire specific form-meaning pairings. As they encounter more instantiations of a pattern, they might develop (partially) abstract representations of the construction.

The correlations between scores in the word formation task and relative frequency of the items' morphemes would be explained in the form of a difference in activation level. If a morphologically complex word contains a morpheme or stem form which is very frequent, the link to the representation of that word or morpheme will be influential because it is strongly activated on a regular basis. When a particular complex word is relatively frequent compared to its morphemic elements, this activation is weaker. The frequency effect indicates that children mainly rely on the stored specific lexical items. If they had used abstract representations, the frequency of individual lexical items would not have been a strong predictor.

The existence of a morphological family size effect in the lexical decision task also has implications for the MultiRep Model. If derivations and compounds contribute to the recognition of a mono-morphemic word that is a stem in these complex words, we must assume that there are links between the stored complex words and the mono-morphemic word. The fact that this is a type and not a token effect seems to exclude the possibility that the complex words are not stored separately, but decomposed when they are encountered.

Acceptability ratings on novel instantiations of the *-baar* construction, finally, indicate that speakers, in this case both children and adults, have abstract representations available to them for the evaluation of such forms. Performance on the definition task, however, which also saw children confronted with new words ending in *-baar* (and other morpheme constructions), was quite varied: responses showed considerable differences between items and between participants.

This raises the question what it really means to have acquired a morpheme construction: being able to use specific forms, defining new words, or evaluating novel instantiations? While the first is most realistic, that is, part of natural language use, it does not provide information about the cognitive reality of more abstract representations (as in Figure 5). Different linguistic tasks tap into different levels of representation. This need not be problematic in linguistic research, or in proficiency assessment, as long as the use of specific forms is not seen as evidence for knowledge of the abstract pattern. The results of these experiments indicate that both specific representations and partially abstract ones are part of speakers' linguistic knowledge, even if this might seem redundant. As Achard and Niemeier put it: "The goal of a usage-based-model is not to achieve mathematical elegance, but to depict the complexity of language use. Consequently, it is composed of an eclectic array of expressions at different levels of complexity, abstraction, and generality. Individual lexical items cohabitate in the system with idioms, conventionalized idiosyncratic collocations, and fully productive grammatical constructions" (Achard and Niemeier 2004: 5).

A number of the different levels Achard and Niemeier mention can be identified in the representations given in Figures 1 through 5: individual lexical items (Figure 1), conventionalized collocations (Figure 2) and productive constructions

(Figure 5). By assuming that lexically specific, partially schematic constructions and highly underspecified patterns are stored in similar ways, differing only in level of specificity, the dichotomy between lexicon and syntax is clearly abandoned. In this complex system, morpheme constructions figure right in the middle of the continuum ranging from words to abstract patterns.

References

Achard, Michel, and Susanne Niemeier. 2004. *Cognitive Linguistics, Second Language Acquisition, and Foreign Language Teaching.* Berlin: Mouton de Gruyter.

Anglin, Jeremy M. 1993. *Vocabulary Development: A Morphological Analysis.* Chicago, IL: University of Chicago Press.

Baayen, R. Harald, Richard Piepenbrock, and Leon Gulikers. 1995. The CELEX lexical database [Computer software]. University of Pennsylvania, Philadelphia, PA: Linguistic Data Consortium.

Backus, Ad M., and Maria B. J. Mos. 2011. Islands of (im)productivity in corpus data and acceptability judgments: Contrasting two potentiality constructions in Dutch. In *Converging Evidence*, Doris Schönefeld (ed.), 165–194. Amsterdam: John Benjamins.

Berko, Jean. 1958. The child's learning of English morphology. *Word* 14: 150–177.

Boas, Hans C. 2008. Determining the structure of lexical entries and grammatical constructions in Construction Grammar. *Annual Review of Cognitive Linguistics* 6: 113–144.

Bybee, Joan. 1995. Regular morphology and the lexicon. *Language and Cognitive Processes* 10: 425–455.

De Jong, Nivja H., Robert Schreuder, and R. Harald Baayen. 2000. The morphological family size effect and morphology. *Language and Cognitive Processes* 15: 329–365.

Duñabeitia, Jon A., Manuel Perea, and Manuel Carreiras. 2008. Does darkness lead to happiness? Masked suffix priming effects. *Language and Cognitive Processes* 23: 1002–1020.

Ellis, Nick C. 2005. At the interface: Dynamic interactions of explicit and implicit language knowledge. *Studies in Second Language Acquisition* 27: 305–352.

Feldman, Laurie B. 2000. Are morphological effects distinguishable from the effects of shared meaning and shared form? *Journal of Experimental Psychology: Learning, Memory, and Cognition* 26: 1431–1444.

Goldberg, Adele E. 1995. *Constructions: A construction grammar approach to argument structure.* Chicago, IL: University of Chicago Press.

Goldberg, Adele E. 2006. *Constructions at work: The nature of generalization in language.* Oxford: Oxford University Press.

Hulstijn, Jan H. 2005. Theoretical and empirical issues in the study of implicit and explicit second–language learning. *Studies in Second Language Acquisition* 27: 129–140.

Langacker, Ronald W. 1987. *Foundations of Cognitive Grammar: Vol. 1 Theoretical Prerequisites.* Stanford, CA: Stanford University Press.

McDonald, Janet L. 2008. Grammaticality judgments in children: The role of age, working memory and phonological ability. *Journal of Child Language* 35: 247–268.

McNamara, Tim P. 2005. *Semantic Priming: Perspectives from Memory and Word Recognition.* New York, NY: Taylor & Francis.

Mos, Maria B. J. 2010. *Complex lexical items*. LOT: Utrecht.

Schneider, Walter, Amy Eschmann, and Anthony Zuccolotto. 2002. E-*Prime user's guide*. Pittsburgh, PA: Psychology Software Tools, Inc.

Schreuder, Robert, and R. Harald Baayen. 1997. How complex simplex words can be. *Journal of Memory and Language* 37: 118–139.

Schrooten, Walter, and Anne Vermeer. 1994. *Woorden in het basisonderwijs: 15 000 woorden aangeboden aan leerlingen* [Words in primary school education: 15.000 words offered to children]. Tilburg: Tilburg University Press.

Sorace, Antonella. 1996. The use of acceptability judgments in second language acquisition research. In *Handbook of Second Language Acquisition*, William C Ritchie, and Tej K. Bhatia (eds.), 375–409. San Diego, CA: Academic Press.

Sorace, Antonella, Ludovica Serratice, Francesca Filiaci, and Michela Baldo. 2009. Discourse conditions on subject pronoun realization: Testing the linguistic intuitions of older bilingual children. *Lingua* 119: 460–477.

Tomasello, Michael. 2003. *Constructing a language: A Usage-Based Theory of Language Acquisition*. Cambridge, MA: Harvard University Press.

Van der Werf, Rintse, Geke Hootsen, and Anne Vermeer. 2008. Automated user-centered task selection and input modification in language learning. *ITL Review of Applied Linguistics* 155: 1–22.

Verhoeven, Ludo, and Anne Vermeer. 1993. *Taaltoets allochtone kinderen bovenbouw. Diagnostische toets voor de vaardigheid Nederlands bij allochtone en autochtone kinderen in de bovenbouw van het basisonderwijs* [Language test migrant children grades 4–6. Diagnostic test for migrant and Dutch children's Dutch proficiency in the later grades of elementary school]. Tilburg: Zwijsen.

Wulff, Stefanie. 2009. Converging evidence from corpus and experimental data to capture idiomaticity. *Corpus Linguistics and Linguistic Theory* 5: 131–159.

Elma Nap-Kolhoff

7 The development of Dutch object-naming constructions in bilingual Turkish-Dutch children receiving low amounts of Dutch language input

1 Introduction

Turkish migrants have been present in the Netherlands since the 1960s. Although they generally have a strong orientation toward the Dutch society, their ethno-linguistic vitality remains strong as well (Extra et al. 2002). This is exemplified in the fact that many second generation parents, who are also fluent in Dutch, prefer to speak Turkish to their children in their first years of life. Infant health care institutions, such as the *consultatiebureau* 'consultation bureau', acknowledge the importance of a strong basis in a first language and advise parents to use their first language at home. At the same time, they encourage parents to send their children to centers for early childhood education (*voor- en vroegschoolse educatie*), where Dutch is the language of interaction. These programs start at age two and are provided by daycare centers available to parents who both have a job, and by pre-school playgroups available to all. From these field experiences questions have arisen about the nature of bilingualism that migrant children acquire in these programs.

From the literature on child bilingualism it is not easy to provide an answer. Studies on very young children (age 2–3) often focus on types of bilingualism in which both languages are more or less equally present in the child's life. That is clearly not the case with these children. Although they are still in the first years of acquiring their first language, they usually have at least a high receptive proficiency in Turkish, and they often have already started producing sentences in this language. The immersion in a Dutch early childhood program is experienced by these children as an introduction to a new language environment, with a language that is still mostly unknown to them. Studies on successive bilingualism, however, generally deal with children above age four.

In order to gain insight into this type of 'second language acquisition' – since that is how it is experienced by the children, as well as by their parents and teachers – in early childhood, two longitudinal multiple case-study projects were carried out in the 1990s and early 2000s. Both research projects studied

DOI 10.1515/9781501505492-008

two- and three-year-old Turkish-Dutch children and recorded their speech, both Dutch and Turkish, over a period of a year or more.

In this chapter, a specific Dutch language construction in both datasets is investigated, i.e. the *object-naming construction*. Children often name objects (e.g. *this is a cat*), and the construction is interesting because it poses several 'learning problems' to the Turkish child who has to learn it. First, the child has to learn to use the Dutch copula, which might be difficult because Turkish has no copula. Second, the child has to acquire the distribution of Dutch demonstrative pronouns specific to this particular construction, while its Turkish equivalent accepts all available demonstrative pronouns. Because of these issues, it remains to be seen whether Turkish children follow the same developmental path as monolingual children learning Dutch, who also need time to acquire the object-naming construction.

We believe that tracking the development of this construction in the speech of the Turkish-Dutch bilingual children provides valuable insight into the process of second language acquisition in early childhood. We employ a usage-based approach to language acquisition as a framework for our study, because it seems well fitted for researching such a specific construction (see Section 2). Especially the work of Wray (2002, 2008a, 2008b) is relevant for interpreting the results within a usage-based model of second language acquisition at different ages.

In this chapter, we will first discuss usage-based approaches to second language acquisition in early childhood (compare Tribushinina and Gillis, *this volume*). We then expand on the Dutch object-naming construction and its acquisition by monolingual Dutch children, before describing the background and results of the present study.

2 Usage-based approaches to early child second language acquisition

Usage-based approaches to language learning claim that the cognitive mechanisms underlying first and second language acquisition are the same (e.g. Ellis 2008; Tomasello 2003). This claim is relevant to us, because it fundamentally absolves us from the task to decide whether the Turkish-Dutch toddlers in our study are learning Dutch as a first or a second language. The claim, however, is not uncontroversial. Researchers within the Chomskyan generative paradigm of linguistics state that the two processes are rather different. In their view, first language acquisition is driven by a language acquisition device which makes use of an innate universal grammar. These innate processes are not, or only partially, available to the adult second language learners (White 1990). In the study of child second language acquisition, widely discussed issues are at what age a child must start learning a second language for it to be the same as first language acquisition (De Houwer 1990; McLaughlin 1978; Meisel 2004) and whether there is a critical age for learning a second language successfully (Hyltenstam and Abrahamsson 2003).

The Chomskyan generative paradigm answers these questions mainly by investigating linguistic phenomena that are close to the so-called core grammar of language. In order to explain more peripheral phenomena, such as vocabulary or less abstract constructions, they often admit that general cognitive learning mechanisms should be taken into account. In usage-based theories these are the only mechanisms at work in language acquisition, since they do not accept any language-specific mechanisms.

Usage-based theories of language thus reject the concept of an innate language acquisition device, as well as the existence of a critical period. They claim that the processes that are at work in the learning, storage, and use of a first language are also employed for languages learned later in life. Like first language grammars, grammars of second languages can be described as inventories of constructions built up from experience with that language. The structure of these inventories is formed by entrenchment, categorization, and abstraction of stored conventional expressions (Ellis 2002, 2008).

How do usage-based theories then account for the differences between first and second language acquisition? We will briefly discuss two explanation models: learned attention, which results in what is known as first language transfer, and age-related changes in cognitive learning styles.

2.1 Learned attention

According to Ellis (2008), the main difference between first and second language acquisition is that second language speakers have, through their experience in the first language, learned to 'hear' specific things in the input, and to disregard others. This *learned attention*, as he calls it, plays a role in memory and in learning in general. In language acquisition, its effect is that patterns that are entrenched in the first language may determine how a speaker of that language categorizes the input received in a second language. A well-known example in language learning is the difficulty Japanese learners have with the English phonemes /r/ and /l/, as these sounds are not distinct phonemes in their first language. It is difficult to 'break up' a category that has become highly entrenched in the first language. Important in Ellis' (2008) usage-based account is that learned attention is a general learning process. First and second language acquisition are still 'similar'. The difference is found in the fact that in second language acquisition there is a stronger, already built-up structured inventory of constructions in the first language, which influences the learning process (see Tribushinina, Valcheva, and Gagarina, *this volume*).

2.2 Cognitive learning styles and age

Learned attention because of the first language is not the only component of general cognition that makes second language learning different. Second language learners are almost per definition older than first language learners. General cognitive mechanisms change with age and may lead to different cognitive learning styles.

Bialystok and Hakuta (1999) present empirical evidence from studies in lifespan cognition demonstrating that general cognitive mechanisms become less efficient or effective with age. In word learning tasks, older learners are more sensitive to timing factors in the presentation of the task material and need longer intervals than younger learners to recall new words. Older learners are also more cautious in giving an answer if they are not sure whether it is correct. In addition, they need more trials to learn lists of associations. Finally, older learners are less proficient at remembering details; they often only recall the gist of a story. Unlike adults, children are still in the process of building and changing categories in their linguistic system, which makes it easier for them to make a new category on the basis of new experiences. The difference is thus one of learning style. According to Bialystok and Hakuta (1999), the change of learning style in adult age is not irreversible: adults may 'overcome' their rigor and become (almost) nativelike in a second language.

According to Wray (2002, 2008a, 2008b), a major difference between adults learning a second language and children learning a first language is that adults analyze the input they receive more and into smaller lexical units. Her model concurs with the usage-based assumption of redundancy: linguistic structures are not necessarily represented as either a rule or a fixed expression, but often as both (see also Mos, *this volume;* Tribushinina and Gillis, *this volume*). Using longer expressions as fixed units has the advantage of a smaller processing load and therefore higher fluency, and of often being more conventional in the choice of words. Adult native speakers of a language generally prefer using common and idiomatic expressions, even though they are able to formulate their thoughts in other ways as well.

Children learning a first language are initially holistic learners. They adhere as much as possible to rather large expressions they hear in the input and only analyze the smaller parts of those expressions when the input provides clear evidence of their existence. Adult second language learners, in contrast, have an analytic learning style. They analyze the input in smaller units and then need additional rules to combine them. Wray (2002, 2008a) does not discuss the nature of these additional rules.

Wray (2002) claims that the difference between holistic versus analytic learning styles in first and (later) second language acquisition can also be observed in second language learners of different ages. Teenage and adult learners tend to focus on learning words and ways of combining words into phrases. Young children, in contrast, initially acquire mostly phrases, and only analyze them into smaller units when the need arises. The transition from holistic to analytical learning starts at about age five or six. It coincides with and is strengthened by the acquisition of literacy with its focus on words as basic units of language.

In this chapter, we use this framework of age-related learning styles to explain our findings on the development of object-naming constructions in Dutch by young speakers of Turkish. The data seem to suggest that young children may also use analytical learning styles if they are pressed by a lack of language input to use holistic learning styles. In the following section, we will present the Dutch object-naming construction under investigation.

3 The object-naming construction

3.1 Object naming in Dutch

Object naming is the communicative act of informing an interlocutor about the name or label for an object or group of objects. The term *object* here refers to concrete persons, animals, or things. Examples of object-naming utterances are *this is grandpa* (pointing at a photograph), *those are mice* (pointing at a picture), or *that is a fork* (answering the question *what is that?*). English and Dutch use copulas in object-naming constructions, but many languages, including Turkish, use juxtaposition (e.g. *bu çatal* 'this fork: this is a fork'). Stassen (1997) uses the term *identity statements* and explains the meaning of object-naming constructions on the basis of a metaphor of labels for files in an archive.[1]

---

1 Stassen's *identity statements* (1997) include what in this chapter are called object-naming constructions, as well as equational identity statements, such as *the Morning Star is the Evening Star*. Equational statements are absent in the child language data studied here.

In interactions with children, adults often name objects to teach them new words. In the case of bilingual children, this may include situations in which a child already has a 'file' with a label in one language, and an adult teaches him the label in the other language. Children, on the other hand, often name objects to show they know labels for words, even though they are usually aware of the fact that this is not new information for the adult interlocutor.

The most frequent object-naming construction in adult Dutch is [$_{neuter}$DEMpro COP NP]. Nap-Kolhoff (2010) analyses the use of Dutch object-naming constructions in adult speech data. The construction contains a demonstrative pronoun, which refers deictically to the object being named. An interesting 'twist' of the Dutch construction is that only the two neuter demonstrative pronouns are used in this construction: *dit* 'this' or *dat* 'that'. The meaning difference between *dit* (and *deze*) and *dat* (and *die*) is related to actual or discourse related proximity.

It is remarkable that only neuter demonstratives appear in the construction, because neuter as well as non-neuter demonstrative pronouns (*die* or *deze*) can occur in similar constructions expressing property (e.g. *dit/dat/deze/die is mooi* 'this/that is beautiful') or possession (e.g. *dit/dat/deze/die is van mij* 'this/that is of me [mine]') (Donaldson 1997). Although the latter two constructions look very similar to the object-naming construction, the main difference is that the referent to which the demonstrative pronoun refers and the 'label' it has, are already known. When the label is known, the gender of the referent is known as well, and the demonstrative pronouns can be used in forms that correspond to that gender. In object-naming constructions, however, the label of the referent is the subject of discussion, and the demonstrative pronoun takes its neutral form: *dit* or *dat*.

Another part of the construction is the copula in the third-person form. The inflectional paradigm of the copula is highly irregular. In the present tense indicative, the copula form *is* 'is' is used, whereas with plural referents the form *zijn* 'are' appears. The past tense forms are *was* 'was' for the singular and *waren* 'were' for the plural, respectively. In the object-naming construction, the singular present tense for *is* is most frequent, followed by *zijn* 'are' in cases of plural reference. The past tense form is highly infrequent and restricted to specific pragmatic contexts, since the objects that are named are typically present at the time of conversation.

The last element of the object-naming construction is the name for the object itself. As the examples presented so far show, the object is usually expressed by a noun indicating the name and the indefinite article *een* 'a'. The exact structure of this part of the object-naming construction is not analyzed in detail in the analyses presented here. The main reason is that our bilingual children have not yet acquired the use of articles in their Dutch during the period of data collection (i.e. until age 3;6–4;0).

A final matter to be considered is the word order of the components of the object-naming construction. Characteristic of copular constructions is that the order can be reversed, without changing the propositional meaning. In the case of the object-naming construction, this reversal results in [NP COP $_{neuter}$DEMpro]. Indeed, utterances such as *een paard is dat* 'a horse is that' are found in adult speech data. From a Construction Grammar perspective, it is not expected that the meaning of the 'label-first' order and the 'normal' order are identical, because a difference in form usually implies a difference in meaning (Croft, 2001). An analysis of label-first constructions in adult speech shows their function can be defined as giving additional focus on the label. Additional focus can for example be given if the child interlocutor has used another (often incorrect) label before, or if the adult realizes the label was difficult for or new to the child. The label-first construction is not further examined in this study. There are not enough instances of this construction in the child dataset, although it seems clear that the children do not give the meaning of additional focus on the label to this word order.

3.2 Object naming in child language

Object naming is one of the first functions for which children use multiword utterances (Brown 1973; Tomasello 2003). Schaerlaekens (1973: 92, 167) attested the utterances in (1) in the speech of two children learning Flemish-Dutch as a first language.[2]

(1) a. *dat ananas*   (Diederik)
       that pineapple
       'that is a pineapple'

   b. *dat bolleke*   (Diederik)
       that candy
       'that is a candy'

   c. *dat auto*   (Diederik)
       that car
       'that is a car'

---

2 From the context it was clear that the children were using an object-naming construction (although without copula), rather than producing one deictic word phrase (e.g. *[ik wil] dat paardje* '[I want] that horse').

    d.   *dat*   *paardje*   (Arnold)
           that   horse-DIM
           'that is a horse'

    e.   *dat*   *bal*   (Arnold)
           that   ball
           'that is a ball'

The absence of a copula in these child utterances constitutes a deviation from the adult norm. The utterances produced by the children can be characterized as *pivot schemas* (Braine and Bowerman 1976; Tomasello 2003). Pivot schemas are word combinations in which one word is fixed (the 'pivot'), usually in a specific position. This fixed word determines the speech-act function of the utterance (Tomasello 2003), in this case object naming. The data in (1) can be characterized as instances of the pivot schema [*dat* X]. Similar pivot schemas are found in the early word combinations of children acquiring other languages, such as English [*that* X], Swedish [*den* X], and Hebrew [*ze* X] (Braine and Bowerman 1976). These pivot schemas are not only used for object naming, but they sometimes also express possessive relationships, as in *this Nina* 'this is Nina's' (boy Jonathan, in Braine and Bowerman 1976: 34). However, object naming is the most frequent function encountered in our different data sets.

In order to obtain more information about the acquisition of the object-naming construction by monolingual Dutch children, Nap-Kolhoff (2010) studied the CHILDES corpus (MacWhinney 2000). The construction was tracked in transcripts for three children between age 1;6–2;0 and 3;4–4;0: Sarah in the Van Kampen corpus (Van Kampen 1994; Van Kampen and Corver 2004) and Matthijs and Josse in the Groningen corpus (Wijnen and Verrips 1998).

As observed before, and as illustrated in (1), the earliest object-naming constructions contain no copula. From the beginning, all three children use different demonstrative pronouns in the construction. In about half of the cases they use the neuter forms *dit* or *dat*, which are correct in the target construction. In the other cases they used *deze* or *die*. One child also used a fixed construction in this first stage, a construction with unanalyzed parts. Josse produced *is dat* in an object-naming construction, while he never used the copula *is* in any other utterance. We assume he had not yet acquired this form of the copula, but used it as a fixed expression in ...*is dat*.

In the second stage, the children used object-naming constructions both with and without a copula. For two children it could be observed that they initially only used the copula *is* in the object-naming construction, and later added other forms (plural and past tense). As soon as children used the copula in the object-naming construction, they also used the correct (neuter) form of the demonstrative.

In the final stage, the children only used the target construction with a copula form. Apart from an incidental use of the non-neuter demonstrative pronoun, the children generally used the correct neuter form in the object-naming construction.

The monolingual Dutch children enter the first stage between age 1;6 and 2;1, and the second stage three to five months later. The stage in which they use both kinds of constructions lasts six to eleven months. From age 2;6–2;8 onwards, the monolingual children in the dataset only use constructions with a copula.

A usage-based approach to language learning accounts well for the developmental pattern observed here. Initially, children 'make do' with the first words they have acquired: juxtaposing a demonstrative pronoun and words for the object they want to name. Then they start noticing the target construction in the language input they receive. They try to align their productions to what they hear in their input, and thus simultaneously pick up the copula as well as the correct demonstrative pronouns. Since usage-based approaches see language learning as building a language inventory, it is also not surprising that the two different constructions appear alongside each other for some time. Redundancy is an important characteristic of a person's language inventory, and for quite some time both constructions can be used, until finally the correct construction is firmly established.

4 The present study

The aim of the present study is to gain more insight into the process of the acquisition of a second language at a young age. In order to do so, we have investigated the object-naming construction in the speech production of 2- and 3-year-old Turkish children learning Dutch. In Section 3.2 we have shown that monolingual Dutch children follow a developmental path in the acquisition of the construction: they start out with utterances like *die poes* 'that cat' (meaning 'that is a cat'), before learning the target construction with a copula and only neuter demonstrative pronouns (*dit, dat*, as in *dat is een poes* 'that is a cat'). During this process there is a phase in which they use both constructions.

In this section we will formulate five hypotheses with respect to the acquisition of the object-naming construction by the Turkish children.

4.1 Second language acquisition = first language acquisition

Following a usage-based perspective, we take the position that first and second language acquisition are essentially the same. We therefore expect the Turkish children to follow the same developmental path in their acquisition of Dutch as the monolingual Dutch children we described in Section 3.2.

H1   *The bilingual children follow the same developmental path as monolingual Dutch children.*

This first hypothesis could be formulated on the basis of many theories of language acquisition, because linguists generally believe that second language acquisition before the age of four is the same as first language acquisition. However, from a usage-based perspective, we do not expect the first hypothesis to fully hold. As we discussed before, there are two cognitive mechanisms in language learning that make second language acquisition different from first language acquisition: learned attention and cognitive learning style. Both mechanisms, however, in general become stronger when a learner is older. We do not know yet to what extent we expect their influence in the acquisition process of the very young children in the present study.

Usage-based models of language acquisition state that children learn a language from the language input they receive. Since the Turkish children in this study receive much lower amounts of Dutch language input than the aforementioned monolingual Dutch children do, we expect them to need much more time to learn the construction. We therefore also formulate the following hypothesis:

H2   *The pace of acquisition of the bilingual children is slower in comparison to monolingual Dutch children, and is related to the amount of Dutch language input the children receive.*

4.2 Learned attention (L1 transfer)

Because of learned attention, a learner may be inclined to notice some elements in a new language quicker than others. Let us consider to what extent the Turkish object-naming construction differs from the Dutch one.

The Turkish language knows three demonstrative pronouns: *bu, şu,* and *o.* The difference in meaning is related to differences in real or discourse-related distance, with *bu* being closest (cf. 'this'), *o* most distant (cf. 'that'), and *şu* in between. All three demonstrative pronouns can be used in the object-naming construction. Turkish has no copula in simple utterances like the object-naming construction. A translation of 'that is a cat' would thus be *o kedi* 'that cat'.

If the first language of the Turkish children is affecting their acquisition of Dutch, we expect them to have more difficulty than monolingual Dutch children in finding out that only neuter demonstrative pronouns can be used in the Dutch construction, because they are already using a language in which all demonstrative pronouns can be used in the object-naming construction. In addition, we expect them to have more difficulty learning the copula, because of its absence in their first language. These expectations lead to the following hypotheses:

H3   *The bilingual children have more difficulty than monolingual Dutch children in acquiring that only neuter demonstratives are used in the object-naming construction.*

H4   *The bilingual children have more difficulty than monolingual Dutch children in acquiring the copula in the construction.*

From the Turkish language data from the children in the present study, we know that they all already produce the Turkish object-naming construction at the outset of the data collection. However, since 2- or 3-year-old children are still in the process of acquiring the basics of their first language, they may not have that strong a learned attention yet.

4.3 Cognitive learning style

Wray (2008b) explains that when learners grow older, their cognitive learning style changes. In general, younger learners are more holistic learners, who, when learning a language, focus on longer, more formulaic expressions in the input. Older learners try to analyze the language input into smaller units. This means that younger learners are often more target-like in their productions, while older learners need more time to 'unlearn' the non-target-like expressions they formed before. Wray gives the age range of 8–12 as an indication for the transition from holistic to analytic learning. We thus expect the child learners in our study to still be using a holistic learning style.

In Section 3.2 we saw that when monolingual children learn the Dutch object-naming construction, the use of the copula and the neuter demonstrative pronoun are acquired simultaneously. It can be argued that that is the result of a holistic learning style: rather than learning the different parts of the construction at different times, they learn the construction as a whole, once they pick it up from the input. This leads to the fifth and final hypothesis:

H5   *Like monolingual Dutch children, the bilingual children learn the correct form of the demonstrative simultaneously with the copula in the construction.*

5 Method

In order to explore the hypotheses, we investigated speech samples of seven Turkish children learning Dutch between the age of two and three. In this section, we first describe the data and the background of the informants. Next, we explain the procedures used for finding utterances with object-naming constructions in the datasets and assigning a level of schematicity to them.

5.1 Informants and data

Data for three bilingual Turkish-Dutch boys, Mehmet, Batuhan, and Yunus, are available in the Nap-Kolhoff bilingual corpus (Nap-Kolhoff 2010). All three children have one parent who is a second (or "intermediate", Backus 1996) generation Turkish immigrant to the Netherlands, and one parent who is of the first generation and immigrated at about the age of 18–19 for marriage. From the age of 2;0 onwards, all children visited a Dutch pre-school playgroup for 11–12 hours per week, where they received their main Dutch language input. Data were collected between age 2;3–2;7 to 3;9–4;0.

Additional data for four bilingual Turkish-Dutch girls, Selma, Berrin, Filiz, and Şükran, are available in the Van der Heijden bilingual corpus (Van der Heijden 1999). They were born in the early 1990s and their parents were all first generation immigrants. Selma attended a daycare center for 40 hours per week. Filiz attended a daycare center for 24 hours per week until the age of 2;0 and for 40 hours per week after that age. Berrin started visiting a pre-school playgroup at age 3;4 for about seven hours per week. Şükran did not attend a pre-school center at all. Both Berrin and Şükran received Dutch language input at home from their older siblings. Data were collected between age 2;1–2;2 to 3;6.

All data were collected in spontaneous speech settings in the homes of the children and/or the pre-school centers they attended. All recordings were transcribed in CHAT format (MacWhinney 2000). The total corpus contains 15,479 Dutch child utterances.

5.2 Data analysis: level of schematicity

The analyses in this chapter are based on an inventory of all object-naming utterances of the form [DEMpro (COP) (Adverb) NP] in the child data.[3] By reading

---

3 DEMpro = demonstrative pronoun; COP = copula; NP = nominal phrase. The elements between brackets may have been absent in the utterance. The adverb is disregarded in the analyses presented here.

the transcripts and taking into account the context of these utterances, it was possible in all cases to establish that they were indeed intended for object naming. If we report an utterance such as *die poes* 'that cat', it was clear from the context that it actually meant 'that is a cat'. In total, 253 such utterances were found.

The next step was to establish the level of schematicity of the utterances in the list. The concept *level of schematicity* is derived from the notion that constructions are acquired through schematization on the basis of specific utterances in specific contexts. Schematization can occur when learners notice commonalities between utterances in the input and between the specific contexts in which those utterances are used. For example, a child who knows the words *poes* 'cat' and *hond* 'dog' can infer that *dat is een* X 'that is an X' is an object-naming construction when she hears (and understands) the utterances *dat is een poes* 'that is a cat' and *dat is een hond* 'that is a dog' in contexts in which an adult names animals. This construction can become more abstract when the child starts noticing differences with similar kinds of utterances, such as the plural *dat zijn poezen* 'those are cats' (*dat* COP X).

When looking at actual productions of children, the schematicity of the expressions has to be inferred from the variation in similar utterances. For example, if a child spontaneously produces *dat is een poes* 'that is a cat' and *dat is een hond* 'that is a dog', it can be inferred that she is employing the schematic construction [*dat is een* X]. Alternatively, if no other instances of the demonstrative pronoun *dat* and/or the copula *is* are found, the unit *dat+is* can be considered formulaic or fixed. Table 1 shows the guidelines we used for establishing the level of schematicity of the demonstrative pronouns in children's object-naming constructions (ONCs).

Table 1: Level of schematicity for demonstrative pronouns.

dit+	Fixed specific demonstrative pronoun, not used outside ONCs
dit	Specific demonstrative pronoun, also used outside ONCs
DEMpro-(non-)neuter	Both (non-)neuter demonstrative pronouns, also used outside ONCs
DEMpro	At least three demonstrative pronouns, also used outside ONCs

Table 2 shows the guidelines for the copula. In most cases, KWAL and COMBO commands in the CLAN software program (MacWhinney 2000) could be used for finding all utterances containing specific words and their contexts.[4]

---

4 See http://childes.psy.cmu.edu/ for the free software.

Table 2: Level of schematicity for copula forms.

+*is*	Fixed *is*, not used outside ONCs
is	*Is*, also used outside ONCs
COP	At least two forms of the copula, also outside ONCs

It is important to understand that in order to determine the level of schematicity, not only the 253 object-naming constructions were taken into consideration, but all utterances the child produced. Even if children like Selma and Berrin produced only nine object-naming construction in the dataset, the analyses of these utterances are still based on a comparison with the other utterances of these children in the dataset. Since both demonstrative pronouns as well as copula forms tend to occur frequently in the recordings once a child starts using them, this seems to be a valid way of establishing the level of schematicity in these cases.

Of course, it cannot be determined whether the child actually used the more abstract construction, as cognitive linguistics assumes that speakers have constructions available at several levels of abstraction (Langacker 2008; Tomasello 2003). For child data, however, it can at least be concluded that children have the data available in their productive repertoire to be able to reach a specific level of abstraction. Whether they actually use it, is another question.

6 Results

The Dutch object-naming constructions produced by the seven Turkish children can be divided into three groups: constructions without a copula, constructions with a fixed or formulaic element, and constructions with a copula. We will discuss the results for each group of object-naming constructions and compare them to what we presented before about the three monolingual Dutch children. We will finish this section with findings about the developmental path the Turkish children take in the acquisition of the Dutch object-naming construction.

6.1 Constructions without a copula

Similar to the monolingual Dutch children in the first stage of the acquisition of the construction, the Turkish children produce constructions of the form *[DEMpro X]. Often, the Turkish children have a strong preference for a specific demonstrative pronoun. Their object-naming construction are better described as *[dieX] or *[deze X]. All seven children use such constructions without a copula (see Table 3).

Table 3: Frequency of the children's object-naming constructions without a copula.

Child	*[die X]	*[deze X]	*[non-neuterDEMpro X]	*[DEMpro X]
Mehmet	48	–	–	2
Batuhan	136	–	–	–
Yunus	9	4		–
Şükran	7	–	–	–
Filiz	1	10	4	–
Berrin	2	8	–	–
Selma	–	–	–	3

However, two remarkable differences are observed between these Turkish children and the monolingual Dutch children presented before. First, the monolingual children generally use several different demonstrative pronouns in this construction, whereas the Turkish children more often stick to a specific demonstrative pronoun (mostly *die* and sometimes *deze*).

A second difference is found in the specific demonstrative pronouns the children use. Figure 1 presents an overview of the specific demonstrative pronouns used in the constructions without a copula by the monolingual and bilingual children. On the one hand, we observe that on average the monolingual children use the four demonstrative pronouns more or less equally often. On the other hand, the bilingual children have a strong preference for *die* (89%). *Deze* occurs in 9% of their object-naming constructions without a copula and *dit* and *dat* hardly ever at all.

The only exception to this picture is the second language learner Selma, whose profile resembles that of the first language learners. In fact, Selma is the second language learner who started learning Dutch at a very young age and received relatively high amounts of Dutch language input.

The differences between the bilingual and monolingual children are significant for all instances of *die, dit,* and *dat* (Fisher's Exact Test; $p < .001$). The differences for *deze* are also significant if all bilingual and all monolingual children are taken together ($p < .001$), but the statistical significance disappears if Batuhan or Filiz are excluded. The differences for *deze* can thus be attributed to the individual usage patterns for these two children, while the differences for the other demonstrative pronouns hold for the bilingual versus the monolingual groups as a whole.

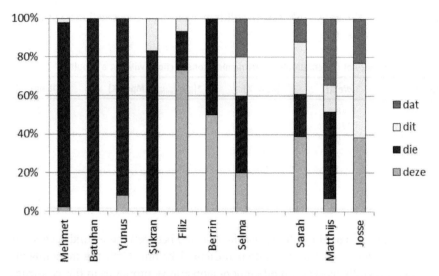

Figure 1: Frequency of use of demonstrative pronouns in object-naming constructions without a copula, in bilingual Turkish-Dutch and monolingual Dutch children (on the right: Sarah, Matthijs, and Josse).

6.2 Constructions with a fixed element

The second group of object-naming constructions are those containing a fixed or formulaic element. Such constructions appeared only sporadically in the data (see Table 4). They are produced by three bilingual children. In all formulaic constructions, the fixed unit contains the copula *is*, which the children did not use at that point of their development in other contexts, and appears to be restricted to the object-naming construction. In the monolingual data, one instance of a construction with a fixed element was found ([X *is+dat*] for Josse, see Nap-Kolhoff 2010).

Table 4: Frequency of object-naming constructions with a fixed element.

Child	Construction	Frequency
Mehmet	[*dat+is* X]	2
	[*dit+is* X]	2
Batuhan	[X *is+dat*]	1
Berrin	[*het+is deze* X]	1

6.3 Constructions with a copula

The third group of constructions are those that contain a copula and are used by children who also use the copula in utterances and constructions of other kinds (see Table 5). Of the Turkish children, only Mehmet, Filiz, and Selma produce those constructions. They only use the copula *is*, and never its plural form *zijn* or past tense *was*.

The monolingual children presented before went through a stage in which they used only *is*, but later started using other forms of the copula before. Apparently, the Turkish children never reached this stage during the period of data collection.

Moreover, when the monolingual children started producing the object-naming construction with a copula, they simultaneously started using the correct neuter demonstrative pronoun. This is not the case with the Turkish children. Mehmet only uses non-neuter *die* in his construction with a copula, and Selma both *die* and neuter *dit*. Berrin produces two constructions with a copula, and both with a correct demonstrative (*dit*).

Table 5: Frequency of object-naming constructions with a copula.

Construction	Mehmet	Filiz	Selma
*[die is X]	6	–	3
*[deze is X]	–	–	–
[dit is X]	–	2	3
[dat is X]	–	–	–
*[non-neuter DEMpro is X]	–	–	–
[neuter DEMpro is X]	–	–	–
[neuter DEMpro COP X]	–	–	–

6.4 Developmental patterns

The Turkish children enter the first stage with only constructions without a copula or fixed expressions between age 2;1 and 3;2.[5] The only exception to this general pattern is Selma, who starts out with constructions with a copula. It is not unlikely, however, that she had already been in the first stage before the data collection started. It is also possible that she was in the stage of producing both utterances with and without copulas, but that the utterances without a

---

5 Or possibly earlier, as there are no recordings available before the age of 2;1.

copula did not turn up in the rather sparse amount of data on object-naming constructions available for her.

Four of the bilingual children, Batuhan, Yunus, Berrin, and Şükran, remain in the first stage of only using object-naming constructions without a copula or with the copula only in fixed expressions during the whole period of observation. Three children, Mehmet, Filiz, and Selma, reach the second stage in which they use both constructions with and without a copula. Only Mehmet reaches the third stage of only using object-naming construction with a copula, during the last recording at age 4;0.

7 Discussion and conclusion

This chapter investigated the acquisition of the Dutch object-naming construction by young Turkish children receiving different, but generally low, amounts of Dutch language input. We can summarize the results as follows. In general, the Turkish children follow the same developmental path as monolingual Dutch children. Like the monolingual children, the Turkish children in this study start with constructions without a copula in which a demonstrative pronoun and the 'name' are juxtaposed. For both groups of children a period follows in which both a construction with a copula is used and the former construction without a copula. In the final stage, they only use constructions with a copula. Not all of the Turkish children reach this stage during the period of data collection.

However, some differences can be observed as well. Among the Turkish children we encountered more constructions with formulaic elements (e.g. with unanalyzed *dat+is*). In their constructions without a copula, they had a preference for one or two demonstrative pronouns, in none of the cases the neuter forms of the target construction. Even in their constructions with a copula, they kept this preference for specific demonstrative pronouns. Unlike the monolingual Dutch children, they did not show the simultaneous acquisition of the copula and the correct neuter demonstrative pronoun.

We formulated five hypotheses about the process of acquisition based on a usage-based approach to language learning. In this section we will discuss the hypotheses in light of the presented results.

H1 *The bilingual children follow the same developmental path as monolingual Dutch children.*

Although the general path of development is the same, we cannot fully confirm this hypothesis, since we also found differences in the acquisition process. Do we have to conclude that second language acquisition is basically different from first language acquisition? We already argued that from a usage-based perspective, we should not be surprised to find differences, although we were not sure whether we would find them in children of this young age. We will take a closer look at these differences in the discussion of hypotheses 3–5.

H2 *The pace of acquisition of the bilingual children is slower in comparison to monolingual Dutch children and related to the amount of Dutch language input the children receive.*

The pace of acquisition of the Turkish children is indeed slower than that of the monolinguals. The Turkish children appear to need much more time before they start using the copula in (some) object-naming constructions. Only three out of seven bilingual children started using the copula at all during the period of data collection. A (rough) calculation of the amount of Dutch language input the children received shows that this is not surprising. If monolingual children receive 70 hours of language input per week, as Tomasello and Stahl (2004) estimate, and they need 3–5 months to leave the first stage, they would need about 900–1500 hours of language input. A child like Batuhan received Dutch language input mainly during his visits to the pre-school playgroup, which amounts to about 12 hours (distributed over 4 days) of Dutch language input per week. Hence, he would need about 18–30 months before receiving enough language input to enter the second stage. He only visited the playgroup for 24 months and did not leave the first stage. Mehmet visited the same playgroup and entered the second stage after 23 months. These rough estimations indicate that the slower pace of acquisition of the Dutch object-naming construction may very well be related to the low amounts of Dutch language input the children received. Of course, we would need more information about the exact quantity as well as quality of language input to draw more definite conclusions. The first indications in this study, however, seem to suggest that we can confirm the hypothesis that the amount of language input is one of the determiners of the language acquisition process.

H3 *The bilingual children have more difficulty than monolingual Dutch children in acquiring that only neuter demonstratives are used in the object-naming construction.*

The Turkish children indeed have more difficulty in acquiring that only neuter demonstratives are used in the object-naming construction. As a matter of fact, all children except Selma use the non-neuter demonstrative pronouns (especially *die*) in overwhelming majority, both in constructions with and without a copula.

The hypothesis was formulated to test the potential influence from the first language. In their Turkish object-naming constructions, *o* is the most frequently used demonstrative, which is the closest translation of Dutch *die*. Hence, it is indeed possible that the children directly 'translate' their Turkish constructions into Dutch. Although the children are still young, the already acquired Turkish construction seems to lead to patterns of learned attention in the acquisition of a second language.

H4   The bilingual children have more difficulty than monolingual Dutch children in acquiring the copula in the construction.

We are not able to confirm this hypothesis on the basis of the data presented here. The Turkish children do start with object-naming constructions without a copula, but so do monolingual Dutch children. The Turkish children stay in this stage of language acquisition for a much longer period of time, but we already discussed before (see Hypothesis 2) that this seems to be related to the low amounts of Dutch language input they receive.

H5   The bilingual children learn, like monolingual Dutch children, the correct form of the demonstrative simultaneously with the copula in the construction.

This hypothesis is falsified by the results of the present study. Whereas monolingual Dutch children simultaneously acquire the copula form in the construction and the correct choice of neuter demonstrative pronouns, this is not the case with the Turkish children. Not all Turkish children acquire the copula during the period of observation, but if they do, they still keep on using non-neuter demonstratives.

Hypothesis 5 was formulated to test whether the young second language learners take a holistic cognitive learning style like their monolingual Dutch peers. The data seem to suggest the possibility that the Turkish children in this study were using more analytical cognitive learning styles.

In sum, it seems to be the case that several factors play a role in the acquisition of Dutch object-naming constructions by Turkish immigrant children learning Dutch at ages two and three. They are presumably influenced by factors determining both first and second language acquisition, such as input frequency and intensity of Dutch language input. Differences with first language acquisition by monolingual Dutch children are partly due to learned attention: cross-linguistic influence from their first language. Moreover, they might be employing a less holistic (Wray 2008b) approach to the target language than their monolingual Dutch peers. Although the data presented in this chapter do not provide conclusive evidence on this matter, it would be an interesting issue to pursue in further research, because this difference in language learning styles is usually said to appear at a much later age (ca. age 8–12; Wray 2008b). It is very well possible that at a more fine-grained level, such as the constructions investigated in this chapter, differences are visible at a much younger age. Especially if children receive only low amounts of input, they might feel 'forced' to search for other ways to categorize their newly learned linguistic knowledge. In addition, it is a difference that is probably only visible during a specific stage in the process of acquisition, as most (or even all) of the bilingual children will eventually acquire Dutch at a native-like level, including full use of target-like object-naming constructions.

References

Backus, Ad. 1996. *Two in One: Bilingual Speech of Turkish Immigrants in the Netherlands.* Tilburg: Tilburg University Press.

Bialystok, Ellen, and Kenji Hakuta. 1999. Confounded age: Linguistic and cognitive factors in age differences for second language acquisition. In *Second Language Acquisition and the Critical Period Hypothesis,* David Birdsong (ed.), 161–181. Mahwah, NJ: Lawrence Erlbaum.

Braine, Martin D.S., and Melissa Bowerman. 1976. *Children's First Word Combinations.* Chicago: University of Chicago Press.

Brown, Roger. 1973. *A First Language: The Early Stages.* Cambridge, MA: Harvard University Press.

Croft, William. 2001. *Radical Construction Grammar: Syntactic Theory in Typological Perspective.* Oxford: Oxford University Press.

De Houwer, Annick. 1990. *The Acquisition of Two Languages From Birth: A Case Study.* Cambridge: Cambridge University Press.

Donaldson, Bruce C. 1997. *Dutch: A Comprehensive Grammar.* New York: Routledge.

Ellis, Nick C. 2002. Frequency effects in language processing: A review with implications for theories of implicit and explicit language acquisition. *Studies in Second Language Acquisition* 24 (2), 143–188.

Ellis, Nick C. 2008. Usage-based an form-focused language acquisition: The associative learning of constructions, learned attention, and the limited L2 endstate. In *Handbook of Cognitive Linguistics and Second Language Acquisition,* Peter Robinson, and Nick C. Ellis (eds.), 372–405. New York: Routledge.

Extra, Guus, Rian Aarts, Tim van der Avoird, Peter Broeder, and Kutlay Yağmur. 2002. *De Andere Talen van Nederland Thuis en Op School* [The Other Languages of the Netherlands at Home and at School]. Bussum: Coutinho.

Hyltenstam, Kenneth, and Niclas Abrahamsson. 2003. Maturational constraints in SLA. In *The Handbook of Second Language Acquisition,* Catherine J. Doughty, and Michael H. Long (eds.), 539–588. Malden, MA: Blackwell.

Langacker, Ronald W. 2008. *Cognitive Grammar: A Basic Introduction.* New York: Oxford University Press.

MacWhinney, Brian. 2000. *The CHILDES Project: Tools For Analyzing Talk*. 3rd ed. Mahwah, NJ: Lawrence Erlbaum.

McLaughlin, Barry. 1978. *Second-Language Acquisition in Childhood*. Hillsdale, NJ: Lawrence Erlbaum.

Meisel, Jürgen M. 2004. The bilingual child. In *The Handbook of Bilingualism*, Tej K. Bhatia, and Williams C. Ritchie (eds.), 91–113. Oxford: Blackwell.

Nap-Kolhoff, Elma. 2010. *Second Language Acquisition in Early Childhood: A Longitudinal Multiple Case Study of Turkish-Dutch Children*. Utrecht: LOT.

Schaerlaekens, Anne M. 1973. *The Two-Word Sentence in Child Language Development: A Study Based on Evidence Provided by Dutch-Speaking Triplets*. The Hague: Mouton.

Stassen, Leon. 1997. *Intransitive Predication*. Oxford: Oxford University Press.

Tomasello, Michael. 2003. *Constructing a Language: A Usage-Based Theory of Language Acquisition*. Cambridge: Harvard University Press.

Tomasello, Michael, and Daniel Stahl. 2004. Sampling children's spontaneous speech: How much is enough? *Journal of Child Language* 31 (1), 101–122.

Van der Heijden, Hanneke. 1999. Word formation processes in young bilingual children. In *Bilingualism and Migration*, Guus Extra, and Ludo Verhoeven (eds.), 123–140. Berlin/New York: Mouton de Gruyter.

Van Kampen, Jacqueline. 1994. The learnability of the left branch condition. In *Linguistics in the Netherlands*, Gertjan Postma, Reineke Bok-Bennema, and Crit Cremers (eds.), 83–94. Amsterdam: John Benjamins.

Van Kampen, Jacqueline, and Norbert Corver. 2004. Diversity of possessor marking in Dutch child language and Dutch dialects. In *Proceedings of the 39th Linguistic Colloquium 2004*, Maurice Vliegen (ed.), 385–398. Berlin: Peter Lang.

White, Lydia. 1990. Second language acquisition and Universal Grammar. *Studies in Second Language Acquisition* 12 (2), 121–133.

Wijnen, Frank, and Maaike Verrips. 1998. The acquisition of Dutch syntax. In *The Acquisition of Dutch*, Steven Gillis, and Annick de Houwer (eds.), 223–229. Amsterdam: John Benjamins.

Wray, Alison. 2002. *Formulaic Language and the Lexicon*. Cambridge: Cambridge University Press.

Wray, Alison. 2008a. *Formulaic Language: Pushing the Boundaries*. Oxford: Oxford University Press.

Wray, Alison. 2008b. The puzzle of language learning: from child's play to 'linguaphobia'. *Language Teaching* 41 (2), 253–271.

Anne Vermeer
8 Acquisition order of connectives in stories of Dutch L1 and L2 children from 4 to 8

1 Introduction

Coherence relations play an important role in the representation of texts in people's minds. They are responsible for the proper connections in discourse between words, segments, clauses and sentences. Generally speaking, two types of coherence relations can be distinguished: referential coherence, expressed by connectives such as *he, her, him* and *those*, relating nominal groups to the same referent; and relational coherence, often expressed by connectives like *and, but, then, until, before, because*, and *while*, relating discourse segments through coherence relations like CAUSE-CONSEQUENCE. This chapter focuses on the emergence of the latter coherence relations. When do children start expressing relational coherence through the use of various additive, temporal and causal connectives?

Within a cognitive theory of coherence relations (Sanders, Spooren, and Noordman 1992, 1993; Spooren and Sanders 2008, summarized in Sanders and Spooren 2009), predictions are made about the order in which coherence relations and their linguistic expressions are acquired. These predictions are based on their increasing cognitive complexity. Experiments show that a categorization into a restricted set of 'cognitive primitives' is valid. In naturalistic data, Evers-Vermeul (2005; Evers-Vermeul and Sanders 2009) investigated three of these cognitive primitives: *Basic Operation* (additive versus causal), *Polarity* (positive versus negative), and *Temporality* (temporal order or not). In each case, the former is assumed to precede the latter in the acquisition process, i.e., additive precedes causal, positive precedes negative, and non-temporal precedes temporal. She did, however, investigate only four connectives (the Dutch counterparts of *and, but, then, because*) in twelve children aged 1;5–5;6, as other (more infrequent and complex connectives) do not yet show up very frequently within that age range. She found evidence for her claims: the causal connective *because* did not appear before the additive, the negative connective *but* did not occur before the positive, and all children came up with *then* only after they had

Anne Vermeer, Tilburg University

DOI 10.1515/9781501505492-009

produced a*nd*. Other and more complex relational connectives were hardly used or not used at all by the children in that age range.

In the current longitudinal study of the development of story telling skills of Dutch monolingual and bilingual children, these claims were further investigated. Over a period of almost four years, at five moments in time, (audio)recordings were made of 93 children aged 4;7 to 8;3 (46 monolinguals and 47 bilinguals), while they were telling the course of events in two picture stories. Their use of various additive, temporal and causal connectives was analyzed qualitatively and quantitatively for positives (*and, because*) as well as negatives (*but, while*). Only correct and creative (i.e., no echo) uses of connectives were taken into account. On the basis of these data it was investigated (1) whether the acquisition order in the emergence of these coherence relations and their linguistic expressions can be explained from their increasing cognitive complexity, (2) whether monolinguals and bilinguals show different patterns, and (3) whether there are differences between boys and girls.

This chapter is structured as follows. In the next section, examples of various connectives in the stories of the children are given. Subsequently, the claims on cognitive complexity and acquisition order are presented in Section 3. In Section 4, the research procedure is explained. The results are presented in Section 5, followed by conclusions and discussion in the last section.

2 Relational coherence

The relation between clauses or sentences can be expressed implicitly or explicitly. Young language learners start off expressing coherence relations implicitly by putting sentences next to each other (juxtaposition), as in example (1). In the examples, t1 to t5 refer to the measuring moments 1 to 5 in this longitudinal study on story telling, and these are followed by the number of the child in question.

(1)   *De kar gaat tegen de boom. Ze vallen allebei. Ach de kar is kapot.*
      Ze huilen allebei. (t5.3201)
      'The cart crashes into the tree. They both fall. Ah the cart is broken.
      They both cry.'

From the description of the story by the child it is clear that there is a relation between the accident of the soap-box (cart) bumping into the tree and the children falling, and also that the broken soap-box is the reason why the children cry.

The listener connects these events in a causal manner on the basis of his knowledge and experience of the world.

However, these relationships are clearer if they are expressed explicitly by connectives and other lexical markers, such as the causal connectives in (2) to (6).

(2) *Ze vallen er vanaf **want** ze botsen tegen een boom* (t1.0214)
     'They fall down **for** they crashed into a tree'

(3) *Hun huilen **omdat** de kar kapot is* (t2.0212)
     'They cry **because** the cart is broken'

(4) ***Doordat** ze tegen een boom aanrijden* (t2.6604)
     '**Because** they crashed into a tree'

(5) ***Daarom** gaat de ballon wegvliegen* (t4.5402)
     '**Therefore** the balloon flies away'

(6) *en pakte 't meisje op **zodat** ze weer op kon staan* (t5.1206)
     'and grabbed the girl **so that** she could stand up again'

Additive connectives such as *and* and *but* in (7) to (10) connect two sentences or clauses without there being an implicational relation, and therefore they express a weaker relation than causal connectives.

(7) *Meisje zit in die kar **en** een jongetje* (t2.0413)
     '(The) girl sits in that cart **and** a boy'

(8) *De vader die kijkte naar de kinderwagen **en** de jongen heeft zo een stang vast* (t4.4003)
     'The father he looked at the baby-buggy **and** the boy is holding a bar'

(9) *En toen was allemaal dat niet stuk, **maar** dit wel* (t1.6505)
     'And then not everything was broken, **but** this was'

(10) *De kinderen wouden in de kinderwagen rijden, **maar** dat kon niet!* (t4.2405)
     'The children wanted to ride in the baby-buggy, **but** that was not possible!'

In the examples of these additive, causal, and temporal connectives, the relations can be positive or negative (the cognitive primitive of *Polarity*, see Introduction), as is the case with *en* 'and' in (7) and *maar* 'but' in (9), which are both additive and non-temporal, but differ in polarity. The same applies to the temporal connectives *toen* 'then' in (11) and *terwijl* 'while' in (13). Temporal connectives explicitly indicate an aspect of time in the events expressed in the stories, as in (11) to (15).

(11) *Toen viel ze ineens **en toen** ging de hand los **en toen** ging de ballon de lucht in* (t2.5804)

'**Then** she fell suddenly **and then** her hand let go **and then** the balloon went into the sky'

(12) *Gingen ze heel hard naar beneden **en daarna** gingen ze naar de boom botsen* (t5.0201)

'They went down very fast **and after that** they crashed into the tree'

(13) ***Terwijl** Tom in de kar zit is Kim hem aan het duwen* (t4.2704)

'**While** Tom is sitting in the cart, Kim is pushing him'

(14) *En ze gingen huilen **totdat** ze waren weer blij* (t5.0806)

'And they were crying **until** they were happy again'

(15) *Dan zegt de meneer: "Uitkijken hoor **voordat** je weer uitglijdt"* (t5.1901)

'Then the man says: "Look out **before** you slip again"'

In all the stories of the children in this dataset, the positive, causal, non-temporal connectives *want* 'for', *omdat* 'because', *doordat* 'as a result' and *daarom* 'therefore' do occur, but their 'negative' counterpart *hoewel* 'however' does not occur even once.

3 Coherence relations in a cognitive perspective

As was indicated in the introduction, the cognitive theory of coherence relations (Sanders et al. 1992, 1993; Spooren and Sanders 2008) makes predictions about the order in which these coherence relations and their linguistic expressions are acquired (cf. Evers-Vermeul and Sanders 2009). These predictions are based on their increasing cognitive complexity. As additives express a weaker relation than causal connectives, additives are supposedly acquired earlier: causal connectives add more information than additives do. Negative relations, too, are cognitively more complex than positive ones, because they deny the relationship between the propositions. So, positive connectives are supposedly acquired before negative ones. Finally, expressing a certain temporal aspect (a specific order of events, or a simultaneity) is cognitively more complex than the absence of an indication of temporality. So, non-temporal connectives are supposedly acquired before temporal ones.

In some aspects, the orders of acquisition mentioned above are in line with those reported in the research of Bloom (1991; Bloom et al. 1980), carried out

among four 3-year-old children: additives were acquired before temporal connectives, causal connectives were next, and adversatives (negative connectives)
were acquired last. However, the uni-dimensional character of this order poses a
problem, as Evers-Vermeul and Sanders (2009) point out. It is for that reason
that Bloom characterizes the successive relations as a cumulative complexity,
defining, for instance, 'causal' as 'additive+temporal'. This fails to offer an
account for non-causal or non-temporal adversatives that are acquired at an
early stage, such as *maar* 'but'. Moreover, even among these four children
Bloom found variation in the order of acquisition that cannot be accounted for
on the basis of the uni-dimensional model used.

A cognitive approach such as that of Sanders and Spooren (Sanders et al.
1992, 1993; Spooren and Sanders 2008) does not capitalize on a fixed order of
acquisition, but rather focuses on an increasing cognitive complexity of various
general conceptual dimensions underlying coherence relations. Thus, their
approach is by definition multidimensional, with each dimension having a
relatively simple and a relatively difficult pole, leaving room for variation in
acquisition. The three dimensions investigated in our longitudinal study are
Basic Operation (additive versus causal relations, the latter being more complex),
Polarity (positive versus negative, the latter being more complex), and *Temporality*
(non-temporal versus temporal order, the latter being more complex). So, in line
with the study of Evers-Vermeul (2005; Evers-Vermeul and Sanders 2009), we
further investigated the claims made by Sanders and Spooren, using the same
three dimensions, but involving more and older children in the research, who
uttered more complex relational connectives. The hypotheses that emerge from
the claims about the assumed cognitive complexity within these three dimensions are indicated schematically in Figure 1 (after Evers-Vermeul and Sanders
2009).

In Figure 1, the three dimensions of cognitive primitives are indicated for
seven types of connectives, all of which are represented by at least one linguistic
expression in Dutch, illustrating that nine different orders (the nine arrows in
Figure 1) are possible. The arrows indicate the assumed order of acquisition.
In Figure 1, the placement of a type on a lower level implies that the connective
in question is acquired later than any type on a higher level. Placement of a type
on the same level implies that no acquisition order is predicted. The figure
clearly shows that with cumulative complexity (e.g. both causal and temporal)
a fixed order of acquisition is predicted, and that interaction between the three
dimensions predicts both uniformity and variety in the order of acquisition.

In the next section, the claims with regard to cognitive complexity and order
of acquisition are investigated in a quantitative analysis of longitudinal data of
93 children. Do their expressions of relational connectives emerge in the same
order as that indicated in Figure 1? Apart from this, it is investigated whether

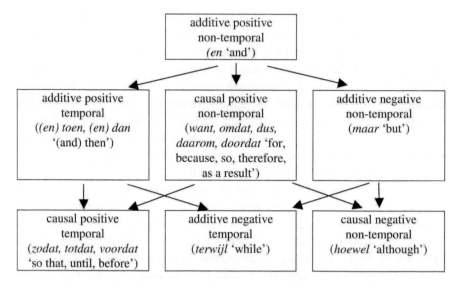

Figure 1: Assumed order of acquisition of relational connectives.

there are differences in the order of acquisition between children who have Dutch as their first language (L1), and children who started later with their acquisition of Dutch (Dutch as a second language, L2), and who lag behind in Dutch language proficiency (Verhoeven and Vermeer 2006). How did they perform compared to their Dutch monolingual peers? Finally, it is investigated whether boys and girls differ in the speed and order of emergence of relational connectives, because girls (up to a certain age) supposedly have the edge over boys in cognitive and linguistic development (Bornstein, Hahn and Haynes 2004; Galsworthy et al. 2000). Studies suggest that girls tend to be more verbal and demonstrate better linguistic skills than boys in terms of syntactic complexity, making their speech more coherent than that of boys. However, this tendency seems to decrease beyond the age of three (Coates 2004). Do girls use more relational connectives than boys, also at a later age?

4 Research methods and design

4.1 Informants

In a longitudinal study on the linguistic development of Dutch monolingual and bilingual children between the ages of four and eight (Verhoeven and Vermeer 2001, 2006), (audio)recordings were made of children while they were telling the course of events in two picture stories. The sample was stratified according to region, socio-economic backgrounds of the parents (i.e. low vs. high levels of education) and the degree of urbanisation characteristic of the school setting. There were 93 children with complete datasets taking part: 46 Dutch mono-lingual and 47 Dutch bilingual children (44 boys and 49 girls). Most bilingual children were from second and third generation Turkish and Moroccan immi-grant families, where Dutch is not used as a home language. At five moments in time, from Kindergarten 1 (mean age 4;7, SD 0;4) to primary school grade 2 (mean age 8;3), the same picture stories were shown. In Table 1, the mean ages at the five measuring moments are given.

Table 1: Mean age of the children (SD = 0;4) at the five measuring moments.

Measuring moment		Mean age
t1	Start of Kindergarten 1	4;7
t2	Start of Kindergarten 2	5;6
t3	End of Kindergarten 2	6;3
t4	End of grade 1 Primary School	7;3
t5	End of grade 2 Primary School	8;3

4.2 Stimulus materials

The data were recorded on the basis of two picture stories. The children were asked to tell what happened in the story. In the first story (see Figure 2) the

Figure 2: Stimulus: picture story 1: the soap-box.

father of two children is asked to turn a pram into a soap-box, which the children subsequently drive down from a slope and crash into a tree. The soap-box is broken, but their father is kind enough to fix it, and the children are happy again. The second story is about a girl with a balloon who slips over a bag of chips in the street, carelessly thrown away by a man. As she falls, the balloon slips from her hand, but happily the man gives her a new one. Both stories are constructed so as to elicit expressions of coherence relations, in particular temporal and causal connectives.

4.3 Procedure

The picture stories are shown individually at each measuring moment by a well-trained experimenter outside the classroom. The utterances of the children (and those of the experimenter) are recorded on audio tape and transcribed in CHAT (MacWhinney 2000). All stories are analyzed qualitatively and quantitatively with respect to the number and the kind of referential elements and relational connectives that are used, their correctness (is the intended and appropriate coherence relation expressed?), and whether or not the use is an echo of what the experimenter has just said.

In order to test the hypotheses, and to gain insight into the development of the use of relational connectives over time, the technique of implicational scaling was used: the rank orders of the various connectives (in terms of frequency) are equated to the acquisition sequence of these connectives (see Klein Gunnewiek 1999: 52 for some critical remarks on this technique). To find out possible differences in speed and order between monolingual and bilingual children in the use of relational connectives, and between boys and girls, analyses of variance (repeated measures) in SPSS were conducted. Only correct and creative (i.e. no echo) uses of relational connectives were taken into account.

5 Results

The complete corpus (93 children × 2 stories × 5 measuring moments) consisted of about 77,000 tokens for the child utterances alone. The stories of the first measuring moment, at the start of Kindergarten 1, showed a mean of 122 tokens per child for the two stories, those of the second and subsequent measuring moments about 170 tokens for each child. The stories of the monolingual children were slightly longer than those of the bilingual children, and those of the girls were sometimes longer than those of the boys, but in both cases no more than ten tokens, and not significant (boys/girls: F (1, 88) = .33, p = .57; L1/L2: F (1, 88) = 0.00, p = .99). In Tables 2 and 3, the number of correctly used connectives are presented for all informants at all five measuring moments.

Table 2 shows that the children at the first measuring moment at the start of Kindergarten 1 (mean age 4;7) mainly used additive and temporal connectives. Causal connectives were rare: *want* 'for' was used only eleven times and *omdat* 'because' three times. The negative additive *maar* 'but' emerged only nineteen times for all children. In the course of Kindergarten 2 (mean age 5;6) neither the use of causal connectives (starting out at 17 times) nor that of negatives (starting out at 21 times) increased much, ending as they did at the end of Kindergarten 2 (mean age 6;3) at 12 causal connectives, and 26 negatives. It was not until the end of grade 1 (mean age 7;3) that causal connectives started being used in substantial numbers with 32 cases reported. It is only at the end of grade 2 (mean age 8;3) that more complex connectives such as *terwijl, totdat, zodat* en *voordat* ('while, until, so that, before') started being used by the children.

Table 2: Number of connectives used in five measuring moments (t1–t5) for all children (N = 93).

	t1	t2	t3	t4	t5
en 'and'	258	414	387	351	469
(en) dan 'and then'	134	264	266	314	261
(en) toen 'and then'	147	377	374	308	282
(en) daarna 'and after that'	4	11	15	10	38
maar 'but'	13	12	21	21	37
maar toen/dan 'but then'	6	9	5	3	4
want 'for'	11	8	6	12	12
omdat 'because'	3	8	4	8	6
daarom 'therefore'	–	–	1	4	4
dus 'so'	–	–	1	6	11
other*	1	1	–	2	13

* other connectives used: t1: *en nu* 'and now'; t2: *doordat* 'as a result'; t4: *terwijl* 'while' (twice); t5: *ineens* 'all at once', *terwijl* 'while', *totdat* 'until', *zodat* 'so that', *voordat* 'before', *opeens* 'suddenly' (twice), and *en nu* 'and now' (six times).

On the basis of these quantitative data, it can be concluded that the nine claims about the order of acquisition of connectives (see Figure 1) are correct, as the frequencies of the connective(s) mentioned first (before the > symbol) are in all nine cases significantly higher than those of the connective(s) mentioned second (after the > symbol):

1. additive > causal (positive, non-temporal):
   en 'and'> *want, omdat, daarom, dus, doordat* 'for, because, therefore, so, as a result'

2. additive > causal (positive, temporal):
   en toen, en dan 'and then' > *zodat* 'so that'

3. additive > causal (negative, non-temporal):
   maar 'but' > *hoewel* 'although' (not in the data)

4. positive > negative (additive, non-temporal):
   en 'and' > *maar* 'but'

5. positive > negative (additive, temporal):
   en toen, en dan 'and then' > *terwijl* 'while'

6. positive > negative (causal, non-temporal):
   want, omdat, daarom, dus, doordat 'for, because, therefore, so, as a result' > *hoewel* 'although' (not in the data)

7. non-temporal > temporal (additive, positive):
   en 'and' > *toen, dan, daarna* 'then, after that'

8. non-temporal > temporal (causal, positive):
   want, omdat, daarom, dus, doordat 'for, because, therefore, so, as a result' > *totdat, voordat* > 'until, before'

9. non-temporal > temporal (additive, negative):
   maar 'but' > *terwijl* 'while'

Thus, the conclusion is that, in line with the predictions made on the basis of the cognitive theory of coherence relations (Sanders et al. 1992, 1993; Spooren and Sanders 2008), the increasing cognitive complexity of the relative coherence relations is reflected in the acquisition order in the emergence of these coherence relations and the linguistic elements that express these cognitive relations.

Next to this, it was investigated whether monolingual Dutch children differ from bilingual Dutch children in speed and order of acquisition. Because the number of children was different for each subgroup, the analyses were conducted on the mean number of uses of a particular type of connective per child. In Table 3, the means and standard deviations of additive, temporal and causal connectives are presented.

Table 3: Means (and standard deviations) of additive, temporal and causal connectives per monolingual (L1) and bilingual (L2) child, at five measuring moments (t1–t5).

		t1	t2	t3	t4	t5
Additive	L1	0.87 (2.00)	0.87 (1.28)	0.89 (0.94)	1.13 (1.65)	1.47 (1.16)
	L2	0.59 (1.15)	0.83 (1.70)	0.89 (1.08)	0.85 (1.43)	1.76 (1.55)
Temporal	L1	0.51 (1.02)	1.04 (1.43)	1.28 (1.51)	2.11 (1.87)	1.43 (1.28)
	L2	0.72 (1.59)	1.91 (3.24)	1.74 (1.72)	1.57 (1.77)	1.26 (1.25)
Causal	L1	0.13 (0.40)	0.13 (0.35)	0.11 (0.31)	0.38 (0.82)	0.26 (0.61)
	L2	0.13 (0.50)	0.20 (0.58)	0.15 (0.42)	0.13 (0.40)	0.37 (0.83)
Total	L1	1.51 (2.39)	2.04 (1.90)	2.28 (1.81)	3.62 (2.80)	3.15 (1.73)
	L2	1.43 (2.26)	2.93 (3.36)	2.78 (2.30)	2.54 (2.39)	3.39 (2.25)

What is striking in Table 3 are the high standard deviations: there are enormous differences between the children. The high standard deviations for temporal connectives at the second measuring moment for bilingual children are also remarkable. Since in the next analyses of variance the sphericity assumptions are not met (the Mauchly tests are significant), Huynh-Feldt corrected F-values will be applied. However, we will report the degrees of freedom in round figures. An analysis of variance (GLM Repeated Measures) shows that the children used more and more relational connectives in the course of time (F (4, 364) = 8.83, $p < .001$, $\eta_p^2 = .09$), for both L1 and L2 children (as the time*L1/L2 interaction was not significant). There were no differences between monolingual and bilingual children (F (1, 91) = 0.12, $p = .73$). The same results are found in separate analyses on the three types of connectives: significant increases over time, with no differences between monolingual and bilingual children (i.e. no main effect of L1/L2 and no significant time*L1/L2 interactions), in the emergence of additive (F (4, 364) = 11.80, $p < .001$, $\eta_p^2 = .06$) and temporal (F (4, 364) = 25.58, $p < .001$, $\eta_p^2 = .07$) connectives, and almost significant for causal connectives (F (4, 364) = 2.15, $p = .08$, $\eta_p^2 = .08$). Table 3 shows that the bilingual children in Kindergarten 2 (t2 and t3) used a lot more temporal connectives than the monolingual children, but this difference is not significant. Also, the increase of causal connectives seems to take place earlier for monolingual children (at the end of grade 1) than for bilingual children (occurring only at the end of grade 2), but this difference is not significant either.

Finally, it was investigated whether the speed and the order of acquisition of connectives differed between boys and girls. The qualitative analysis already showed that at the first measuring moment in Kindergarten 1, the cognitively more complex connectives, such as *want* 'for' and *omdat* 'because' were used mostly by girls (eleven times, vs. three times by boys). In the last grade, too, cognitively more complex temporal connectives (*voordat* 'before', *totdat* 'until', *zodat* 'so that') were used by girls. Quantitative analyses showed that at all five measuring moments girls used more connectives than boys. Analyses of variance confirm that for both groups the use of connectives increased over time (F (4, 364) = 8.48, $p < .001$, $\eta_p^2 = .09$), and that the groups did not differ in speed (interaction time*gender is not significant), but that the differences in use between boys and girls in the number of connectives is significant (F (1, 91) = 11.29, $p = .001$, $\eta_p^2 = .09$). This difference was mainly a consequence of the more frequent use of causal connectives by girls (F (1, 91) = 7.81, $p = .006$, $\eta_p^2 = .08$), of temporal connectives (F (1, 91) = 5.85, $p = .02$, $\eta_p^2 = .06$), and to a lesser extent, of the more frequent use of additive connectives (F (1, 91) = 3.81, $p = .054$, $\eta_p^2 = .04$). In Figure 3, the development of the use of causal connectives by girls (top line) and boys (bottom line) is displayed graphically.

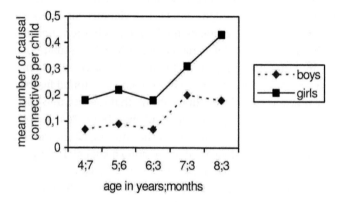

Figure 3: Mean number of causal connectives used per child, for girls (top line) and boys (bottom line), at five measuring moments, from the start of Kindergarten 1 (age 4;7) to the end of grade 2 of primary school (age 8;3).

6 Conclusion and discussion

In this longitudinal study on the development of story telling skills of 93 Dutch monolingual and bilingual children aged 4;7 to 8;3, it was investigated when the children expressed relational coherence explicitly by means of positive and negative additive, temporal and causal connectives. It was investigated whether the emergence of these relationships confirm the claim of the cognitive theory of coherence relations (Sanders et al. 1992, 1993; Spooren and Sanders 2008) that the increasing cognitive complexity of these relationships is reflected in the acquisition order of the linguistic elements that express them. Using the technique of implicational scaling in which the rank orders of the various connectives (in terms of frequency) are equated to the acquisition sequence of these connectives, we found evidence for all the hypotheses emerging from this theory (Evers-Vermeul and Sanders 2009): on the whole, additive connectives (*en* 'and', *maar* 'but') do emerge earlier than causal connectives (*want* 'for', *omdat* 'because', *daarom* 'therefore', *dus* 'so', *doordat* 'as a result'). Positive connectives (*en* 'and') appear before negative ones (*maar* 'but', *terwijl* 'while'), and non-temporal connectives (*omdat* 'because') occur before temporal ones (*totdat* 'until', *zodat* 'so that', *voordat* 'before'). This is in line with the study by Evers-Vermeul (2005; Evers-Vermeul and Sanders 2009), who investigated these claims with twelve children aged 1;5 to 5;6 with respect to the four connectives *en, maar, toen,* and *want* ('and', 'but', 'then' and 'for').

From the data, it is clear that the children use more and more relational connectives in the course of time, but it is not until the end of grade 1 (mean age 7;3) that causal connectives emerge in any substantial way. More complex connectives such as *terwijl, totdat, zodat* and *voordat* ('while, until, so that, before') are used by very few children at the end of grade 2 (mean age 8;3). However, in this study only relatively short texts are available (mean number of 122 tokens per child at the start of Kindergarten 1, and 180 tokens at the end of grade 2), and the time span between two recordings is relatively long (9–12 months). To get a more precise answer to the question when these and other complex connectives are used by children, more data from older children, and preferably from longer texts, should be collected, with a shorter time span between the recordings.

There were no significant differences between monolingual and bilingual children in the order and speed of acquisition of additive, temporal and causal connectives. Bilinguals do tend to use more temporal connectives around age six, but this is not significant, and their use of causal connectives seems to increase towards the end of grade 2 (mean age 8;3), whereas Dutch mono-linguals already show an increase there one year earlier, but this difference is not significant either. The absolute numbers of these more complex connectives in our study is quite low (see Tables 2 and 3); more data and data from older children are needed to get a more precise picture (cf. the recommendations in Van den Bergh and Evers-Vermeul, *this volume*), and to find out whether this difference may be the result of a later start in the acquisition of Dutch by bilinguals, and/or of less input of Dutch at home.

Finally, girls use significantly more connectives than boys do at all periods in time. This difference is due mainly to a more frequent use of causal connectives and temporal connectives, and to a lesser extent, additive connectives. In contrast to boys, girls also use the cognitively more complex temporal causal connectives *voordat, totdat* and *zodat* ('before, until, so that'). In an earlier study involving a writing task to be carried out by older children using the same picture stories (Verhoeven and Vermeer 1996), girls wrote longer stories that were more precisely formulated and more elaborate than those written by the boys. As part of this difference, perhaps, girls used connectives more often than boys, who describe the stories much less precisely. An analysis of referential coherence in these stories (Van der Veen 2008), shows that girls are better able than boys to use the correct referential elements, such as pronouns and posses- sives. So, in the use of relational and referential coherence, too, the reputation of girls being more proficient than boys of the same age is (once again) con- firmed. We did not find any support for Coates' (2004) claim that the verbal difference between boys and girls disappears in the first years of school, as the girls' more frequent use of connectives remains constant from age four to eight.

The enormous variation between the children is striking: at the age of eight, some of the children hardly use any causal connectives, while the picture stories are explicitly constructed to elicit cause-consequence relations. The abundant use of the temporal *(en) toen, (en) dan* '(and) then' may indicate that the children are trying to express the causal relation that way, because they have not yet found the correct words to use. On the other hand, however, it might also be due to the experimenters trying to prompt children to continue their story, by saying *en verder?* 'so what happens next?', thereby triggering the use of the temporal connective *en toen* 'and then'.

We found evidence for Spooren and Sanders' cognitive theory of coherence relations on the basis of the technique of implicational scaling, in which fre- quencies of connectives are equated to their acquisition sequences. However, the increasing cognitive complexity is not the only factor that predicts the order in which coherence relations are acquired. Frequency of language input is an important factor, too (Lieven and Tomasello 2008), which holds also for the acquisition of connectives (Van Veen et al. 2009). In our data, we found that the more complex temporal causal connectives in particular – *voordat, totdat* and *zodat* ('before, until, so that') – were hardly ever used. Apart from cognitive complexity, a possible explanation for this might be that these words are very infrequent in the daily input children get, so that there may have been very few opportunities for the children to acquire these forms. The correlations between the frequencies of the connectives in our data, and the frequencies in the daily input children in primary education get (on the basis of the frequency corpus of Schrooten and Vermeer 1994) are high ($r = .67$; $p = .02$ for the absolute frequencies). So, frequency of input may be a simpler and therefore more attrac- tive explanation for the findings (see Behrens 2009). To determine the relative contribution of both cognitive complexity and input frequency in the order of acquisition of relational connectives in children, research in which both factors are taken into account simultaneously is required.

References

Behrens, Heike. 2009. Usage-based and emergentist approaches to language acquisition. *Linguistics* 47: 383–411.

Bloom, Lois. 1991. *Language Development From Two to Three.* Cambridge: Cambridge University Press.

Bloom, Lois, Margaret Lahey, Lois Hood, Karin Lifter, and Kathleen Fiess. 1980. Complex sentences: Acquisition of syntactic connectives and the semantic relations they encode. *Journal of Child Language* 7 (2): 235–261.

Bornstein, Marc H., Chun-Shin Hahn, and O. Maurice Haynes. 2004. Specific and general language performance across early childhood: Stability and gender considerations. *First Language* 24 (3): 267–304.

Coates, Jennifer. 2004. *Women, Men and Language: A Sociolinguistic Account of Gender Differences in Language.* 3rd ed. London: Pearson.

Evers-Vermeul, Jacqueline. 2005. The development of Dutch connectives. Change and acquisition as windows on form-function relations. Ph.D. diss., Utrecht University. Utrecht: LOT. Available at: http://www.lotpublications.nl/Docu-ments/110_fulltext.pdf.

Evers-Vermeul, Jacqueline, and Ted Sanders. 2009. The emergence of Dutch connectives: How cumulative cognitive complexity explains the order of acquisition. *Journal of Child Language* 36 (4): 829–854.

Galsworthy, Michael J., Ginette Dionne, Philip S. Dale, and Robert Plomin. 2000. Sex differences in early verbal and non-verbal cognitive development. *Developmental Science* 3 (2): 206–215.

Klein Gunnewiek, Marian. 1999. Acquisition sequence of German: A comparison of cross-sectional versus longitudinal data. In *Utrecht Institute of Linguistics OTS Yearbook 1998–1999*, Jan Don, and Ted Sanders (eds.), 48–57. Utrecht: Utrecht Institute of Linguistics OTS.

Lieven, Elena V. M., and Michael Tomasello. 2008. Children's first language acquisition from a usage-based perspective. In *Handbook of Cognitive Linguistics and Second Language Acquisition*, Peter Robinson, and Nick C. Ellis (eds.), 168–196. New York/London: Routledge.

MacWhinney, Brian. 2000. *The CHILDES Project: Tools for Analyzing Talk.* 3rd ed. Mahwah, NJ: Lawrence Erlbaum.

Sanders, Ted. 2005. Coherence, causality and cognitive complexity in discourse. In *Proceedings/ Actes SEM-05. First International Symposium on the Exploration and Modelling of Meaning*, Michel Aurnague, Myriam Bras, Anne Le Draoulec, and Laure Vieu (eds.), 105–114. Toulouse: University of Toulouse-le-Mirail.

Sanders, Ted, and Wilbert Spooren. 2009. The cognition of discourse coherence. In *Discourse, of course*, Jan Renkema (ed.), 197–212. Amsterdam: Benjamins.

Sanders, Ted J. M., Wilbert P. M. Spooren, and Leo G. M. Noordman. 1992. Toward a taxonomy of coherence relations. *Discourse Processes* 15: 1–35.

Sanders, Ted J. M., Wilbert P. M. Spooren, and Leo G. M. Noordman. 1993. Coherence relations in a cognitive theory of discourse representation. *Cognitive Linguistics* 4 (2): 93–133.

Schrooten, Walter, and Anne Vermeer. 1994. *Woorden in het basisonderwijs. 15.000 woorden aangeboden aan leerlingen.* [Words in primary education: 15,000 words offered to students] Tilburg: TUP. Available at www.woordwerken.annevermeer.com.

Spooren, Wilbert, and Ted Sanders. 2008. The acquisition order of coherence relations: On cognitive complexity in discourse. *Journal of Pragmatics* 40 (12): 2003–2026.

Van der Veen, Suzanne. 2008. 'Meneer ging geld geven naar de mevrouw, want de meneer wou patat kopen': Ontwikkeling in het gebruik van coherentie door NT1 en NT2 jongens en meisjes ['Mister gave money to madame, because the mister wanted to buy French fries': Development in the use of coherence by Dutch L1 and L2 boys and girls]. Masterthesis Communication Design, Humanities Faculty, Tilburg University.

Van Veen, Rosie, Jacqueline Evers-Vermeul, Ted Sanders, and Huub van den Bergh. 2009. Parental input and connective acquisition in German: A growth-curve analysis. *First Language* 29 (3): 267–289.

Verhoeven, Ludo, and Anne Vermeer. 1996. *Taalvaardigheid in de bovenbouw: Nederlands van autochtone en allochtone leerlingen in het basis- en mlk-onderwijs* [Language proficiency in grades 6-8: Dutch for L1 and L2 students in primary and special education]. Tilburg: Tilburg University Press.

Verhoeven, Ludo, and Anne Vermeer. 2001. *Taaltoets Alle Kinderen. Diagnostische toets voor de mondelinge vaardigheid Nederlands bij kinderen van groep 1 tot en met 4* [Language Test All Children: Diagnostic test for Dutch oral skills for children in grades 3 to 6]. Arnhem: Cito.

Verhoeven, Ludo, and Anne Vermeer. 2006. *Verantwoording Taaltoets Alle Kinderen (TAK)* [Account of Language Test All Children]. Arnhem: Cito. Available at www.toetswijzer.nl/html/tg/10.pdf.

Elena Tribushinina, Eva Valcheva and Natalia Gagarina

9 Acquisition of additive connectives by Russian-German bilinguals: A usage-based approach

1 Introduction[1]

The ability to produce a coherent discourse is a crucial milestone in the linguistic development of a child. Acquisition of discourse coherence is a long process that continues far beyond age four when basic morphosyntactic structures have already been acquired (Berman and Slobin 1994; Gagarina 2012; Gülzow and Gagarina 2007b; Hickman 2003; Hudson and Shapiro 1991; Peterson and McCabe 1983; Ripich and Griffin 1988; Spooren and Sanders 2008). In order to be able to produce a coherent discourse children have to acquire various devices expressing referential and relational coherence. Referential coherence involves repeated reference to the same entities throughout a discourse, and relational coherence involves establishing logical relations between two or more discourse segments (Sanders and Spooren 2007). Prototypical markers of relational coherence are connectives such as *and, but* and *because*.

Several studies of first language acquisition have shown that connectives are acquired in a particular order. This order is determined by syntactic complexity and by conceptual complexity. Syntactically, children proceed from less integrated to more integrated clause structures (Diessel 2004). For example, the Dutch coordinator *want* 'because' is acquired before the synonymous subordinator *omdat* 'because', since subordinate clauses are more integrated into the main clause (e.g. by means of intonation, word order) than coordinate clauses and are more complex in this respect (Evers-Vermeul and Sanders 2009). Conceptually,

1 This research was supported by a Marie Curie International Research Staff Exchange Scheme Fellowship within the 7th European Community Framework Programme (grant number 269173) and by Bundesministerium für Bildung und Forschung (BMBF) (grant number 01UG0711). We thank Marina Akkuzina and Elena Limbah for collecting and transcribing the Russian data. Franziska Kriester kindly assisted in collecting and transcribing the German data. We are also grateful to all children, parents and teachers who made this investigation possible.

Elena Tribushinina, UiL OTS – Utrecht University
Eva Valcheva, Freie Universität Berlin
Natalia Gagarina, Leibniz-Zentrum Allgemeine Sprachwissenschaft

DOI 10.1515/9781501505492-010

each connective can be characterized in terms of a limited set of cognitive primitives, such as basic operation (additive *vs.* causal), polarity (positive *vs.* negative) and source of coherence (content, epistemic and speech act relations) (Sanders, Spooren, and Noordman 1992). Connectives expressing a positive relation (e.g. *and, then*) are usually acquired before connectives denoting a negative relation (e.g. *but, however*). Further, the acquisition of conceptually more complex causals such as *because* was shown to lag behind the acquisition of additives such as *and* (Berman and Slobin 1994; Bloom et al. 1980; Evers- Vermeul 2005; Evers-Vermeul and Sanders 2009; Knjazev 2007; Spooren and Sanders 2008).

Recently, the cumulative complexity approach has been applied to second language acquisition (Dekker 2007; Vermeer, *this volume*). Still it is not clear whether and to what extent patterns of connective use in a second language (L2) are different from patterns observed in a first language (L1). On the one hand, findings reported in Dekker (2007) and Pishwa (2002) indicate that child L2 learners have difficulty acquiring complex connectives such as causals. On the other hand, Vermeer (*this volume*) found no significant differences between monolingual and early L2 learners of Dutch in their use of additive, temporal and causal connectives (even though bilinguals had a tendency to use fewer causals than monolinguals).

Notice that the above studies have only focused on connective use in a bilingual child's second language. The study reported in this paper will extend this line of research and trace frequencies and functions of connectives in both languages of a bilingual child in order to pinpoint possible interactions between the connective systems in a child's L1 and L2. To this end, we will investigate a distribution of additive connectives, such as 'and' and 'but' in the narratives elicited from bilingual children with L1 Russian and L2 German and compare them to narratives elicited from monolingual speakers of Russian and German.

The outline of the paper is as follows. Section 2 summarizes relevant semantic properties of the connectives under study. Section 3 presents the experimental hypotheses. Materials and method are described in Section 4. Results are reported in Section 5. Main conclusions of this research and their implications are discussed in Section 6.

2 Additive connectives

2.1 Conceptual space

A comparison between Russian and German connective systems is particularly interesting because additive connectives in Russian rely on a different package of cognitive primitives than their counterparts in German. More specifically, the conceptual space covered by the German additive connective *und* 'and' is divided between two Russian connectives – *i* 'and' and *a* 'and/but'. Similarly, the functional domain of the Russian connective *a* 'and/but' is covered by three German connectives – *und* 'and', *aber* 'but' and *sondern* 'but'. Thus, although the additive connectives in the two languages involve more or less the same cognitive primitives, the way these primitives are packaged into connective semantics and the way connectives function in discourse largely differ. The main properties of the connectives selected for this investigation are summarized below.

2.2 The Russian connectives

2.2.1 Russian i 'and'

Jasinskaja and Zeevat (2008, 2009) convincingly demonstrate that the application of *i* 'and' is mainly restricted to contexts with a single discourse topic. Compare, for example, (1) and (2). Both sentences in (1) have the same topic – the dog; therefore, the use of *i* 'and' is grammatical. In contrast, (2) has two topics – the cat and the bird, which renders the use of *i* awkward. In such cases, *a* 'and/but' is preferred. Thus, *i* is generally used for topic maintenance, where *a* is used to mark topic switch (see Section 2.2.2).

(1) *A*   *tam*   *vot*   *sobačka*   *sidit.*   *I*   *ona*   *tixo*   *vot*
     and/but   there   PART   dog   sits   and   she   quietly   PART

     idët,   *čtoby*   *kisku*   *pojmat'.*   (BR5-071[2])
     walks   so.that   pussy   catch

     'And there a/the dog is sitting. And it is walking slowly in order to catch the cat.'

(2) *Koška*   *prišla*   **i*   *ptička*   *letit.*   (BR6-077)
     cat   came   and&ERR   bird   flies
     'A/the cat came and a/the bird is flying.'

---

2 These examples come from the narrative database used in this study (see Section 4). The first letter in the subject code refers to a linguistic background of the speaker (B – bilingual, M – monolingual). The second letter refers to the language in which the story was elicited (R – Russian, G – German). The following number (4, 5 or 6) indicates the age group. The last three digits form a unique subject code.

I 'and' can coordinate not only clauses as in (1), but also noun phrases as in (3) and verb phrases as in (4).

(3) *A   tut   ložechka   i   viločka.* (BR4-041)
and/but here spoon-DIM and fork-DIM
'And here is a spoon and a fork.'

(4) *Koška podošla i   xotela zabrat'sja, čtoby s"est' ptenčikov.* (MR4-031)
cat   came.by and wanted climb.up so.that eat   chicks-DIM
'The cat came by and wanted to climb the tree in order to eat the baby-birds.'

In child speech, as in adult language, *i* 'and' is also used to denote a causal relation; witness (5).

(5) *A   orël   ee   prjamo   za   spinu vot   svoim*
and/but eagle her straight by   back PART own

kljuvom sxvatil i   ona ispugalas'. (MR6-062)
beak   grabbed and she scared

'And the eagle pecked her [=fox] right on her back with his beak,
and [=therefore] she was frightened.'

In this sentence, the child establishes a causal relation between the eagle's act of pecking and the fox's state of fear by using the semantically under-specified additive connective *i* 'and' instead of choosing a connective with a more specific causal meaning, such as *poétomu* 'so'. It should be mentioned that *i*, unlike the English *and* and the German *und*, has an obligatory causal interpretation in contexts with topic shift. When two clauses conjoined by *i* have two different topics and no causal relationship can be established between the propositions of these clauses, *a* 'and/but' must be used.

2.2.2 Russian *a* 'and/but'

The use of *i* 'and' in Russian is constrained by the presence of a conjunction with a semi-negative additive meaning – *a* 'and/but'. As specified in the previous section, *a* is preferred when an additive relation is established between two topics. Russian semantic literature distinguishes between three senses of *a*: parallel/contrast, topic switch and inconsistency (Kreidlin and Paducheva 1974). These senses will be considered in order.

In the parallel/contrast sense, *a* is used to coordinate two clauses – one describing activity/state A performed/experienced by subject A', and the other describing a parallel or contrastive activity/state B performed/experienced by subject B'. A parallel sense is illustrated in (6) and a contrast relation is exemplified by (7).

(6) *A   zdes' koška zalezla   na derevo, **a**   sobaka*
     and/but here cat   climbed.up on tree   and/but   dog

     uže   dërnula ee   za xvost. (MR6-063)
     already pulled   her by tail

     'And here the cat has climbed up the tree and the dog has already pulled her by the tail.'

(7) *Oni *možut   letet', **a**   koški net.* (BR4-059)
     they may/can&ERR fly   and/but cats   NEG
     'They [=birds] can fly and cats can't.'

A 'and/but' can also be used to denote a topic switch. For example, in (8) *a* marks a transition from one topic (the eagle) to a new topic (the fox).

(8) *Potom on priletel   na derevo. **A**   k   nemu*
     then   he came.flying on tree   and/but to him

     podošla lisa. (MR6-049)
     came.by fox

     'Then he [=eagle] came flying to the tree. And a fox came up to him.'

When the same topic is maintained across the two clauses, *i* 'and' should be used instead of *a* 'and/but'. For example, the child correctly uses *i* in (9), because the topic of wanting the fish is sustained throughout the clauses.

(9) *Vorona xočet s"est' rybku. Ona vzjala rybku. **I**   lisa*
     crow   wants eat   fish   she took   fish   and   fox

     xočet s"est' rybku. (MR4-176)
     wants eat   fish

     'The crow wants to eat the fish. She grabbed the fish. And the fox wants to eat the fish.'

Just like *i* 'and', *a* 'and/but' may have a causal interpretation. However, *i* has a positive causal reading of 'therefore', whereas *a* is used to express a negative causal meaning of inconsistency. In the case of *a* two situations are not supposed to go together. For example, in (10) the speaker is surprised that the eagle does not fall from the fox's back even though the fox is running.

(10) *Lisa   bežit,   **a**   on   ne   otcepljaetsja.*   (MR6-048)
      fox   runs   and/but   he   not comes.unhooked
      'The fox is running, but he [=eagle] still holds her fast.'

Finally, *a* can also be used to express correction, as in (11). In this case, it is similar to the German *sondern* 'but' (Jasinskaja and Zeevat 2008).

(11) *Ptica   sidit   ne   na   stole,   **a**   na   dereve.*
      bird   sits   not on   table   and/but   on   tree
      'The bird is not sitting in the tree, but on the table.'

It should also be mentioned that in Russian *a* 'and/but', but not *i* 'and' is used in the sequential connectives such as *a potom* 'and then' and *a teper'* 'and now'.

2.2.3 Russian *no* 'but'

Perhaps the most prominent function of *no*, at least in juvenile narratives, is denial of expectation, whereby the clause introduced by *no* 'but' cancels the expectation or conclusion prompted by the previous clause or context. In (12), for instance, the preceding context creates an expectation that the cat had pain because the dog was pulling her by the tail. In contrast to this expectation, the child hopes that the cat was not hurt.

(12) *Zdes'   ona   *vskarabknulas',   a   sobaka   ee   za*
      here   she   climbed.up   and/but   dog   her by

      *xvost   deržit.   **No**   ja   nadejus',   čto   ej   ne   bol'no.*   (MR6-051)
      tail   holds   but   I   hope   that her not painful

      'Here she [=cat] has climbed the tree and the dog is holding her by
      the tail. But I hope it does not hurt her.'

In conversations, *no* is often used to express an objection to the other speaker's prior utterance (cf. Diessel 2004: 164). Since the material dealt with in this study included only monologues, our data do not contain such uses. The argumentative function of *no* described by Anscombre and Ducrot (1977) and by Jasinskaja and Zeevat (2008) is not realized in children's narratives either.

2.3 The German connectives

2.3.1 German *und* 'and'

The German *und* 'and' has a broader meaning than its Russian counterpart *i*. Unlike *i*, *und* is not restricted to additive relations with a single topic as in (13), but can also be used to coordinate clauses with two different topics as in (14).

(13) | *Jetzt* | *ist* | *und* | *jetzt* | *ist* | *ein* | *Wolf* | *gekommen.* | ***Und*** | *er* |
|---|---|---|---|---|---|---|---|---|---|
| now | is | and | now | is | a | wolf | come | and | he |

wollte	*ihn*	*fressen.*	(BG5-101)
wanted	him	eat	

'Now and now a wolf came. And he wanted to eat him.'

(14) | *Und* | *die* | *Katze* | *rennt* | *weg.* | ***Und*** | *die* | *Mutter* | *gibt* |
|---|---|---|---|---|---|---|---|---|
| and | the | cat | runs | away | and | the | mother | gives |

den	*kleinen*	*Kindern*	*etwas*	*zu*	*essen.*	(BG5-046)
the	small	children	something	to	eat	

'And the cat is running away. And the mother gives her small children something to eat.'

Similar to the Russian *i* 'and', *und* may also have a causal interpretation. For instance, in (15) the bird's act of opening its beak caused the fish to fall out of its mouth. The relation between the two events is made explicit by *und*.

(15) | *Und* | *der* | *Vogel* | *hat* | *seinen* | *Schnabel* | *aufgemacht.* | ***Und*** |
|---|---|---|---|---|---|---|---|
| and | the | bird | has | his | beak | opened | and |

der	*Fisch*	*fliegte*	*nach*	*unten.*	(BG6-035)
the	fish	flew	towards	below	

'And the bird opened her beak. And the fish fell down.'

Unlike the Russian *i* 'and', *und* can also be used to denote a contrastive relation illustrated in (16). In this case, Russian would require *a* 'and/but'.

(16) | *Und* | *dann* | *ist* | *die* | *Mutter* | *weggeflogen.* | ***Und*** | *die* |
|---|---|---|---|---|---|---|---|
| and | then | is | the | mother | flown.away | and | the |

Kinder	*waren*	*noch*	*da.*	(BG6-036)
children	were	still	there	

'And then the mother flew away. But the children were still there.'

Finally, *und* is often used as a part of sequential connectives such as *und dann* 'and then', *und da* 'and then' and *und jetzt* 'and now'.

2.3.2 German aber 'but'

Yet again, the conceptual space covered by the German adversative connective *aber* does not show a one-to-one correspondence to the semantic make-up of its Russian counterpart *no*. Like *no*, *aber* can be used to express denial of expectation as in (17). A major difference between the two connectives is that only *aber* can denote contrast as in (18). In such cases, Russian prefers *a* 'and/but'.

(17)   *Und*   *er*   *wollte*   *den*   *Fisch*   *haben,*   *der*   *Vogel.*
       and   he   wanted   the   fish   have   the   bird

       Aber   *er*   *hat*   *den*   *Fisch*   *nicht.*   (BG6-035)
       but   he   has   the   fish   not

       'And he wanted to have the fish, the bird. But he did not have the fish.'

(18)   *Die*   *hatte*   *vier*   *hm*   *drei*   *Kinder.*   ***Aber***   *das*   *ist*
       DEM   had   four   hm   three   children   but   this   is

       ein   *Vogel.*   (BG6-036)
       a   bird

       'She had four hm three children. But this is a bird.'

2.3.3 German sondern 'but'

As explained above, the adversative domain in German is covered by two connectives – *aber* and *sondern*, both roughly corresponding to the English *but*. While *aber* has a fairly broad adversative meaning, *sondern* is only used as a correction marker, as in example (19) from Jasinskaja and Zeevat (2009). In Russian this function is fulfilled by *a* 'and/but'.

(19)   *Peter*   *ist*   *nicht*   *in*   *Berlin,*   ***sondern***   *in*   *Paris.*
       Peter   is   not   in   Berlin   but   in   Paris

       'Peter is not in Berlin, but in Paris.'

To anticipate the discussion in Section 5, no instances of *sondern* were attested in our data.

3 Hypotheses

Considering peculiarities of (bilingual) child language acquisition and differences between the Russian and the German connective systems, we make predictions with respect to i) the order in which connectives are acquired; ii) the frequencies of additive connectives in the speech of bilingual children; and iii) the interaction of language systems in a bilingual mind. These predictions will be discussed in turn.

First, following the cognitive theory of coherence relations (Sanders et al. 1992) and the cumulative complexity approach to connective acquisition (Evers-Vermeul 2005; Evers-Vermeul and Sanders 2009), we hypothesize that connectives denoting negative relations (Ger. *aber, sondern*; Ru. *no*) will be acquired later than connectives denoting positive relations (Ger. *und*; Ru. *i*). Since the Russian connective *a* 'and/but' may have both a positive and a negative additive reading, we hypothesize that the acquisition of negative senses (contrast, inconsistency) will lag behind the development of the positive senses (parallel activities, topic switch). This order of acquisition should be attested in the speech of both monolingual and bilingual children.

Second, we predict that child L2 learners will over-use positive additive connectives for maintaining discourse coherence in order to compensate for a delayed acquisition of more complex coherence devices. The frequency of 'and' in both monolinguals and bilinguals should decrease with age in favour of connectives with more specific meanings (e.g. causal, relative, temporal), which are acquired later (cf. Dekker 2007; Pishwa 2002; Sebastián and Slobin 1994: 278).

Third, we expect to find an interaction between the language systems of a bilingual child. Following a usage-based approach to language acquisition, we assume that frequency is one of the essential factors in language acquisition and processing (Bybee 2001; Dąbrowska 2004; Diessel 2004; Gülzow and Gagarina 2007a; Langacker 1987; Tomasello 2003, see also Tribushinina and Gillis, *this volume*). The more a child is exposed to a particular construction, the more entrenched this construction will be in her mind. This explains why bilingual children tend to over-generalize linguistic structures from the language they hear more often to the language in which they receive less input (Döpke 1998, 1999; Tomasello 2003: 198). In other words, distributional properties of a dominant language may pre-empt relevant distinctions in a minority language. Applying this idea to connective acquisition in a Russian-German bilingual context, we hypothesize that bilingual children will re-analyze the conceptual space of additivity in their L1 (Russian) under the influence of the more dominant L2 (German). For example, the conceptual space of *i* may be over-extended to include uses involving referent switch and contrast relations which are characteristic of the German counterpart *und*.

4 Methodology

4.1 Participants

Sixty bilingual children participated in the study: twenty four-year-olds (age range 4;1–4;11, mean age 4;6), twenty five-year-olds (age range 5;1–5;10, mean age 5;7) and twenty six-year-olds (age range 6;0–7;2, mean age 6;7). All children were L1 speakers of Russian acquiring German as L2 from around age 2;6. Length of exposure to German varied from 13 months to 65 months (mean length of exposure: 39 months).

The performance of bilingual children was compared to that of ninety monolingual controls. Forty-five children were monolingual speakers of Russian, including fifteen four-year-olds (age range 3;9–4;2, mean age 4;0), fifteen five-year-olds (age range 4;7–5;0, mean age 4;10) and fifteen six-year-olds (age range 5;7–6;5, mean age 5;11). Forty-five children were monolingual speakers of German, among them fifteen four-year-olds (age range 3;8–4;2, mean age 4;0), fifteen five-year-olds (age range 4;7–5;0, mean age 4;10) and fifteen six-year-olds (age range 5;8–6;3, mean age 5;11).

The two monolingual groups were matched for age with each other. The monolingual and the bilingual group were matched for language age in German; therefore, the monolingual groups are (chronologically) younger than the corresponding bilingual groups. The bilinguals and the monolingual German-speaking children were recruited from schools and kindergartens in Berlin. The Russian monolinguals were recruited through kindergartens in Saint Petersburg.

4.2 Materials and procedure

Two picture stories were used to elicit children's narratives – the Fox story (Gülzow and Gagarina 2007b) and the Cat story (Hickmann 2003). Each story contains six pictures. The children were interviewed individually in a quiet room by a native speaker of the language in which the story was elicited. The investigator asked the child to tell the story in pictures and placed all pictures one after another on the table in front of the child. After the child looked through all the pictures and acknowledged to have understood the story, the experimenter put all the pictures away and afterwards placed only the first picture in front of the child and said: "Please, start telling the story". When the child finished describing picture 1, the investigator placed picture 2 next to picture 1 so that the child could see two pictures at the same time. When the child finished picture 2, the investigator moved it on top of picture 1 and placed picture 3 next to picture 2 on the table, etc. If the child fell silent in the middle of the story, the investigator encouraged her to continue by saying: "Anything else?", "Continue, tell me some more", "Let's see what else happens in the story", etc.

The bilingual children were tested in both languages using two different stories, with a maximum interval of two weeks between the sessions. The mono-lingual children were randomly assigned to one of the two stories. Forty-five of them told the Fox Story and forty-five the Cat Story.

The sessions were audio-recorded and later transcribed into CHAT format according to the CLAN conventions (MacWhinney 2000) by competent research assistants who were native speakers of German and Russian, respectively. The mean number of word tokens and the mean number of utterances per narrative are presented in Table 1.

Table 1: Mean length of the elicited narratives (standard deviations in brackets).

	4-year-olds		5-year-olds		6-year-olds	
	Tokens	Utterances	Tokens	Utterances	Tokens	Utterances
German						
bilingual	89.8	16.6	88.9	14.0	102.9	16.9
	(28.1)	(5.5)	(35.1)	(5.3)	(28.4)	(4.7)
monolingual	62.3	10.9	71.1	10.7	84.3	14.5
	(22.9)	(2.6)	(26.9)	(3.5)	(25.4)	(4.0)
Russian						
bilingual	80.7	14.1	79.5	11.8	80.5	11.9
	(35.8)	(5.5)	(26.7)	(4.8)	(22.3)	(3.5)
monolingual	48.1	12.9	86.6	15.3	102.5	18.9
	(23.0)	(4.6)	(61.1)	(6.7)	(55.6)	(7.9)

4.3 Coding

Six connectives were targeted for analyses: the Russian *i* 'and', *a* 'and/but', *no* 'but' and the German *und* 'and', *aber* 'but' and *sondern* 'but'. The searches were made by means of the CLAN software. Direct repetitions and particle uses of *aber* were not counted. This resulted in a subcorpus of 1,645 connective tokens. Each connective was assigned one of the following functions (see Section 2): additive (noun-phrase coordination, verb-phrase coordination, clausal coordina-tion with referent maintenance, clausal coordination with referent shift), parallel, contrast, causal relation, sequential relation, denial of expectation, inconsistency, topic switch and correction. Within each function, we coded all inappropriate uses as errors. Cases such as (20) where it was impossible to identify the func-tion were coded as unclear.

(20) *Teper'*   *rybka*   *u*   *lisički*   *i* ...   (MR4-037)
     now   fish-DIM   by   fox-DIM   and
     'Now the fox has the fish and ...'

All (semi-)idiomatic expressions such as *vzjal i upal* 'fell all of a sudden' and *vot i vsë* 'and that's all' were coded as irrelevant.

5 Results

5.1 Frequency of use

5.1.1 The Russian data

The mean frequencies of the positive additive connective *i* 'and' per utterance in the narratives of Russian-German bilinguals and Russian monolinguals are presented in Figure 1. A 3x2 ANOVA with age group (4-, 5-, vs. 6-year-olds) and background (monolingual vs. bilingual) as between-subject factors revealed a significant main effect of background (F (1, 99) = 23.7, $p < .001$, η_p^2 = .19); bilinguals used *i* more often than monolinguals. There was also a significant effect of age group (F (2, 99) = 4.6, $p < .05$, η_p^2 = .09). Posthoc Bonferroni comparisons showed that six-year-olds used *i* significantly more often than four-year-olds ($p = .006$). The differences between the other age groups were not significant. There was no significant age group by background interaction (F (2, 99) = 0.82, $p = .45$).

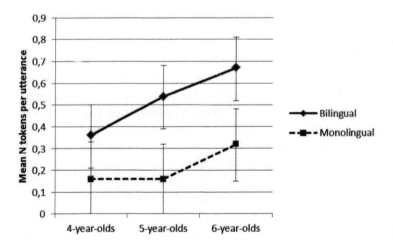

Figure 1: Mean number of tokens of i 'and' per utterance (error bars indicate 95% confidence intervals).

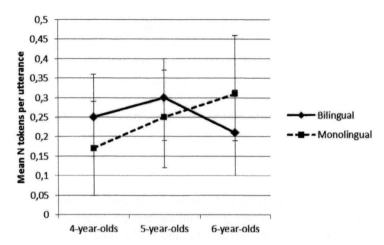

Figure 2: Mean number of tokens of a 'and/but' per utterance (error bars indicate 95% confidence intervals).

The mean frequencies of the semi-negative connective *a* 'and/but' are summarized by age group and language background in Figure 2. A 3x2 ANOVA was performed with age group (4-, 5-, vs. 6-year-olds) and background (monolingual vs. bilingual) as between-subject factors. There were no significant main effects of age group (F (2, 99) = 0.58, p = .56) and background (F (1, 99) = 0.04, p = .84). The age group by background interaction was not significant either (F (2, 99) = 1.40, p = .25).

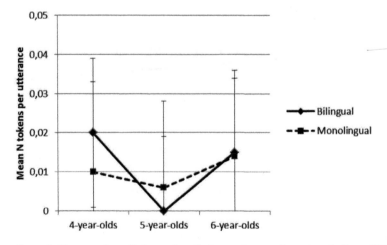

Figure 3: Mean number of tokens of no 'but' per utterance (error bars indicate 95% confidence intervals).

As is evidenced by Figure 3, the adversative connective *no* 'but' was used rarely across all groups and the variance was large in both the bilingual and the monolingual group. A 3x2 ANOVA with age group (4-, 5-, vs. 6-year-olds) and background (monolingual vs. bilingual) as between-subject factors revealed no significant effects of age (F (2, 99) = 0.84, p = .44) and background (F (1, 99) = 0.03, p = .87). The age by background interaction was not significant either (F (2, 99) = 0.27, p = .76).

5.1.2 The German data

Figure 4 summarizes the mean number of tokens of *und* 'and' per utterance in the narratives of Russian-German bilinguals and German monolinguals. A 3x2 ANOVA with age group (4-, 5-, vs. 6-year-olds) and background (monolingual vs. bilingual) as between-subject factors showed a significant main effect of background (F (1, 99) = 5.21, p < .05, η_p^2 = .05). The narratives of bilingual children contained more tokens of *und* per utterance than the narratives of the monolingual comparison group. The effect of age group (F (2, 99) = 0.98, p = .38) and the background by age group interaction (F (2, 99) = 0.51, p = .60) were not significant.

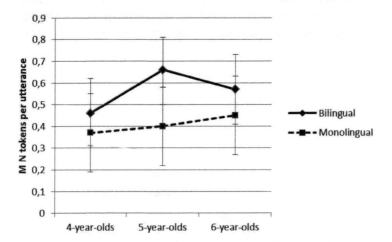

Figure 4: Mean number of tokens of und 'and' per utterance (error bars indicate 95% confidence intervals).

Like in Russian, adversative connectives were very infrequent in the German narratives. There were no instances of *sondern* 'but' in our data. The mean frequencies of *aber* 'but' were very low, as evidenced by Figure 5.

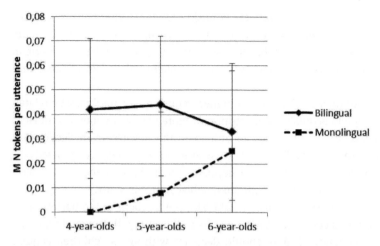

Figure 5: Mean number of tokens of aber 'but' per utterance (error bars indicate 95% confidence intervals).

A 3x2 ANOVA with age group (4-, 5-, vs. 6-year-olds) and background (mono-lingual vs. bilingual) as between-subject factors revealed a significant main effect of background (F (1, 99) = 5.10, $p < .05$, $\eta_p^2 = .05$). Bilingual subjects used *aber* more often than the monolingual comparison group. There was no signifi-cant effect of age (F (2, 99) = 0.13, $p = .88$) and no significant age by background interaction (F (2, 99) = 0.71, $p = .49$).

5.1.3 Summary and discussion

Prior research shows that children heavily rely on the additive connective 'and' (Berman and Slobin 1994; Bloom et al. 1980). One reason is that they have not acquired more complex connectives yet, but attempt to produce a coherent discourse (Diessel 2004; Evers-Vermeul and Sanders 2009). Another possible explanation is that younger children rarely use markers of global plot-based connectivity; rather they maintain local connectivity by marking a shift from one picture to another. In this case, 'and' can be characterized as "utterance-initial discourse filler, with no semantic or thematic motivation other than to indicate that 'more is still to come'" (Berman and Slobin 1994: 176). The results of our study indicate that bilingual children rely on 'and' even more than mono-lingual children in both languages (cf. Gagarina 2012). It might be the case that L2 learners of German over-use *und* 'and' in order to compensate for a delayed acquisition of more complex coherence devices (cf. Dekker 2007) and of the lexicon and grammar in general (cf. Polinsky 2008). Furthermore, bilinguals may over-use *und* because there is no counterpart of *a* 'and/but' in German. The fact that the functions of the Russian *a* partly correspond to the German *und* may explain why bilinguals use *und* more frequently than monolingual children of the same age.

In the case of their L1 (Russian), a higher frequency of *i* 'and' may be related to either incomplete acquisition or attrition of more complex coherence devices (cf. Maher 1991: 68). Furthermore, to anticipate the discussion in Section 5.2, bilinguals tend to use *i* 'and' in contexts where the semi-negative connective *a* 'and/but' is preferred. This probably happens under the influence of German, the environment language of the bilingual subjects in this study.

Thus, the hypothesis that 'and' would be more frequent in the narratives of bilingual children is confirmed by the results in this study. However, the prediction that the frequency of 'and' should decrease with age as children acquire complex connectives with more specific meanings is not borne out by the data. Older Russian-speaking subjects used more tokens of *i* 'and' than younger participants. In German, there were no differences between the age groups. It might be the case that the frequency of 'and' drops at a later age not covered by the present investigation.

Adversative connectives were very infrequent in both Russian and German narratives and their frequencies did not change with age. This pattern is probably attributable to both lower frequencies of adversatives in the adult input and a greater conceptual complexity of negative connectives (cf. Evers-Vermeul 2005; Evers-Vermeul and Sanders 2009; Spooren and Sanders 2008). Bilingual children used *no* 'but' as often as monolingual Russian-speaking children did. In contrast, they used *aber* 'but' more frequently than their monolingual German-speaking peers. As in the case of *und*, this finding may be explained by the fact that there is no counterpart of the frequent Russian connective *a* 'and/but' in German. Hence, bilingual children may try to compensate for the absence of *a* by transferring its functions to both *und* and *aber*, which leads to higher frequencies of these two connectives. Some of the functions of *a*, such as expressing a parallel relation and a topic switch, may be realized by asyndetic structures in German.

The frequencies of the Russian semi-negative connective *a* 'and/but' did not differ between the monolingual and the bilingual group, and did not change with age. Thus, the elements for which there is no counterpart in a second (environment) language of bilingual children do not seem to be affected by attrition and/or cross-linguistic interference.

5.2 Functional properties

Relating to the discussion of the various functions of additive connectives in Russian and German in Section 2, we will now consider the distribution of the different functions in the children's narratives. Only correct uses are discussed here; erroneous, unclear and irrelevant uses were not included. In view of relatively low frequencies of each function, we collapsed the data from different age groups.

5.2.1 The Russian data

An overview of the functions fulfilled by *a* 'and/but' in the elicited narratives is presented in Table 2. The numbers represent percentages of uses with a specific function out of all relevant uses.

Table 2: Distribution of a 'and/but' over functions (%).

	Bilinguals (N = 177)	Monolinguals (N = 161)
Parallel	57	71
Sequential	30	17
Topic switch	9	6
Contrast	3	4
Inconsistency	1	2

As hypothesized, negative uses of *a* (contrast, inconsistency) are relatively infrequent in child speech, probably because of their conceptual complexity. Children overwhelmingly use *a* to coordinate two parallel events. Further, in line with our prediction, language learners heavily rely on sequential connectives such as *a potom* 'and then' for maintaining coherence.

Comparing the performance of bilinguals to that of monolinguals, we found a significant difference in the distribution of *a* across functions (χ^2 (4) = 11.6; $p < .05$). The examination of standardized residuals did not reveal any significant differences between the two groups as far as specific functions are concerned (no z-values above 1.96 or below −1.96).

Let us now turn to the functions of the main competitor of *a* in the domain of additivity – the conjunction *i* 'and'. The distribution of its functions attested in the narratives is summarized in Table 3. The category 'additive' includes not only cases of pure conjoining, but also cases of coordination involving a temporal relation of sequence or simultaneity.

Table 3: Distribution of i 'and' over functions (%).

	Bilinguals (N = 241)	Monolinguals (N = 146)
Additive: verb-phrase coordination	32	53
Additive: clausal coordination with referent maintenance	17	21
Additive: clausal coordination with referent shift	35	14
Additive: noun-phrase coordination	9	8
Causal	6	6

There were significant differences between bilinguals and monolinguals in the distribution of i over functions (χ^2 (4) = 26.0, p < .001). The proportion of i used for verb-phrase coordination was over-represented in the narratives of the monolingual group (z = 2.4), whereas the proportion of i coordinating clauses with two different referents was higher than expected in the narratives of bilinguals (z = 2.4).

Since there are very few tokens of *no* in our data (N = 14), only few cautious observations about its use in the narratives can be made. All of the attested uses have the same function of denial of expectation. Most of these instances are realizations of the same constructional schema – 'X wanted to do Y, but s/he could not'. See, for example, (21).

(21) *I*   *potom*   *lisička*   *pribežala,*   *i*   **xotel*
      and   then   fox   came.by.running   and   wanted&ERR

      rybu   *s''est',*   **no**   *ne*   *dostala.*   (BR6-043)
      fish   eat   but   NEG   reached

      'And then the/a fox came and wanted to eat the fish, but couldn't reach it.'

Thus, it is plausible to assume that children acquire the function of denial of expectation by rote-learning a frequent frame and extending it to similar situations later on (cf. Diessel 2004; Tomasello 2003). Another prominent function of *no* in child language – objection to what a conversation partner has said – was not attested in our data, most likely, due to the monologic character of the narratives.

5.2.2 The German data

The functions of *und* 'and' in the narratives of monolingual and bilingual children are listed in Table 4. The distribution of *und* over functions differed significantly between groups (χ^2 (6) = 12.9, $p < .05$). The examination of standardized residuals showed that monolinguals used *und* more often for noun-phrase coordination ($z = 2.0$). No other significant differences were found.

Having considered the functions of the positive additive connective *und* 'and' we now turn to the adversative connective – *aber* 'but'. As indicated above, *aber* is relatively infrequent in the stories. Table 5 shows the proportion of different uses of *aber* in the narratives.

Table 4: Distribution of *und* 'and' over functions (%).

	Bilinguals (N = 461)	Monolinguals (N = 191)
Sequential	50	40
Additive: clausal coordination with referent shift	26	34
Additive: verb-phrase coordination	13	13
Additive: clausal coordination with referent maintenance	4	4
Additive: noun-phrase coordination	3	6
Causal	4	2
Contrast	2	2

Table 5: Distribution of *aber* 'but' over functions (%).

	Bilinguals (N = 39)	Monolinguals (N = 9)
Denial of expectation	41	67
Contrast	28	11
Topic switch	10	22
Sequential	10	0
Inconsistency	10	0

No significant difference between the two groups in the distribution of *aber* across functions was found (χ^2 (4) = 4.6, $p = .33$). As evidenced by Table 5, denial of expectation was the most common function of *aber* in the narratives of both groups. Like in Russian, denial of expectation was repeatedly realized in the modal frame 'X wanted to do Y, but could not'.

5.2.3 Summary and discussion

To recapitulate, the distribution of additives over different functions is largely similar in the narratives of monolinguals and bilinguals. However, bilinguals use 'and' for noun-phrase coordination significantly less often than monolinguals in both languages. At the same time, bilinguals over-use the Russian *i* 'and' in cases of clausal coordination with referent shift. This is likely to be a manifestation of cross-linguistic interference. The German *und* can be used for both reference maintenance and shift, whereas the Russian *i* has a strong preference for maintenance. Hence, bilinguals appear to use *i* in contexts where *a* 'and/but' is preferred because the German counterpart of *i* allows such uses.

Further, as predicted, children in both groups often use additives in sequential constructions, which confirms earlier findings demonstrating that sequential connectives such as *and then* are children's "most favored connective device" (Berman and Slobin 1994: 178, cf. Polinsky 1995b). The proportion of negative uses of *a* 'and/but' (contrast, inconsistency) is very low in both groups. Thus, children start using *a* predominantly in the positive sense, which is consonant with the cumulative complexity hypothesis of connective acquisition (Evers-Vermeul and Sanders 2009). This view is also corroborated by the finding that adversative connectives are rarely used by children and that their use is predominantly restricted to recurrent modal frames.

5.3 Analysis of errors

Table 6 shows the frequency of inappropriate uses for each connective.

Table 6: Number and percentage of errors.

	i	*a*	*no*	*und*	*aber*
Bilinguals	138 (39%)	6 (3%)	0	4 (0.8%)	1 (2%)
Monolinguals	9 (6%)	3 (2%)	0	0	0

The most surprising result is that the bilingual children make fewer errors with *und* than with *i*, i.e. they use 'and' more correctly in their second language. This might be an indication of L2-induced attrition of the children's first language and their higher proficiency in the L2. The proportion of inappropriate uses of *a* does not differ between monolinguals and bilinguals (χ^2 (1) = 0.78, p = .38). By contrast, the proportion of inappropriate uses of *i* is significantly higher in the stories produced by bilingual subjects (χ^2 (1) = 63.6, p < .001).

About 64% of the erroneous uses of *i* involves the use of the wrong sequential *i potom* 'and then' – which is a loan translation of the German *und dann* – instead of the standard Russian *a potom*. The monolingual Russian children used *i potom* only in two cases. In 34% of the instances, the bilingual children used *i* in contexts involving a double topic, which clearly require *a* 'and/but', as, for example in (2). Thus, early L2 learners transfer the general additive meaning of *und* to *i*. This is a process of meaning extension in which "the meaning of a word in L1 is generalized to include the meaning of another word in L1, on analogy to the range of meaning of the equivalent word in L2" (Seliger and Vago 1991: 8). Meaning extension is very common in the process of L1 attrition (Silva-Corvalán 1991). The remaining 2% of errors involves using *i* instead of *no* for expressing denial of expectation as in (22).

The finding that attrition affects only *i* 'and', but not *a* 'and/but' is consonant with the results of earlier studies suggesting that L1 attrition is selective and only affects items having a counterpart in L2, because similar linguistic structures in L1 and L2 are in competition with each other (Gürel 2004; Seliger 1996, cf. MacWhinney 2008). If L2 is more dominant than L1, it pre-empts the conceptual categories of L1 that are in competition with similar categories in L2 (cf. Keijzer 2010). Hence, the semantics of *a* 'and/not' is not affected by L2-induced attrition because there is no counterpart of *a* in German.

(22) *I*   *koška* *xočet* *ix,*   *ptiček*   *zabrat'*   *i*
      and   cat   wants   them   birds-DIM take.away   and

      s"est'. ***I***   *ona* *ne*   *mogla* *dostat'.* (BR4-059)
      eat   and&ERR   she   NEG   could   reach

      'And the cat wants to take them, birds, away and eat them.
      And she couldn't reach them.'

Before turning to the German data, it is worth pointing out that both monolingual and bilingual children sometimes use *a* 'and/but' in a way that is not ungrammatical, but rather pragmatically immature. As explained earlier, *a* 'and/but' is a default marker of double topics. When *i* 'and' is used to coordinate two topics, it usually presupposes a causal relation between the two events (Jasinskaja and Zeevat 2008; Sannikov 1989). Thus, in contexts such as (23) and (24) we would expect to find *i* rather than *a*, because the latter construes the two events without a causal link.

(23) *I*   *sobaka* *košku* *ispugala,* *?a*   *koška* *ubežala.* (BR6-034)
      and   dog   cat   frightened   and/but   cat   ran.away
      'And the dog frightened the cat, and the cat ran away.'

(24) *Ona* *upala,* *kostočka,* *?a*   *lisa* *xotela* *ee*   *sxvatit'.* (MR6-062)
      she   fell   bone-DIM   and/but   fox   wanted   her   grab
      'It fell, the bone, and the fox wanted to grab it.'

In German, all the errors with additive connectives directly or indirectly involve *aber* 'but'. In one case, *aber* is infelicitously used in a context that requires the use of *und* 'and'; see (25). The remaining errors involve the use of *und* in contexts where *aber* should have been used, as in (26).

(25) | *Und* | **das* | *Rabe* | *hat* | *aus* | *Versehen* | *geguckt* | *und* |
|------|--------|--------|-------|------|-----------|-----------|--------|
| and | the&ERR | raven | has | out | mistake | looked | and |

hat	*aus*	*Versehen ...*	*und*	*wollte*	*ihn*	*was*	*sagen.*
has	out	mistake	and	wanted	him	what	say

*Aber	*hat*	*den*	*Mund*	*aufgemacht.*	(BD6-052)
but&ERR	has	the	mouth	opened	

'And the raven looked by mistake and by mistake ... and wanted to tell him something. But opened his mouth.'

(26) | *Und* | *die* | **Babyvogeln* | **willen* | *mitkommen.* | ****Und*** |
|------|-------|---------------|------------|-------------|------------|
| And | the | baby.birds&ERR | want&ERR | come.with | and&ERR |

die	**kannen*	*nicht*	*fliegen.*	(BD4-011)
DEM	can&ERR	not	fly	

'And the baby-birds want to go with her. And they cannot fly.'

The observed error pattern in Russian and German corroborates the view that negative and causal coherence relations are more complex and, therefore, take longer to acquire (Evers-Vermeul 2005; Evers-Vermeul and Sanders 2009; Spooren and Sanders 2008). Similarly, an experimental study reported in Paltiel-Gedalyovich (2003) demonstrated that the interpretation of *aval* 'but' by Hebrew-speaking children is not adult-like even at age 9;6. The results further indicate that bilingual children tend to seek alternative means in their second language to compensate for the missing counterpart of a functionally important item in their first language. At the same time, language-specific packages of cognitive primitives constituting the semantic make-up of connectives in L1 may be re-arranged under the influence of a child's L2.

6 Conclusions and discussion

The outcomes of this study are, by and large, consistent with the cumulative complexity approach to connective acquisition (Evers-Vermeul and Sanders 2009). The adversative connectives – Russian *no* 'but' and German *aber* 'but' – are very infrequent in the narratives of four- to six-year-old children. Moreover, the use of these connectives appears to be mainly restricted to rote-learnt frequent frames such as 'X wanted to do Y, but could not'. Lower frequencies and item-based usage of adversatives in child speech may be caused by lower frequencies in the input, as well as by a greater conceptual complexity of negative connectives.

The finding that might present a challenge to the cumulative complexity approach is that the semi-negative connective *a* 'and/but' is frequently used by Russian-speaking children across all age groups. Notice, however, that the youngest subjects in our study were four years of age. It is plausible to assume that the acquisition of *a* lags behind the acquisition of *i* early in development, but levels up by age four. To determine whether this is indeed the case, future research will have to consider data from younger children (around age two) and to combine corpus analyses with comprehension experiments. A result that is definitely consistent with the cumulative complexity hypothesis is that the children in this study rarely use *a* in the negative senses of contrast and inconsistency, which are conceptually more complex than the positive functions of expressing parallel and sequential relations.

The hypothesis that early sequential bilinguals over-use additive connectives in their L2 is also confirmed by the data. One plausible explanation of this pattern is that additive connectives compensate for a delayed acquisition of more complex coherence devices by L2 learners (cf. Vermeer, *this volume*). Another reason why Russian-German bilinguals over-use both *und* 'and' and *aber* 'but' is that in the absence of a German counterpart of *a* 'and/but', children transfer its functions partly to *und* and partly to *aber*. Interestingly, the frequency of the Russian *i* 'and' is also higher in the speech of bilingual children. The analysis of functions of *i* in Section 5.2 reveals that bilingual children over-use this connective in contexts where the German *und* is felicitous and where Russian prefers *a* 'and/but'. A higher frequency of *i* may, therefore, be related to L1 attrition in the dominant German environment.

The prediction that the frequency of 'and' in both languages decreases with age is not borne out by the data. In Russian, six-year-old children used *i* more often than four-year-olds. In German, there were no differences between the age groups. This result might be explained by the findings reported in Peterson and McCabe (1987) demonstrating that children up to nine years of age over-use *and* employing it for a wide range of semantic functions even though their connective inventory already contains connectives with more specific meanings. Thus, the frequencies of 'and' are likely to drop beyond age six.

Finally, the results show that the semantics of the Russian connective *i* 'and' in the language of the bilingual children is over-extended under the influence of the German *und*. Bilingual children use *i* 'and' in contexts of reference shift, where *a* 'and/but' is preferred. As against this, the functions of *a* in the speech of bilingual children seem to remain intact. Furthermore, the frequencies of *a* in the narratives of bilingual children were not different from the narratives of the monolingual group.

Taken together, these findings corroborate a usage-based view of language acquisition as an active process of analyzing and generalizing over distributional patterns in the input (Dąbrowska 2004; Diessel 2004; Tomasello 2003). It is clear from the results that the categories and their functions in child language are not stable; they are constantly changing in the process of distributional learning. Since the bilingual subjects in our study were raised in a dominant German-speaking environment, more frequent input from German pre-empted relevant conceptual distinctions in the semantics of the additive connectives in the children's L1, which has lead to a re-construction of the conceptual space of additivity. However, L1 attrition appears to be selective – only elements for which there is a counterpart in L2 were re-conceptualized in L1; language-specific elements having no competitor item in L2 remained intact.

References

Anscombre, Jean-Claude, and Oswald Ducrot. 1977. Deux mais en français? *Lingua* 43 (1): 23–40.

Berman, Ruth A., and Dan Isaac Slobin (eds.). 1994. *Relating Events in Narrative: A Cross-linguistic Developmental Study.* Hillsdale, NJ: Lawrence Erlbaum Associates.

Bloom, Lois, Margaret Lahey, Lois Hood, Karin Lifter, and Kathleen Fiess. 1980. Complex sentences: Acquisition of syntactic connectives and the semantic relations they encode. *Journal of Child Language* 7 (2): 235–261.

Bybee, Joan. 2001. *Phonology and Language Use.* Cambridge: Cambridge University Press.

Dąbrowska, Eva. 2004. *Language, Mind, and Brain: Some Psychological and Neurological Constraints on Theories of Grammar.* Edinburgh: Edinburgh University Press.

Dekker, Annelieke. 2007. Causale domeinmarkering en taalverwerving: Een onderzoek naar de verwerving van Nederlandse causale connectieven door meertalige kinderen [Causal domain marking and language acquisition: A study into the acquisition of Dutch causal connectives by multilingual children]. Unpublished Master's thesis, Departement of Dutch Language and Culture, Utrecht University.

Diessel, Holger. 2004. *The Acquisition of Complex Sentences.* Cambridge: Cambridge University Press.

Döpke, Susanne. 1998. Competing language structures: The acquisition of verb placement by bilingual German-English children. *Journal of Child Language* 25 (3): 555–584.

Döpke, Susanne. 1999. Cross-linguistic influences on the placement of negation and modal particles in simultaneous bilingualism. *Language Sciences* 21 (2): 143–175.

Evers-Vermeul, Jacqueline. 2005. *The Development of Dutch Connectives: Change and Acquisition as Windows on Form-Function Relations.* (LOT Dissertation Series 110) Utrecht: LOT.

Evers-Vermeul, Jacqueline, and Ted Sanders. 2009. The emergence of Dutch connectives: How cumulative cognitive complexity explains the order of acquisition. *Journal of Child Language* 36 (4): 829–854.

Gagarina, Natalia. 2012. Discourse cohesion in the elicited narratives of early Russian-German sequential bilinguals. In *Multilingual Individuals and Multilingual Societies*, Kurt Braunmüller, and Christoph Gabriel (eds.), 101–119. Amsterdam: John Benjamins.

Gülzow, Insa, and Natalia Gagarina. 2007a. *Frequency Effects in Language Acquisition*. (Studies on Language Acquisition 32) Berlin: de Gruyter.

Gülzow, Insa, and Natalia Gagarina. 2007b. Noun phrases, pronouns and anaphoric reference in young children narratives. In *Intersentential Pronominal Reference in Child and Adult Language*, Dagmar Bittner, and Natalia Gagarina (eds.), 203–223. Berlin: ZAS Papers in Linguistics.

Gürel, Ayşe. 2004. Selectivity in L2-induced L1 attrition: A psycholinguistic account. *Journal of Neurolinguistics* 17 (1): 53–78.

Hickmann, Maya. 2003. *Children's Discourse: Person, Space, and Time Across Languages*. Cambridge: Cambridge University Press.

Hudson, Judith A., and Lauren R. Shapiro. 1991. From knowing to telling: The development of children's scripts, stories, and personal narratives. In *Developing Narrative Structure*, Allyssa McCabe, and Carole Peterson (eds.), 89–136. Hillsdale, NJ: Lawrence Erlbaum.

Jasinskaja, Ekaterina, and Henk Zeevat. 2008. Explaining additive, adversative and contrast marking in Russian and English. *Revue de Sémantique et Pragmatique* 24: 65–91.

Jasinskaja, Ekaterina, and Henk Zeevat. 2009. Explaining conjunction systems: Russian, English, German. In *Proceedings of Sinn und Bedeutung 13*, Arndt Riester, and Torgrim Solstad (eds.), Stuttgart.

Keijzer, Merel. 2010. Inside the attriter's mind: A comparative exploration of the cognitive constraints in Dutch L1 attrition in an L2 English environment and advanced Dutch L1 acquisition. In *Cognitive Processing in Second Language Acquisition*, Martin Pütz, and Laura Sicola (eds.), 227–239. (Converging Evidence in Language and Communication Research 13) Amsterdam/Philadelphia: John Benjamins.

Knjazev, Jurij P. 2007. Ontogenez značenij obuslovlennosti [Ontogeny of causal meanings]. In *Semantičeskie Kategorii v Detskoj Reči* [Semantic categories in child speech], Stella N. Cejtlin (ed.), 339–358. St. Petersburg: Nestor-Istorija.

Kreidlin, Grigorij E., and Elena V. Paducheva. 1974. Značenie i sintaksičeskie svojstva sojuza *A* [Meaning and syntactic properties of the conjunction A]. Naučno-Tehničeskaja Informacija 2: 31–37.

Langacker, Ronald W. 1987. *Foundations of Cognitive Grammar*, Vol. 1. Theoretical prerequisites. Stanford, CA: Stanford University Press.

MacWhinney, Brian. 2000. *The CHILDES Project: Tools for Analyzing Talk*. Mahwah, New Jersey: Lawrence Erlbaum Associates.

MacWhinney, Brian. 2008. A unified model. In *Handbook of Cognitive Linguistics and Second Language Acquisition*, Peter Robinson, and Nick Ellis (eds.), 341–371. New York: Routledge.

Maher, Julianne. 1991. A cross-linguistic study of language contact and language attrition. In *First Language Attrition*, Herbert W. Seliger, and Robert M. Vago (eds.), 67–84. Cambridge: Cambridge University Press.

Paltiel-Gedalyovich, Leah R. 2003. Towards an explanation of first language acquisition of Hebrew coordination. Ph.D. diss., Department of Foreign Literatures and Linguistics, Ben-Gurion University.

Peterson, Carole, and Allyssa McCabe. 1983. *Developmental Psycholinguistics: Three Ways of Looking at a Child's Narrative*. New York: Plenum Press.

Peterson, Carole, and Allyssa McCabe. 1987. The connective 'and': Do older children use it less as they learn other connectives? *Journal of Child Language* 14 (2): 375–382.

Pishwa, Hanna. 2002. Language learning and vantage theory. *Language Sciences* 24 (5–6): 591–624.

Polinsky, Maria. 1995a. American Russian: Language loss meets language acquisition. *Formal Approaches to Slavic Linguistics.* Cornell Meeting, 370–406. Ann Arbor: Michigan Slavic Publications.

Polinsky, Maria. 1995b. Cross-linguistic parallels in language loss. *Southwest Journal of Linguistics* 14 (1–2): 87–123.

Polinsky, Maria. 2008. Heritage language narratives. In *Heritage Language Education: A New Field Emerging*, Donna M. Brinton, Olga Kagan, and Susan Bauckus (eds.), 149–164. New York/London: Routledge.

Ripich, Danielle N., and Penny L. Griffin. 1988. Narrative abilities of children with learning disabilities and non-disabled children. *Journal of Learning Disabilities* 21 (3): 165–173.

Sanders, Ted J., Wilbert P.M. Spooren, and Leo G. Noordman. 1992. Toward a taxonomy of coherence relations. *Discourse Processes* 15 (1): 1–35.

Sannikov, Vladimir Z. 1989. *Russkie Sočinitel'nye Konstrukcii* [Russian coordinating constructions]. Moscow: Nauka.

Sebastián, Eugenia, and Dan Isaac Slobin. 1994. Development of linguistic forms: Spanish. In *Relating Events in Narrative: A Crosslinguistic Developmental Study*, Ruth A. Berman, and Dan Isaac Slobin (eds.), 239–284. Hillsdale, NJ: Lawrence Erlbaum Associates.

Seliger, Herbert W. 1996. Primary language attrition in the context of bilingualism. In *Handbook of Second Language Acquisition*, William C. Ritchie, and Tej J. Bhatia (eds.), 605–626. New York: Academic Press.

Seliger, Herbert W., and Robert M. Vago. 1991. The study of first language attrition: An overview. In *First Language Attrition*, Herbert W. Seliger, and Robert M. Vago (eds.), 3–15. Cambridge: Cambridge University Press.

Silva-Corvalán, Carmen. 1991. Spanish language attrition in a contact situation with English. In *First Language Attrition*, Herbert W. Seliger, and Robert M. Vago (eds.), 151–171. Cambridge: Cambridge University Press.

Sanders, Ted, and Wilbert Spooren. 2007. Discourse and text structure. In *Handbook of Cognitive Linguistics*, Dirk Geeraerts, and Hubert Cuykens (eds.), 916–941. Oxford: Oxford University Press.

Spooren, Wilbert, and Ted Sanders. 2008. The acquisition order of coherence relations: On cognitive complexity in discourse. *Journal of Pragmatics* 40 (12): 2003–2026.

Tomasello, Michael. 2003. *Constructing a Language: A Usage-Based Theory of Language Acquisition*. Cambridge, MA/London: Harvard University Press.

III Implications for language teaching and translation

Hana Gustafsson and Marjolijn Verspoor
10 Development of chunks in Dutch L2 learners of English

1 Introduction

Evidence from various research disciplines has demonstrated that a substantial part of native speaker repertoire consists of a wide range of conventionalized expressions (Ellis 2008; Sinclair 1991; Wray 2002) which in this paper are generally referred to as *chunks*. Many chunk types are part of traditional phraseology and clearly recognizable as fixed units, such as *of course, living room, grow up, the sky is the limit*, but those most pervasive in native-like repertoire are simply "normal ways of saying things" (Granger and Paquot 2008: 35; Langacker 2008: 84). These are the preferred ways of expressing certain notions out of all the grammatically correct options available: Compare for example *Will you marry me?* and *Would you like to become my spouse?* (Pawley and Syder 1983). Although many chunks are highly context-specific, in general the proportion of chunks in native-like written language has been estimated at about 50% (Erman and Warren 2000) and it tends to be even higher in native-like spoken language (Ellis 2008: 4).

Since chunks are such a pervasive feature of a native-like repertoire, they are also a crucial aspect of second language (L2) development. Verspoor, Schmid, and Xu (2012) have shown that the number of chunks used in written texts is one of the better measures to distinguish among five L2 English proficiency levels (from beginner to high intermediate). Chunks contribute to fluency and authenticity of L2 use and may also speed up general linguistic development. However, it is precisely this feature of the target language that is often the greatest obstacle for L2 learners. Although the classroom context does focus on chunks, the range is limited (Eyckmans, Boers, and Stengers 2007) and often does not include "normal ways of saying things" as they are not part of traditional phraseology, grammar or lexicon (Langacker 2008: 84). Most importantly, classroom context often provides only limited exposure to authentic input, which from a usage-based perspective is absolutely crucial.

Note: This work was partly supported by the Research Council of Norway through its Centers of Excellence funding scheme, Project number 223 265; and partly by the Center for Language and Cognition Groningen (CLCG), PhD project *Chunks in L2 development: A usage-based perspective.*

Hana Gustafsson, University of Oslo
Marjolijn Verspoor, University of Groningen

DOI 10.1515/9781501505492-011

From a usage-based perspective, L2 development is primarily driven by frequency and salience of structures in the surrounding input (Ellis and Cadierno 2009). In theory, this means that sufficient exposure to authentic input in the target language – where chunks are very frequent – will drive the learning of chunks of the target language. But even when immersed in authentic input, L2 learners' attention tends to be focused on individual words rather than on word combinations (Wray 2002: 6). Individual words such as *school* are learned separately and earlier than two-word expressions such as *at school*, because for L2 learners single words tend to be more salient as units than multi-word expressions (chunks). Similarly, "preferred ways of saying things" may not be sufficiently salient as a unit in order to be learned as a chunk. The sensitivity to how words go together in authentic language is crucial for the learning of chunks and is most likely heightened by more exposure to authentic input (Ellis and Cadierno 2009). There are numerous individual differences in how L2 learners learn and use chunks (Schmitt and Carter 2004), which is also in line with the usage-based perspective assumption that individual learners construct their L2 differently depending on their exact experience of the L2. Moreover, as Verspoor and Smiskova (2012) maintain, L2 learners may also show great variability in their development of chunks over time. In this study, individual differences will be considered in relation to the amount and kind of input L2 learners are receiving and in relation to individual variability in development over time.

In short, learning chunks is an important part of L2 development and tracking learners' use of chunks can give us valuable insight into the process of L2 development. In this paper, we will report on a data driven study in a group of 22 Dutch L2 English learners; 11 in a semi-immersion instructional (high-input) condition and 11 in regular instructional (low-input) condition. Our main aim is to track the development of chunks in these learners, with a close focus on the potential differences between the high- and low-input conditions. Taking a usage-based perspective, we expect that the learners' use of chunks will reflect the amount and kind of input they are receiving. We expect the learners to use chunks that are generally frequent and/or salient in L2 English and chunks that are frequent and/or salient in their specific L2 environment. The high-input learners are expected to use more chunks and a greater range of chunk types than the low-input learners. To gain insight into the actual developmental process of using chunks over time, we zoom in on two learners selected from our group and conduct a case study from a dynamic usage-based perspective (Verspoor and Smiskova 2012).

Since chunks are a complex linguistic phenomenon and our study of chunks in L2 development is data driven, we will first explain our operationalization of chunks and give a detailed description of the method employed in our study.

Next, we will present and discuss the findings of our longitudinal study of chunk development. With our findings we hope to show that chunks, as we define them, develop differently in high- and low-input learners and that tracking learners' use of chunks can give us important insights into L2 development from a usage-based perspective.

2 Operationalizing chunks

In order to track the development of chunks in learner data we need an exact definition of a *chunk*. However, as a linguistic phenomenon, chunks are notoriously difficult to capture. The exact operationalization depends on the purpose of the study and the nature of the data in question (Wray 2002). Since this study investigates the development of native-like chunks in learner language from a usage-based perspective, we need a highly inclusive definition. In order to build this definition, we followed a cyclical process of definition and identification of chunks in our data (Wray 2002: 19). First, we consulted the learners' writings to see what types of chunks they contain; next, based on this exploratory stage we built a general definition of a chunk; and finally, this data-derived definition then served to identify more instances of chunks in the data. This is a dynamic approach that fits well with a usage-based perspective and our data-driven study.

The exploratory stage revealed that the learners in our study used not only multi-word expressions which are part of traditional phraseology (such as *human body; sick and tired; boss around*) but also expressions that are the preferred ways of saying certain things (see Smiskova, Verspoor, and Lowie 2012). Compare *when I grow up* and *when I am a grown up adult* in the following two excerpts from learner texts:

(1) *When I am a grown up adult i would like to be a neurosurgeon. I would like to be a neurosurgeon when i am a grown up because i really like biology and i think i am quite good at it. I also think the human body is very interesting. It's so special how everything is organised so well and that most of the time works.*

(2) *I seriously have no idea what kind of job I'd like to do. And I'm getting sick and tired of people who ask me that. Just because of that I'm in eight grade, I'm probably supposed to know what I want to do when I grow up...*
  I absolutely don't like it when people boss me around.

Based on the exploratory stage, we defined a chunk as a conventionalized word sequence expressing a certain concept. The same concept could also be expressed by a word sequence which, while following rules of syntax correctly, is not a preferred word combination; compare *at school* vs. *in school; do homework* vs. *make homework; when I grow up* vs. *when I am a grown up adult.* In other words, a chunk for the purposes of this study is defined as a combination of two or more orthographic words[1], which may also include variable slots, expressing an idea (concept) in a conventionalized way. Such definition is in line with Langacker's (2008) notion of units representing normal ways of saying things:

> A substantial proportion of what is needed to speak a language fluently tends to be ignored because it is part of neither lexicon nor grammar as these are traditionally conceived. What I have in mind are the countless units representing normal ways of saying things. Native speakers control an immense inventory of conventional expressions and patterns of expression enabling them to handle a continuous flow of rapid speech. While they can certainly be included, I am not referring to lexical items of the sort found in dictionaries, nor even to recognized idioms. At issue instead are particular ways of phrasing certain notions out of all the ways they could in principle be expressed in accordance with lexicon and grammar of the language. These units can be of any size, ranging from standard collocations to large chunks of boilerplate language. These can be fully specific or partially schematic, allowing options in certain positions. (Langacker 2008: 84)

In order to distinguish between different types of chunks identified in the learner data, our aim was to classify the identified chunks in established typological categories. In fact, we found that using a typology of established chunk types was also helpful in the initial identification stage. Based on our definition, we were aiming for a typology of chunks which would include both established phraseological chunk types and "preferred ways of saying things". Since this is precisely what Granger and Paquot (2008) advocate, we chose to follow their classification approach. They propose the integration of two major approaches: the traditional *phraseological approach*, which is based on linguistic analysis, strictly distinguishes between phraseology and syntax and is mostly concerned with specific phraseological categories, most often non-compositional (idiomatic, semantically opaque, such as *kick the bucket*) and/or syntactically irregular (such as *by and large*). The second is a *corpus-based, frequency-distributional approach*, which has produced extensive evidence of frequently occurring semantically and syntactically regular word combinations, which are not part of traditional phraseology.

The formal typology of phrasemes proposed by Granger and Paquot (2008: 43–44) served as basis for the typology of chunks we used in this study (See Table 1 in Appendix). The original typology has three functional categories: *referential* (chunks which refer only to content and have no pragmatic function),

---

[1] Compounds which are hyphenated or written together as an orthographic word are also included (e.g. *however*).

textual (chunks with a discourse structuring and organizational function) and *communicative* (chunks with a communicative function, e.g. addressing inter-locutors). These functional categories are then subdivided on the basis of struc-tural types and degrees of non-compositionality (idiomaticity). In our study, we further grouped these into organizational levels (phrase or sentence level). Finally, we included "preferred ways of saying things" (namely, conventionalized sentences and conventionalized sentence stems), and additional categories based on the exploratory analysis of our data: structures, variable idioms (Stefanowitsch and Gries 2003: 43) and constructions. Table 1 in Appendix shows the modified typology including examples from our data.

However, when using any typology for a fine categorization of chunks it is important to bear in mind that we are imposing a fixed structure on a fuzzy, emergent phenomenon that may not have entirely fixed categories. The defining characteristics of chunks – such as non-compositionality, fixedness, function – tend to be present to a certain degree. This means that each formal category defined by these characteristics has prototypical examples, but there may also be word sequences in that category that do not display the defining charac-teristics to the same degree. Compare for instance the varying degrees of non-compositionality (idiomaticity) in *blow a fuse – blow your own trumpet – blow the gaff* (Granger and Paquot 2008). This is due to the fact that these defining characteristics form a continuum rather than clear-cut categories; and this in turn is caused by the overlap between morphology, syntax, semantics and discourse (Granger and Paquot 2008: 37). Moreover, many chunks are nested, i.e. consisting of smaller, often overlapping chunks (Wray 2002: 28), such as in *[[[The only thing] I [[know [for sure]]*, which can complicate the process of counting and classifying chunks.

Therefore, the typology of chunks presented here is intended as a helpful inventory of prototypes that may be further refined on the basis of more data analysis. Its categories should be perceived as dynamic and open rather than fixed and mutually exclusive; for instance, a chunk can display the defining characteristics of several categories (e.g. *however* is a linking adverbial in its function as well as a compound in its structure).

In resolving these and other complexities involved in researching chunks, it is crucial to closely adhere to the aim and background of the study (Wray 2002: 28). In our case, this involved making decisions in line with the usage-based perspective in order to tease out differences in development between our high- and low-input learners. In the following section, we describe in detail how chunks were identified and classified in this study and how we ensured con-sistency of the process.

3 The study

This paper reports on two longitudinal studies investigating the development of chunks in learners' language over about 2.5 years in high- and low-input conditions. The first is a group study, in which two groups of learners in two conditions (high- and low-input) are compared at the beginning and the end of the study. The second is a case study, in which the development of chunks is traced of two selected learners across 12 data points over time.

3.1 Input and production frequencies

Our participants are 22 Dutch high school learners who attend the same Dutch school, have a similar socio-economic background, and a similar scholastic aptitude (Verspoor et al. 2010). Both groups have an interest in language as the high-input group opted for a bilingual Dutch-English stream and the low-input group for monolingual (Dutch) stream that includes classical languages. At the start of the study the learners were about 11 years old in their first year at high school. The high-input group attended an education program in which subjects, such as geography and history, were taught in English. This group also had five hours of English as subject taught by a native speaker of English. In the high-input condition, students were exposed to a great amount of spoken English by both non-native and native speakers of English; most of their course materials were the same as used by native speakers. The low-input group attended a Dutch regular education program with all subjects taught in Dutch. This group had 2 hours of English a week also taught by a native speaker of English, but the course materials, even though communicative contained quite a bit of explicit grammar instruction. This group also had 2 hours in Latin and Greek.

The learners were asked to write about once a month on informal topics such as *My new school* or *My vacation*; *Write about the rules at home*; *Do you think they are fair?*; *What do you want to be when you grow up?*; *Write about a film or a book you like.* Most of the writings were written directly on computer, where the word limit was 200 words; some were handwritten in class. There was no time limit for the writings, but the students usually wrote no longer than 10 minutes.

3.2 Identification of chunks in written texts

First, we used researcher intuition to identify multi-word expressions which could match our general definition of a chunk. To help validate such intuitive decisions, we used Wray's (2008: 113–127) list of diagnostic criteria. Following Wray's instructions (2008: 115), we only used the criteria to validate expressions we had already intuitively identified as chunks, rather than using the criteria to initially identify chunks. If needed, which was mostly in the case of "preferred ways of saying things", intuitive judgments were further validated with the help of reference corpora. The reference corpora were used to confirm that a multi-word expression we intuitively identified as a chunk indeed frequently occurred in the corpora as a conventionalized unit. This step was based on the underlying notion of frequency, but not on detailed frequency or mutual strength counts.[2] In principle, this step gives further support to the criterion in point H of Wray's list of diagnostic criteria: "By my judgement, based on direct evidence or my intuition, there is a greater than chance-level probability that the writer will have encountered this precise formulation before in communication from other people" (Wray 2008: 120).

In addition to standardized reference corpora, such as the British Narional Corpus (BNC) (Davies 2004) and the Corpus of Contemporary American English (COCA) (Davies 2008), we also used the WebCorp search engine (Renouf, Kehoe, and Banerjee 2007), which allowed us to search the World Wide Web as a reference corpus. WebCorp is particularly relevant in our study since we are following young teenagers who tend to have a great deal of exposure to the language of the Internet; moreover, a number of conventionalized expressions that do not occur in standardized corpora are frequently found on the Internet (e.g. *The only thing I know for sure is that* +clause).

As already mentioned, larger chunks were often nested, i.e. they contained smaller, overlapping chunks. The larger chunks were mostly "preferred ways of saying things", such as *the only thing I know for sure*, which includes a verb complement (*know*+clause) and a particle (*for sure*). In these cases, the smaller chunks were not counted separately, as the composite larger chunk was perceived as a separate form-meaning/function unit in itself.

Finally, all identified chunks were categorized for type following our typology (Table 1 in Appendix). In the cases of chunks which display the defining characteristics of several categories, functional categories were given preference, since they are the more fundamental distinction in our typology. For instance, *however*, which is a compound in its structure as well as a linking adverbial in its function, was classified as a linking adverbial rather than a compound.

To ensure consistency of the identification process, all intuitive judgments were made by the first author, discussed and fine-tuned with the second author

---

2 We were unable to use word association measures as at the time of our study Webcorp did not provide this type of statistical information (Renouf et al. 2007: 53).

and validated as described in this section. To ensure all chunks were categorized consistently, the first author went through the coding process twice.

3.3 Method of analysis

In the cross-sectional study we used the procedure described in the previous section to identify chunks in texts written by the high-input learners (N = 11) and low-input learners (N = 11) at the start of the study (October 2007) and towards the end of the study (May 2009).[3] Next, we established several measures of chunk use in order to tease out differences between the groups and within the groups over time.

First, we recorded the raw token frequencies of all chunk types in Oct 07 and May 09 to see which chunk types were most frequently used in each group and if their distribution changed over time. To discover variety in chunk use, we counted the number of different chunk types per text (chunk types/text). To be able to compare learners and groups, we calculated relative frequencies by taking text length into account: for relative token frequency we calculated the ratio of all chunk tokens per 100 words of text (chunks/100 words); for relative token frequency of each chunk type we calculated the type-token ratio of each chunk type per 100 words (type-token [chunk type]/100 words). To gain more insight into the use of chunks in relation to text length, we calculated the correlation between the length of each text and the number of all chunk tokens in it (correlation text length/chunks). To measure overall "chunk coverage" we calculated the percentage of all words used as part of a chunk in each text (%chunk-words/text). Finally, to capture differences in the development of chunk length we calculated the mean chunk length per text (mean chunk length/text).

Next, we performed statistical analyses on all these measures to see where there might be significant differences in development, both between the groups and within the groups over time (potential change from Oct 07 to May 09).

In the case study we used the same procedure for the identification of chunks texts written by two selected high-input and low-input learners. For each measurement over time (i.e. each collected text) we recorded the number of different chunk types and the raw token frequency of each chunk type. This way we obtained a longitudinal chunk profile for each learner, which allowed us to track their individual development in detail over two years (Oct 07 to Nov 09).

---

3 Due to subject dropout we had to take May 09 as the end-point of our cross-sectional group study; the data for our microgenetic study was available until November 09.

4 Results group study

The results show that in Oct 07 the low-input group wrote on average significantly longer texts than the high-input group (low-input mean 114.18, high-input mean 65.09 words, $p < .05$) and in May 09 the high-input group wrote on average significantly longer texts than the low-input group (high-input mean 157.72, low-input mean 103 words, $p < .05$). We will first present the raw token frequencies of all chunk types identified in the texts and then the relative frequencies according to each measure.

4.1 Raw frequencies of chunk tokens and types

In total, 18 chunk types[4] were identified in all the texts together. Figure 1 shows raw token frequencies of each chunk type at the beginning of the study in Oct 07 and Figure 2 at the end of the study in May 09.

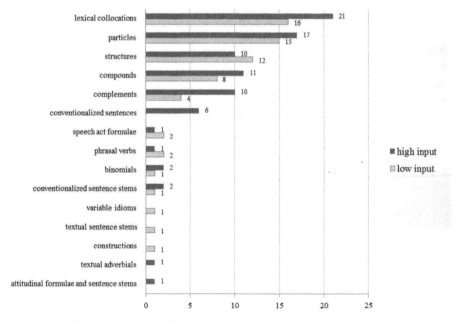

Figure 1: October 2007: Raw token frequency of each chunk type in high- and low-input group.

---

4 Not all of the 22 categories of our typology were expected to appear in the data, which indeed they did not (such as slogans, proverbs, similes and complex textual organizers).

Figure 1 shows that the most frequent chunks at the beginning of our study were lexical collocations (e.g. *strong coffee; main character; first kiss*) followed by particles (e.g. *a lot of; at home; in English*), structures (e.g. *NUMBER years old*), compounds (e.g. *living room*), verb complements (e.g. *would like to; going to; have to; like -ing; think + clause*) and conventionalized sentences (*It's hard to explain*).

Figure 2 shows that at the end of the study the frequency distribution was quite different: verb complements had moved from their fifth place to become the most frequent chunk type; conventionalized sentence stems (e.g. *The only thing I know for sure is that*+clause) and attitudinal formulae (e.g. *I mean*) had moved into the top five most frequent chunk types, and structures moved down from their third place to become much less frequent.

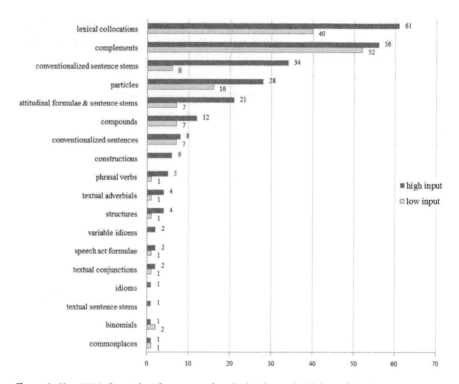

Figure 2: May 2009: Raw token frequency of each chunk type in high- and low-input group.

4.2 Relative frequencies of chunk tokens and types[5]

The relative chunk token frequency: In Oct 07 the high-input group used on average significantly more chunks per 100 words (mean 10.62, $p < .05$) than the low-input group (mean 4.97). Repeated measures ANOVA shows that over time, the measure increased significantly more in the low-input group (F (1, 20) = 5, $p < .05$) than in the high-input group. Figure 3 shows the time/group interaction chart. Post hoc pair-wise comparison (paired samples t-test) shows that there was a significant increase between Oct 07 and May 09 in both low-input ($p < .001$) and high input group ($p = .04$). In May 09 there were no significant differences between the groups in the average number of chunks per 100 words ($p > .05$).

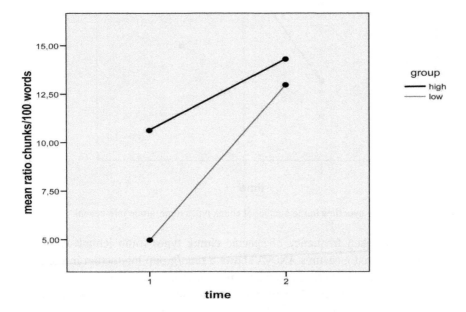

Figure 3: Increase over time in chunks/100 words (time/group interaction).

The relative chunk type frequency: In Oct 07 there was no significant difference between the groups in the number of chunk types. Repeated measures ANOVA shows that over time, the number of chunk types increased significantly more in the high-input group (F (1, 20) = 5, $p < .05$) than in the low-input group. Figure 4 shows the time/group interaction chart. Post hoc pair-wise comparison

---

5 For detailed results of statistical analyses see Table 2 in Appendix.

(paired samples t-test) shows that the increase between Oct 07 and May 09 was significant in the high-input group (p = .001) but not in the low-input group (p = .07). In May 09, the high-input group used significantly more chunks types per text (mean 7.0, p < .001) than the low-input group (mean 4.55).

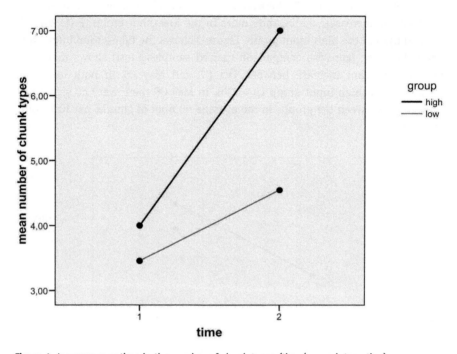

Figure 4: Increase over time in the number of chunk types (time/group interaction).

The relative token frequency of specific chunk types (ratio [chunk type]/100 words): Repeated measures ANOVA shows a time/group interaction in the ratio of two chunk types: verb complements and conventionalized sentence stems.

The ratio of verb complements increased significantly more in the low-input group (F (1, 20) = 5; p < .05) than the high-input group. Figure 5 shows the time/group interaction chart. Post hoc pair-wise comparison (paired samples t-test) shows that the increase in the verb complements ratio between Oct 07 and May 09 was significant in both low-input (p = .001) and high-input group (p = .02).

The ratio of conventionalized sentence stems increased significantly more in the high-input group (F (1, 20) = 10; p < .05) than in the low-input group. Figure 6 shows the time/group interaction chart. Post hoc pair-wise comparison (paired samples t-test) shows that the increase in the ratio of conventionalized sentence stems between Oct 07 and May 09 was significant in the high-input group (p < .001) but not in the low-input group (p = .052).

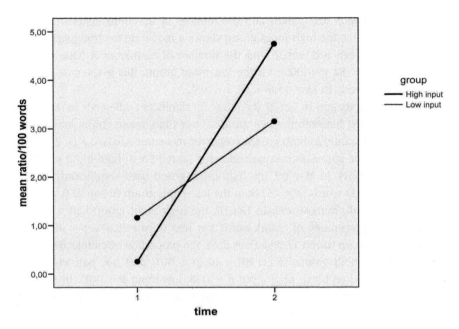

Figure 5: Increase over time in the ratio of verb complements (time/group interaction).

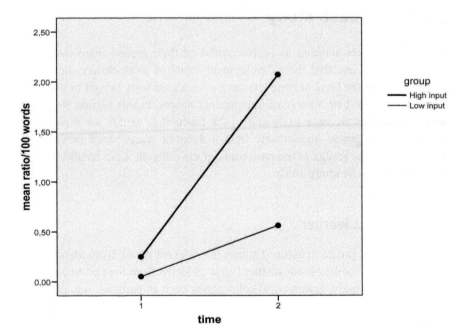

Figure 6: Increase over time in the ratio of conventionalized sentence stems (time/group interaction).

Correlation between text length and the number of all chunk tokens: In both Oct 07 and May 09, the high-input group shows a moderate to strong significant correlation between text length and the number of chunks in it (Oct: $r = .61$, $p < .05$; May: $r = .87$, $p < .001$); for the low-input group, this is the case only at the end of the study in May 09 ($r = .73$, $p < .05$).

Mean chunk length: In Oct 07 there was no significant difference in the mean chunk length/text between the two groups. Over time, mean chunk length/text increased significantly in both groups (repeated measures ANOVA: F (1, 20) = 74, $p < .001$, post hoc pair-wise comparison using paired t-test: high-input $p < .001$, low-input $p < .001$). In May 09, the high-input group used significantly longer chunks (mean 3.13 words, $p < .05$) than the low-input group (mean 2.60 words).

Proportion of chunk-words: In Oct 07, the high-input group had a significantly higher percentage of chunk-words per text (mean 26.8%, $p < .05$) than the low-input group (mean 12.4%). Over time, the proportion of chunks increased significantly in both groups (F (1, 20) = 34, $p < .001$; post hoc pair-wise comparison using paired t-test: high-input $p = .008$, low-input $p < .001$). In May 09, the high-input group had a significantly higher percentage of chunk-words per text (mean 45.6%, $p < .05$) than the low-input group (mean 33.2%).

5 Results case study

Two learners were selected as representative of their groups (high- and low-input), in the sense that their development matched most closely the chunk development at the level of their groups. Both learners were judged to be at the same starting level by a panel of independent judges. In this section we report on the results of the case study and in the Discussion section we explore the learners' development qualitatively from a dynamic usage-based perspective. We also relate the results of the case study to the different input conditions and to the results of the group study.

5.1 Low-input learner

The longitudinal profile in Figure 7 shows the different chunk types identified in texts written by the low-input learner (texts collected from Sept 07 to Nov 09). Throughout the study, grammatical collocations such as particles (e.g. *at home*) and verb complements (e.g. *like -ing*) are the most frequent chunk types; in some texts these grammatical collocations are overused (see Figure 7, May 09). The other two most frequently occurring chunk types are lexical collocations and compounds. After 2.5 years the learner used six chunk types compared to three chunk types at the start of the study. The correlation between the number of chunks and the length of the texts collected over time is rather weak and non-significant ($r = 0.40$, $p > .05$).

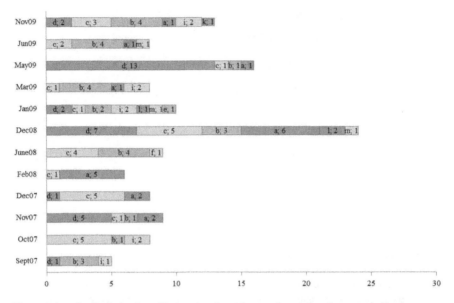

Figure 7: Longitudinal chunk profile in a low-input learner (raw token frequency). Numbers and letters in the bar chart indicate raw token frequencies of individual chunk types: a = compounds, b = lexical collocations, c = particles, d = complements, e = phrasal verbs, f = idioms, i = structures, k = constructions, l = conventionalized sentence stems, m = conventionalized sentences (chunk types are labeled alphabetically following Table 1. in Appendix).

5.2 High-input learner

Figure 8 illustrates the range of chunk types used by the high-input learner over time. Grammatical collocations, such as particles (e.g. *at home*) and verb complements (e.g. *like -ing*) are the most frequent, followed by lexical collocations (e.g. *strong coffee*), conventionalized sentence stems (e.g. *One thing I know for sure is that* +clause) and structures (e.g. **number** *years old*). After 2.5 years the learner used 10 chunk types compared to 1 chunk type at the start of the study. The chunk range includes types with a communicative and discourse organization function (e.g. *I mean; you know; by the way*). There is a strong, significant correlation between the number of chunks and the length of the texts collected over time ($r = .95$, $p < .001$).

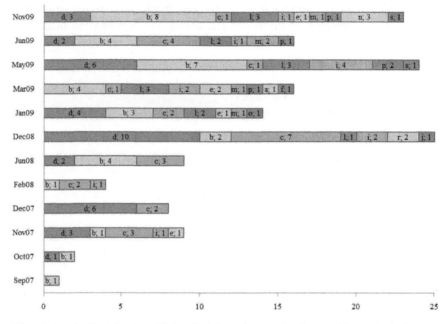

Figure 8: Longitudinal chunk profile in a high-input learner. Numbers and letters in the bar chart indicate raw token frequencies of individual chunk types: a = compounds, b = lexical collocations, c = particles, d = complements, e = phrasal verbs, f = idioms, i = structures, j = variable idioms, l = conventionalized sentence stems, m = conventionalized sentences, n = textual prepositions, o = textual conjunctions, p = textual adverbials, r = speech act formulae, s = attitudinal formulae (chunk types are labeled alphabetically following Table 1. in Appendix).

6 Discussion

6.1 Group study

The chunk measures we used in this study have helped tease out a number of significant tendencies in the development of the two groups. The results show that in both groups there is growth over time in all chunk measures. This is not surprising: since chunks are pervasive in language, both groups learn chunks as they learn other aspects of L2 English. However, there are differences in how much some of these measures increased in each group. We will discuss how these differences could be related to the amount and kind of input the learners were receiving. We will also discuss how the results of these measures are related and which measures seem to distinguish best the differences in development between the high- and low-input learners. We will also illustrate the group tendencies with the results of the case study.

6.1.1 Raw frequencies

The raw frequency counts show that out of the 22 types established in our typology, 18 types were identified in the learner data, with considerable differences in frequency distribution between the different types (Figures 1 and 2 in the Results section). In general, the overall frequency distribution of chunk types appearing in the data at the start of the study was different than at the end of the study. In October 07 the most frequent chunk types were lexical collocations, particles, structures (short slot-fillers), compounds and complements. Most of these chunk types are short and/or grammatically based and tend to be very frequent in L2 English; they are also the ones most often encountered as part of language instruction. The use of these chunks contributes to L2 accuracy but not as much to general fluency and authenticity. Also, in Oct 07 there were only very few "preferred ways of saying things", discourse organizers, communicative formulae and idiomatic chunks – the kind of chunks that greatly contribute to fluency and authenticity and are typical of an authentic native-like repertoire. Such findings indicate rather low levels of L2 proficiency at the start of the study.

As the overall use of chunks increased over time and the learners started using new chunk types, the frequency distribution of different chunk types changed. While the short and/or grammatically based chunks were still very frequent, the order of frequency changed as "preferred ways of saying things", discourse organizers and communicative formulae were more frequently used: in May 09, the most frequent were complements, lexical collocations, particles, conventionalized sentence stems, attitudinal formulae, compounds and conventionalized sentences. Such findings show that as the learners were becoming more proficient and had more contact with the language, they started using the longer chunks that greatly contribute to L2 fluency and authenticity. However, the results also show that some aspects of the frequency distribution and of the changes over time were not the same for both input groups.

6.1.2 Relative frequencies

The relative frequencies show that at the start (Oct 07) the high-input group out-performed the low-input group on two chunk measures: %chunk-words/text and chunks/100 words. This means that in Oct 07 the high-input group already used significantly more chunks, which could be related to the two months of semi-immersion in authentic input the group had already received at the time of the first writing (as opposed to the low-input group, who had received only 2 hours of English instruction weekly). At that point the high-input group was not using significantly more chunk types than the low-input group.

As the learners were becoming more proficient over time and started using more chunks, the relative measures grew in both input groups; however, there was a significant difference in the growth of two of these measures: the number of chunk types increased significantly more in the high-input group and chunks/100 words increased significantly more in the low-input group. In line with our expectations, the high-input learners developed a greater range of chunk types, since they had more exposure to authentic input. The significantly greater increase in chunks/100 words in the low-input group most likely indicates that there was a slight difference in L2 proficiency between the low-input and high-input learners at the time of the first writing. The progress in the low-input group was then more rapid because they started from lower (even zero) levels than the high-input group, who had already established a certain level of the L2.

The relative frequencies show that at the end of the study (May 09) the high-input group again outperformed the low-input group, this time on three chunk measures. Firstly, the high-input group had a significantly higher proportion of chunks in their texts than the low-input group (% chunkwords/text). In fact, the high-input group had approached native-like proportion of chunks in their texts: on average, 46% of the learners' texts consisted of fixed chunks – quite close to Erman and Warren's (2000) estimation that about 50% of native speaker text consists of chunks; in the low-input group the average percentage was 33%.

Secondly, in May 09 the high-input group used significantly longer chunks (mean chunk length/text) than the low-input group. This contributed to the increased percentage of chunk-words in text: since longer chunks contain more words, the percentage of chunk-words per text is higher. From a usage-based perspective, it is interesting to look at *why* the mean chunk length increased. The increased chunk length reflects our findings about the increase over time in certain chunk types: the high-input group increased their ratio of conventionalized sentence stems (e.g. *The only thing I know for sure is that* +clause) significantly more than the low-input group. In addition, the high-input group developed other types of longer chunks, such as textual sentence stems, attitudinal formulae and conventionalized sentences (e.g. *There are more important things in life*). It was mainly the increase in these "preferred ways of saying things" what contributed to the overall increase in chunk length.

What is also interesting about the longer chunks is that they are nested, i.e. consisting of smaller, often overlapping chunks. For instance, consider the example sentence in (3), which contains a conventionalized sentence stem *The only thing I know for sure*+clause. The stem consists of several overlapping word sequences, which in our study could all be considered chunks. As units, they all occur quite frequently in native-like use of English (for illustration, the corresponding numbers show token frequency per 1 million words in COCA), with the frequency of occurrence decreasing with the increased length of the sequence:

(3) *The only thing I know for sure is that I want to travel.*

for sure	5706
know for sure	1161
the only thing	7796
the only thing I know	52
the only thing I know for sure	4

While all these sequences could in principle be also counted separately, in our study we only take into account the original 7-word sequence: it is a conventionalized way of expressing a certain notion (a normal way of saying this), which in its entirety can be regarded as a form/meaning/function mapping in Langacker's terms (2008: 84). In a study of L2 development, the ability to use such expression seems a sign of fluency, authenticity and a certain proficiency in the L2. It also shows that the learner is paying attention to how things are normally said, or, to how individual words are combined into authentically sounding clauses and sentences, and finally into a fluent, native-like discourse (Ellis 2001; Pawley and Syder 1983). Since the use of these longer chunks is prominent in the high-input group, we can conclude that a) frequent exposure to authentic input facilitates the learning of longer chunks, b) that high-input learners develop sensitivity for "normal ways of saying things" and that, possibly, c) high-input learners are able to manipulate the L2 in larger form/function/ meaning units and/or are able to recall longer word sequences.

Finally, in May 09 learners in the high-input group used significantly more chunk types than the low-input group. This reflects the already mentioned use of discourse organizers, communicative formulae and above all "preferred ways of saying things" and is again in line with our expectations: more authentic input means a wider range of chunk types; more exposure to authentic input means greater opportunity to learn a wider range of chunk types.

However, in May 09 the high-input group also wrote significantly longer texts, which could also influence their scores on some of these measures: longer texts increase the chance that more chunk types are used, and longer texts will logically contain more chunk tokens. Still, this is not entirely the case in our data: the length of a text and the number of chunks in it do not always correlate highly. Firstly, in Oct 07 the low-input group wrote significantly longer texts by almost a half than the high-input group; still, the high-input group used significantly more chunks. Secondly, the high-input group shows a strong significant correlation between text length and the number of chunks in it both at the start and at the end of the study; for the low-input group, this was only the case at the end of the study. These findings seem to suggest a different type of development in the two input groups: in native speaker repertoire we would also expect text length and number of chunks to correlate – since language is full of chunks, longer text will contain more chunk tokens. This finding could be a sign of more native-like development in the high-input group.

6.1.3 Individual differences

Our cross-sectional study has also revealed individual differences in the use of chunks, which we have noted not only in the statistical analyses (high standard deviations in almost all measures) but also in qualitative analyses of the data. Some of the chunks our learners use are not what one would expect in relation to the assigned topic, nor are they the kind that frequently appears in everyday language, in standardized corpora or in a classroom setting. Still, they are clearly chunks characteristic of the kind of input the learners are regularly exposed to. In an answer to a topic question (*What would you like to be when you grow up?*) two learners responded in very different ways – and used very different chunks. In example (4), we can detect the jargon of computer games, while in (5) we could guess at movies, TV shows and glossy magazines:

(4) *when i grow up i want to be a **game designer**. then i can make all kinds of games. i already use **game maker 7** where you can **program your own pictures**, you draw them with paint and then you can **let them appear or disappear** and you can **let them fire something or change into something else**. you can **make a sort of super mario** because you can **set the gravity and the jumping height**, but you can also **make a sort of pack man**, you just make a labyrinth and you **let your picture do what you want when you press certain buttons** and you **make other pictures follow you**. then you say that when a **collision** happens **between you and the guy, you delete yourself**. there are also programs that are used for making **3D pictures** and where you can **scan your drawings** to paste them on a way that you can easily **make them 3D**.*

(5) *When I grow up,* ***I want to be famous, I want to be a star, I want to be in*** ***movies.*** *When I grow up,* ***I want to see the world,*** *I want to drive nice cars,* ***I want to have groupies.*** *When I grow up,* ***I want to be on TV,*** *that people know me, be in magazines. When I grow older than that, I want to have a nice, rich, husband that pays everything for me. I want to* ***do nothing at all*** ***and just lay around our pool all day long.*** *When I grow even older* ***I want*** ***to have children*** *and than* ***I hope I will be a good mom.*** *I will* ***make sure*** ***they get everything they need,*** *but I will not spoil them. I don't want to have* ***spoiled children,*** *but I do* ***want them to have a good life.*** *That is what I want to be when I grow up.*

In fact, the first few lines of learner text (5) almost exactly correspond with the chorus in a popular song which was traced back via WebCorp: *When I grow up / I wanna be famous / I wanna be a star / I wanna be in movies / When I grow up / I wanna see the world / Drive nice cars / I wanna have groupies / When I grow up / Be on TV / People know me / Be on magazines* (The Pussycat Dolls, LLC 2008: When I grow up). This is valuable evidence of the influence of input on the learner's use of L2 English.

In short, there are clear individual differences in what chunks learners use and how they use them, which can be related to different kinds of input they are exposed to. This is compatible with the usage-based assumption that everyone's experience of language is slightly different: what may be a completely unknown, highly idiomatic and perhaps a rather useless expression for one person (e.g. *super mario, pack man, set the gravity and the jumping height*) may be a frequently encountered and relevant expression for another. Compared to native speakers our Dutch L2 learners receive limited amounts of English input, and each learner may be surrounded by different kinds of input and developing their language in different ways. As a result, the developmental paths of chunks may be very different for each learner. The texts collected during our study provide evidence: some are more dense with chunks than others and the different chunk types are unevenly spread across the texts written by individual learners.

6.2 Case study

The longitudinal chunk profiles of the high and long-input learner (Figures 7 and 8 in the Results section) suggest qualitative differences in development. The high-input learner uses a range of different chunk types and shows considerable variability in the frequency distribution of chunk types over time, while in the low-input learner this variability is much less pronounced. At the start of the study the low-input learner used more chunks than the high-input learner (compare Figures 7 and 8, Sept 07), but she seems to develop differently and does not experience the same rapid explosion of a wide range of chunk types as the high-input learner. The qualitative differences interpreted here at face value were further analyzed in Verspoor and Smiskova (2012), who argue that from a dynamic usage-based perspective, this difference in variability over time is meaningful and relevant to the learners' L2 development.

The profiles of the two learners also show different patterns in the development of specific chunk types. In the high-input learner, there are interesting relationships over time in the use of lexical collocations, grammatical collocations and "preferred ways of saying things". In the first half of the study she tended to overuse particles and verb complements, while using only a few lexical collocations; in the second half of the study her use of lexical collocations rapidly increased, she started using "preferred ways of saying things" and fewer grammatical collocations. This decrease could be explained by nesting: as the learner starts using longer and more complex conventionalized word sequences, shorter grammatical chunks embedded in them are no longer free-standing and consequently are not counted as such. For the low-input learner, grammatical collocations (verb complements and particles) remain the most frequent types throughout the study, the increase in lexical collocations is much less pronounced than in the high-input learner, and there is no clear emergence of "preferred ways of saying things".

The differing patterns of development can be related to the learners' different input conditions and illustrate in greater detail some of the significant effects identified on group level. The low-input learner, who had less exposure to authentic input, shows a rather limited development of different chunk types (from 3 chunk types to 6), while the high-input learner developed a whole range of different types (from 1 to 10). Next, while the low-input learner uses only very few "preferred ways of saying things", there is a clear emergence of this chunk type in the high-input learner: after 2.5 years, conventionalized sentence stems are the third most frequent chunk type in her text. The rapid increase in lexical collocations in the high-input learner matches the increase in raw token frequency on the group level (although this overall increase in the high-input group was not captured by the ratio type-token colloc/100 words). The high-input learner also uses communicative formulae and discourse organizers (textual and referential chunk types), both of which are an integral part of native-like discourse, while in the low-input learner these chunk types are missing. Finally, while the high-input learner shows a very strong significant correlation between the text length and the number of chunks, the low-input learner only shows a moderate trend, which is not significant. Just as on the group level, these findings seem to indicate a faster and more native-like development in the high-input learner.

7 Conclusion

In this study we explored the development of chunks from a usage-based perspective in two groups of Dutch L2 learners of English, one in a high- and one in a low-input condition. Using an integrated approach we have captured some significant differences in the development of each group over time. Our findings show that over time both groups used increasingly more chunks and developed a greater range of chunk types, among which were traditionally recognized types and so called "normal ways of saying things" (Langacker 2008); both groups also used increasingly longer chunks. Moreover, in line with our usage-based expectations, our findings also show significant differences between the two input groups. The high-input learners, who had more exposure to authentic input, developed a significantly greater range of chunk types including those with a clear discourse function, greater number of "normal ways of saying things" and a greater proportion of chunk-words per text. At the end of the study, this proportion was on average 46% – fairly close to Erman and Warren's (2000) estimate of about a 50% proportion of chunks in native speaker text. Such findings lead to interesting conclusions that would benefit from further usage-based research. The significant differences we identified between the two groups are related to recognized features of a fluent, authentic native speaker repertoire: high chunk density, wide range of chunk types of various structure and function, longer and nested chunks. This suggests that the development of chunks in our high-input learners is more native-like than the development in our low-input learners; as a result, the high-input learners are also using their L2 in a more fluent and authentic way. Finally, we have also identified clear individual differences in what chunks the learners are using and how they are using them – this seems to be not only influenced by the amount and kind of input they are receiving, but also by their individual communicative needs.

References

Davies, Mark. 2004. BYU-BNC: The British National Corpus. Available online at http://corpus. byu.edu/bnc.BYU-BNC [On-line].

Davies, Mark. 2008. The Corpus of Contemporary American English (COCA): 400+ million words, 1990-present. Available online at http://www.americancorpus.org. COCA [On-line].

Ellis, Nick C. 2001. Memory for language. In *Cognition and Second Language Instruction*, Peter Robinson (ed.), 33–68. Cambridge: Cambridge University Press.

Ellis, Nick C. 2008. Phraseology: The periphery and the heart of language. In *Phraseology in Foreign Language Learning and Teaching*, Fanny Meunier, and Sylviane Granger (eds.), 1–13. Amsterdam: John Benjamins.

Ellis, Nick C., and Teresa Cadierno. 2009. Constructing a second language: Introduction to the special edition. *Annual Review of Cognitive Linguistics* 7: 111–139.

Erman, Britt, and Beatrice Warren. 2000. The idiom principle and the open choice principle. *Text* 20 (1): 29–62.

Eyckmans, June, Frank Boers, and Helene Stengers. 2007. Identifying chunks: Who can see the wood for the trees? *Language Forum* 33 (2): 85–100.

Granger, Sylviane, and Magali Paquot. 2008. Disentangling the phraseological web. In *Phraseology: An Interdisciplinary Perspective*, Sylviane Granger, and Fanny Meunier (eds.), 28–49. Amsterdam: John Benjamins.

Langacker, Ronald W. 2008. Cognitive Grammar as a basis for language instruction. In *Handbook of Cognitive Linguistics and Second Language Acquisition*, Peter Robinson, and Nick C. Ellis (eds.), 66–88. New York: Routledge.

Pawley, Andrew, and Frances H. Syder. 1983. Two puzzles for linguistic theory: Native-like selection and native-like fluency. In *Language and Communication*, Jack C. Richards, and Richard W. Schmidt (eds.), 163–199. New York: Longman.

Renouf, Antoinette, Andrew Kehoe, and Jay Banerjee. 2007. WebCorp: An integrated system for web text search. In *Corpus Linguistics and the Web*, Nadja Nesselhauf, Marianne Hundt, and Carolin Biewer (eds.), 47–68. Amsterdam: Rodopi.

Schmitt, Norbert, and Ronald Carter. 2004. Formulaic Sequences in Action: An Introduction. In *Formulaic Sequences: Acquisition, Processing and Use*, Norbert Schmitt (ed.), 1–22. Amsterdam/Philadelphia: John Benjamins.

Sinclair, John M. 1991. *Corpus, Concordance, Collocation*. Oxford: Oxford University Press.

Smiskova, Hana, Marjolijn Verspoor, and Wander Lowie. 2012. Conventionalized ways of saying things (CWOSTs) and L2 development. *Dutch Journal of Applied Linguistics* 1 (1): 125–142.

Stefanowitsch, Anatol, and Stefan Th. Gries. 2003. Collostructions: Investigating the interaction of words and constructions. *International Journal of Corpus Linguistics* 8: 209–243.

Verspoor, Marjolijn, and Hana Smiskova. 2012. Foreign Language Development from a Dynamic Usage-Based Perspective. In *L2 writing development: Multiple perspectives*, Rosa M. Manchón (ed.), 17–46. Berlin: Mouton de Gruyter.

Verspoor, Marjolijn, Monika S. Schmid, and Xiaoyan Xu. 2012. A dynamic usage based perspective on L2 writing. *Journal of Second Language Writing* 21 (3): 239–263.

Verspoor, Marjolijn, Jennifer Schuitemaker-King, Eva van Rein, Kees de Bot, and Peter Edelenbos. 2010. Tweetalig onderwijs: Vormgeving en prestaties. Onderzoeksrapportage.

Wray, Alison. 2002. *Formulaic Language and the Lexicon*. Cambridge: Cambridge University Press.

Wray, Alison. 2008. *Formulaic Language: Pushing the Boundaries*. Cambridge: Cambridge University Press.

Appendix

Table 1: Typology of chunks (closely based on Granger and Paquot 2008: 43–44).

1. Chunk types with a referential function	
1.1 Word and phrase level	
a. Compounds	*sunbathing, two-week holiday, ice-cream* – made up of two elements which have independent status outside these word combinations. They can be written separately, with a hyphen or as one orthographic word.
b. Lexical collocations	*heavy rain, take a dive, strong current, pretty hard, real close, go wrong, hurt badly* – strings of specific lexical items, which co-occur with a mutual expectancy greater than chance and have a semantic dependency relationship; they show compositional structure and do not have pragmatic functions. The "base" of a collocation is selected first by a language user for its independent meaning. The second element is semantically dependent on the "base". One collocation can be embedded in another, as in (take [[strong] measures])
c. Grammatical collocations: Particles	*afraid of, involved in, at school, in English* – restricted combinations of a lexical word and a grammatical word
d. Grammatical collocations: Complements	*avoid -ing; necessary to; want/going/have/ manage to; go -in; keep -ing; would like to; be able to; know+clause; say that+clause* – restricted combinations of a lexical word and a complement structure (infinitive, gerund, reflexive pronoun or a nominal sentence)
e. Phrasal verbs	*blow up, make out, crop up* – combinations of verbs and adverbial particles; can have varying degrees of non-compositionality
f. Idioms	*to spill the beans, to let the cat out of the bag, to bark up the wrong tree* – constructed around a verbal nucleus and characterized by their semantic non-compositionality. Lack of flexibility and marked syntax are further indications of their idiomatic status

g. Similes	*as old as the hills, to swear like a trooper* – stereotyped comparisons; they typically consist of sequences following the frames "as ADJ as (DET) NOUN"and "VERB like a NOUN"
h. Irreversible bi- and trinomials	*bed and breakfast; kith and kin; left, right and center* – fixed sequences of two or three word forms that belong to the same part-of-speech category and are linked by the conjunction *and* or *or*
i. Structures	*Even ADJ+er than; as ADJ as, a year ago, two meters high* – short slot-fillers containing one or more free slots for a lexical item
j. Variable idioms	*pay a price for -ing; end up -ing* – have a slot and are to some degree idiomatic (Stefanowitsch and Gries 2003: 222)

1.2 Clause and sentence level

k. Constructions	*The sooner we are finished, the sooner we can go* – longer slot-fillers containing one or more free slots for a phrase or a clause
l. Preferred ways of saying things: Conventionalized sentence stems	*one thing I know for sure is...; all they can do is...* – a clause or its fragment whose grammatical form and lexical content is wholly or largely fixed; its fixed elements form a standard label for a culturally recognized concept
m. Preferred ways of saying things: Conventionalized sentences	*It's hard to explain. There are more important things in life. I`m just who I am.* – a sentence whose grammatical form and lexical content is wholly or largely fixed; Its fixed elements form a standard label for a culturally recognized concept

2. Chunk types with a textual function
2.1 Word and phrase level

n. Textual prepositions	*in addition to, apart from* – grammaticalized combinations of simple prepositions with a noun, adverb or adjective
o. Textual conjunctions	*so that, as if, even though* – grammaticalized sequences that function as complex conjunctions

p. Textual adverbials	*in other words, last but not least, more accurately, what is more, to conclude, the reason for, however* – linking chunks such as polywords, grammaticalized prepositional phrases, adjectival phrases, adverbial phrases

2.2 Clause level

q. Textual sentence stems	*another thing is*+clause; *it will be shown that*+clause; *I will discuss*+clause – routinized fragments of sentences that are used to serve specific textual or organizational functions and typically involve a subject and a verb

3. Chunk types with a communicative function

r. Speech act formulae	*Good morning; Take care; You're welcome;* suggesting (*why don't we*), concluding (*that's all*) – preferred ways of performing certain functions such as greetings, compliments, invitations
s. Attitudinal formulae and sentence stems	*in fact, to be honest, it is clear that* – used to signal speaker's attitudes towards their utterances and interlocutors
t. Proverbs and proverb fragments	*When in Rome* – express general ideas by means of non-literal meaning (metaphors, metonymies, etc.); equivalent to complete sentences but are often abbreviated
u. Commonplaces	*it's a small world; we only live once; the sky is the limit* – non-metaphorical complete sentences that express tautologies, truisms and sayings based on everyday experience
w. Slogans	*Make love, not war.* – short directive phrases made popular by their repeated use in politics or advertising

Table 2: Statistical analyses of chunk measures in a cross-sectional study (*significant at the .05 level; **significant at the .001 level).

Chunk measures	Oct 07 means (SDs) indep. samples t-test (α = .05)		May09 means (SDs) indep. samples t-test (α = .05)		Effects (p-values) repeated measures ANOVA (α = .05)		
	high-input	low-input	high-input	low-input	time	group	time/group
chunk types/text	4.00 (2.45)	3.45 (1.86)	7.00** (0.89)	4.55 (1.86)	.000	.036	.036
% chunk-words/text	26.8* (16.28)	12.40 (7.29)	45.60* (9.82)	33.2 (10.49)	.000	.002	.652
chunks/ 100 words	10.62* (5.64)	4.97 (2.51)	14.29 (2.15)	12.96 (3.74)	.000	.011	.046
mean chunk length/text	1.65 (0.89)	1.02 (0.56)	3.13* (0.40)	2.60 (0.40)	.000	.005	.760
type-token lex.col/100 words	2.62 (1.94)	1.15 (1.09)	3.26 (1.75)	4.02 (2.95)	.006	.599	.063
type-token compl/100 words	1.16 (2.02)	0.26 (0.44)	3.15 (1.20)	4.75 (3.10)	.000	.562	.041
type-token conv.sent stem/100 words	0.25 (0.55)	0.05 (0.17)	2.07 (1.11)	0.56 (0.81)	.000	.002	.004
mean text length	65.09 (20.23)	114.18* (42.83)	157.72* (39.26)	103.00 (35.45)			
Pearson correlation text length/chunks	.612*	.146	.867**	.726*			

Déogratias Nizonkiza

11 Predictive power of controled productive knowledge of collocations over L2 proficiency

1 Introduction

Collocations are important for second/foreign (L2) language learners if they want to use the language more efficiently and sound more natural (see among others Boers et al. 2006; Granger 1998; Granger and Meunier 2008; Howarth 1998; Meunier and Granger 2008; Nesselhauf 2005; Pawley and Syder 1983; Schmitt 1998; Wray 2002). Over the past decades, researchers have attempted to describe collocations and at the moment, it is clear that studies on collocations have adopted three main approaches (Granger and Paquot 2008; Gyllstad 2007; Handl 2008; Nesselhauf 2004, 2005; Siyanova and Schmitt 2008).

Nesselhauf (2005) has traced two prominent traditions through which collocations have been researched: the frequency-based and the phraseological tradition. She has also observed that some scholars primarily work in either one of the two traditions, but additionally include elements from the other in order to address the limitations of the tradition they follow. The latter constitutes the third tradition that Gyllstad (2007) and Granger and Paquot (2008) refer to as the 'best of the two worlds'. The third tradition endorses Schmitt's (1998) view that frequency, i.e. how often words collocate, and exclusiveness, i.e. how strongly words collocate, are the two determining factors to consider when defining collocations.

The frequency-based tradition is Firthian in nature and advocates frequency of occurrence of word combinations as the major feature that characterizes collocations (see among others Granger and Paquot 2008; Gyllstad 2007; Handl 2008; Li and Schmitt 2009; Nesselhauf 2005; Siyanova and Schmitt 2008). It should be acknowledged that even though frequency of co-occurrence has been traditionally considered as the main characteristic feature of collocations, Granger and Paquot (2008) suggest adopting a distributional approach in defining collocations. The latter consists of two extraction methods: n-gram analysis, which allows for extraction of two or more co-occurring words irrespective of their

Déogratias Nizonkiza, North-West University (Potchefstroom campus)

DOI 10.1515/9781501505492-012

idiomatic nature; and co-occurrence analysis, roughly defined as a statistical identification of significantly co-occurring words.

According to Nesselhauf (2005), among others, the phraseological tradition is largely influenced by the Russian phraseology, and has Cowie (1998) and Howarth (1998) as leading representatives. Within this tradition, words forming a collocation must be syntactically related, where transparency or the varying degrees of fixedness, and commutability or substitutability are the main features of collocations. This implies that collocations are transparent in meaning as opposed to idioms that are opaque. For instance, *apply for a job* is totally transparent as the meaning of the whole is the sum of the meanings of the individual words it consists of. *Face a problem* is, however, less transparent than *apply for a job*, but it is not as idiomatic as *face the music*, which means 'show courage', the meaning of which cannot be worked out from the meanings of the words that compose it.[1] Substitutability/commutability refers to the extent to which one collocate can be replaced with (an)other(s), which Nizonkiza (2011: 118) explains in the following terms: "For example *strong wind* is an adjective + noun combination where *wind* is the node and *strong* the collocate and the combination is transparent. In *strong wind*, *strong* can be interchangeably used with other adjectives like *terrible*, *fierce*, *moderate* etc. but not with *heavy*, which clearly indicates that substitution is possible, but restricted."

Following the growing interest in collocations, many scholars have attempted to understand their nature and test them. Schmitt (1998), however, remarks that even experts still do not know how to best test collocations. According to him, the complex nature of collocations and the available studies on collocations that are entirely descriptive are the reasons that may account for this lack of preciseness on how to test them. Nesselhauf (2005) attributes this to the different angles under which collocations have been researched, a view shared by Eyckmans (2009). Different researchers have indeed explored collocations within their own field of study, resulting in their being ill-defined (Eyckmans 2009; Nesselhauf 2005). Without a clear definition of the concept, capturing its construct remains a serious challenge. The frequency-based and the phraseological approaches referred to above are good examples of attempting to grasp the same concept using, however, different defining criteria.

For Gyllstad (2007) studies on command of collocations fall into two categories and are limited in number. The first category consists of studies that involve analyses of learners' essays in corpora and are not tests as such. Cowie (1998), Granger (1998), Granger and Paquot (2008), Howarth (1998), and Nesselhauf (2005) constitute typical examples. A common observation in these studies is

---

1 These examples were found in Laufer and Waldman (2011: 649).

that collocations cause difficulties for L2 learners. The second category is more experimental and consists of tests, both receptive and productive, presented to participants. My study falls within this category of productive tests. It is worth noting that Bonk (2001), Eyckmans, Boers, and Demecheleer (2004), and Gitsaki (1999) are among the few scholars who have tested the productive aspect of collocations in association with L2 proficiency, all of them pointing to the conclusion that collocational competence develops in parallel to L2 proficiency. Bonk (2001), however, has been criticized for being unsystematic in selecting test items (cf. Gyllstad 2007; Jaén 2007), while Gitsaki (1999) can be criticized for comparing three proficiency groups based on different sets of items, which is "less straightforward" (Gyllstad 2007: 53). Moreover, the two studies did not consider the word frequency levels when selecting items, even though frequency plays an important role in knowing words (cf. Nation 1990, for vocabulary size; Gyllstad 2007 and Nizonkiza 2011, for receptive knowledge of collocation). Eyckmans et al.'s (2004) test is not only time consuming, but was also originally developed as a reading comprehension measure and does not exclusively test collocations (Boers and Lindstromberg 2009). Like Bonk (2001) and Gitsaki (1999), Eyckmans et al. (2004) did not take word frequency into account either. This is a gap that I believe is worth exploring in detail through research and that should be filled.

Furthermore, following Boers et al.'s (2006), Bonk's (2001), Howarth's (1998), and Schmitt's (1998) view that collocation knowledge is more important at the productive level than the receptive level; and Eyckmans's (2009) view that most collocation errors occur in production, there is a great need to further the assessment of the productive collocational competence. Collocations are indeed important at the productive level because using them contributes to sounding nativelike (Pawley and Syder 1983) while failing to use them correctly or using unconventional combinations makes L2 users sound foreign and odd, "making the learners less effective communicators and hindering their acceptance into the speech community" (Siyanova and Schmitt 2008: 431). This is in line with Boers and Lindstromberg's (2009), Laufer and Paribakht's (1998), Van de Poel and Swanepoel's (2003), and Zareva, Schwanenflugel, and Nikolova's (2005) observation that word comprehension does not automatically predict its correct use. The present study was undertaken in light of what precedes and investigated controlled productive knowledge of collocations across proficiency levels among L2 learners (see details in Section 3.1).

The operational definition of collocations put forward in this study adopts the conciliatory approach that considers both frequency of co-occurrence (frequency-based approach) and the syntactic nature of the collocations constituents, transparency, and substitutability (phraseological approach). Collocations should thus, for the purpose of this study, be understood as frequently co-occurring V+N combinations that are within the range of the *Oxford Collocations Dictionary for Students of English* (Crowther, Dignen, and Lea 2002) used as the primary source for selecting collocates (cf. Section 3.3.1 for details). Although the dictionary compilers did not specifically mention how frequent the combinations were, the latter were carefully checked in the British National Corpus. The reference accepts a range of frequent combinations from weak to strong or restricted through medium-strength collocations and excludes totally free combinations and idioms. The dictionary also considers the syntactic categories of collocations' constituents. For instance, if the target word is a noun (e.g. *competition*), its collocations will be listed in the order: adjective-noun (e.g. *international competition*), verb-noun (e.g. *win a competition*), noun-verb (e.g. *competition take place*), etc.[2]

Collocations have proven to be important in many ways, which has already started to have some pedagogical impact. This is the subject of the following section.

2 Related literature

2.1 Role and pedagogical impact of collocations

Both theoreticians and practitioners of second language acquisition have stressed the importance of formulaic sequences – to use Wray's term – which I restrict to collocations (see definition above) in an L2 setting, insofar that they are widespread and of great significance as regards language proficiency (see among others Gyllstad 2007, 2009; Mel'čuk 2006; Pawley and Syder 1983; Sinclair 1991; Wray 2002). Collocations perform various roles, which Wray (2002) has summarized as reducing the speaker's processing effort, manipulating the hearer (his identity and his perception of the speaker's identity), and maintaining his identity as an individual or a group member of a community. It is worth noting that although Wray (2002) uses the term formulaic sequences, collocations are definitely accommodated.

Seen in a wider perspective, collocations provide a linguistic solution to a non-linguistic problem, i.e. promoting/protecting the interests of the speaker (Wray 2002). In order to illustrate the point, Wray (2002: 93) suggests considering "the motivation behind the desire to speak fluently, express identity, organize text and help the hearer to understand what you say." All this is geared to help

---

2 Examples retrieved from the *Oxford Collocations Dictionary for Students of English* (Crowther et al. 2002).

the speaker in his communicative enterprise. Speaking fluently is undoubtedly facilitated by memorized formulaic language, a claim that has gained empirical support showing that the speaker who uses formulaic language rather than novel sentences will be more fluent and sound more natural (Wray 2002). Reducing processing effort by using pre-assembled expressions also helps in the manipulative role of collocations. According to Wray (2002: 95), a string like *I wonder if you would mind...* is intended to make the hearer perceive the speaker as polite and therefore respond in the desired way. This holds for membership that is signaled by using this kind of language (Boers and Lindstromberg 2009), which Wray (2002: 96) quoting Becker (1975) puts as follows: "the use of formulaic sequences that are shared by a speech community offers speakers a powerful way of signaling to their hearers that they are to be identified as members of the group."

Saving the processing effort as a role of collocations has gained support from other scholars, among whom Schmitt (1998), who suggests that we are better at memorizing than at processing. Boers and Lindstromberg (2009) also maintain that pre-fabricated chunks facilitate L1 and L2 fluency in both production and comprehension. A strong statement in this favor that seems to be pedagogically oriented comes from Wray (2002), according to whom L2 learners encounter problems in their language learning because they adopt an analytical approach rather than a holistic one. They process the language in terms of individual words rather than whole units, and therefore production becomes cognitively demanding for them.

Given this fundamental role played by collocations, several calls to teach second/foreign languages with an explicit focus on collocations have been made, with suggestions of approaches to adopt (see among others Boers et al. 2006; Boers and Lindstromberg 2009; Lewis 1993, 1997, 2000; Martynska 2004; Nation 2001; Nattinger and DeCarrico 1992; Singleton 1999; Willis 1990). The success of teaching collocations may reside in maintaining a good balance between "the achieving of successful interactional events and the saving of processing effort" (Wray 2002: 198). Even though the question of how to teach collocations has not yet been fully addressed, different approaches point to the observation that raising learners' awareness can open up new pathways. Notable examples include Barfield's (2009), Boers et al.'s (2006, 2008), Ying and O'Neill's (2009), and Peters's (2009) recent pedagogical experiments (see Barfield and Gyllstad 2009 for details), and Wray (2002). Discussing these studies is beyond the scope of this chapter, but it is worth stressing that they have come to a similar conclusion that raising the learners' awareness is the approach to adopt. This supports the psychological conditions, noticing, retrieving, and generation, put forward by Coxhead (2008), in relation to how to teach multi-word units. In this line of thought, Wray and Fitzpatrick (2008) suggested adopting the psycholinguistic approach according to which memorization can play an important role in learning phraseology.[3] We also note the empirical studies (see Boers and Lindstromberg 2008 for details) that established/highlighted the rationale of implementing a cognitive linguistics inspired pedagogy and its effectiveness in teaching multi-word units.

Having discussed the roles of collocations and their growing pedagogical impact, let me turn to the way their productive aspect has been tested, especially in relation with L2 proficiency

2.2 Productive tests of collocations

Studies on the command of collocations have involved both corpora-oriented analyses and elicitation through administering tests. The latter is more experimental and in line with the present study. In this section, I will briefly review the readily available tests of this nature.

Biskup (1992) is among the first scholars to have tested productive knowledge of collocations. She developed a test that involved Polish and German university students, and that required test-takers to translate verb+noun and adjective+noun combinations from their mother tongues into English. She found that the two groups produced the same number of correct answers, with the Polish students using more restricted collocations than the German students. Conversely, the latter were found to be more risk-taking in using paraphrases when they lacked the appropriate collocation. One of Biskup's major observations is that closeness between L1 and L2 is very important in collocation knowledge. However, the test she used has been criticized for the lack of details about items and reliability measures (Gyllstad 2007; Jaén 2007).

Bahns and Eldaw (1993) tested fifteen verb+noun collocations and involved German English majors (year 1–3). One group was required to translate fifteen German sentences into English. The other group took a cloze test with English sentences in which test-takers were required to supply the missing verb (collocate of the noun). Bahns and Eldaw (1993) did not find any significant difference between the two groups and concluded that collocation knowledge does not correlate with general lexical knowledge. This conclusion was based on two assumed independent variables, which actually were not independent as they were taken from the same data (Gyllstad 2007). The test has also been criticized

---

3 More details on Coxhead's (2008) and Wray and Fitzpatrick's (2008) approaches can be found in Meunier and Granger (2008).

for not presenting reliability measures and for using too few items (Gyllstad 2007; Jaén 2007).

Farghal and Obiedat (1995) tested twenty-two common collocations among Arabic English majors. Two groups were administered two different test formats. The first group took a fill-in-the-blank test that consisted of eleven items in which one half of the collocation was given. The second group was presented with Arabic sentences based on the same collocations as in the first test that had to be translated into English. Farghal and Obiedat (1995) concluded that L2 learners have difficulty coping with collocations because vocabulary is taught as single lexical items, which leads to lexical incompetence. The reliability measures that are not reported and the fairly small number of items constitute a matter of concern in this study (Gyllstad 2007; Jaén 2007).

Gitsaki (1999) tested collocation knowledge of Greek learners of English through translation and elicitation. The tests consisted of translation and fill-in-blank tasks. Participants had to translate ten sentences from Greek into English for the translation task while they had to supply the missing part of the collocations in the fill-in-blank task, where they were presented with English sentences (50, 65, and 90 for the three proficiency groups, respectively). The main findings of the study are: (i) collocation knowledge develops as the general proficiency develops, (ii) lexical collocations, such as the V+N combinations, were the most difficult in both tasks, and (iii) the Adv+Adj, and V+N combinations were more avoided. While the study has come up with interesting results, it has been criticized for having compared three proficiency groups based on different sets of items especially for the fill-in-blank task (Gyllstad 2007).

Bonk (2001) tested collocational knowledge of university students, all speakers of East-Asian languages. The test battery consisted of three subsets of collocation knowledge and Bonk (2001) aimed to compare collocational knowledge and overall English proficiency. The first subset consisted of seventeen English sentences containing collocations of the type verb+object, in which the verb was deleted and had to be supplied. The second subset consisted of seventeen English sentences with verb+preposition type of combination, where the preposition was missing. The third subset was a receptive test presented in a multiple-choice format. Test-takers were presented with four sentences and their task was to decide in which of the four options the verb was not used correctly. Bonk found that collocational knowledge as tested by means of two of the three subsets (the preposition subset failed to test the relationship) highly correlated with his proficiency measure, an adapted version of TOEFL. Bonk has been criticized, however, for having selected the items in an unsystematic way and having presented items in sentences that require some reading and the question is whether he tested collocation knowledge or reading comprehension (Gyllstad 2007).

The Delete-Essentials Test (DET) is another collocation test that can be taken as general proficiency indicator. It was developed by Eyckmans et al. (2004), initially as a reading comprehension test. An authentic text with numbered lines is presented to test-takers with deleted words that have to be indispensable and predictable (Boers and Lindstromberg 2009). They are not indicated to the test-takers who have to infer them from the context and co-text and therefore supply them. Even though DET does not exclusively test collocations, knowledge of collocations, which helps the test-takers to anticipate on the missing words, plays a central role in the test performance. The test allows testing the productive knowledge of collocations beyond mere word recognition, which is an obvious advantage. However, its time-consuming nature, its narrow coverage of collocations tested, and the lack of strict control of tested items make the test less workable (Boers and Lindstromberg 2009).

Jaén (2007) tested both the receptive and productive collocational competence of English majors at the University of Granada (Spain) using definition tasks. She designed an 80 item test to assess both receptive and productive knowledge of collocation and found that participants had a poor collocational competence. Productive knowledge of collocation was found to be fairly lower than receptive knowledge. However, she acknowledged that her study could be taken as a pilot study given the relatively small sample involved in the study; only second year students participated. She appealed to scholars in the area to test especially the productive aspect of collocations, in a longitudinal context for instance, which is likely to yield interesting results with excellent pedagogical implications.

As appears in the above description, progress in terms of measuring productive knowledge of collocations has been made. We now know that closeness between L1 and L2 matters in knowledge of collocations (Biskup 1992) and that collocations pose problems for L2 learners (Farghal and Obiedat 1995; Jaén 2007). What is particularly striking is that the studies described above have used different tasks ranging from cloze procedures (Bahns and Eldaw 1993; Bonk 2001; Eyckmans et al. 2004) to elicitation techniques (Farghal and Obiedat 1995) and translation (Bahns and Eldaw 1993; Biskup 1992; Farghal and Obiedat 1995), and still they yielded more or less comparable results. Most of them for instance point to the conclusion that collocational knowledge tends to grow with proficiency (Bonk 2001; Eyckmans et al. 2004; Gitsaki 1999). This relationship, however, remains inconclusive because studies such as Bahns and Eldaw (1993) point to the opposite. In addition, modeling the testing of productive knowledge of collocations remains a considerable challenge, given the shortcomings these studies suffer from. These shortcomings include a lack of clear criteria in selecting test items, which was observed in almost all the studies, the lack of reliability measures in most of the studies, and the number of items tested, which are either too few or not strictly controled.

3 Measuring controled productive collocational competence across proficiency levels

3.1 Hypotheses

The main issue in this study is the extent to which L2 learners' controled productive collocational competence develops with proficiency level. My assumption is that controled productive knowledge of collocations increases with proficiency level, but cannot reliably predict L2 proficiency. This assumption is based on previous research findings, which have established a strong relationship between receptive collocation knowledge and L2 proficiency (Gyllstad 2007, 2009; Keshavarz and Salimi 2007; Nizonkiza 2011). It might then be logical to assume that this holds for productive knowledge of collocations (cf. Bonk 2001 and Gitsaki 1999), or controled productive in the present case. However, empirical evidence suggests that productive knowledge always lags behind receptive knowledge (Jaén 2007; Laufer 1998; Laufer and Paribakht 1998), which leads me to believe that controled productive collocational competence develops alongside L2 proficiency, but cannot reliably predict it.

The second issue to explore, and which is corollary of the first, is to quantify the amount of controled productive knowledge of collocations gained from one level of proficiency to another. To this end, the study is conducted in a semi-longitudinal context. My assumption is that as controled productive collocational competence of L2 learners increases with proficiency level, collocation knowledge grows from one level to another, but the gain is neither the same nor always significant. This assumption is based on previous research findings that learning vocabulary in general, and receptive and productive aspects in particular, is not a linear process (Laufer 1998; Meara 1996; Melka 1997; Read 2004).

Thirdly, as it has already been proven right that more frequent words are better known (Nation 1983, 1990; Nation and Beglar 2007) at the level of vocabulary size, I believe that this might be the same for controled productive knowledge of collocations. Therefore, I assume that L2 learners master collocations of words from more frequent word bands better than those from less frequent ones. Word bands should be understood as the classification (using frequency as a criterion) of words in bands of 1000 words each. Schmitt, Schmitt, and Clapham (2001) place the cut-off point of frequency at the 2000-word band, which means that they consider the top 2000 words as frequent.

3.2 Participants

The target population of this study consists of English majors at the University of Burundi from which a sample was selected. All the participants are Burundi nationals between the ages of 20 and 26, from year 1 (N = 36), year 3 (N = 44), or year 4 (N = 36).

Following Babbie (1990) and Dagnelie (1992), the random sampling technique was used in selecting the test-takers. Bouma's (1984) suggestion that at least thirty participants should be included in any study for valid statistical analyses helped to decide on the number of participants. They sat a TOEFL test in order to determine their level of proficiency and a controled productive collocation test in order to test the hypotheses of the study (details on the test development in Sections 3.3.1 and 3.3.2).[4]

3.3 The test battery

3.3.1 Word selection

In order to test the hypotheses proposed in this study, a test of productive knowledge of collocations was administered to the target population. As mentioned in Section 1, there are three main approaches to defining/describing collocations, and the approach adopted in this study is the third, which considers both frequency and phraseology (Gyllstad 2007). Frequency of words and their syntactic nature (V+N combinations) guided the selection.

The words included in the test were selected from Nation (2006), one of the most recent databases of word families based on the British National Corpus (BNC), and organized in word frequency bands. It consists of fifteen of these frequency bands, each composed of 1000 word families.[5] However, only the 2000-word, the 3000-word, and the 5000-word bands were considered for item selection. The Academic Word List (Coxhead 2000), which consists of frequent words in academic contexts that do not appear in the first 2000 most frequent words in English, was also considered. These are the bands used by Nation (1983) and most of his followers. The 10000-word band, another band considered by Nation and followers, was excluded from the sample because it consists of

---

4 The tests were administered the same morning. TOEFL requirements were strictly adhered to for grading the proficiency test and I awarded 1 point per correct answer for the collocation test.
5 The frequency list has been updated and consists of 25 frequency bands now.

infrequent words, and given the proficiency level of the target population (see TOEFL scores in Nizonkiza 2011); we would not learn much from scores at this word band.

In this line of thought, Schmitt et al. (2001) advocated that knowledge of the first 3000 words constitutes a threshold that allows learners to read authentic texts. This is in line with and even stressed in Laufer and Nation (1999), according to whom, 75% of the running words in a formal text and 84% of informal spoken use are covered by the first 1000-word band. They also remark that the tenth 1000-word band accounts for less than 1% of the running words in a text. They go on, arguing that the distinction between high frequent and low frequent words is 'cost-benefit', i.e. more time should be spent on what is more important. Quoting Nation and Hwang (1995), they draw the line between high frequent words and low frequent words at the 2000-word band. The distinction is based on (i) frequency, (ii) coverage of text, (iii) size of the high frequency group, (iv) overlap between various word counts, and (v) the starting point of specialized vocabularies.

The test then involves four word bands from which ten words were selected (cf. Nation and Beglar 2007). These words are referred to as nodes and were selected following systematic random sampling (cf. Babbie 1990; Dagnelie 1992), i.e. from a random starting point each nth word was selected. It is worth noting that for the purpose of this study, the node had to be a noun. In case the nth word was not a noun, the next one was selected instead. Their collocates (verbs) were selected from the *Oxford Collocations Dictionary for Students of English* (Crowther et al. 2002). In order to ensure that the test would test knowledge of collocations, but not knowledge of the collocates, the latter had to be from a higher or similar frequency band as the node, in which case the two words could be expected to be known to the same extent (Gyllstad 2007; Nation 1983, 1990). Perfor-mance on the test in this case is likely to reflect knowledge of collocations. The danger of including infrequent collocation constituents is that test-takers may fail to find the collocation because they do not even know the individual words composing it.

The first step in the selection procedure was to find a noun in the frequency bands considered. After a noun was selected, all the verbs that collocate with it in the V+N combination were listed and their frequency band checked in Nation's (2006) frequency list. The verbs from higher or similar frequency band were retained and the final selection was made on the basis of how often they co-occur with the noun. An online 'collocation sampler' was run for cross-checking. This sampler gives different collocates of the node, how often they appear in the Bank of English, how many times they co-occur with the node, and how significantly they do so.[6] It orders the collocates by their degree of significance, with the most significant collocate considered for selection. For instance, the collocates of the word *accuracy* include *of, with, be, correct, checked, ensure, lack, predict, fly,* etc. up to the 100th co-occurring word. *Improve, increase, check, confirm, test, ensure, doubt,* and *question* are presented in the *Oxford Collocations Dictionary for Students of English* (Crowther et al. 2002) as the relevant V+N combinations. *Ensure* was selected because it belongs to the 1000-word band, thus more frequent than *accuracy,* which belongs to the 2000-word band, and because it collocates with it more significantly than the other verbs of the V+N combination.

The collocations investigated in this study were restricted to V+N combinations for the three reasons explained in Gyllstad (2007): (i) they constitute frequent occurrences; (ii) they cause a lot more difficulties for L2 learners; and (iii) they contain the most important information for communication. The collocations of the type N+V were disregarded in order to avoid two directions of the collocation, and thereby make the task more straightforward and less cognitively demanding for the test-takers. Each collocation was presented in a sentential context with the verb to the left of the noun (see description in 3.3.2).

3.3.2 The test format

The test was modeled after Laufer and Nation (1999), in which the target word is included in a sentence. In the present case, once the collocates were selected, authentic illustrative sentences were selected from the *Oxford Collocations Dictionary for Students of English* (Crowther et al. 2002). The dictionary was chosen for the following reasons:
  (i) It was designed as a learning tool.
 (ii) It was compiled on the basis of the BNC (frequency of collocations was checked from the corpus).
(iii) It contains sentences from the BNC, or with minor modifications aimed at making them more accessible for learners, without altering the meaning of the collocations.

The original test was designed to test the controled productive ability, and was developed from Nation's Vocabulary Levels Test (1990). The productive ability refers to "the ability to use a word when compelled to do so by a teacher or

---

6 The collocation sampler is available online at: http://www.collins.co.uk/Corpus/CorpusSearch.aspx

researcher, whether in an unconstrained context such as a sentence writing task, or in a constrained context such as a fill-in task where a sentence context is provided and the missing target word has to be supplied" (Laufer and Nation 1999: 37).

Controled productive ability as defined by Laufer and Nation (1999) refers to either of two tasks: a sentence writing task and a fill-in task. The two tasks are different to some extent, but in both cases, the target word(s) are chosen by the teacher/researcher. Choosing the target words to present to participants is what makes controled productive knowledge differ from free productive knowledge, the other aspect of productive knowledge. The latter consists of essay writing and requires participants to write on a particular topic (cf. Laufer and Nation 1995). Participants are responsible for both word choice and essay writing.

The present study opted for the fill-in task, which seems to be more controled than the sentence writing task. And as Laufer and Nation (1999) suggest, the first two letters of the missing word were provided, which has the benefit of avoiding wildly varying answers. Test-takers were instructed to complete the underlined word (collocate). Then, an example was provided so as to ensure transparency (see example [1]).

(1) Instruction: Complete the underlined words in the sentences below.

    Example: She is conducting campaigns to *at*......... new clients.
                  She is conducting campaigns to *attract* new clients.

3.3.3 Pilot study

The test was trialed on native speakers (2), PhD students (5), MA students (5), and BA students (7) in order to see whether the items worked and to validate them. The test was found to be internally consistent (α = .83). The item facility values were also run, ranging between 29% and 100%. According to Alderson, Clapham, and Wall (1995), the ideal items should be closer to 50%, although in the present test, they were closer to 70%. This can be attributed to the assumed high level of proficiency of the pilot population. The frequency of the items may also have contributed in so far that as many as fifteen items have a facility value of 100%. They are from the 2000-word band (five items), the 3000-word level (four items), the AWL (four items) and a few from the 5000-word band (two items). The corrected item-total-correlation was also performed; four items were below the cut-off point (.19) and would cause alpha to increase if deleted (cf. Section 3.4.1 for details). They were not revised following the assumption that the population was fairly small. The test was then validated as it proved to function quite well.

3.4 Results

3.4.1 Item analysis

Following Pallant's (2007) view that a .7 alpha is acceptable while a .8 alpha is preferable, the present test is internally consistent (α = .77). In order to test if test items discriminated well between the test-takers with different abilities, the corrected item-total correlation (CITC) was carried out. The latter is measured on a scale where the higher the figure, the better the item discriminates between test-takers. In a well-functioning test, the figures should not be below .30 or .25 (Green 2013). In the same vein, Ebel (1979) sets the cut-off point at .19 and suggests the following scale:
-   .40 or higher: definitely good items.
-   .30 to .39: reasonably good items.
-   .20 to .29: marginal items in need of improvement.
-   .19 or lower: poor items, to be revised or eliminated.

Following Ebel's scale, the CITC clearly shows that 70% of the items function well (cf. Table 1). However, twelve items fall below the cut-off point. An in-depth analysis of these items shows that as many as five items (12%) do not cause any change in alpha if deleted, three items (7.5%) cause alpha to drop and four items (10%) make alpha increase if deleted. The four items (2, 11, 23, and 24) which cause alpha to increase if deleted are definitely flawed items which must be changed or revised while the others need improving. Overall, the test can be said to function well although a few items need revising.

Table 1: Corrected item total correlation on Ebel's scale.

CTC	Item number	Total
.40 and higher	4, 10, 36	3 (7.5%)
.30 to .39	5, 8, 13, 16, 17, 25, 31, 33, 34, 35, 38	11 (27.5%)
.20 to .29	3, 6, 9, 12, 15, 18, 20, 26, 27, 28, 30, 32, 37, 40	14 (35%)
Below .19	1, 2, 7, 11, 14, 19, 21, 22, 23, 24, 29, 39	12 (30%)

3.4.2 Controlled productive collocation knowledge develops parallel to L2 proficiency

The chief aim of the study was to evaluate the extent to which controlled collocation knowledge develops across proficiency levels. The proficiency level of the participants was determined by administering a proficiency measure, the

TOEFL. On the basis of the results (see Table 2), and bearing in mind Bouma's (1984) recommendation regarding the number in each group, the group of participants was split into three levels. These will be referred to in the rest of this chapter as level 1, level 2 and level 3. An ANOVA confirmed that the difference in terms of performance between the groups was statistically significant (F (2, 112) = 292.65, $p < .05$). Posthoc Bonferroni comparisons revealed that level 3 scored higher than level 2 ($p < .001$), and that level 2 obtained higher scores than level 1 ($p < .001$).

Table 2: TOEFL and Collocate scores (and standard deviations) per level.

Test	Level 1 (n = 35)	Level 2 (n = 42)	Level 3 (n = 38)
TOEFL (max. = 677)	335.17 (16.18)	386.40 (16.12)	444.63 (24.59)
Collocate (max. = 40)	20.77 (4.07)	21.31 (5.14)	25.97 (4.60)

The same proficiency levels were reflected in the collocation test. A One-way ANOVA showed that scores differed per proficiency level (F (2, 112) = 14.23, $p < .05$). However, as posthoc Bonferroni comparisons show, level 1 and level 2 nearly achieved the same scores ($p = .88$). A significant increase in scores was found only between level 2 and level 3 ($p < .05$). This seems to indicate that controled productive collocation knowledge develops alongside proficiency, but improves significantly as from a particular level. These findings confirm hypothesis 1 of the study that claims that controled productive knowledge of collocation increases with proficiency level, but cannot reliably predict it.

The data were analyzed further by performing a Pearson correlation between scores from both tests. As Figure 1 illustrates, there is a linear relationship between the two tests ($r = .44$, $p < .01$). Following Pallant (2007) in that a correlation is small (.10–.29), medium (.30–.49), or large (.50–1.00), the present correlation is medium. This is further evidence for a parallel growth between overall proficiency and productive knowledge of collocations that supports the first hypothesis from yet another angle.

The second aim of this study was to obtain insight into the gain in collocation knowledge across proficiency levels. As the collocate scores in Table 2 and the accompanying statistical analyses indicate, the levels 1 and 2 achieved almost the same score (the gain between the two is 0.54), whereas the gain from level 2 to level 3 is much bigger (4.66). This confirms hypothesis 2 of the study, which claims that the controled productive collocational competence of L2 learners increases with proficiency level, but the gain is neither the same nor always significant.

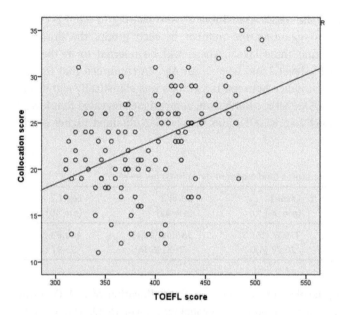

Figure 1: Correlative links between scores on the collocation test and on TOEFL.

3.4.3 The role of word frequency in collocation knowledge

The third aim of the study was to assess the role played by word frequency in collocation mastery. In order to achieve this aim, the target words were selected following word frequency at the 2000-word, 3000-word, 5000-word bands, and the Academic Word List. A repeated measures ANOVA was conducted in order to compare scores across these word frequency bands. The means and standard deviations are presented in Table 3.

Table 3: Mean scores (and standard deviations) per word frequency band.

Word frequency	Level 1 (n = 35)	Level 2 (n = 42)	Level 3 (n = 38)	Overall (N = 115)
2000-word (max. = 10)	5.83 (1.60)	6.52 (1.71)	7.08 (1.49)	6.50 (1.67)
3000-word (max. = 10)	5.49 (1.61)	5.98 (1.90)	7.63 (1.46)	6.37 (1.89)
AWList (max. = 10)	4.94 (1.41)	4.88 (1.90)	6.61 (1.58)	5.47 (1.83)
5000-word (max. = 10)	4.51 (1.54)	3.93 (1.56)	4.66 (1.68)	4.35 (1.60)

The mean scores presented in Table 3 of each level separately and of all participants together show that the test-takers' scores vary following word frequency bands. As indicated by the repeated measures ANOVA with the Sphericity Assumed correction test, the differences between scores at frequency bands appear to be statistically significant for all groups together (F (3, 342) = 60.07, p < .001), for level 1 (F (3, 102) = 6.58, p < .001), for level 2 (F (3, 123) = 27.90, p < .001), as well as for level 3 (F (3, 111) = 43.30, p < .001).

Posthoc Bonferroni tests reveal that for all groups together, scores at each two successive frequency bands differ significantly (p < .05) except between the 2000-word and 3000-word bands (p = 1.00). The absence of significant differences between scores at the 2000-word and 3000-word bands holds at each of the proficiency levels (level 1: p = 1.00; level 2: p = .35; level 3: p = .27). For the other word bands, results seem to be inconsistent. At proficiency level 1, for instance, no successive frequency bands show significant differences. At proficiency level 2, significant differences only occur between the 3000-word and the AWL (p < .05). Proficiency level 3 is the level where results match the ones for all groups together, as differences between the 3000-word band and the AWL and between the AWL and the 5000-word band are statistically significant (p < .05). These findings suggest that performance on collocations follows frequency band, with collocations of words from higher frequency bands mastered first. However, level of proficiency plays a role as well; I shall come back to this in the Discussion section. This finding confirms hypothesis 3 of the study according to which L2 learners master collocations of words from more frequent word bands better than those from less frequent ones.

4 Discussion

The present study attempted to assess controlled productive knowledge of collocations associating it with L2 proficiency among English majors at the University of Burundi. With the first aim of the study, I examined the relationship between controlled productive knowledge of collocations and L2 proficiency. Using the TOEFL test in order to determine the level of proficiency of participants, three groups were distinguished. The same groups were reflected in the scores on the collocation test that also correlated significantly with TOEFL. However, levels 1 and 2 nearly achieved the same score on the collocation test, which tells us that controlled productive knowledge of collocation of L2 learners develops alongside their general proficiency, but it improves significantly as proficiency increases. This is in line with Laufer (1998: 266), who observed that after a year of instruction, controlled active vocabulary progressed faster among the 11th graders than the 10th graders, two groups of students who participated in her study. Her question was whether this non-linearity in vocabulary progress reflects "the nature of L2 vocabulary learning, which may proceed slowly in the first years and gain momentum later." She tentatively concluded so by stressing that although the 11th graders added 850 words in one year, it does not imply that this is what they had been doing over the previous years of exposure to the language.

The current study also supports Bonk (2001) and Gitsaki (1999), who found a correlation between productive collocation knowledge and L2 proficiency, with a slight distinction. While the present study established a relationship between controled productive knowledge and L2 proficiency that becomes stronger as proficiency increases, the two studies did not report any such observation. Two interpretations are possible. On the one hand, different tests were used, and hence may test two different aspects of collocation (controled vs. elicitation). The present study used a test modeled after Laufer and Nation's (1999) Vocabulary Levels Test active version while Gitsaki (1999) used L1 to L2 translation, L2 sentence cloze, and analysis of L2 essays. Bonk (2001) used L2 sentence cloze for the productive aspect and L2 receptive recognition task for the receptive aspect. On the other hand, the levels of proficiency of the participants may be the reason. Participants in the present study are beginners and low intermediates while participants in the two other studies range from low intermediate to advanced (Bonk 2001) and post-beginners to post-intermediate (Gitsaki 1999). Although only empirical data can clarify the matter, I side for the second option, in line with Laufer's (1998) observation above, assuming that collocation growth is slow at low levels, gains momentum at intermediate levels and stabilizes and even reaches a plateau at very advanced levels.[7] For the latter aspect, I get support from Li and Schmitt (2009), who did not find any progress at all in collocation production among postgraduate Chinese students of English at MA level. Their level of proficiency was very high (640 in TOEFL or 6.5 in IELTS) after four/five years of teaching experience.

The second aim of the study was to explore the gains of controled productive knowledge of collocation across proficiency levels. The means were calculated and cross-examined following the proficiency levels. The results show that the gains are only significant from level 2 to level 3. This finding empirically supports Laufer's (1998) hypothesis that vocabulary growth is slow in beginning levels and gains momentum as proficiency increases, as discussed above.

The third aim of the study was to determine the role of word frequency in controled productive knowledge of collocation. To this end, words were selected from different frequency bands, hoping to see test-takers performing gradually better, from the less frequent to the more frequent word bands. Results of the

---

7 This was confirmed in a replication of this study extended to include more levels of proficiency, the results of which are reported in Nizonkiza (2012).

study show that, overall, this is the case as the scores increase with word frequency bands, highlighting the crucial role played by frequency in knowing words (cf. Nation 1983, 1990; Nation and Beglar 2007). At the vocabulary size level, with no doubt, the more frequent words are the best known, which seems to be the case with controled productive knowledge of collocations as results from this study indicate. However, differences between scores at the 2000-word and 3000-word bands are not significant. This could be attributed to the cut-off point of frequency that used to be placed at the 2000-word band (Schmitt et al. 2001), but that has recently been raised to the 3000-word band (Schmitt and Schmitt 2014). Furthermore, level 1 students did not show any significant differ-ence between performance at two successive word bands, while level 2 students only showed significant scores between the 3000-word band and the AWL. Only level 3 students performed differently on two successive word bands, except the 2000-word and 3000-word bands. This is indicative not only of the slow growth of collocations among L2 learners (Laufer and Waldman 2011), but it also reveals learners' tendency to go quantitative rather than qualitative in their learning of words (Henriksen and Stenius Stæhr 2009). Henriksen and Stenius Stæhr (2009: 225) explain this in the following terms: learners "perceive lexical learning as a process of accumulating new language elements rather than refining and restructuring their existing knowledge, for example, in relation to developing collocational knowledge of already acquired lexical items."

5 Conclusion

The results of the study suggest that controled productive collocation knowledge develops parallel to L2 proficiency, indicating that the levels of proficiency dis-tinguished by means of TOEFL scores are reflected in the collocation test scores. However, they are only significant between level 2 and level 3. Similarly, con-troled productive knowledge of collocation is found to increase from one level of proficiency to another, but the gains are not significant at low levels of profi-ciency. Moreover, frequency is found to be a key factor in determining controled productive knowledge of collocations. The test-takers gradually scored better from the less frequent to the more frequent word bands, with proficiency level also playing a role.

On the whole, the present study has achieved its objectives; and now that the question of teaching collocations is much more related to what aspects to teach and how to teach them (Granger and Meunier 2008), it is hoped that this study has made a considerable step in this direction. Testing the productive aspect of collocations, especially quantifying their growth across proficiency and word frequency levels, may allow us to develop a syllabus with focus on collocations, taking into account both proficiency level and word frequency. It would therefore constitute one of the interesting pedagogical implications of the study by complementing previous studies that have addressed the issue of how collocations should be explicitly taught. These studies have proposed new pathways, without however, taking word frequency and proficiency levels into account. I believe that the awareness raising approach reported in Barfield and Gyllstad (2009), Boers and Lindstromberg (2009), and Wray (2002), the psychological and psycholinguistic approaches (Coxhead 2008 and Wray and Fitzpatrick 2008, respectively), and the cognitive linguistics inspired pedagogy, reported in Boers and Lindstromberg (2008), coupled with word frequency and proficiency levels could take this debate a step further.

While it can argued that the results obtained from this study come from a controled type of test – the usage-based paradigm of which may be questionable – there seems to be an obvious advantage of this approach, especially for teaching purposes. According to Nizonkiza (2014), an experimental study where pre-determined items – and thus controled – are tested might contribute greatly towards gaining better insights into the measurability of collocations and also into their difficult nature in the sense that it allows comparing both participants' performance and items to one another. By doing so, the researcher can identify which collocations are more problematic than others, and also quantify their growth, which I believe lays basic groundwork for modeling not only the testing of collocations, but also their teaching. Furthermore, the construct through which knowledge of collocations is operationalized in this study is close to usage-based in the sense that it provides authentic examples as extracted from the British National Corpus and included in the *Oxford Collocations Dictionary for Students of English* (Crowther et al. 2002) for teaching/learning purposes.

References

Alderson, J. Charles, Caroline Clapham, and Dianne Wall. 1995. *Language Test Construction and Evaluation*. Cambridge: Cambridge University Press.

Babbie, Earl R. 1990. *Survey Research Methods*. California and Belmont: Wordsworth Company.

Bahns, Jens, and Moira Eldaw. 1993. Should we teach EFL students collocations? *System* 21 (1): 101–114.

Barfield, Andy. 2009. Following individual L2 collocation development over time. In *Researching Collocations in Another Language*, Andy Barfield, and Henrik Gyllstad (eds.), 208–223. New York: Palgrave Macmillan.

Barfield, Andy, and Henrik Gyllstad (eds.). 2009. *Researching Collocations in Another Language*. New York: Palgrave Macmillan.

Biskup, Gabrys D. 1992. L1 influence on learners' rendering of English collocations: A Polish/ German empirical study. In *Vocabulary and Applied Linguistics*, Pierre J. Arnaud, and Henri Béjoint (eds.), 85–93. London: MacMillan.

Boers, Frank, June Eyckmans, Jenny Kappel, Hélène Stengers, and Murielle Demecheleer. 2006. Formulaic sequences and perceived oral proficiency: Putting the lexical approach to the test. *Language Teaching Research* 10 (3): 245–261.

Boers, Frank, and Seth Lindstromberg (eds.). 2008. *Cognitive Approaches to Teaching Vocabulary and Phraseology*. Berlin: Mouton De Gruyter.

Boers, Frank, and Seth Lindstromberg. 2009. *Optimizing a Lexical Approach to Instructed Language Acquisition*. New York: Palgrave Macmillan.

Boers, Frank, Seth Lindstromberg, Jeanette Littlemore, Hélène Stengers, and June Eyckmans. 2008. Variables in the mnemonic effectiveness of pictorial elucidation. In *Cognitive Linguistic Approaches to Teaching Vocabulary and Pedagogy*, Frank Boers, and Seth Lindstromberg (eds.), 189–218. Berlin: Mouton de Gruyter.

Bonk, William J. 2001. Testing ESL learners' knowledge of collocations. In *A Focus on Language Test Development: Expanding the Language Proficiency Construct across a Variety of Tests*, Thom Hudson, and James Dean Brown (eds.), 113–142. Honolulu: University of Hawaii Second Language Teaching and Curriculum Center.

Bouma, Gary D. 1984. *The Research Process*. Oxford: Oxford University Press.

Cowie, Anthony Paul (ed.). 1998. *Phraseology: Theory, Analysis, and Applications*. Oxford: Clarendon Press.

Coxhead, Averil. 2000. A new academic word list. *TESOL Quarterly* 34 (2): 213–238.

Coxhead, Averil. 2008. Phraseology and English for academic purposes: Challenges and opportunities. In *Phraseology in Foreign Language Learning and Teaching*, Fanny Meunier, and Sylviane Granger (eds.), 149–161. Amsterdam: John Benjamins.

Crowther, Jonathan, Sheila Dignen, and Diana Lea (eds.). 2002. *Oxford Collocations Dictionary for Students of English*. Oxford: Oxford University Press.

Dagnelie, Pierre. 1992. *Principes d'Expérimentation* [Principles of Experimentation]. Gembloux: Presses Agronomiques de Gembloux.

Ebel, Robert L. 1979. *Essentials of Educational Measurement*. New Jersey: Prentice Hall.

Eyckmans, June. 2009. Toward an assessment of learners' receptive and productive syntagmatic knowledge. In *Researching Collocations in Another Language*, Andy Barfield, and Henrik Gyllstad (eds.), 139–152. New York: Palgrave Macmillan.

Eyckmans, June, Frank Boers, and Murielle Demecheleer. 2004. The Deleted-Essentials Test: An effective and affective compromise. *Humanising Language Teaching* 6 (4). Available from www.hltmag.co.uk.

Farghal, Mohammed, and Hussein Obiedat. 1995. Collocations: a neglected variable in EFL. *International Review of Applied Linguistics in Language Teaching* 33 (4): 315–331.

Gitsaki, Christina. 1999. *Second Language Lexical Acquisition: A Study of the Development of Collocational Knowledge*. San Francisco: International Scholars Publications.

Granger, Sylviane. 1998. Prefabricated patterns in advanced EFL writing: Collocations and formulae. In *Phraseology: Theory, Analysis and Applications*, Anthony P. Cowie (ed.), 145–160. Oxford: Oxford University Press.

Granger, Sylviane, and Magali Paquot. 2008. Disentangling the phraseological web. In *Phraseology: An Interdisciplinary Perspective*, Sylviane Granger, and Fanny Meunier (eds.), 27–49. Amsterdam: John Benjamins.

Granger, Sylviane, and Fanny Meunier (eds.). 2008. *Phraseology: An Interdisciplinary Perspective*. Amsterdam: John Benjamins.

Green, Rita. 2013. *Statistical Analyses for Language Testers*. Basingstoke: Palgrave McMillan.

Gyllstad, Henrik. 2007. Testing English collocations. Unpublished Ph. D. diss., Lund University.

Gyllstad, Henrik. 2009. Designing and evaluating tests of receptive collocation knowledge: COLLEX and COLLMATCH. In *Researching Collocations in Another Language*, Andy Barfield, and Henrik Gyllstad (eds.), 153–170. New York: Palgrave Macmillan.

Handl, Susanne. 2008. Essential collocations for learners of English: The role of collocational direction and weight. In *Phraseology in Foreign Language Teaching and Learning*, Fanny Meunier, and Sylviane Granger (eds.), 43–66. Amsterdam: John Benjamins.

Henriksen, Birgit, and Lars Stenius Stæhr. 2009. Processes in the development of L2 collocational knowledge: A challenge for language learners, researchers and teachers. In *Researching Collocations in Another Language*, Andy Barfield, and Henrik Gyllstad (eds.), 224–231. New York: Palgrave Macmillan.

Howarth, Peter. 1998. Phraseology of second language proficiency. *Applied Linguistics* 19 (1): 24–44.

Jaén, María M. 2007. A corpus-driven design of a test for assessing the ESL collocational competence of university students. *International Journal of English Studies* 7 (2): 127–147.

Keshavarz, Mohammad H., and Hossein Salimi. 2007. Collocational competence and cloze test performance: A study of Iranian EFL learners. *International Journal of Applied Linguistics* 17 (1): 81–92.

Laufer, Batia. 1998. The development of passive and active vocabulary in a second language: same or different? *Applied Linguistics* 19 (2): 255–271.

Laufer, Batia, and Paul Nation. 1995. Vocabulary size and use: Lexical richness in L2 written production. *Applied Linguistics* 16 (3): 307-322.

Laufer, Batia, and Paul Nation. 1999. A vocabulary-size test of controlled productive ability. *Language Testing* 16 (1): 33–51.

Laufer, Batia, and T. Sima Paribakht. 1998. The relationship between passive and active vocabularies: Effects of language learning contexts. *Language Learning* 48 (3): 365–391.

Laufer, Batia, and Tina Waldman. 2011. Verb-noun collocations in second language writing: A corpus analysis of learners' English. *Language Learning* 61 (2): 647–672.

Lewis, Michael. 1993. *The Lexical Approach: The State of ELT and the Way Forward*. Hove: Language Teaching Publications.

Lewis, Michael. 1997. *Implementing the Lexical Approach: Putting Theory into Practice*. Hove: Language Teaching Publications.

Lewis, Michael. 2000. *Teaching Collocations: Further Development in the Lexical Approach*. Hove: Language Teaching Publications.

Li, Jie, and Norbert Schmitt. 2009. The acquisition of lexical phrases in academic writing: A longitudinal case study. *Journal of Second Language Writing* 18 (2): 85–102.

Martynska, Malgorzata. 2004. Do English language learners know collocations? *Investigationes Linguisticae* 11: 1–12.

Meara, Paul. 1996. The dimensions of lexical competence. In *Competence and Performance in Language Learning*, Gillian Brown, Kirsten Malmkjaer, and John Williams (eds.), 35–53. New York: Cambridge University Press.

Mel'čuk, Igor. 2006. Collocations: Définition, rôle et utilité [Collocations : Definition, role and usefulness]. In *Les Collocations: Analyse et Traitement*, Francis Grossmann, and Agnès Tutin (eds.), 23–31. Amsterdam: De Werelt.

Melka Teichroew, Francine. 1997. Receptive versus productive vocabulary. In *Vocabulary: Description, Acquisition, and Pedagogy*, Norbert Schmitt, and Michael McCarthy (eds.), 84–102. New York: Cambridge University Press.

Meunier, Fanny, and Sylviane Granger (eds.). 2008. *Phraseology in Foreign Language Learning and Teaching*. Amsterdam: John Benjamins.

Nation, Paul. 1983. Testing and teaching vocabulary. *Guidelines* 5 (1): 12–25.

Nation, Paul. 1990. *Teaching and Learning Vocabulary*. Rowley, MA: Newbury House.

Nation, Paul. 2001. *Learning Vocabulary in Another Language*. New York: Cambridge University Press.

Nation, Paul. 2006. How large a vocabulary is needed for reading and listening? *Canadian Modern Language Review* 63 (1): 59–82.

Nation, Paul, and David Beglar. 2007. A vocabulary size test. *The Language Teacher* 31 (7): 9–13.

Nation, Paul, and Kyongho Hwang. 1995. Where would general service vocabulary stop and special purposes vocabulary begin? *System* 23 (1): 35–41.

Nattinger, James R. and Jeanette S. DeCarrico. 1992. *Lexical Phrases and Language Teaching*. Oxford: Oxford University Press.

Nesselhauf, Nadja. 2004. What are collocations? In *Phraseological Units: Basic Concepts and their Application*, David J. Allerton, Nadja Nesselhauf, and Paul Skandera (eds.), 1–21. Basel: Schwabe.

Nesselhauf, Nadja. 2005. *Collocations in a Learner Corpus*. Amsterdam: John Benjamins.

Nizonkiza, Déogratias. 2011. The relationship between lexical competence, collocational competence, and second language proficiency. *English Text Construction* 4 (1): 113–145.

Nizonkiza, Déogratias. 2012. Quantifying controlled productive knowledge of collocations across proficiency and word frequency levels. *Studies in Second Language Learning and Teaching* 2 (1): 67–92.

Nizonkiza, Déogratias. 2014. The relationship between productive knowledge of collocations and academic literacy among tertiary level learners. *Journal for Language Teaching* 48 (1): 149–171.

Pallant, Julie. 2007. *SPSS Survival Manual*. Buckingham and Philadelphia: Open University Press.

Pawley, Andrew, and Frances Hodgetts Syder. 1983. Two puzzles for linguistic theory: Nativelike selection and nativelike fluency. In *Language and Communication*, Jack C. Richards, and Richards W. Schmidt (eds.), 191–226. London: Longman.

Peters, Elke. 2009. Learning collocations through attention-drawing techniques: A qualitative and quantitative analysis. In *Researching Collocations in Another Language*, Andy Barfield, and Henrik Gyllstad (eds.), 194–207. New York: Palgrave Macmillan.

Read, John. 2004. Plumbing the depths: How should the construct of vocabulary knowledge be defined? In *Vocabulary in Second Language*, Paul Bogaards, and Batia Laufer (eds.), 209–227. Amsterdam: John Benjamins.

Schmitt, Norbert. 1998. Measuring collocational knowledge: Key issues and an experimental assessment procedure. *ITL Review of Applied Linguistics* 119–120: 27–47.

Schmitt, Norbert and Diane Schmitt. 2014. A reassessment of frequency and vocabulary size in L2 vocabulary teaching. *Language Teaching* 47 (4): 484–50.

Schmitt, Norbert, Diane Schmitt, and Caroline Clapham. 2001. Developing and exploring the behaviour of two new versions of the vocabulary levels test. *Language Testing* 18 (1): 55–88.

Sinclair, John. 1991. *Corpus, Concordance, Collocation*. Oxford: Oxford University Press.

Singleton, David. 1999. *Exploring the Second Language Mental Lexicon*. Cambridge: Cambridge University Press.

Siyonava, Anna, and Norbert Schmitt. 2008. L2 learners production and processing of collocation: A multi-study perspective. *The Canadian Modern Language Review* 64 (3): 429–458.

Van de Poel, Kris, and Piet Swanepoel. 2003. Theoretical and methodological pluralism in designing effective lexical support for CALL. *Computer Assigned Language Learning* 16 (2–3): 173–221.

Willis, Dave. 1990. *The Lexical Syllabus: A New Approach to Language Teaching*. London: Collins ELT.

Wray, Alison. 2002. Formulaic language and the lexicon. Cambridge: Cambridge University Press.

Wray, Alison, and Tess Fitzpatrick. 2008. Why can't you just leave it alone? Deviations from memorised language as a gauge of nativelike competence. In *Phraseology in Foreign Language Learning and Teaching*, Fanny Meunier, and Sylviane Granger (eds.), 123–147. Amsterdam: John Benjamins.

Ying, Yang, and Marnie O'Neill. 2009. Collocation learning through an 'AWARE' approach: Learner perspectives and learning process. In *Researching Collocations in Another Language*, Andy Barfield, and Henrik Gyllstad (eds.), 181–193. New York: Palgrave Macmillan.

Zareva, Alla, Paula Schwanenflugel, and Yordanka Nikolova. 2005. Relationship between lexical competence and language proficiency: Variable sensitivity. *Studies in Second Language Acquisition* 27 (4): 567–595.

Karen Sullivan and Javier Valenzuela

12 Comparing word sense distinctions with bilingual comparable corpora: A pilot study of adjectives in English and Spanish

1 Introduction

Amidst the recent surge of interest in the applications of corpora in Cognitive Linguistics, and the wide range of methodologies now available (e.g. Gries and Stefanowitsch 2006), the types of corpora employed and their applications in translation and L2 instruction still has the potential for further expansion. The current chapter draws attention to one of the areas in which the field has the potential for growth, and suggests the gains it may have to offer translation and Second Language Acquisition (SLA). These points are then illustrated with examples from a pilot corpus study conducted on a set of adjectives in English and Spanish.

The pilot study is suggestive of the potential role of bilingual comparable corpora, that is, sets of non-parallel matched monolingual corpora, each in a different language, as an approach to comparative lexical semantics. This method is argued to hold several advantages over the more traditional lexical studies employing monolingual corpora and bilingual parallel corpora. The study sorts a set of adjective senses from an English corpus and a Spanish corpus on the basis of distributional variables (such as whether adjectives occur in predicative or attributive position), which allows a detailed analysis of the relatedness of the senses of each word in each language. The networks of related senses in the two languages can then be compared, and it can be seen which senses are similar or different in the two languages. This can serve as a guide for L2 students, translators and lexicographers interested in finding the best approximation for a given source-language meaning in a target language.

2 Types of corpora and their applications

Many types of corpora are currently available, several of which have been, or could be, employed in studies with implications for SLA or translator training.

Karen Sullivan, University of Queensland
Javier Valenzuela, University of Murcia

DOI 10.1515/9781501505492-013

To date, relatively few of the available types of corpora have been taken advantage of in translation studies. Granger (2003: 21) provides a summary of available corpus types and those that have been employed in contrastive linguistics and translation studies, a list updated to some extent in Marzo et al. (2010). The circumscribed range of corpus usage can be attributed in part to the relative newness of the field. For instance, the use of corpora in translation studies was not suggested until Baker (1995). The integration of corpora in SLA is slightly older, dating back at least to Johns and King (1991).

Types of corpora with past or potential applications within translation studies and SLA include (bilingual) parallel corpora, monolingual comparable corpora, and bilingual comparable corpora. We will briefly mention some of the relevant work done with these types of corpora, and the advantages and disadvantages of each type for SLA applications.

Parallel corpora are probably the most widely used corpora in translation studies. These are "corpora that contain a series of source texts aligned with their corresponding translations" (Malmkjaer 1998: 539, quoted in Granger 2003: 20). Translated texts without their source texts may also be used. These may be termed *translation* (or *translational*) *corpora* (Baker 1999). Parallel corpora may be employed either to study translation itself or as a basis for comparing the structure of two languages (Mason 2001). However, as Mason (2001) notes, parallel corpora may give deceptive results for research comparing linguistic structure, as their target language material will differ from non-translated data from that language. It may be influenced by the source language, or may be subject to artifacts stemming from the process of translation itself (see Olohan 2004: 26–28 for a discussion of examples). Some of these effects can be controlled for by employing two parallel corpora, one translated from language A to B and one translated from B to A (Johansson 1998; referred to as *bilingual parallel corpora* in Zanettin 1998).

In translation studies, artifacts arising from translation are an important focus of study in their own right. Largely for this reason, the use of monolingual comparable corpora is on the rise in translation studies (see Olohan 2004, Chapter 4). These corpora consist of translated and non-translated texts in a single language, examined "in order to explore how text produced in relative freedom from an individual script in another language differs from text produced under the normal conditions which pertain in translation, where a fully developed and coherent text exists in language A and requires recoding in language B" (Baker 1993: 233, quoted in Olohan 2004: 36). These corpora allow researchers to identify features of translated texts, some of which are outlined in Baker (1996). Although parallel corpora may be useful for understanding or conducting translation, they appear to be less immediately useful in SLA. For

SLA students, it may be more productive to be exposed to non-translated, rather than translated, data from the L2 (Johansson 2007).

Monolingual corpora of learner data are probably the most frequent type of corpus employed in SLA studies. The International Corpus of Learner English (initiated and directed by Sylviane Granger), for example, collects essays from 2nd- and 3rd-year university students studying English, representing sixteen L1s. Several studies have used this corpus to compare native speaker data with learner data from speakers of an L1, or a set of L1s, in order to draw attention to L1 transfer or interference effects, such as the frequency of the use of grammatical constructions (as in Valenzuela and Rojo 2008) or of particular lexical items (as in Ringbom 1998).[1] These results can be integrated into SLA instruction to help students avoid typical learner patterns of overuse or underuse.

Despite the gains made with monolingual comparable corpora, relatively little research has so far been conducted using bilingual comparable corpora. When these corpora have been employed, they have focused on the study of specific genres, such as printed public notices in English and German (Schäffner 1998) or medical research articles (Williams 2010), or for the study of collocational frequency (Noël and Colleman 2010; Zanettin 1998). Bilingual comparable corpora have been proposed for use in monolingual Word Sense Disambiguation (WSD) (Kaji 2003) – that is, "translation equivalents" in one language can be used to define the various senses of a given word in a different language – but this procedure has little direct application for translator training and even less for SLA. It seems evident that comparable data from multiple languages are necessary if L2 learners and translators are to use corpus data to find the nearest equivalent, in a target language, for a lexical item in a source language. This suggests that bilingual comparable corpora as well as monolingual corpora are a potentially valuable resource for SLA and translation studies addressing lexical semantics.

3 Options in corpus analysis

Besides the choice of corpus type, several other decisions must be made by researchers interested in employing corpora in SLA studies. A study may focus on word senses, words, or phrases in the corpora, for example. It is also necessary to select the parameters that are taken into account, such as the words

---

1 Numerous studies of this type are collected in an online Learner bibliography by the Centre for English Corpus Linguistics. See: http://sites-test.uclouvain.be/cecl/projects/learner_corpus_bibliography.html.

or syntax that co-occur with the items of interest. This section will address the choice of parameters, and the selection of words versus senses, selected in previous research and available for future investigations relevant to applications in SLA and translation. The discussion will focus on hierarchical cluster analyses (HCA), an exploratory data grouping method that has proven its usefulness in studies of monolingual polysemy (Gries and Divjak 2009; Sullivan 2012) and translational corpora (Jenset and Hareide 2013; Ke 2012). HCA also has the advantage that its results can be assessed with bootstrapping, a method by which data are shuffled and then re-clustered to statistically evaluate the validity of the clusters (Divjak 2010; Glynn 2010; Suzuki and Shimodaira 2011).

Perhaps the most readily available variables that can be employed in clustering consist of the items' collocations, that is, other items that tend to occur in proximity to the items in question (an approach adopted in Kaji 2003, and in monolingual corpus studies including Gibbs and Matlock 2001, and Kishner and Gibbs 1996). However, there are several reasons why the use of predominantly syntactic variables may allow for a more accurate impression of cross-linguistic equivalence than the more traditional reliance on collocations. Collocations tend to be highly language-specific, which is the primary reason that translators-in-training need to be exposed to the concordances of items in the target language, because they are likely to differ from the source language (see Hadley 2002 for discussion). This trait, which renders concordances a productive part of translator training, makes them less useful in comparisons between languages, since collocations are likely to often be too different between the two languages for meaningful comparisons to be made. Of course, languages have different syntactic structures as well as different concordance patterns, but we argue it is more revealing to compare syntactic structures between languages (i.e. adverbial modification) than to find analogous collocates (i.e. co-occurrence of *skin* with *soft* in English and that of *piel* 'skin' with *suave* 'soft/smooth' in Spanish). Additionally, individual collocates can distort a cluster analysis, particularly one comparing word senses (Gries and Divjak 2009), and reliance solely on collocates may do little to reveal ties between senses, since collocates can co-occur with only one sense.

The variables that are considered can be selected and manipulated in many different ways. Gries and Divjak (2009) employ morphosyntactic or semantic variables in their analysis which they call "ID tags". Though clustering analyses based primarily on syntactic data present several advantages, it must be acknowledged that tagging syntactic IDs is currently far more labor intensive than collecting collocations. Future advances in automatic corpus tagging could simplify the ID-tagging process, allowing even long-distance syntactic relations and large-scale syntactic structures to be identified and tagged automatically. Improved availability of comparable corpora in multiple languages with any degree of tagging beyond POS-tagging (for example, tagging of nouns and/or adjectives for plurality) would reduce the number of variable values that must be manually identified and assigned as ID tags in a given study.

In addition to the type of data chosen for annotation and consideration, corpus studies dealing with polysemy can choose whether to compare the various senses of individual words, thereby charting the structure of polysemy networks, or to ignore the different senses of each item and compare instead different words with each other, mapping the relatedness of "near synonyms" (Gries 2008; Divjak 2010) and discovering which words in a semantically related set are most similar based on their distribution and syntactic, semantic, and other properties.

Examining the concordances of one item at a time, in one language at a time, offers applications for translation and potentially for SLA (Hadley 2002). However, we suggest that there are also advantages to analyzing the connections between senses of various items, and in comparing these networks of senses in multiple languages. A speaker or translator will typically need to find the best approximation for one sense of a source-language item in a target language. Examining concordances of a single item in the target language may give learners and translators a general feel for the usage range of a particular item, but may be less directly applicable to the everyday task of word translation than a corpus-based tool that compares multiple words and senses in both the target and source languages. This can be accomplished through the use of clustering of word senses in bilingual comparable corpora.

As seen in the previous section, most clustering studies – and all of those employing the methodological choices described above – have been employed with monolingual corpora (Divjak and Gries 2008; Gries 2006; Sullivan 2012). Which of the choices explored above are most compatible with the use of bilingual corpora? It has already been suggested that syntactic, as opposed to collocational, data, are more appropriate to cross-linguistic studies. In terms of the choice between "near synonyms" and word senses, it seems that the latter may prove more useful. No L2 speaker or translator would want to always equate one specific lexical item in the source language, such as English *soft*, with one specific item in the target language, such as Spanish *suave*. It seems more realistic that one specific sense of *soft* might, indeed, always be best translated as *suave*. There may in turn be a specific sense of *suave* that can always be felicitously translated into English as *soft*. It may be most useful in SLA and translation, therefore, to look for similarity between word senses rather than between words. For this, studies of bilingual comparable corpora with clustering of word senses may prove the most productive choice.

4 Pilot study: method

As a preliminary assessment of the effectiveness of word sense clustering using bilingual comparable corpora, our sample study collected 300 examples of each of four adjectives: English *soft* and *smooth* and Spanish *suave* and *blando*. English examples were randomly selected from all instances of the lemmas *soft* and *smooth* tagged as adjectives in the British National Corpus, and Spanish examples were randomly selected from all instances of the lemmas *suave* and *blando* tagged as adjectives in the Corpus del Español. These examples were assigned ID tags and analyzed in context to identify the sense instantiated by each corpus example. Identification of senses and annotation of ID tags for *blando* and *suave* was assisted by a team of undergraduate native speakers of Spanish. Senses in both English and Spanish were chosen by consensus among the authors and the undergraduate team, and the choice of which senses should be considered as separate was continually reassessed as data were analyzed. The senses of each word were clustered based on the ID tags.

As discussed, the ID tags in our study were primarily syntactic. In addition to the reasons discussed above for using syntactic versus collocational tags, we chose syntactic over semantic tags because we aimed to make the annotation as objective and unbiased as possible. We found evaluations of syntactic features to be more consistent across annotators than semantic judgments.

Given the preliminary nature of the study, only nine ID tags were included for each language. Eight were the same for both languages and one tag was used for each language that was not applicable for the other. For both English and Spanish, ID tags were assigned for the type of construction in which the adjective appeared (attributive, predicative or resultative); modification of the adjective by one or more adverbs; presence of other adjectives modifying the same noun; presence of a PP complement on the modified NP; presence of the NP within a PP; whether the modifiee was expressed anaphorically; whether the modified noun was a mass or count noun, and its number (singular or plural). English ID tags included *tough*-movement, which does not exist in Spanish, and Spanish ID tags included pre- or post-nominal position of the adjective, which is far more variable in Spanish than in English. Adjective gender was not included as an ID tag in Spanish because it is largely semantically arbitrary, an observation confirmed by the apparently randomizing effect its inclusion had on the resultant cluster analysis. We intend to expand the number of ID tags in subsequent studies on texture adjectives in English and Spanish, though we will continue to emphasize syntactic variables.

In all clustering studies of sense relatedness, no matter how objective the ID tags, sense labeling itself is subjective to some degree. The application of criteria such as those of the principled-polysemy approach (Evans 2005: 41; Tyler and Evans 2001; discussed in Gries and Divjak 2009) can make the process of distinguishing senses less arbitrary, but total objectivity or agreement between all researchers is almost impossible. The main problem for distinguishing senses is granularity (i.e. at which level similar senses should be distinguished). Granularity was resolved partly based on frequency: senses with three or fewer examples were preferentially grouped with others rather than put in the "other" category; and also on classification accuracy. An overly high granularity is unproblematic when there are an adequate number of examples of each sense, because similar senses cluster together. High granularity only becomes truly problematic when there are few examples of each sense – as was occasionally the case in our small-scale study – because a small set of examples cannot be expected to be representative of the contexts in which a given sense occurs, leading to inaccurate clustering.

In the procedure used here, ID tags were annotated in columns in an Excel file in the format shown in Table 1. Note that the "sense" label is purely for convenience, and that these one-word labels are not taken in any way to be descriptions or definitions of the senses, but merely as labels for senses which are treated as distinct from other senses. We argue that it is neither necessary nor desirable for SLA or translator training to define word senses using a one-word "synonym" in either the same language or in a different language (see Kaji 2003), as is common practice in WSD. These "synonyms" are a necessity in machine translation, but for human corpus users they are less useful than more exact definitions. It is convenient to have a short label for word senses, especially as a shorthand in annotating and as inputs to analysis software, but for human audiences these labels can be accompanied by in-depth explanations of the nuances of each particular sense, the semantic range of the sense, and its boundaries with other senses. These explanations should not be *a priori*, but should be based on observations and examples from the corpus itself. The semantics of any word sense are likely to be complex, and we see no advantage to artificially constraining or simplifying the descriptions of senses.

The ID tags for each item form a behavioral profile vector (the set of variables the values of which are represented by ID tags), which can be inputted into a hierarchical agglomerative cluster (HAC) analysis. This can be done in a number of ways. Here, we are following the procedure described in Gries and Divjak (2009), using the Behavioral Profiles (BP) program for R written by Gries (2008). Among other functions, this script performs a HAC that sorts the examples on the basis of their behavioral profiles. This results in a tree-like clustering diagram, called a "dendrogram", in which similar senses are clustered. The current

Table 1: Sample senses and ID tags of *soft*.*

Sense	Syn.	PP comp	In PP	Adv.	Other adjs.	Count N?	Number of N	
Consistency	a	yes	no	yes	no	yes	s	for the table, continues on to an arugula salad with dates and a meltingly **soft** pork shank with rye gnocchi and sauerkraut.
Flexible	a	no	no	no	no	yes	pl	are very uncommon in snowboarding. And at the same time, you're wearing **soft** boots that you can run around in,
Force	a	no	yes	no	no	yes	s	his eyes brushing my neck, my jaw, and my mouth with a **soft** force, and then resting deep inside my eyes.
Gentle	p	no	no	no	yes	yes	s	guy is about 5' 5", 130 pounds, sweetheart, intelligent, **soft** and gentle. Not someone who's prone to be a tough guy.
Humanities	a	no	yes	no	no	yes	pl	business, engineering, and the like – has clearly decided to write off the **soft** disciplines, namely the humanities and the arts.
Indirect	a	no	no	no	no	no	n	Well put... we need the most severe changes to restrict the **soft** money which, as I say a couple of times, is a blight on...
Noise	p	no	no	yes	no	yes	s	it as best as he can. The sound, however, is still understandably **soft**. # STARKS waits and then reaches for the knob on...

* a = attributive; p = predicative; s = singular; pl = plural; n = not applicable

study utilized the Canberra similarity metric to make the best use of the relatively small data set, and used the Ward amalgamation strategy, in order to encourage clusters of an easily interpretable size.

The BP script for R also incorporates the pvclust script (Suzuki and Shimodaira 2011) that assesses the reliability of the HAC analysis with bootstrap resampling. That is, the instances of each word or sense are repeatedly shuffled and then re-clustered. In the BP script, data are re-clustered 10,000 times. The results of this resampling are reported as Approximately Unbiased (AU) *p*-values, which are assigned to each cluster and which report how often the cluster emerged in the resamplings. For example, an AU *p*-value of 70% would mean that a particular cluster occurred in 70% of the resamplings. The apparent cluster is less likely to be due to chance than a cluster with a lower AU *p*-value, and more likely to be a chance occurrence than a cluster with a higher AU *p*-value.

5 Pilot study: results and analysis

The outcome of the HAC analysis can be represented in dendrograms such as Figures 1–4. Distance ("height") between points of amalgamation represents the difference between the clusters. As this is a preliminary study, which involved the use of relatively few ID tags and small corpus samples, "height" is fairly low and height distinctions are small, meaning that clusters could be subject to change with the addition of more data. Nevertheless, even these preliminary results give some indications of the potential applications of clustering of senses found in bilingual comparable corpora.

The AU *p*-values are given above each cluster and to the right. When these are low, the apparent cluster does not replicate well and is probably due to chance. Higher AU *p*-values indicate clusters that are more strongly supported by the data.

As might be expected, our trial study confirmed that polysemy networks across languages demonstrate frequent mismatches. Of course, similar-seeming items, such as English *smooth* and Spanish *suave*, have some senses that they share and others that they do not (see Figures 1 and 2). For example, both items can refer to texture, as in *textura suave* or *smooth texture* (labeled as "textura" and "slick", respectively). On the other hand, *smooth* has an "efficient" sense that *suave* lacks, as in *smooth efficiency*, and *suave* has a "gentle" sense not expressed by *smooth*, as in *soplo suave* 'gentle breeze'.

Not only does each item each have senses not shared by their near equivalents in another language, but items typically have some senses that are better expressed with one word in an L2 and other senses that are better expressed with a different L2 word. Some senses of English *soft* are close equivalents of senses of Spanish *suave*, and some can be more closely equated with Spanish *blando* (compare Figure 3 with Figures 2 and 4).

For example, senses shared by *soft* and *suave* refer to the texture of skin (the sense labeled "skin" in *soft skin* and the "piel" sense in *suave piel;* but #*blanda piel*) and to silkiness of hair or fur (*soft curls;* these senses are labeled "silky" and "sedoso" in Figures 3 and 2). On the other hand, *soft* and *blando* share a set of senses referring to gentle forces (*soft push;* senses labeled "force" and "fuerza" in Figures 3 and 4), squishy surfaces (*soft mud;* labeled "squishy" and "malleable"), yielding springy surfaces (*soft cushions;* "yielding" and "mullido"), and internal consistency (*soft butter;* "consistency" and "consistencia"). The "yielding", "force", "squishy" and "silky" senses of *soft* cluster together in Figure 3, and therefore behave similarly in English, even though some senses resemble *blando* and some *suave* in Spanish. The "yielding" / "force" / "squishy" /

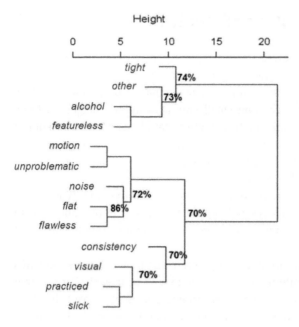

Figure 1: Dendrogram for *smooth* with AU values (values below 70% not shown).

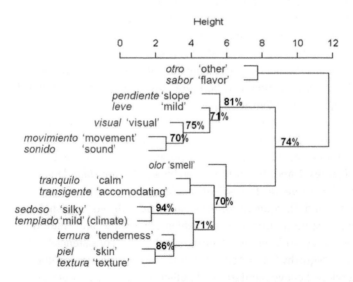

Figure 2: Dendrogram for *suave* with AU values (values below 70% not shown).

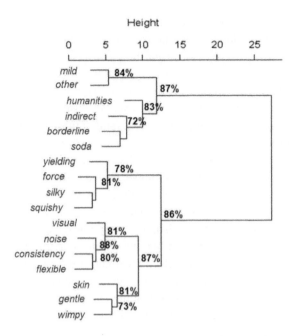

Figure 3: Dendrogram for *soft* with AU values (values below 70% not shown).

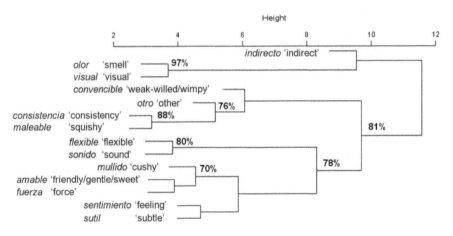

Figure 4: Dendrogram for *blando* with AU values (values below 70% not shown).

"silky" cluster had an AU *p*-value of 78%, meaning that the cluster recurred in 78% of the bootstrap resamplings (see Figure 3). It therefore occurs with the majority of possible initial orders, and does not depend to a great extent on the initial order of the data.

Although this type of observation may be facilitated by the use of corpora, it could be achieved by careful study alone. A unique contribution of clustering based on word senses is that this analysis can reveal how clusters of senses, as well as individual senses, are related across languages. Our results suggest that many of the senses which are shared between *blando* and *soft*, but not by similar adjectives such as Spanish *suave* and English *smooth*, cluster closely together in English and also to some extent in Spanish. If several of these senses (such as those related to internal consistency and squishy surfaces) are closely related in both languages, it may be no accident that all senses in the cluster are expressed by the same lexical item in each language. Instead, the senses are probably related by underlying semantic commonalities, and may even be predicted, based on these commonalities, to be expressed by a common lexical item in languages other than English and Spanish. Learning the clusters of senses that are near-equivalents in two languages may be an efficient way for L2 learners to understand how to best express a given meaning in their L2, by looking at the clusters of meanings expressed by each L2 item and comparing these with the meanings in their L1. Learning corresponding clusters of senses in the two languages is more efficient than memorizing all the corresponding senses individually.

Cluster analyses based on syntactic features take advantage of more shared variables between senses than analyses based solely on collocations (such as Kaji 2003), in that slightly different senses are far more likely to share syntactic structures than to share individual collocates. Examples (1)–(3) are from the texts taken from the British National Corpus and Corpus del Español and used in the current study (as are all subsequent examples). Each excerpt in (1)–(3) represents a different sense of *soft*, and few collocates are shared by the different senses. However, the shared syntactic structures are immediately evident. The cluster of senses of *soft* that can be characterized as referring to skin texture – "skin" in Figure 3, as in example (1), as well as gentleness of personality "gentle", as in (2), and weakness of will "wimpy", as in (3) – demonstrates syntactic attributes typical of the cluster, such as the use of the copula, the predicative position of the adjective, and the presence of other adjectives coordinated with *soft*. The "skin" / "gentle" / "wimpy" cluster has an AU *p*-value of 81%.

(1) *You want the skin there to be as smooth and **soft** as possible*
(2) *the guy is about 5' 5", 130 pounds, sweetheart, intelligent, **soft** and gentle*
(3) *she's very well spoken, but she's pretty **soft***

ID tags typical of this cluster include the use of multiple adjectives (as in *smooth and soft*), predicative use of *soft* (*to be… soft, is… soft*) and adverbial modification (*pretty soft*). These uses of *soft* almost always modify singular nouns, typically count nouns (such as *the guy*). For the latter two senses exemplified above, these nouns are also typically animate and human, but this type of semantic information was not taken into consideration in this analysis – a choice which allowed clustering such as with the sense in (1) to come through more strongly. The ID tags listed above are of course not shared by every instance of a sense in the cluster, but did help to typify the cluster relative to senses outside the cluster.

To give a Spanish example, a cluster is formed by the senses of *blando* referring to (4) springy cushiness ("mullido"), (5), weak or gentle force ("fuerza") and (6) mildness or sweetness of personality or behavior ("amable"). This cluster has an AU value of 70% (see Figure 4).

(4) *me acomodaba en los **blandos** almohadones de un coche del ferrocarril*
     'I got settled on the **soft** cushions of a train car'
(5) *el rostro sonrosado por los **blandos** golpes de la espuma...*
     'the face rosy from the **soft** splashes of the spray...'
(6) *¿Y si los **blandos** halagos de esta niña pudiesen cicatrizar las úlceras de mi corazón?*
     'and if the **soft** praises of this girl could heal the wounds in my heart?'

These uses were often in the plural (e.g. *blandos golpes* 'soft splashes/blows'). The adjective *blando* was typically attributive and pre-nominal (*blandos almohadones* 'soft cushions' vs. *almohadones blandos*) and often occurred in a noun phrase with a PP modifier (*de un coche, de la espuma, de esta niña* 'of a car, of the spray, of this girl').

Clustering based on syntax can prove useful where both collocates and intuitions are misleading. For example, both Spanish *suave* and English *smooth* modify nouns denoting motion, as in *suave movimiento* and *smooth motion*. However, the sense of *suave* referring to motion ("movimiento" in Figure 2) and the sense of *smooth* describing motion ("motion" in Figure 1) are not comparable. A "smooth" motion is a graceful or practiced motion, whereas *suave movimiento* refers to a weak or feeble movement. This sense of *suave* should probably never be translated as, or equated with, *smooth*, and vice versa, despite the superficial similarity of the expressions that might prompt the senses to be viewed as near-equivalents. The difference in meaning is, however, apparent in the clustering of the senses of *suave* and *smooth* in each language. In Spanish, this sense of *suave* appears to cluster with senses referring to dim visual stimuli ("visual") and weak audio stimuli ("sonido"), and (less closely) with mildness of a condition, such as a disease ("leve") (see Figure 2; this cluster has an AU value of 71%). This suggests that the sense refers to a low position on a scale of intensity – in this case, intensity of the motion described. In English, on the other hand, *smooth* referring to motion ("motion" in Figure 1; as in example [7]) clusters with the sense of *smooth* referring to the unproblematic accomplishment of a goal ("unproblematic"; as in [8]). This cluster has an AU value of only 56%, but is nevertheless worth mentioning due to its incontrovertible difference from the Spanish pattern.

(7)   *His gait was **smooth**, as if his hip sockets had been oiled...*
(8)   *As moose rescues go, this was a **smooth** one, says Sinnott...*

This clustering suggests that the sense of *smooth* referring to swift unimpeded motion is metaphorically related to the sense referring to swift unhindered accomplishment of a goal. This is a different type of association to that suggested by the clustering of the "movimiento" sense in Spanish. Awareness of this type of clustering can draw attention to the difference in meaning between the two superficially similar senses of *smooth*.

In general, our analysis suggests that metaphoric senses such as *smooth* "unproblematic" do not cluster exclusively with other metaphoric senses in either Spanish or English, but instead cluster with specific non-metaphoric senses. For example, in Spanish, the "amable" sense of *blando* referring to 'kindness' or 'sweetness' clusters with "mullido" ('yielding surface'; AU value 70%), whereas the "convencible" ('weak-willed') sense clusters more closely with "consistencia" ('liquid consistency'; though with an AU value of only 60%); that is, a friendly human being is *blando* in the manner of a comfortable chair, whereas a weak-willed human being is "malleable" like a semi-liquid jelly. English *soft* lacks an "amable" sense referring to sweet behavior or character (expressions such as *soft-hearted* have suggestions of this sense, though these were not well-represented in the corpus). On the other hand, the "wimpy" sense of *soft* in English is connected to "consistency" (as part of a larger cluster with AU value 87%), as in Spanish. The patterns of semantic extension in the languages therefore appear similar, in that specific metaphoric senses are tied to specific non-metaphoric senses, but the resultant networks differ in their details. Awareness of these distinctions is a key to the correct usage of these senses with the appropriate connotations. For example, a Spanish speaker learning English might be unaware that English *soft* lacks some of the positive connotations of the Spanish "amable", but that the negative sense "convencible" translates well as English *soft* "wimpy". The other members of the clusters of these senses in each language make it clear which senses are closer in meaning between the languages. This can be especially useful in understanding metaphoric senses, for which the connections to other senses may not be apparent to an L2 learner.

6 Conclusion

Recent advances in corpus applications have contributed much to Cognitive Linguistics, and increasingly to translation studies and SLA. However, the types of corpora that have been adopted for SLA applications remain largely limited to monolingual corpora. These corpora have proven their utility in translation studies and SLA: monolingual untranslated corpora can give SLA students a feel for the native usage of lexical items and constructions in their L2, and monolingual learner corpora allow SLA students to avoid common mistakes in their L2. We suggest here that bilingual comparable corpora may prove equally well-suited for SLA studies of vocabulary and lexicon. In particular, a comparison of sense clustering in an L1 and L2 can allow students to recognize which types of senses of an item in their L1 correspond most closely to particular items in the L2. For example, this type of analysis demonstrates graphically which groups of senses of English *soft* resemble senses of Spanish *blando*, and which senses of *soft* more closely resemble senses of Spanish *suave*. At the same type, these analyses can draw attention to mismatches between deceptively similar L1 and L2 items, such as English *smooth* and Spanish *suave*, both of which can modify nouns denoting types of motion, but which have very different meanings and hence different positions in the dendrograms of these English and Spanish adjectives. The clusters can also help students choose lexical items with the intended connotations, by drawing attention to the relatedness of these senses with other clearly positively or negatively connotated senses, as in the above example comparing English *soft* and Spanish *blando*. Finally, clusters can aid students in the appropriate use of metaphoric senses, by illustrating how these senses are connected to less metaphoric senses, the meaning and use of which may help clarify the items' metaphoric meanings.

Results from bilingual comparable corpus studies are a long way from being integrated in the SLA classroom. We argue that this lack of progress can be attributed at least in part to the relative paucity of corpus studies aimed at SLA applications, and the lack of diversity in the studies that do exist. Our results, though tentative, suggest that additional types of corpus studies may be productive for SLA. We have also suggested certain methodological choices that may be pursued in order to generate benefits for SLA. It is hoped that recognition of the varied types of corpora and methodologies available for SLA research will lead to the expansion of corpus studies aimed at SLA application, and ultimately the productive integration of these studies and their results in the SLA classroom.

References

Baker, Mona. 1995. Corpora in translation studies: An overview and some suggestions for future research. *Target* 7 (2): 223–243.

Baker, Mona. 1996. Corpus-based translation studies: The challenges that lie ahead. In *Terminology, LSP and Translation: Studies in Language Engineering, in Honour of Juan C. Sager*, Harold Somers (ed.), 175–186. Amsterdam: John Benjamins. 1999. The role of corpora in investigating the linguistic behaviour of professional translators. *International Journal of Corpus Linguistics* 4 (2): 281–298.

Divjak, Dagmar. 2010. *Structuring the Lexicon: A Clustered Model for Near-synonymy*. Berlin: Mouton de Gruyter.

Divjak, Dagmar, and Stefan T. Gries. 2008. Clusters in the mind? Converging evidence from near-synonymy in Russian. *The Mental Lexicon* 3 (2): 188–213.

Gibbs, Raymond W., and Teenie Matlock. 2001. Psycholinguistic perspectives on polysemy. In *Polysemy in Cognitive Linguistics*, Hubert Cuyckens, and Britta Zawada (eds.), 213–239. Amsterdam: John Benjamins.

Gilquin, Gaëtanelle, and Stefan T. Gries. 2009. Corpora and experimental methods: a state-of-the-art review. *Corpus Linguistics and Linguistic Theory* 5 (1): 1–26.

Glynn, Dylan. 2010. Synonymy, lexical fields, and grammatical constructions. A study in usage-based Cognitive Semantics. In *Cognitive Foundations of Linguistic Usage-Patterns*, Hans-Jörg Schmid, and Susanne Handl (eds.), 89–118. Berlin/New York: Mouton de Gruyter.

Granger, Sylviane. 2003. The corpus approach: a common way forward for CL and TS. In *Corpus-based Approaches to Contrastive Linguistics and Translation Studies*, Sylviane Granger, Jacques Lerot, and Stephanie Petch-Tyson (eds.), 17–30. Amsterdam/New York: Rodopi B.V.

Gries, Stefan T. 2006. Corpus-based methods and cognitive semantics: the many meanings of *to run*. In *Corpora in Cognitive Linguistics: Corpus-Based Approaches to Syntax and Lexis*, Stefan T. Gries, and Anatol Stefanowitsch (eds.), 57–99. Berlin/New York: Mouton de Gruyter.

Gries, Stefan T. 2008. Behavioral Profiles 1.0. A program for R 2.7.1 and higher. Available from the author.

Gries, Stefan T., and Dagmar Divjak. 2009. Behavioral profiles: a corpus-based approach to cognitive semantic analysis. In *New Directions in Cognitive Linguistics*, Vyvyan Evans, and Stephanie Pourcel (eds.), 57–75. Amsterdam: John Benjamins.

Gries, Stefan T., and Anatol Stefanowitsch (eds.). 2006. *Corpora in Cognitive Linguistics: Corpus-Based Approaches to Syntax and Lexis*. Berlin/New York: Mouton de Gruyter.

Jenset, Gard B., and Lidun Hareide. 2013. A multidimensional approach to aligned sentences in translated text. *Bergen Language and Linguistics Studies* 3 (1): 195–210.

Johansson, Stig. 1998. On the role of corpora in cross-linguistic research. In *Corpora and Cross-Linguistic Research: Theory, Method and Case Studies*, Stig Johansson, and Signe Oksefjell (eds.), 3–24. Amsterdam: Rodopi.

Johansson, Stig. 2007. *Seeing Through Multilingual Corpora: On the Use of Corpora in Contrastive Studies*. Amsterdam/Philadelphia: John Benjamins.

Johns, Tim F., and Philip King (eds.). 1991. *Classroom Concordancing*. Birmingham: Centre for English Language Studies.

Kaji, Hiroyuki. 2003. Word sense acquisition from bilingual comparable corpora. In *Proceedings of the 2003 Conference of the North American Chapter of the Association for Computational Linguistics on Human Language Technology – Volume 1*, 32–39. Edmonton: Association for Computational Linguistics.

Ke, Shih-Wen. 2012. Clustering a translational corpus. In *Quantitative Methods in Corpus-Based Translation Studies: a Practical Guide to Descriptive Translation Research*, Michael P. Oakes, and Meng Ji (eds.), 149–174. Amsterdam: John Benjamins.

Kishner, Jeffrey M., and Raymond W. Gibbs. 1996. How *just* gets its meanings: Polysemy and context in psychological semantics. *Language and Speech* 39 (1): 19–36.

Malmkjaer, Kirsten. 1998. Love thy neighbour: Will parallel corpora endear linguists to translators? *Meta: Journal des Traducteurs* 43 (4): 534–541.

Marzo, Stefania, Kris Heylen, and Gert de Sutter (eds.). 2010. *Corpus Studies in Contrastive Linguistics*. Amsterdam/Philadelphia: John Benjamins.

Mason, Ian. 2001. Translator behaviour and language usage: Some constraints on contrastive studies. *Hermes* 26: 65–80.

Noël, Dirk, and Timothy Colleman. 2010. Believe-type raising-to-object and raising-to-subject verbs in English and Dutch: A contrastive investigation in diachronic construction grammar. In *Corpus Studies in Contrastive Linguistics*, Stefania Marzo, Kris Heylen, and Gert de Sutter (eds.), 7–31. Amsterdam/Philadelphia: John Benjamins.

Olohan, Maeve. 2004. *Introducing Corpora in Translation Studies*. New York: Routledge.

Ringbom, Håkan. 1998. Vocabulary frequencies in advanced learner English: A cross-linguistic approach. In *Learner English on Computer*, Sylviane Granger (ed.), 41–52. London/New York: Addison Wesley Longman.

Schäffner, Christina. 1998. Parallel texts in translation. In *Unity in Diversity? Current Trends in Translation Studies*, Lynne Bowker, Michael Cronin, Dorothy Kenny, and Jennifer Pearson (eds.), 83–90. Manchester: St Jerome.

Sullivan, Karen. 2012. It's hard being soft: Antonymous senses vs. antonymous words. *The Mental Lexicon* 7 (3): 307–326.

Suzuki, Ryota, and Hidetoshi Shimodaira. 2011. Pvclust v1.2-2: Hierarchical clustering with p-values via multiscale bootstrap resampling. [Software] Osaka: Ef-prime. Available from http://cran.r-project.org/web/packages/pvclust/index.html.

Valenzuela, Javier, and Ana M. Rojo. 2008. What can language learners tell us about constructions? In *Cognitive Approaches to Pedagogical Grammar*, Sabine de Knop, and Teun de Rycker (eds.), 197–230. Berlin/New York: Mouton de Gruyter.

Williams, Ian A. 2010. Cultural differences in academic discourse: Evidence from first-person verb use in the methods sections of medical research articles. *International Journal of Corpus Linguistics* 15 (2): 214–239.

Zanettin, Federico. 1998. Bilingual comparable corpora and the training of translators. *Meta: Journal des Traducteurs* 43 (4): 616–630.

Index